STUDIES IN BAPTIST HIS
VOLUM.

Tracks and Traces

Baptist Identity in Church and Theology

Studies in Baptist History and Thought

Series Editors

Anthony R. Cross	Centre for Baptist History and Heritage, Regent's Park College, Oxford
Curtis W. Freeman	Duke University, North Carolina, USA
Stephen R. Holmes	King's College, London, England
Elizabeth Newman	Baptist Theological Seminary at Richmond, Virginia, USA
Philip E. Thompson	North American Baptist Seminary, Sioux Falls, South Dakota, USA

Series Consultants

David Bebbington	University of Stirling, Stirling, Scotland
Paul S. Fiddes	Regent's Park College, Oxford, England
Stanley J. Grenz	Carey Theological College, Vancouver, British Columbia, Canada
Stanley E. Porter	McMaster Divinity College, Hamilton, Ontario, Canada

A full listing of all titles in this series
appears at the close of this book

STUDIES IN BAPTIST HISTORY AND THOUGHT
VOLUME 13

Tracks and Traces

Baptist Identity in Church and Theology

Paul S. Fiddes

PATERNOSTER PRESS

Copyright © Paul S. Fiddes 2003

First published 2003 by Paternoster Press

Paternoster Press is an imprint of Authentic Media
P.O. Box 300, Carlisle, Cumbria, CA3 0QS, U.K.
and P.O. Box 1047, Waynesboro, GA 30830–2047, U.S.A

09 08 07 06 05 04 03   7 6 5 4 3 2 1

The right of Paul S. Fiddes to be
identified as the Author of this Work has been asserted by him
in accordance with the Copyright, Designs
and Patents Act 1988

British Library Cataloguing in Publication Data
A catalogue record for this book is available from the British Library

ISBN 1–84227–120-2

Typeset by A.R. Cross
Printed and bound in Great Britain
for Paternoster Press
by Nottingham Alpha Graphics

Series Preface

Baptists form one of the largest Christian communities in the world, and while they hold the historic faith in common with other mainstream Christian traditions, they nevertheless have important insights which they can offer to the worldwide church. Studies in Baptist History and Thought will be one means towards this end. It is an international series of academic studies which includes original monographs, revised dissertations, collections of essays and conference papers, and aims to cover any aspect of Baptist history and thought. While not all the authors are themselves Baptists, they nevertheless share an interest in relating Baptist history and thought to the other branches of the Christian church and to the wider life of the world.

The series includes studies in various aspects of Baptist history from the seventeenth century down to the present day, including biographical works, and Baptist thought is understood as covering the subject-matter of theology (including interdisciplinary studies embracing biblical studies, philosophy, sociology, practical theology, liturgy and women's studies). The diverse streams of Baptist life throughout the world are all within the scope of these volumes.

The series editors and consultants believe that the academic disciplines of history and theology are of vital importance to the spiritual vitality of the churches of the Baptist faith and order. The series sets out to discuss, examine and explore the many dimensions of their tradition and so to contribute to their on-going intellectual vigour.

A brief word of explanation is due for the series identifier on the front cover. The fountains, taken from heraldry, represent the Baptist distinctive of believer's baptism and, at the same time, the source of the water of life. There are three of them because they symbolize the Trinitarian basis of Baptist life and faith. Those who are redeemed by the Lamb, the book of Revelation reminds us, will be led to 'fountains of living waters' (Rev. 7.17).

Dedicated to the memory of
Ernest A. Payne, C.H.

Contents

Preface and Acknowledgements

The chapters of this book began, with one exception, as separate papers or articles. These, moreover, were mostly written for meetings for discussion with fellow-Baptists or with ecumenical partners, so that I am immensely indebted to a whole host of people, too numerous to name, for the shaping of their contents. Behind the papers there lies an experience of good talk, good company and shared worship, and the gift of generous hospitality from fellow-Christians in many parts of the world. The following list of chapters and their origins should make this debt clear.

1. 'Introduction: The Question of Identity' is an edited version of the chapter entitled 'Theology and a Baptist Way of Community', printed in *Doing Theology in a Baptist Way*, edited by Paul S. Fiddes (Oxford: Whitley Publications, 2000), pp. 19-38, ©2000 author and Whitley Publications. This paper was originally given at the first Consultation of 'Baptists Doing Theology in Context' in Oxford, August 1999.

2. ' "Walking Together": The Place of Covenant Theology in Baptist Life Yesterday and Today' was first published in *Pilgrim Pathways. Essays in Baptist History in Honour of B.R. White*, edited by W. H. Brackney, P. S. Fiddes and John H.Y. Briggs (Macon, GA: Mercer University Press, 1999), pp. 47-74, ©1999 Mercer University Press, used by kind permission of the publishers.

3. 'Beginning a New Millennium: Doctrinal Themes of Strategic Significance for Baptists' was first given to the BWA Commission on Baptist Doctrine and Interchurch Cooperation, meeting in July 1996 in Hong Kong. A shorter version was published in *Baptist Faith and Witness. Book 2. The Papers of the Study and Research Division of the Baptist World Alliance, 1995-2000*, edited by L.A. (Tony) Cupit (McLean: Baptist World Alliance, 1999), pp. 13-22, ©1999 the Baptist World Alliance, used by kind permission of the publishers.

4. 'Church and Trinity: A Baptist Ecclesiology of Participation' is a revised version of a paper first published in *Gemeinschaft am Evangelium. Festschrift für Wiard Popkes*, edited by E. Brandt, P.S. Fiddes and J. Molthagen (Leipzig: Evangelische Verlagsanstalt, 1996), pp. 37-54, ©1996 Evangelische Verlagsanstalt, Leipzig, used by kind permission of the publishers.

5. 'Authority in Relations between Pastor and People: A Baptist Doctrine of Ministry' is an expanded and updated version of a paper given to the BWA Commission on Church Leadership, meeting in July 1991 in Montreal, Canada. A shorter version was published under the title

'Authority in People-Pastor Relations' in *Baptist Faith and Witness. The Papers of the Study and Research Division of the Baptist World Alliance 1990-1995*, edited by William H. Brackney and L.A. Cupit (Samford University Press, Samford, 1995), pp. 59-63, ©1995 Baptist World Alliance, used by kind permission of the publishers.

6. 'Baptism and Creation' was first published in *Reflections on the Water. Understanding God and the the World through the Baptism of Believers*, edited by Paul S. Fiddes (Regent's Study Guides 4: Macon: Smyth & Helwys/Oxford: Regent's Park College, 1996), pp. 47-67, ©1996 the author and Regent's Park College. The paper had its origin in a study group of British Baptist ministers and theologians, meeting from 1989-1995, the members of which all contributed papers to *Reflections on the Water*.

7. 'Believers' Baptism: An Act of Inclusion or Exclusion?' is a considerably expanded version of a paper published by the Hertfordshire Baptist Association in 1999, as part of a series *Signposts for a New Century. Exploring Baptist Distinctives*, ©1999 the author. This chapter also includes material from my paper 'Baptism and the Process of Christian Initiation', published in Stanley E. Porter and Anthony R. Cross (eds.), *Dimensions of Baptism. Biblical and Theological Studies* (JSNT Supplement Series 234; Sheffield: Sheffield Academic Press, 2002), pp. 280-303, ©2002 Sheffield Academic Press, used by kind permission of the publishers. Earlier versions of this chapter have been presented and discussed in various places: at a meeting of the Hertfordshire Baptist Association in 1999; at a Joint Working Group of the World Council of Churches and the Roman Catholic Church, meeting in Antelias, Lebanon, in May 2000; at a World Council of Churches Faith and Order Consultation on Baptism, meeting in Faverges, France in September 2001; and at informal conversations between the Baptist Union of Great Britain and the Church of England, meeting in London in January 2001, and at Oxford in February 2002.

8. 'The Church as a Eucharistic Community: A Baptist Contribution' has been specially written for this book.

9. 'The Church's Ecumenical Calling; A Baptist Perspective' is a much expanded version of an unpublished paper given to the Melbourne School of Ministry, meeting in Whitley College, Melbourne, Australia, in June 2001. This chapter also contains some material from my paper 'Salvation and the Church: a Comparison of Baptist and Orthodox Thinking' in *Ecumenism and History. Studies in Honour of John H.Y. Briggs*, edited by Anthony Cross (Carlisle: Paternoster Press, 2002), pp. 120-48, ©2002 author and Anthony R. Cross, used by kind permission of the publishers.

10. 'The Understanding of Salvation in the Baptist Tradition' is an edited version of a paper published in *For Us and For Our Salvation.*

Seven Perspectives on Christian Soteriology, edited by Rienk Lanooy (Utrecht-Leiden: Interuniversitair Instituut voor Missiologie en Oecumenica, 1994), pp. 15-38, ©1995 Interuniversitair Instituut voor Missiologie en Oecumenica, used by kind permission of the publishers. The paper was originally given as a lecture at the Inter-University Institute in Leiden, in 1993.

11. 'Mission and Liberty: A Baptist Connection' is an expanded version of an unpublished paper, given under the title 'Mission: the Essence of the Church?', at conversations between the Baptist World Alliance and the Orthodox Ecumenical Patriarchate of Constantinople, in Oxford in May 1997.

There are other acknowledgements to be made for the use of two pieces of poetry in the book. In chapter 6, extracts from the poem by Adrian Mitchell, 'Stufferation', ©1991 Adrian Mitchell, and printed in *Adrian Mitchell's Greatest Hits – The Top Forty* (Newcastle upon Tyne: Bloodaxe Books, 1991), are used by kind permission of the author and the publishers.

In chapter 8, the poem 'In Great Waters', by R.S. Thomas, first printed in *Frequencies* (1978), and reprinted in R.S. Thomas, *Collected Poems 1945-1990* (London: Phoenix Press, 2001), ©1993 R.S. Thomas, is used by kind permission of the Estate of R.S. Thomas and the publishers, J.M. Dent.

In the light of the many conversation-partners, as indicated above, who have contributed to the final form of these papers, it seems invidious to mention only a couple of names. But I am glad to acknowledge here the companionship in theological discussion, over the past twenty-five years, of two fellow-Baptist ministers: Richard Kidd and Brian Haymes. I am also very grateful for the encouragement and efforts of the General Editor of the series in which this book appears, Anthony Cross, who has spent a good deal of his own time on preparing the copy for the press.

Because these chapters began as separate pieces, there is some overlap between them, and the sense now and then of 'starting again'. However, I should make clear that I have edited, expanded and adapted the papers as originally offered, with the kind consent in each case of the publisher concerned. My aim has been to produce a study which is thoroughly unified, and which is a coherent Baptist vision of the Christian church in its faith and practice. In quest of this integration, I have also supplied a number of links between the chapters in the footnotes, and I ask the indulgence of my readers for the frequent invitation to page-hunting.

I believe that the idea of Baptist identity which emerges from these pages is in continuity with a recognizable strand of Baptist thinking during the last hundred years, though hopefully adding some surprising twists within it. I am thinking of the 'track' of Baptist heritage which has been trodden by some of those who have gone before me as members and staff of Regent's Park College, and notably by Henry Wheeler Robinson, E. A. Payne, Neville Clark, Morris West and Barrie R. White. Indeed, I dedicate this book to the memory of one of them, Dr. Ernest A. Payne, who ordained me to the Christian ministry thirty years ago this year. Presiding over my ordination as a representative of the Baptist Union of Great Britain, he was also at the time a President of the World Council of Churches. In this he exemplified in himself the Baptist vision which places the community of Baptist Christians clearly within the fellowship of the church universal.

Regent's Park College
University of Oxford
Michaelmas Term, 2002

CHAPTER 1

Introduction:
The Question of Identity

Tracks and Traces

To speak of 'making tracks' evokes images of bare footprints left along a sandy beach, the ruts of a tractor across muddy fields, the hacked trail of an explorer through a jungle and the path made by boots in a fall of snow. At any rate, there is a definite path which has been marked out and a direction to be observed. To use this metaphor of the heritage of a church community implies that there are pathways trodden in the past which still have definite meaning and relevance for the present, and for which the technical term is 'tradition'. The group of Christians called 'Baptist' has had some interest in such tracks, but has also shown characteristic impatience with being limited by them. Part of the purpose of this book is to recall tracks made by Baptists in the past that have the potential still to offer guidance for the present day, to affirm that Baptists belong to the long story of the church universal (the 'catholic church') and, within a shorter horizon, that they are children of the Reformation of the church and so share pathways with others who have travelled that way.

The term 'traces' belongs more to our present age. It evokes the picture of a shadowy after-image, or a scarcely worked-out trajectory; it hints at uncertainty, at ambiguity in both knowledge and direction. In its most extreme use in our contemporary culture, it indicates doubts about the relation between words and the objects in the world that they supposedly describe. The notion of a 'trace' questions whether 'signifiers' have any direct connection with the reality to which they refer ('things signified'), or whether they offer only hints and clues which point to it, and which mark out a path towards other traces which are yet to be.[1] Baptists have characteristically shared this doubt in some

---

1   Jacques Derrida, *Speech and Phenomena, and Other Essays on Husserl's Theory of Signs*, trans. D.B. Allison (Evanston: North Western University Press, 1973), pp.

areas, notably with regard to the power of reference of creeds and the sacraments; they have suspected that some church dogmas, despite professed intentions, have tended to confuse the signifier with the thing signified. They have thus refused to be bound by the words of creeds, and have drawn careful *distinctions* between the signs of the sacraments and the benefits of salvation to which they point, though many have warned also against *separating* the external expression and the 'good' offered in Christ.[2]

For all that, the Baptist tradition has not doubted that there *is* a covenant between the word and the world, which belongs to God's covenant of grace. In particular, Baptists have been confident about the referential power of the words of scripture, to inform us about the reality of human life and alert us to the ways of God in the world. While Baptists have sometimes been *too* confident about this, claiming, for instance, a direct continuity between their own form of church and the commands of Christ in the New Testament, Baptists have also produced Baptist biblical scholars who have been in the forefront of critical scholarship.[3] What has been consistent has been an expectation that scripture can be relied upon to witness to the Word of God in Christ. Such a confidence in scripture was held in the twentieth century by the Reformed theologian Karl Barth, who also however reminds us that even words of scripture are only traces in themselves.[4] Even the best human words are frail, and collapse under the weight of reference. As poets discover, words 'slip, slide, perish/ Decay with imprecision, will not stay in place'.[5] Especially with regard to the realities of God, human words have no capacity in themselves to refer what is incomparable and transcendent. As Barth perceived, they must be seized hold of by revelation to become the Word of God, to enable them to refer to anything beyond the finite world, and this means nothing less than an encounter with the self-revealing God.[6]

135–41. On the idea of a 'trace', see Paul S. Fiddes, *The Promised End. Eschatology in Theology and Literature* (Challenges in Contemporary Theology; Oxford: Blackwell, 2000), pp. 31–8.

2   For instances, see ch. 8, pp. 164–6; cf. ch. 7, pp. 129–30.

3   There has been a particular Baptist contribution to Old Testament studies. When the German Old Testament scholar Otto Eissfeldt produced the second edition of his magisterial *Introduction to the Old Testament* in 1955 (English translation; Oxford: Basil Blackwell, 1966), he dedicated it 'to the Representatives of three generations of Old Testament Scholarship: Theodore H. Robinson, Harold H. Rowley, Aubrey R. Johnson.' These were all Baptists. To these names should be added H. Wheeler Robinson and – in more recent times – R.E. Clements and Rex A. Mason.

4   Karl Barth, *Church Dogmatics*, trans. and ed. G.W. Bromiley and T.F. Torrance (14 volumes; Edinburgh: T. & T. Clark, 1936–77), I/1, pp. 107–110, 165–9, 196–8.

5   T.S. Eliot, 'Burnt Norton', V, from *Four Quartets* in *The Complete Poems and Plays of T.S. Eliot* (London: Faber, 1969), p. 175.

6   Barth, *Church Dogmatics*, I/1, p. 340; II/1, pp. 186–90, 214–20.

It is, then, a proper humility to regard all talk about God as 'traces' of the truth, though we may rely upon the divine faithfulness to align these traces in the right direction, to make them correspond to *whom* God really is. While we can never describe God in human words, 'traces' can point to God and enable us to participate in God's life.

Part of the purpose of this book is to sketch out such 'traces' of a doctrine of God which may form a basis for what are sometimes called 'Baptist principles'. These are not tracks which we can examine and by which we can hunt God down. They are traces of a God who has 'just passed by' and of whose back we are graciously allowed to catch a glimpse.[7] They are traces of the God who is both disclosed and hidden, unveiled and veiled, in the face of Jesus Christ.[8] If we are to sketch out a path into the future, taking into account the tracks of the past, we must trace out the nature and purpose of the God who has a future. This study of Baptist identity is thus not only, or even mainly, a study of the trodden paths of history. It is a venture upon the traces of theology, which appear only in the context of community.

Theology and Community

Baptists have always resisted the idea that there is a distinctively 'Baptist theology', at least in terms of there being a Baptist version of such basic doctrines as Trinity, Christology, anthropology and eschatology. Baptists have written, and do write, theology on such topics, but they think of themselves as simply contributing to a common storehouse alongside other Christian theologians. But is there a Baptist way of *doing* theology, of approaching the theological task? There is a phrase that has some currency among Baptists at present, which is 'the Baptist way of being the church'.[9] If there is such a thing as this, then I suggest that there *must* also be a Baptist way of doing theology. As long as we can identify a Christian community, or family of communities, as something called 'Baptist', then there must be a Baptist mode of theologizing. Of course, this is only one mode among others; there is nothing exclusive about it. But it is there, amid the glorious plurality and diversity of theological methods. The American Baptist theologian, James McClendon, defines theology as 'the discovery, understanding and transformation of the

---

7   Exodus 33:22–3. Cf. Emmanuel Levinas, 'Meaning and Sense' in A. Peperzak, S. Critchely, R. Bernasconi (eds.), *Emmanuel Levinas. Basic Philosophical Writings* (Bloomington and Indianapolis: Indiana University Press, 1996), p. 63: 'He shows himself only by his trace, as it is said in Exodus 33.'

8   Barth, *Church Dogmatics*, I/1, pp. 165–9, 174–7.

9   See, for example, Nigel Wright, *Challenge to Change. A Radical Agenda for Baptists* (Eastbourne: Kingsway Publications, 1991), p. 22.

convictions of a convictional community',[10] and it is this necessary relation between community and theology that we should now explore. For this project, we may call three witnesses in support.

The Experience of a Community

First, from the shadows of the nineteenth century, steps as witness the figure of Friedrich Schleiermacher, who has often been called 'the Father of modern Protestant Theology'. His insight was that since theology was a reflection on *experience of God*, it must belong to a particular community with its own corporate sense of Christ as Redeemer in its midst. There was, he thought, a universal human consciousness or feeling of 'absolute dependence' upon God as the source of life and being, but this sense of God never occurred in a merely general form. It was always specific to the community in a particular time and place in which the Redeemer was present, to shape and purify this experience. His concern was not, we notice, individual, subjective experience but the shared experience of a group.

Schleiermacher, in his own church setting, thus proposed that there must in Germany be a Protestant theology and a Catholic theology, as long as these communities of faith were distinct from each other in their life and worship.[11] He was, we might say, being realistic about the tragic situation of a broken church universal. As long as the church of Christ is rent asunder into different communities of belief, there will be different styles of theology. Schleiermacher hastens to affirm that we must work to overcome division in the visible form of the church, as something which is 'merely temporary'. Moreover, he urges that the separations that exist at present must not prevent us from seeking as much fellowship as is possible.[12]

We might take issue with Schleiermacher's focus on 'feeling', though it would be fairer to translate this as 'intuition' since what he had in view was not something as driven by emotion as the English word 'feeling' portrays. He wanted to get away from the split between 'knowing' and 'doing' into which the philosopher Kant had plunged Christian thinking, isolating Christian belief as he had to the area of 'doing' or morality. In face of this, Schleiermacher wanted to affirm 'feeling' as a way of

---

10   James Wm. McClendon Jr., *Systematic Theology*, Vol. 1, *Ethics* (Nashville: Abingdon Press, 1986), p. 23.

11   F. Schleiermacher, *The Christian Faith*, trans. H. R. Mackintosh and J.S. Stewart (Edinburgh: T. & T. Clark, 1968), pp. 88–93; Schleiermacher, *Brief Outline on the Study of Theology*, trans. Terence N. Tice (Richmond: John Knox Press, 1966), pp. 94–7, 113–15.

12   Schleiermacher, *The Christian Faith*, pp. 682–7.

knowing God. We should certainly bring the *practices* of a community, its actions inside or outside its boundaries, more firmly together with experience than Schleiermacher did at times. Yet for all this, Schleiermacher was making the important point that as long as communities have differences in their 'consciousness' of God and each other, there will be differences in the theologies that reflect on that experience.

Schleiermacher's insight is still alive today; it is embodied in German universities by there being two separate faculties of theology – Protestant and Catholic. From the British scene we tend to feel rather critical and even superior about this. *Our* university faculties of theology are (to put it negatively) non-confessional and (to put it positively) ecumenical. Baptist colleges in the UK, for instance, are connected to universities within the public system of higher education, and are committed to doing theology across the boundaries of the churches. To write personally for a moment, in my own situation in Oxford, candidates are formed for Baptist ministry in a university faculty which includes not only a good number of Baptists, but members of the United Reformed and Methodist churches, Anglicans who are canons of Christ Church Cathedral or teachers in Anglican theological colleges, Roman Catholic theologians who are members of four orders (Benedictine, Jesuit, Dominican and Franciscan), and a Greek Orthodox bishop who is an internationally-known patristics scholar. All happily teach alongside each other. When theological colleagues come to visit us from elsewhere in Europe – especially Germany – or from seminaries in North America, they greatly appreciate the novel experience of working together in seminars across the denominations.

Despite, however, all these advantages of a non-confessional stance of theology in the universities, we in Britain have also paid a price for it. Theology in some university faculties has become detached from the life and mission of the church. It has become a field of study using the same methods of investigation and research as other humanities, and has often obtained respectability by becoming simply identified with religious studies – an important discipline but a separate one from theology.[13] Unlike German courses in theology, Christian ethics has become an optional module rather than being an inseparable part of the study of systematic theology. Courses that combine theology and pastoral studies, or offer a considerable amount of reflection on the practice of the Christian community, have increasingly migrated from university

---

13   So John Webster, *Theological Theology. An Inaugural Lecture delivered before the University of Oxford on 27 October 1997* (Oxford: Clarendon Press, 1998), pp. 22–25, urges the re-establishing of 'theology's relation to the culture of Christian faith and practice from which it so often finds itself dissociated' and for 'the integration of academy and congregation'.

faculties into courses at theological colleges which are *accredited* by the universities, and this has tended to increase a sense of separation within the universal Christian church. In universities where courses in pastoral study and degrees in 'practical theology' *are* embedded in the interior life of university faculties – and I am glad to name Oxford as one of these – those who teach them may nevertheless be mainly those who are employed by churches or by church colleges, rather than those who hold posts on the establishment of the university itself.

In a variety of ways, then, a 'non-confessional' approach to theology at university level may result in the sundering of academic theology from the experience and the practice of actual church communities. A better way forward is surely a 'multi-confessional' one, enabling students to reflect on a plurality of ways of life in community, across the separated Christian families. In such an approach the distinctive life-style of Baptist communities, marked by a particular Baptist experience, will have a part to play.

What then is this 'Baptist experience' which shapes theology? In the first place, the presence of the kingdom of God which can be known in all the world is experienced in the church as the rule of Christ in the congregation. The liberty of local churches to make decisions about their own life and ministry is not based in a human view of autonomy or independence, or in selfish individualism, but in a sense of being under the direct rule of Christ who relativizes other rules. This liberating rule of Christ is the foundation of what makes for the distinctive 'feel' of Baptist congregational life, which allows for spiritual oversight (*episkope*) both by the *whole* congregation gathered together in church meeting, and by the minister(s) called to lead the congregation.[14] This oscillating movement between corporate and individual oversight is difficult to pin down, and can lead to disasters when it begins to swing wildly from one side to another, but it is based in taking the rule of Christ seriously. Since the same rule of Christ can be experienced in assemblies of churches together,[15] there is also the basis here for Baptist associational life, and indeed for participating in ecumenical clusters. Flexible though it is in its actualization, and taking different forms as it does among different cultures, there is something about this response to the rule of Christ which Baptists recognize as familiar wherever they meet it in the world.

Another familiar experience arises from the practice of believers' baptism, in which the candidate is expected to be able to affirm that

---

14   See *The Confession of Faith of those Churches which are commonly (though falsly) called Anabaptists* (London: printed by Matthew Simmons, 1644), hereafter called the 'London Confession', in William L. Lumpkin, *Baptist Confessions of Faith* (Chicago: Judson Press, 1959); art. XLIV, p. 168.

15   See the London Confession (1644) in Lumpkin, *Baptist Confessions*, Introduction (p. 155) and art. XLVII, pp. 168–9.

'Jesus Christ is Lord' for himself or herself. This is not to say that baptism is a witness to faith *rather than* a moment of objective encounter with the transforming grace of God, nor that it is an individual act *rather than* a corporate act of the church in its own faithfulness. The sacrament is all these things at once, and this is the intensity of its meaning and effectiveness. My concern here is simply with aspects of the 'Baptist experience', and part of this is being part of a community in which it is expected that any member will be able and willing – if asked – to witness to her or his own sense of being called by Christ into a life of discipleship, both individual aِd shared with others. Such a baptismal word of witness is also a prophetic word, challenging the powers and structures of society around with the call of Christ to a life marked by compassion and justice. This does not require a high degree of intellectual understanding and assent, nor a standard form of words (the more surprising the better); moreover, in the case of those who are severely handicapped in mind or body, others in the community may need to employ a spiritual imagination and insight to discern a witness, perhaps offered in non-verbal ways.

Linked with this experience is a third, that all members are gifted in leading others in worship of the triune God, and that no equipment or resources are needed (neither prayer book nor overhead projector) except the presence of two or three Christian disciples gathered together. This does not neglect the discipline of training in the leading of worship; it does not undermine the special calling of the pastor by Christ to lead worship representatively and regularly; it does not deny that any congregation which fails to draw upon the liturgical riches of the church universal will soon become impoverished. All these elements are part of the Baptist experience. But at the centre is a freedom to worship unconstrained by forms which are sanctioned either by tradition or human law. Liturgies are the more meaningful when they are used because there is no requirement to use them. Led by others in worship like this, the Baptist Christian will also expect to hear the word of God mediated through fellow members as they read and interpret the scriptures in their own context of daily life and work.

I have tried here to identify some aspects of the experience of being part of a Baptist community of worship and mission, rather than making a list of Baptist principles. It is the experience of walking together under a rule which liberates from human rule, the experience of being with others who can witness to being called to follow Christ's way of life, and the experience of being led by each other into the interweaving life of the triune God. This is the experience of a group of people who – in Britain – have been for the most part from the working classes, until the last century largely self-educated, for much of their history oppressed or excluded from positions in society, and who have been throughout their

history advocates for liberty of religion and conscience for all. In some
parts of the world today this is still their social profile. I do not mean to
claim that this is an experience exclusive to Baptists, but that wherever it
happens theology will be shaped by it; it does happen among Baptists,
and so there is a Baptist way of doing theology. Theological concepts
such as the rule of God and authority will have to take reflection on this
experience into account.

The Confession of a Community

In case readers are becoming uncomfortable with this appeal to
experience, I call the witness of Karl Barth, to whom I have already
appealed. Theology for Barth is, in the first place, the *confession* of the
church in response to God's self-revelation. God speaks a word to us and
enables us to speak it back to God. 'Theology' is talk *about* God and
talk *to* God at the same time; it is, in human terms, impossible – but God
requires us to do the impossible with the help of grace. With God all
things are possible, even the overcoming of the infinite gap of speech
between Creator and created. First-order theology is thus not the
theological works written by an Augustine, Luther, Schleiermacher or
even a Karl Barth, but the confession of the church in its worship, its
creeds, its preaching, its works of love and its testimony through
individual believers. For Barth, what we usually call 'theology' is a
second-order activity of examining the witness of the church; it is the
critical discipline of assessing the content of the church's talk about
God, and so can be called 'Church Dogmatics'.[16]
  If this is so, then we need to listen to the way that a community talks
about God. Theology will be shaped not only by the experience of the
community but by its confession. Barth regards the great, historic
statements of faith as a kind of Christian proclamation or preaching, and
the task of theology is to reflect upon them, to test them against the
disclosure of the Word of God and to use them in turn to help us
understand the Word.[17] Barth himself makes little distinction between
creeds and confessions in this venture, though the difference is quite
important in the Baptist way of doing theology. While the 'creeds' have
been generally seen as binding belief and conscience, Baptists have not
been reluctant to compile 'confessions' for use in teaching, for making
clear the basis on which they covenant together, and for explaining their
belief and practice to those outside Baptist communities.

---

16   For the above, see Barth, *Church Dogmatics*, I/1, pp. 71–87.
17   See for example, Barth's use of the Nicene Creed in developing a doctrine of the
'eternal Son': *Church Dogmatics*, I/1, pp. 423–7.

The distinction then is not an absolute one, and is rather more about the way that statements of faith are used. In many Baptist confessions, the major creeds of the world-wide church have in fact been explicitly acknowledged as trustworthy witnesses to faith. A General Baptist confession of 1679, for instance, affirms that the Creed of Nicaea and the so-called Athanasian Creed were to be 'received' and 'believed' and 'taught by the ministers of Christ'.[18] At the very first Congress of the Baptist World Alliance, in London in 1905, the chairman Dr Alexander McLaren called on the vast gathering to repeat together the words of the Apostles' Creed as 'a simple acknowledgement of where we stand and what we believe.' In the later twentieth century the German-language Baptist confession used in Germany, Austria and Switzerland declares that 'it presupposes the Apostles' Creed as a common confession of Christendom',[19] and the Norwegian Baptists have affirmed 'the content' of both the Apostles' and the Nicene Creed.[20] The model covenant service, recently produced by the Baptist Union of Great Britain for use in churches in 2001, provides in its main text the alternatives of either the Apostles' Creed or a selection of scripture verses as a means of confessing the Christian faith, and includes the Nicene Creed in further resources.[21]

In early Baptist life, a confession was often associated with the 'covenant' by which the community renewed its pledge of faithfulness to its Lord, and committed itself to a common life and mutual caring. The church book, for instance, might contain both a confession and a form of covenant, adjacent to each other. In the early years of Baptist churches in England, there was an ambiguity about the link between the confession of faith adopted by a church and its covenant document.[22] While the two might be adjacent, the one was not *included* in the other. As I am going to argue extensively in later chapters, covenant is about relationship and trust, about 'walking together' which is in some mysterious way part of the very journey of salvation. Such an open journey cannot be finally fixed in a document. Nevertheless, in doing theology in a Baptist way we

---

18 *An Orthodox Creed, Or A Protestant Confession of Faith* (London: 1679), art. XXXVIII, in Lumpkin, *Baptist Confessions*, pp. 326–7.

19 G. Keith Parker, *Baptists in Europe. History and Confessions of Faith* (Nashville: Broadman Press, 1982), p. 57. So also the Confession of the Baptist Union of Finland on p. 111.

20 Parker, *Baptists in Europe*, p. 111.

21 *Covenant 21. Covenant for a Gospel People* (London: Baptist Union, 2000), pp. 10–11.

22 See Roger Hayden, 'Baptists, Covenants and Confessions' in Paul S. Fiddes, Roger Hayden, Richard L. Kidd, Keith W. Clements and Brian Haymes, *Bound to Love. The Covenant Basis of Baptist Life and Mission* (London: Baptist Union, 1985), pp. 26–8.

will pay attention to the confessions which have been produced by different Baptist communities in different contexts. They will not be tests of membership, but they are important examples of 'proclamation', in the Barthian sense. Baptist theologians should be familiar with the Baptist early confessions, and the way that they affirm Reformation insights into grace, faith, ministry and covenant in the setting of seventeenth-century England. They should be aware of a range of modern Baptist confessions, and reflect on those that have arisen in Europe in the context of a prevailing Catholic, Orthodox or Lutheran environment (confessions from Italy, Romania and Germany are good examples here[23]). Finally, it is worth reflecting theologically on the statements produced by the world communion of Baptists in assembly together – such as the declarations about evangelism (Seoul 1990, Madras 1995), racism (Harare 1992, Atlanta 1999) and worship (Berlin 1998).[24] These are examples of proclaiming the faith in the world today, and they are resources for theology as 'Church Dogmatics'.

The Stories of a Community

Third, in case readers are becoming uncomfortable about an appeal to theologians from the German tradition alone (one Lutheran and one Reformed), we should call the witness of the American Baptist theologian, James McClendon, to whom I have already referred. He begins his *Systematic Theology* with the affirmation that this is to be in a 'baptist mode'[25] of doing theology. Among other reasons, this is because the narrative of scripture must always shape the narrative of a particular community: story will transform story.[26]

It is, of course, fairly current theological coin at the moment to speak about the scriptural narrative as the 'grammar' of a Christian community, providing the structure for its speaking and acting. But McClendon understands the Baptist vision to be nothing other than a shared awareness that the present Christian community *is* the early Christian community and *is* the eschatological community. Baptists understand themselves, he suggests, as living *immediately in* the scriptural story and

---

23   For the modern confessions of German and Romanian Baptists, see Parker, *Baptists in Europe*, pp. 57–76. The Confession of Faith of the Christian Evangelical Baptist Union of Italy is published by Il Seminatore, Piazza S. Lorenzo in Lucina, 35, Roma.

24   See Tony Cupit (ed.), *Baptist World Alliance Covenants and Declarations 1990–2000* (McLean: Baptist World Alliance, 2000).

25   McClendon himself deliberately uses a lower-case 'b' in 'baptist', as I explain below.

26   McClendon, *Ethics*, pp. 31–5.

in the story of the day of judgement, and it is this that shapes their convictions and their ethics. We may differ about whether or not this is the *central* organizing principle for a baptist theology. But if theology is at all about the interaction of the story of scripture with the story of a community, then this story is a particular one, held by a particular people. There is what McClendon calls a 'community of reference' for theology; Baptists have a shared story, so they must have a theology.

McClendon suggests that Baptist theology should thus draw upon a rich variety of material from the narrative life of the community – hymns, journals, stories, as well as confessions. In his American context he points to the recovery of the story of blackness among Baptists, such as the way that slaves deliberately lived in the story of the Exodus.[27]

In both Britain and North America Baptists have significant stories about the struggle for liberty on which they can reflect. Thomas Helwys died in prison in 1616 (the date is not exact) because of his plea for religious liberty for all, whether Christians, Jews, Moslems or 'heretics'. Roger Williams was exiled into the New England wilderness, the 'Siberia' of the time, for refusing to accept the restrictions laid on people by the idea of a 'Christian nation'. John Bunyan wrote his dream of the pilgrim from a Bedford jail because he would not conform to the limits imposed on preaching the gospel of Christ. William Knibb led the fight against slavery in the British colony of Jamaica, and was vilified by the landowners as 'Knibb the Notorious'. Martin Luther King Jr. proclaimed his dream of a non-segregated American South and paid for the dream with his life. These stories of dissent shape the community, and they need to influence theology too.

In England we surely also need to recover the hidden stories of *women* in the churches. To take just one example, there was the circle of literary women to which the Baptist poet and hymn-writer Anne Steele belonged in the mid-eighteenth century. Her niece, under the pen-name Silvia, wrote much poetry on the subject of friendship, and it is this theme that forms the basis for her passionate advocacy of liberty, especially for the American colonists.[28] The renewed interest in the place of friendship in gender-relations in our time makes the thought and experience of these women of special interest in Baptist theologizing. Perhaps we have moved on just a little from one reviewer of Silvia's verse, who commented that 'There is an excellence in this poem which few writers attain, and which from a female pen especially is not always expected.'[29]

---

27 McClendon, *Ethics*, p. 39.

28 See 'Liberty. An Ode', printed at the end of *Danebury. The Power of Friendship*, a long poem published anonymously (Bristol: W. Pine, 1779).

29 Reviewed in the *Monthly Review*, 61 (1779), p. 43. See Marjorie Reeves, 'Literary Women in Eighteenth-Century Nonconformist Circles', in Jane Shaw and Alan

Our three witnesses – Schleiermacher, Barth, McClendon – tell us that the experience, the confession and the stories of a community shape theology. In this sense, as long as there is a Baptist community, there will be a Baptist theology. But this leads to a further problem: how can a Baptist community be identified? *Which* communities are these which give rise to a Baptist way of doing theology?

Identifying a Baptist Community

We can readily name a number of convictions that belong to a Baptist community – notably the gathered church, the priesthood of all believers, the final authority of Christ, believers' baptism, the call to faithful corporate discipleship, and religious freedom. These convictions in themselves are not unique to Baptists, but the way that Baptists have held them is still important. We might say further, I think, that there is something distinctive about the way that Baptists have *held these convictions together*; the combination or constellation is more distinctive than the single items.[30] There is especially something distinctive about the way that the convictions have been held together within a particular worship-life and practice of church meetings.

But having said this, there might well be communities naming themselves 'Baptist' and holding these convictions, or versions of them, which other Baptists find it hard to identify with. To make the problem concrete, I divert for the moment into recalling an instalment of the recent American TV sit-com, *Ally McBeal*, set in a lawyer's office.[31] This particular episode featured the male editor of a feminist magazine who had been fired by the woman owner because he was a Southern Baptist, and the Southern Baptist Convention had recently declared as a point of principle that a wife should 'submit to the servant leadership of her husband'. The editor himself disagreed strongly with this declaration, and stated his own convictions in court. He won his case against unfair dismissal, because it turned out that the woman editor was not interested in his personal view; it was enough for her that he was a Baptist, and that

---

Kreider (eds.), *Culture and the Nonconformist Tradition* (Cardiff: University of Wales Press, 1999), p. 20.

30 'American Baptists, A Unifying Vision', a resource document for the Commission on Denominational Identity of American Baptists, printed in *American Baptist Quarterly* 6/2 (1987), p. 114, suggests that convictional 'genes' are woven together with a particular 'tone'.

31 *Ally McBeal* (Fox), season 2, episode 'It's My Party', first screened 19 October 1998.

the Baptist Convention had made this statement – and has since, indeed, embodied it in its confession of faith.[32]

This little story raises some interesting questions of Baptist identity. Within the story itself, was the owner right to identify the editor with other Baptists who held certain views about women? In what sense could the editor identify *himself* with those whom he disagreed with on a fundamental issue? But outside the story, what about the viewers? Several million people in the UK who saw the episode may now assume that Baptists in general hold this view about the status of women; they have no idea about the differences between Baptists in different areas of the world. And do British Baptists regard themselves as fellow-Baptists with all Southern Baptists, or just selected ones – such as the editors of feminist magazines? One notable Baptist defender of civil liberties writes, 'In Washington when I tell someone "Yes, I'm a Baptist and I work for Baptists," their response often drips with snide. I hurriedly say, "But I'm a Bill Moyers, Jimmy Carter, Barbara Jordan kind of Baptist"'.[33] But does making a personal list of those who are to be approved as fellow-Baptists make a community in the sense we have explored it above? How, then, is a Baptist community to be identified? There are perhaps two ways of approaching this question.

Not 'Baptist', but 'baptist'?

The first approach is that adopted by James McClendon, who writes 'Baptist' with a small 'b'. By 'baptist' he means a certain approach to faith and life which he roots in the Radical Reformation, and which is actualized, however imperfectly, in a wide range of communities.[34] Some of these might not call themselves Baptist, and others which *do* call themselves Baptist he would not recognize as embodying baptist principles (with a small 'b'). So we take a universal characteristic and see where it might be localized. Those who deny being 'Baptist with a capital B' usually do so for the commendable reason of wanting to recover and preserve principles that have marked Baptist tradition, especially its beginnings in a Reformation form of dissent, but which seem lamentably absent today.

---

32   Revised version of The Baptist Faith and Message of the Southern Baptist Convention, USA (adopted 14 June 2000), article XVIII 'The Family' (amended 1998); text available from www.sbc.net/bfm/.

33   James M. Dunn, 'Yes, I am a Baptist' in Cecil P. Staton (ed.), *Why I am a Baptist. Reflections on Being Baptist in the 21st Century* (Macon: Smyth and Helwys Publishing, 1999), p. 48.

34   McClendon, *Ethics*, pp. 19–21, 34–5.

This approach, in terms of our book title, focuses on finding 'tracks' from the past. It may also relieve people from the real discomfort of relating to actual Baptist churches whose views and practices are alien to them. Thus, they still regard themselves as 'baptist' without being an active member of any Baptist congregation. The problem, however, is that they might end up with a highly personalized view of what it is to be baptist. Or they might be seeking for the same kind of homogeneous fellowship which appears in certain theories of church growth, and which has been rightly criticized as refusing the disturbing challenge of living with those who are 'not like us'. As Jürgen Moltmann has emphasized, a characteristic of the church is for it to be the fellowship of the 'unlike'.[35] While James McClendon's own course of life demonstrated clearly and courageously the acceptance of 'otherness', there is a danger that others might take the 'baptistic' principle in another direction.

Identity as Identification

A second way of approaching the question of identity is not to begin from baptistic universals, but from the particular form of Baptist life into which Christ has called a disciple (through many human circumstances) for worship of God and mission to the world. This 'local' form might be a national union, or it might even be the associational life of churches within a region of a union; in its particularity it will have an identity that comes from its own history and heritage of thought as well as its activities today. This present book about Baptist identity constantly takes its point of departure, for instance, from the story of Baptist and Nonconformist life in England. Owning this immediate identity does not mean an uncritical reception of all its aspects, and belonging will require trust and mutual acceptance. Identity contains a strong element, that is, of willing identification. At the same time, a Baptist Christian will know that he or she is a member of the body of Christ which is the church of all the redeemed, universal in time and space. So from a particular place of Baptist belonging, it is then possible to answer the summons of Christ to enter *as wide a fellowship as is possible*. This also will be the way of trust, not a demand for absolute sameness.[36]

In a broken situation of the church universal there can only be a world-wide fellowship through world communions, or what are often despised as 'denominations'. These are imperfect signs of a universal

---

35   Jürgen Moltmann, *The Church in the Power of the Spirit. A Contribution to Messianic Ecclesiology*, trans. M. Kohl (London: SCM Press, 1977), pp. 182–9.

36   See Richard L. Kidd (ed.), *On the Way of Trust. Jointly written by the Principals of the four English Colleges in membership with the Baptist Union of Great Britain* (Oxford: Whitley Publications, 1997), pp. 21–7.

church, and Baptists have kept the future open with an eschatological symbol – that is, declining to call their wider ecclesial structures '*The Baptist Church*'. But there will never be meaningful, committed and costly relations with those in other cultures without international communions. Of course, members of one society can pick and choose individuals in other societies with whom they want to align themselves and whom they may support with practical aid, but this will inevitably be satisfying to those members' own concerns and limited to their own knowledge of the world. Commitment to a world *communion* of churches will bring the surprises and challenges of links with places which were not originally in a private horizon of interests, and with people who are different and are to be valued for whom they are.

Not only individuals within churches, but churches and unions of churches can make covenant with others for fellowship and mission, and out of faithful obedience to Christ who is the Lord of the one church universal, *identify* with those whom they cannot agree with about everything – or sometimes it seems, not much at all. To use the language of our title, we can be content with 'traces' in our communion with each other, satisfied to be able to catch echoes of the story that is also ours. The only qualification is that others are willing to make covenant with us, with the same openness to living in trust on the journey. In a first stage this is likely to mean the forming or affirming of a particular world communion, but this should be regarded as only provisional, always penultimate on the way to making visible the one church of Christ.

This introductory chapter, being about identity, necessarily has a personal tone. It seems appropriate then to say that I have myself caught these echoes and found these traces among Baptists throughout the world. I have stood with fellow Baptists at a service in Sam Sharpe Square in Montego Bay, Jamaica, a place named in memory of the Baptist deacon and slave who was executed for his protest against the British slave system. I have prayed with fellow Baptists by the side of the Han river in Seoul, Korea, and witnessed several thousand young people being baptized – not in a media spectacle, but each one greeted personally by his or her pastor. I have lectured with fellow Baptists in the University of Timisoare, Romania, near the square where more than fifty young people were killed in the revolution of 1989 as they demonstrated for freedom, shouting 'God exists'. I have talked with Portuguese Baptists in Lisbon, where the great earthquake of 1755 is still remembered as the event which shook people's faith in a good creator, and destroyed a whole system of natural theology. I have shared in a Sunday morning service in the black township of Tembisa near Johannesburg where the previous night Zulu Inkata terrorists had massacred nearly a hundred people, and I have experienced Zulu and Chosa Baptists worshipping together in acceptance of each other. I have sat with Baptists in Cuba, listening to the way that they understand mission in their neighbourhood, led by a pastor who was serving as a Deputy in the government of Fidel Castro, and suffering rejection by fellow Christians because of this involvement in politics. I have received hospitality from Baptists in Myanmar, and admired the way that the many ethnic groups express their faith, and their hopes for their common society, through their different styles of song and dance. Through these experiences, my thinking has been shaped in a way that would not have been possible without a shared identity as Baptists.

Identity, I suggest, is more about *identification* than about being *identical*. It is an identification which is not a mere human effort, but is enabled by that identification of God with humanity that we call incarnation. Later in this book I want, then, to make clear that my appeal to the act of identifying does not conform the church to the secular model of a voluntary society, though there will always be something intentional about it;[37] nor am I ignoring the truth that we share a common identity as members of the body of Christ through baptism.[38] However, a theology of identification will be bound to envisage visible unity as being covenantal at heart, rather than (say) a recovery of any *particular* structure of episcopal oversight which has precedent in history.[39] It will lean more on the openness of the trace than the boundaries of a track. With regard to Baptist identity in particular, the mood is caught by an American Baptist historian, who ends his answer to the question 'why are you a Baptist?' with the words: 'Religion at its best is not generic; it has specificity and peculiarity. Being a Baptist is messy, controversial, divisive, and energizing.'[40] It is not that we share an already-existing identity through establishing a common list of agreed items, but we willingly *identify* ourselves with others who want to make or keep covenant with us because they catch an echo of their story in us. This desire and our response will take us, often, into depths of shared life beyond what is possible at present in ecumenical sharing *between* communions, and will give us an identity which will bring a richness to the ecumenical fellowship. In short, identity is about covenant-faithfulness, and this appeal to covenant brings me to a final question about the Baptist way of doing theology. Is there something particularly Baptist about the *content* of theology as well as method?

---

37   See below, ch. 2, pp. 40–55.
38   See below, ch. 7, pp. 150–2.
39   See below, ch. 9, pp. 221–7.
40   Bill Leonard, 'Being Baptist. Hospitable Traditionalism', in Staton (ed.), *Why I am a Baptist*, p. 88.

A Baptist Focus in Theology

In an article exploring what the Baptist way of doing theology might be, Brian Haymes has usefully identified four characteristics of *method* in theology, rooted in distinctive Baptist convictions about the nature of the church. A Baptist approach to theologizing, he suggests, is marked by a continual re-making, an imaginative living in the biblical story, a generous pluralism, and a collegiality in which doing theology is shared between experts and those who simply live out their theology in a practical way.[41] With regard to the *content* of theology, I have already observed that Baptists have been reluctant to admit that there are any particular Baptist forms of basic Christian doctrines. Baptists usually, however, make an exception for the doctrine of the church and baptism, not always realizing how deeply intermeshed ecclesiology and sacramental theology are with concepts of salvation and the nature of the triune God.

Thus, what we have explored above about the effect of the experience, the confession and the stories of a community must lead us to suppose that there will be a distinctively Baptist focus to the *content* of the theology too. Being in a particular community will give its thinkers a kind of guiding interest, a theme which remains as a kind of *cantus firmus*, an underlying melody beneath the counterpoint of detail, even when it does not become overt. Other Christian communions have such a theme which has generally appeared within the work of major theologians in their story. I will take the risk of crude generalization, and suggest that the Reformed tradition is interested in the theme of the sovereignty of God, exemplified by Calvin; Lutherans cannot write much without returning to the theme of justification by faith, exemplified by Luther; Catholic theology still organizes a great deal of its thought around the transformation of nature by grace, as expounded in Scholastic thought and notably by Thomas Aquinas; the Orthodox church continually explores the theme of *theosis* or the divinization of human life, as found in the Eastern Church Fathers but given firm outlines by St Maximus the Confessor.

Baptists do not have such formative theologians. But they do have a theological theme that was of central importance for several centuries, and is gradually being recovered in our day. I mean the idea of *covenant*, which I have already placed at the centre of thinking about the nature of identity. It is a theme which Baptists share with others in the Reformed tradition, and especially with English Congregationalists – now part of the United Reformed Church – but which took its own particular form in

---

41 Brian Haymes, 'Theology and Baptist Identity' in Paul S. Fiddes (ed.), *Doing Theology in a Baptist Way* (Oxford: Whitley Publications, 2000), pp. 1–5.

Baptist congregational life. In the next chapter I intend to explore this idea in detail, but what I want to stress here is that the making of a covenant by a local congregation in the seventeenth and eighteenth centuries was not simply regarded by them as a *human* act of commitment to each other. In covenanting together, they believed there to be an intersection between the promise-making of members of a local congregation, and God's eternal covenant of grace. In some mysterious way this eternal covenant, made from God's side and by God's own initiative, became actual in time and space when believers bound themselves to each other in faithful fellowship. There was an integration of the horizontal and vertical dimensions of covenant. Now, there has been a good deal of recent reflection among British Baptists on the implications of covenant for *ecclesiology*, for associating together not only locally, but at regional and national levels. But here for a moment I want to consider how this theme might guide the doing of theology in general. Briefly, I offer three suggestions.

First, it should mean that Baptist theologians will be interested in the theological idea of 'participation' in God.[42] If the covenant fellowship of local Christians somehow shares in the covenant fellowship of God's own life, then the whole of theology should reflect this being 'in God.' The link between human community and divine communion is in fact a guiding thought in the attempt of Stanley Grenz to write a systematic theology from a Baptist perspective, called *Theology for the Community of God*. This is a massive and formative work to which Baptists should be much indebted, although I would want to go one stage further myself in relating communion and covenant. Grenz proposes that the Baptist notion of the church as a covenanting people 'focuses our attention on its actual manifestation in human history'; so *covenant* roots us in time and space, while the idea of the church as *community* or *communion* 'lifts our conception beyond the activity of God in history to the life of the triune God himself, which provides the foundation for that activity.'[43] I suggest that covenant and communion in God are in fact mysteriously intertwined in *both* time and eternity, and that in this interaction there is a distinctive Baptist theme. It has some affinity, though in its own Baptist way, to the Orthodox theology of *theosis*, or 'divinization', which does

---

42   Graham Watts makes a similar plea in his paper, 'The Spirit and Community. Trinitarian Pneumatology and the Church', *Theology in Context* 1 (2000), pp. 71–3. I have myself attempted such a theology in Paul S. Fiddes, *Participating in God. A Pastoral Doctrine of the Trinity* (London: Darton, Longman & Todd, 2000).

43   Stanley J. Grenz, *Theology for the Community of God* (Nashville: Broadman and Holman, 1994, p. 628. Grenz, pp. 603–10, 630, thus concentrates on the idea of making a covenant community through voluntary commitment. For a complementary view, stressing the initiative of divine grace, see ch. 2 below, pp. 42–4.

not mean 'becoming God' but sharing to the most intimate degree in the fellowship of the divine life.

Second, the theme of covenant means that Baptist theologians will always be working and struggling with the relation between divine grace and human freewill. Covenant brings together human responsibility in keeping covenant, and divine initiative in making covenant in the first place. No one can enter into a church covenant without being presented with both these truths: as Benjamin Keach put it in 1697, '*we* give up ourselves, through the *everlasting* covenant.'[44] In our own story, Baptists have brought these truths together for the sake of mission. Andrew Fuller did this on the verge of the nineteenth century with his book called *A Gospel worthy of All Acceptation*, combining a confidence in God's sovereign purpose in atonement with the human moral duty to respond to it.[45] This provided a theological foundation for the work of the newly founded Baptist Missionary Society. At the beginning of the twentieth century, faced by the need for a united mission in England, General and Particular Baptists came together into a Union, so uniting the truths of divine sovereignty and human responsibility in their own bodies.[46] At the beginning of the twenty-first century there are new ways that we need to work at bringing these truths together: for instance, in the face of the scientific challenge we need to think about what free-will means in the form of the self-creativity of living things and processes. How do creaturely human response and divine grace come together in the interacting web of organic life? And how can both divine grace and human freedom come together in another interacting web, the network of electronic communications?

Third, the theme of covenant should interest us in the place of promises within human life in general. This can be viewed from several angles. The political philosopher, Hannah Arendt, writes that societies can only get over their evil from the past, and change for the better, through two faculties: forgiveness, and the power to make and keep promises. Promises, she suggests, deal with 'the ocean of uncertainty' in the future by setting up 'islands of security' which make it possible for relationships to continue and endure.[47] Government requires agreement

---

44 Benjamin Keach, *The Glory of a True Church, and Its Discipline Display'd* (London, 1697), p. 71 (my italics).

45 Andrew Fuller, *The Gospel Worthy of all Acceptation,* 2nd edition (1801), in *The Complete Works of the Rev. Andrew Fuller,* ed. A.G. Fuller. A New Edition (5 volumes; London: William Ball, 1837), II; see, for example, pp. 55–8, 82.

46 See Ernest A. Payne, *The Baptist Union. A Short History* (London: Carey Kingsgate Press, 1959), pp. 113–43.

47 Hannah Arendt, *The Human Condition. A Study of the Central Conditions Facing Modern Man* (New York: Doubleday Anchor Books, 1959), pp. 212–13.

between human persons and a reliance on promise, but it seems we are living in a society at present in which people find commitment difficult, and distrust the promises made by elected leaders. While covenant is a deeper theological concept than a voluntary social contract there are connections between these ideas, and Baptist theology may have particular resources for exploring the theme of promise in society and fostering a renewal of mutual trust. Further, societies are shaped (even perhaps created) by language, and promising has become a significant theme in the philosophy of language, as an important example of performative speech. In this way of thinking, words do not just refer to things, but 'get things done'; they are not only signs, but promote actions. Biblically, the idea of promise is at the heart of covenant between God and human partners: a God who promises gives us security while leaving the future open for surprising fulfilments of the promise. A God who promises 'gets things done', but in such a way that in the coming of fulfilment there is plenty of room for human contribution to God's project.

In such ways as these, the concept of covenant among Baptists can make a considerable contribution to social, political, philosophical and biblical studies. Moreover, a theology that interacts with these disciplines will be shaped by a Baptist *community* that regards itself as living in covenant relationship. This is to travel the pilgrim way with the guidance of established tracks, yet aware that we walk into the future only with the help of traces.

CHAPTER 2

'Walking Together': The Place of Covenant Theology in Baptist Life Yesterday and Today

Covenant and Identity

Baptists have never been much interested by historic moments and places in their story. They do not look back readily to an Augsburg or a Dort or even to a Chalcedon. It seems to be a mark of Baptist life to adapt to the present and constantly to seek to re-invent itself, which at best can be seen as openness to the Spirit of God and at worst as a neglect of the lessons which the Spirit has wanted to teach the church during its history. But if one place and time were to be fixed upon as formative for Baptist Christians, it might well be at Gainsborough near Lincoln in 1606 or 1607, when a congregation of English Separatists made a covenant together. As William Bradford recalled the event years later in America, the members

> joyned them selves (by a covenant of the Lord) into a Church estate, in the fellowship of the gospell, to walke in all his wayes, made known, or to be made known unto them, according to their best endeavours, whatsoever it should cost them, the Lord assisting them.[1]

They were not yet a Baptist church, but within a year the part of the congregation that gathered in Gainsborough would be in exile in Amsterdam with their pastor, John Smyth, and within two years would have adopted the practice of believers' baptism. Some members of that church would return to England in 1611 with Thomas Helwys as their pastor to found the first General Baptist church on English soil. The other part of the original covenanting group, who worshipped in Scrooby, were to follow their fellow believers to Holland, though not into similar Baptist convictions. From their church in Leiden, served by John

---

1   William Bradford, *History of Plymouth Plantation, 1620–1647*, ed. W.C. Ford (2 volumes; Boston: Massachusetts Historical Society, 1912), I, pp. 20–22.

Robinson as its pastor, many of them would sail for America on the Mayflower and contribute to the story of Congregationalism in New England.

This covenanting at Gainsborough was a defining moment. It exemplifies the continuity between Baptists and the earlier movement of separatism from the newly established Church of England. Its language reflects the Separatist heritage, from Robert Browne onwards, of conceiving covenant in two dimensions at once, vertical and horizontal; that is, the church was gathered by the members' making a covenant or solemn agreement *both* with God *and* with each other. There is the characteristic pledge 'to walk in the Lord's ways', which reaches back to the earlier congregational covenant of the Separatist church led by Francis Johnson,[2] and forward to the many covenants of local General and Particular Baptist churches from the late seventeenth century onwards.

Significant too is the openness to the future expressed in the phrase 'to be made known to them', which recalls a similar 'further light' clause in the covenant of Johnson's church ('all ways ... whether as yet seen or not'),[3] and the later much celebrated saying of John Robinson that 'the Lord has more truth and light yet to break forth out of his holy word'.[4] In a recovery of interest in the theme of covenant among British Baptists in our own time, a good deal of stress has been laid on the openness to the unknown that is implied by the metaphor of 'walking together'. The image is a dynamic one, of pilgrimage and process, and its use by some modern Baptists has been influenced by 'theologies of hope' which have stressed that God's promise opens up a future with a quality of newness which constantly challenges the institutions of the present with the unexpected.[5] The openness of 'walking together' on the way of trust in covenant has thus also been contrasted with the more closed boundaries

---

2   See the account by Henry Ainsworth, *The Communion of Saincts* (Amsterdam, 1615), p. 340.

3   F. Johnson, *An inquirie and answer of Thomas White his discoverie of Brownisme* (Amsterdam, 1606), p. 35. This, however, is a negative reference to discerning evil ways. Ainsworth's account (previous note) is more positive, referring to 'the paths of God as he shall teach them'.

4   From notes of Edward Winslow on John Robinson's parting speech to those leaving his Leyden congregation to sail on the *Mayflower* in 1620.

5   See e.g. Richard Kidd, 'The Documents of Covenant Love' in Fiddes et al., *Bound to Love*, pp. 43–4; Brian Haymes, 'Covenant and the Church's Mission', ibid., pp. 66–72; Richard Kidd (ed.) *Something to Declare. A study of the Declaration of Principle jointly written by the Principals of the four English Colleges in membership with the Baptist Union of Great Britain* (Oxford: Whitley Publications, 1996), pp. 12–16, 24–5, 31–2; Paul Ballard, 'Baptists and Covenanting' in *BQ* 24/8 (1972), pp. 377–8.

of a confession of faith. So the concept of covenant has been appealed to in our day, not only as a means of understanding the nature of the local congregation, but in support of the risks of ecumenical partnership, as a theological basis for association between churches, and as a way of conceiving identity as a union of churches on a national level.

All this may seem a great distance from Gainsborough. If the seed is present in the phrase 'to be made known', it must be confessed that the search for future guidance in that turbulent period often led to the growth of dissension rather than mutual trust. The two parts of the original covenanting group were to be alienated from each other on the issue of believers' baptism, and John Smyth's congregation was to split over the issue of whether, having adopted believers' baptism, it should apply to join the Mennonites. The congregation led by Francis Johnson, already in Amsterdam when the Gainsborough-Scrooby groups arrived, was not only divided on its reaction to John Smyth's self-baptism, but was rent internally over the matter of the interpretation of Matthew 18:17 regarding church discipline. But, from the perspective of the present day, it may be a source of encouragement that both paedo-baptists and believer-baptists share a common story in the covenant of Gainsborough. It is as we are willing to discern obedience to the ways of the Lord in the two somewhat different paths taken thereafter by Congregationalists and Baptists that we may learn to 'walk together' in the wider ecumenical context of the present day.

These opening remarks should already have made clear that this chapter is not intended to be limited to a strictly historical study. The place of covenant in the thought of English radical Puritans and Separatists in the late sixteenth and early seventeenth centuries has already been considered in a number of modern studies;[6] a pioneering work in this area was *The English Separatist Tradition* by B. R. White,[7] and notable further works were published by two of his doctoral pupils at Oxford, R. T. Kendall[8] and Stephen Brachlow.[9] White's thesis that Separatist theologies of covenant were central to John Smyth's thought

---

6   See Perry Miller, *The New England Mind* (New York: Norton Press, 1939); David Zaret, *Heavenly Contract: Ideology and Organization in Pre-Revolutionary Puritanism* (Chicago: University of Chicago Press, 1985), p. 106.

7   B.R. White, *The English Separatist Tradition. From the Marian Martyrs to the Pilgrim Fathers* (Oxford: Oxford University Press, 1971). The essay which was the original form of this chapter was written in Barrie White's honour.

8   R.T. Kendall, *Calvin and English Calvinism to 1649* (Oxford: Oxford University Press, 1979).

9   Stephen Brachlow, *The Communion of Saints. Radical Puritan and Separatist Ecclesiology 1570–1625* (Oxford: Oxford University Press, 1988).

has been subject to some criticism,[10] but I believe that my present essay will offer support for his account. However, I am not only concerned with the origins of the covenant tradition among Baptists in their early days, but with its development in the next two centuries, its widespread demise in the nineteenth century and its resurgence among us in the last two decades. Nor will these be simply historical reflections; I hope to show that a renewed theology of covenant will be fruitful for several concerns that face Baptists in the context of the 'inter-church process' and the secular culture of today, and especially through the tendency of covenant towards openness to others and the whole of creation.

Indeed, one of the attractions of the concept of covenant for early Baptists was that it provided a larger sense of identity to those who had separated from the national church; in answer to those who accused them of losing continuity with the Catholic (i.e. universal) church it enabled them to claim a continuity with the whole covenant people of God throughout the ages. This is the spirit of the covenant of New Road Baptist Church, Oxford, made in 1780 when it re-formed a church life which was already more than a century old, daring to call itself a 'Protestant Catholic Church'.[11]

The Meaning of 'Covenant'

When Stephen Brachlow refers to the 'rich texture of puritan covenant theology',[12] he has in mind a complex relationship between unconditional and conditional understandings of the covenant relationship between God and human beings. He rightly protests against a too simple polarization, as if it were only the *most* radical of Puritans who took a conditional view of the covenant, insisting that it would be invalid unless the conditions of ethical obedience to God's laws were fulfilled, especially in the area of church discipline.

This was certainly the view of Separatists such as Robert Browne, Henry Barrow and Francis Johnson, and was later the view of Baptists such as John Smyth and Thomas Helwys. For them, therefore, the covenant relationship between God and the national English church was broken and void. However, Brachlow observes that radical Puritans who remained within the establishment could take a conditional view when it suited their argument in urging internal reforms within the church. William Perkins, for example, could define covenant as '[God's] contract with man

---

10   See James R. Coggins, 'The Theological Positions of John Smyth', *BQ* 30/6 (1984), pp. 247–59.

11   Printed in W. Stevens and W.W. Bottoms, *The Baptists of New Road, Oxford* (Oxford: Alden Press, 1948), p. 25.

12   Brachlow, *Communion of Saints*, p. 34

concerning the obtaining of life eternal, upon a certain condition.'[13] But Puritans such as Perkins could equally lay stress upon the unconditional aspect of the covenant when opposing separation from the established church, and especially when seeking to counter the case for believers' baptism. Separatists such as Johnson could also appeal to the unconditional nature of the covenant when opposing the adoption of believers' baptism by fellow Separatists, arguing that infant baptism was analogous to the everlasting covenant of grace made with Abraham 'and his seed for ever'.[14]

Here Brachlow ventures to take issue with B. R. White, who had suggested that the conditional view of the covenant among Separatists was a departure from their Calvinistic Puritan tradition. Brachlow notes that the ambiguity between conditional and unconditional aspects was already present in Puritan thought, and that this mirrors the tensions within the Old Testament itself in its account of covenant, containing as it does both unconditional forms (notably the covenants with David and Abraham) and conditional ones (especially the covenant made through Moses).[15] We shall return to this issue when considering the relation between covenant and salvation, but for the moment we need to put it in a wider context of meaning. We can observe, I suggest, at least four threads of significance of the term 'covenant' within the cloth of English Puritan and Separatist theology. Failure to identify these will undoubtedly lead to confusion in any discussion, as will failure to notice where they are woven together in a harmonious pattern or even into a single multiple-stranded thread.

In the first place, 'covenant' referred to an eternal 'covenant of grace' which God has made with human beings and angels for their salvation in Jesus Christ. Calvin was influential in developing this idea, which for him included the restriction of the covenant to the elect.[16] Again from Calvin is the belief that there is only one eternal covenant, but that it takes a different form of application or dispensation in the two eras of the Old Testament and the New Testament. Under either testament the covenant is made through Christ as mediator, but under the old Christ is present in

13   William Perkins, *A Golden Chaine* (Cambridge, 1591), p. 31; as quoted in Brachlow, *Communion of Saints*, p. 33.

14   Francis Johnson, *A brief treatise against two errours of the Anabaptists* (Amsterdam, 1609), p. 17. On this issue, see Stephen Brachlow, 'Puritan Theology and General Baptist Origins', *BQ* 31/4 (1985), pp. 187–9.

15   Brachlow, *Communion of Saints*, pp. 4–13, 34–40. On types of covenant in the Old Testament, see below, chapter 4, pp. 74–6.

16   E.g. John Calvin, *Institutes of the Christian Religion*, trans. H. Beveridge (2 volumes; London: James Clarke, 1949), I, 2, vi:1–4, pp. 293–8; II, 3, xxi:6–7, pp. 208–11.

shadowy types whereas he is fully manifested in the new.[17] So John Smyth begins his discourse on *Principles and Inferences concerning the Visible Church* with the definition:

> Remember that there be alwaies a difference put betwixt the covenant of grace; and the manner of dispensing it, which is twofold: the form of administring the covenant before the death of Christ, which is called the old testament; and the forme of administring the covenant since the death of Christ which is called the new Testament or the kingdome of heaven.[18]

Significantly, Smyth goes on immediately to say that his treatise on the nature of the church which follows is actually concerned with the 'dispensing of the covenant' since the death of Christ, a clue we shall follow up in a moment.

Second, the divine covenant could refer to a transaction between the persons of the triune God, in which the Son is envisaged as consenting to the will of the Father to undertake the work of the salvation of the elect. While Calvin depicts the atonement in Christ as a transaction in which the Son satisfies the justice of the Father, he only hints that this might be regarded as a *covenant* relationship between the two persons. This idea was fully developed by seventeenth-century Calvinist theologians, and is embodied in the Westminster Confession. Thus, while the Particular Baptist London Confession of 1644 refers only to 'the blood of the everlasting covenant', the Second London Confession of 1677 specifies the eternal covenant as a being 'a transaction between the Father and the Son about the Redemption of the Elect'.[19] In his treatise on the Covenant, *The Display of Glorious Grace* (1698) the Baptist pastor Benjamin Keach regards the 'federal' agreement between the Father and the Son[20] as the primary meaning of the covenant of grace. In the 'Holy Covenant' between the Father and Son, 'Jesus Christ struck hands with God the

---

17   Calvin, *Institutes*, I, 2, x:23; 2, xi:4–10, pp. 385, 391–6; cf. John Gill, *Complete Body of Doctrinal and Practical Divinity* (1770). *A New Edition in Two Volumes* (Grand Rapids: Baker Book House, 1978 = London: 1795 repr. 1839), I, bk.2, p. 308.

18   John Smyth, *Principles and Inferences concerning the Visible Church* (1607); printed in W.T. Whitley (ed.), *The Works of John Smyth* (2 volumes; Cambridge: Cambridge University Press, 1915), I, p. 250.

19   *Confession of Faith Put Forth by the Elders and Brethren Of many Congregations Of Christians (baptized upon Profession of their Faith), In London and the Country* (London: 1677), hereafter called the 'Second London Confession', ch. VII.3, in Lumpkin, *Baptist Confessions,* p. 260.

20   Benjamin Keach, *The Display of Glorious Grace. Or, The Covenant of Peace Opened. In Fourteen Sermons* (London, 1698), p. 285.

Father, in behalfe of all God's Elect'.[21] So Keach agrees with those
theologians who maintain that:

> 'Christ is the covenant primarily... With Christ the covenant was made as with the
> chief Party; with Believers it was made in subordination to him; with him it was
> made at first Hand, with us at second Hand.'[22]

In the later higher Calvinism of John Gill, the covenant between the
Father, Son and Spirit has become virtually the *only* meaning of the
covenant of grace. The elect participate in the benefits of this transaction,
but it is not *made with* them even in the secondary way envisaged by
Keach, since Gill can find no mutuality of conditions or reciprocal
freedom in the relationship between God and creatures.[23] Instead, Gill
portrays a scene in the heavenly council in which the covenant is made,
which though colourful has just a touch of bathos in it (and at least a
passing resemblance to a Baptist church meeting!):

> In the eternal council [Jehovah] moved it, and proposed it to his Son, as the most
> advisable step that could be taken to bring about the designed salvation, who
> readily agreed to it, and said, *Lo, I come to do thy will, O God*, Heb.x.7, from Psalm
> xl.7,8; and the Holy Spirit expressed his approbation of him to be the fittest
> person to be the Saviour, by joining with the Father in the mission of him ... The
> pleasure and satisfaction the three divine persons had in this affair, thus advised to,
> consulted, and approved of, is most clearly to be seen and observed at our Lord's
> baptism.[24]

Third, the term 'covenant' could refer to an agreement which God
makes corporately with his church, or with particular churches. For
instance, a radical Puritan who remained in the established church,
Thomas Cartwright, asserted against the Separatists that God's covenant
with the Church of England remained unbroken, despite disobedience
over matters of church order: 'the Lord is in covenant; this he does to
our assembly in England, therefore they are the Lord's confederates.[25]
When portraying the covenant bond between God and his people as
organized into the form of a society or institution (the 'church estate'),
writers tend to appeal to the covenant formula of God with Israel – 'I will
be their God and they shall be my people' – and its forms in the New
Testament referring to the church.[26] At first this may seem identical with

---

21   Keach, *Display of Glorious Grace*, p. 243.
22   Keach, *Display of Glorious Grace*, p. 294, quoting 'a worthy writer'.
23   Gill, *Body of Divinity*, I, bk. 2, p. 309
24   Gill, *Body of Divinity*, I, bk. 2, p. 305.
25   Cit. Brachlow, *Communion of Saints*, p. 47.
26   2 Cor. 6:16–18; Heb. 8:10, quoted by John Smyth, *Paralleles, Censures,
Observations* (1609) in *Works*, II, pp. 386–7.

the first meaning, the covenant of grace with the elect, but there are subtle differences in the way that the idea of the covenant is handled. For instance, Calvin could envisage God's making a 'general covenant' with Israel as a nation, while only bestowing on the elect the 'Spirit of regeneration, by whose power they persevere in the covenant even until the end.'[27] He then drew the parallel with the church of Christ as a way of explaining how some *seem* to be in covenant relationship with God and yet fail to persevere. Again, and rather differently, some who thought that the covenant bond between God and his elect unquestionably stood firm, could still debate the question as to whether it had come to an end with a particular church.

This of course complicates the issue as to whether the 'covenant' was unconditional or conditional upon obedience; what covenant is in mind? In his answering the question as to how a church 'must be planted and gathered' under the lordship of Christ, Robert Browne clearly sets out a conditional view of the covenant bond, with two sides to it:

> (36) First, by a couenant and condicion, made on God's behalfe. Secondlie by a couenant and condicion made on our behalfe.... The couenant on Gods behalf is his agreement or partaking of condicions with us that if we keepe his lawes, not forsaking his gouernment, hee will take vs for his people, & blesse vs accordingly.... (37) What is the covenant or condicion on our behalfe? We must offer and geve vp our selues to be of the church and people of God.[28]

But this discussion is not explicitly related to the eternal covenant of grace in Christ, so we do not know whether Browne thought that this was conditional too; rather, Browne is immediately concerned with the nature of the local congregation as being under the direct *government* of Christ, and obliged to keep his laws. If we were to attempt to systematize these different uses of covenant, we might envisage the first sense identified above as God's agreement with the invisible church of the elect, and the third sense as God's partnership with a particular, visible church, whether local or national.

But there are dangers in being *too* tidy. Keach and Gill refer to those who try to distinguish between a 'covenant of redemption' and a 'covenant of grace', the former being the covenant in which Christ achieved peace with God in eternity, and the latter which was 'made with the elect, or believers, in time'.[29] Both Keach and Gill protest with some

---

27   Calvin, *Institutes*, II, 3, xxi:7, pp. 210–11.

28   Robert Browne, *A Booke which sheweth the life and manners of all true Christians* (Middelburgh: 1582), reprinted in A. Peel and L. Carlson (eds.), *The Writings of Robert Harrison and Robert Browne* (London: Allen and Unwin, 1953), pp. 254–6.

29   Keach, *Display of Glorious Grace*, p. 212; Gill, *Body of Divinity*, I, bk. 2, p. 311.

justice that there can only be one gracious covenant of God. Perhaps it is better to see the Puritan, Separatist and (later) Baptist theologians as registering an ambiguity, or mysterious area, when the eternal decree of God actually takes form in time and space, and to this recognition of mystery I intend to return.

The fourth sense of covenant has already been implied in our considering of Browne's account. That is, 'covenant' can refer to the agreement undertaken and signed by church members when a particular local church was founded, and subsequently by new members on entering it. It seems that the early Separatist churches associated with Browne, Barrow, Johnson and Smyth were constituted through such a covenanting, and Smyth defines a church by this way of gathering it:

> A visible communion of Saincts is of two, three or more Saincts joyned together by covenant with God & themselves....[30]

That he is envisaging a literal act of covenant-making is clear from his assertion that:

> the outward part of the true forme of the true visible church is a vowe, promise, oath, or covenant betwixt God and the Saints.... This covenant hath 2 parts. 1. Respecting God and the faithful. 2. Respecting the faithful mutually.[31]

Typical phrases in such covenants express the twofold dimension of a contract made by the members 'vertically' with God and 'horizontally' with each other: members promise to 'give themselves up to God' *and* to 'give themselves up to each other'; to 'walk in the ways of the Lord' *and* 'to walk together'; to obey the 'rules of Christ' *and* to 'watch over each other'. These covenants were common among the Congregationalist descendants of the Separatists from the early decades of the seventeenth century onwards, and Geoffrey Nuttall well expresses the advantages of what was a physical as well as spiritual act:

> The drawing up of a covenant and the committing of it to writing added to its solemnity; while the appending of the signatures (or marks) of those who entered into it both underlined its binding character and satisfied their self-consciousness as individuals.[32]

---

30   Smyth, *Principles and Inferences*, in *Works*, I, p. 252.

31   Smyth, *Principles and Inferences*, in *Works*, I, p. 254.

32   G. Nuttall, *Visible Saints. The Congregational Way 1640–1660* (Oxford: Basil Blackwell, 1957), p. 78.

Covenant-making like this appeared rather rarely after Smyth among churches that required believers' baptism for membership,[33] until the last years of the seventeenth century, when the publication of their church covenants by both Benjamin and Elias Keach (father and son) seem to have exercised a considerable influence on Baptist practice. These covenants from Horsley Down and the city of London respectively (both published in 1697) were often copied or modified, and the popularity of making church covenants among both General and Particular Baptists increased to the extent that when the church at Downton, Wiltshire, was re-established in 1793 it assumed that the making of a covenant was 'the usage of all organized Churches of the faith of Jesus Christ';[34] it employed Keach's model. John Gill asserts that baptism in itself does not make someone a member of a church, but only 'mutual consent and agreement, in their covenant and consideration with each other.'[35]

It was probably in fact the adoption of believers' baptism as the moment of entry into the local church that diminished the usage of a written covenant among Baptists for a period in the seventeenth century. The part of John Smyth's Amsterdam congregation that had returned to London in 1611/12 with Thomas Helwys as their pastor certainly replaced entry to membership by covenant promises by entry through baptism. Among Particular Baptists in London, Hanserd Knollys in 1645 refuted the charge that his and other independent churches required potential members to make a covenant. Knollys was not only himself opposed to this practice as having no foundation in scripture, but insisted that none of the churches he knew in London that practised the baptism of believers 'make any particular covenant with Members upon admittance'.[36]

In accord with this, the London Confession of 1644, of which Knollys was one of the signatories, makes no mention of gathering a church through a covenant, and nor is there any such explicit reference in any of the seventeenth-century Baptist confessions of faith, Particular or General. However, the definition of a church in the 1644 Confession echoes the same covenant ideas that had been expressed in Separatist church covenant-making, following quite closely in wording the *True Confession* of 1596 which had been issued by Johnson's church. The visible church is defined as:

---

33   Those which accepted both infant and believers' baptism often seem to have had covenants, for example the church at Hitchin.

34   See the unsigned article 'Church Covenants', *BQ* 7/5 (1935), p. 231.

35   Gill, *Body of Divinity*, II, bk. 4, pp. 565–7.

36   Hanserd Knollys, *A Moderate Answer unto Dr. Bastwick's Book; Called, Independency not Gods Ordinance* (London, 1645), pp. 13–14.

a company of visible Saints, called & separated from the world ... being baptized into that faith, and joyned to the Lord, and each other, by mutuall agreement, in the practical injoynment of the Ordinances, commanded by Christ their head and King.[37]

There is typical covenant thought in the language of being joined to the Lord and each other 'by mutual agreement', as in the next article which speaks of being under the direct government of Christ, and being given 'his promises, and ... the signes of his Covenant.' This is a *concept* of a local covenant, entered by mutual consent and carrying obligations between members, which goes beyond the general theological idea of a covenant between God and the church (the third meaning I have distinguished above). The language of 'walking together' also regularly appears in early Baptist confessions,[38] including the Second London Confession of 1677/89 which echoes the wording of covenant promises when it states that members of the church 'do willingly consent to walk together according to the appointment of Christ, giving up themselves, to the Lord & one to another'.[39]

For the most part of the seventeenth century, then, Baptists clearly thought of the gathering of the local church in covenant terms, even if they did not have the 'outward form'. As John Fawcett was to put it at the end of the next century:

it is the custom in many of our churches to express this [covenant or mutual compact] in writing... though this circumstance cannot be thought essentially necessary to the constitution of a church...[40]

The Relation between the Eternal and the Local Covenant

Having picked out four separate threads of the Puritan-Separatist tapestry of covenant thought, we can now see more clearly how they are woven

---

37   The London Confession (1644), art. XXXIII, in Lumpkin, *Baptist Confessions*, p. 165; cf. *A True Confession of the Faith* (1596), arts. 17, 27, in Lumpkin, *Baptist Confessions*, pp. 165, 90.

38   E.g. *The Faith and Practise of Thirty Congregations, Gathered According to the Primitive Pattern* (London: Will Larnar, 1651), art. 52, in Lumpkin, *Baptist Confessions*, p. 183; *Sixteen Articles of Faith and Order* (The 'Midland Association Confession'), 1655, art. 15, in Lumpkin, *Baptist Confessions,* p. 199; *A Confession of the Faith of Several Churches of Christ* (The 'Somerset Confession') (London: Henry Hills, 1656), art. XXIV, in Lumpkin, *Baptist Confessions*, p. 209.

39   Chap. XXVI.6, in Lumpkin, *Baptist Confessions*, p. 286.

40   John Fawcett, *The Constitution and Order of a Gospel Church Considered* (Halifax, 1797), p. 12.

together. It is no accident of words that the very same term 'covenant' is
used for the mutual agreement of church members and the eternal decree
of God, that is, both for the local and eternal covenant. Some modern
writers seem to assume that it *is* merely coincidental,[41] and James Coggins
argues explicitly that the covenant ecclesiology of John Smyth 'should
not be confused with Calvinist covenant theology'.[42] He considers that
the difference between the idea of an eternal covenant of God with the
elect and a 'covenant among individual men and women' is too great for
them to be brought together. Here he takes issue with B. R. White, who
had found a stroke of originality by Smyth in fusing the two together,
maintaining that:

> it seems that for him, in the covenant promise of the local congregation the eternal
> covenant of grace became contemporary and man's acceptance of it was actualized
> in history.[43]

White further points out that the relation between the local covenant
bond and the eternal covenant offered to all humankind will be
analogous to the relation between a particular local congregation and
'the invisible company of all God's elect.' This means, I suggest, that a
Baptist ecclesiology built on the concept of covenant must take a strong
view of the church universal. The universal church cannot just be an
adding together of many local communities, as Baptists have sometimes
depicted it; rather, there is a universal reality which *pre-exists* any local
manifestation of it, as God's eternal covenant with humankind pre-exists
the local covenant bond. Covenant and catholicity belong together.

A dislocation between the covenant of the local church and the eternal
covenant of grace is encouraged by the secular use of 'covenant' to
mean nothing more than a voluntary society, and I intend to discuss this
further below. Thus, Baptist unions in Europe which actually use the
biblical word for 'covenant' in their titles – for example *Förbundet* in
Sweden and *Bund* in Germany – have had little or no theological
reflection on the relevance of covenant theology for fellowship at union
level. Since the word 'covenant' is used for many secular organizations,
it has become a dead metaphor. I suggest that the theological 'depth' of
the concept of covenant needs to be recovered, that is, its rooting in the
life and mission of the triune God, and that the witness of Separatists and
early Baptists can prompt us to do this.

---

41   See Roger Hayden, 'The Particular Baptist Confession 1689 and Baptists
Today', *BQ* 32/8 (1988), p. 413: 'in the local church, covenant signified something
different [from the Covenant of Grace].'

42   Coggins, 'Theological Positions of John Smyth', p. 249.

43   White, *The Separatist Tradition*, p. 128.

If we refer to the four meanings of covenant I have isolated above, then it is clear that Robert Browne brings the third and fourth together. God's making of covenant with the church is simultaneous with the making of covenant *by* the church. The act of local covenant-making is not simply a human enterprise, a promise by believers to be faithful; it is the gracious act of God to take the church 'to be his people', and God's 'promise to be our God and Saviour'.[44] Thus the ambivalence between the divine and the human making of covenant which White finds original to Smyth is already present in Browne. It is indeed embedded in the Separatist (and later, Baptist) conviction that through covenant a local community is under the direct rule of Christ and so has been given the 'seals of the covenant' – that is, the power to elect its own ministry, to celebrate the sacraments of baptism and the Lord's Supper, and to administer discipline (the authority to 'bind and loose').

Smyth, however, does use expressions which draw the first meaning of 'covenant' more clearly together with the third and fourth than in Browne. As I have already noted, he evidently intends his treatise on the nature of the church to be a working out of the 'ordinances of Christ for the dispensing of the covenant since his death', and this is the eternal covenant of grace 'established by the blood of Christ'. God's part in the 'vowe, promise, oath or covenant' of the visible church is 'to give Christ' and 'with Christ al things els'.[45] Through the covenant bond, 'the Lord chose vs to be his', and 'by vertue of the covenant God made with us ...God is our God & our Father, only in Chr[ist] & through him: & al the promises of God in Christ are yea and Amen.'[46] When Coggins maintains that 'Smyth hardly ever discussed covenant theology at all' he misses the significance of the scripture references which Smyth attaches to such statements as: 'Vnto whome the covenant & Christ is given, vnto them al the promises are given'[47] or 'God with them maketh his covenant, & they are his sonnes & daughters, & he is their Father.'[48] Texts like 2 Cor. 1:20, Gal. 3:14-16 and Heb. 8:10 are exactly those which would be appealed to in any discussion of the eternal covenant of grace made through Christ as mediator. In sum, when the church makes its covenant promise it receives 'the promise' of God,[49] and the covenant of grace was understood in Calvinist tradition precisely as God's promise to humankind:

---

44   Browne, *A Booke which sheweth*, in *Writings*, pp. 37–8, pp. 254–6; cf. *A True and Short Declaration* (?1583), in *Writings*, pp. 422–3.

45   Smyth, *Principles and Inferences*, in *Works*, I, p. 254.

46   Smyth, *Paralleles*, in *Works*, II, p. 387.

47   Smyth, *Paralleles*, in *Works*, II, p. 389.

48   Smyth, *Paralleles*, in *Works*, II, p. 386.

49   Smyth, *Paralleles*, in *Works*, II, p. 403.

> We say the Church or two or three faithful people Seperated from the world and joyned together in a true covenant, have both Christ, the covenant, & promises...

We notice the easy slipping here from one sense of 'covenant' to another; those who are joined in [church] covenant 'have the covenant [of grace]'. The way that these aspects of covenant are connected is not of course worked out systematically, and it remains tantalizing not only in Smyth, but in the later model covenant of Benjamin Keach at Horsley Down (1797). This begins with the pledge:

> to give up ourselves to the Lord, in a Church state according to the Apostolical Constitution that he may be our God, and we may be his People, through the Everlasting Covenant of his Free grace, in which alone we hope to be accepted by him, through his blessed Son Jesus Christ, whom we take to be our High Priest, to justify and sanctify us....[50]

In this drama of the 'solemn covenant of the church', the members are not just recalling that they *have been* included in God's eternal covenant, but envisage themselves as somehow entering it at that very moment. How is it possible to square this with Keach's (moderate) Calvinism? There is a clue in an extended quotation from Isaac Chauncey which Keach includes in *The Display of Glorious Grace* to support his argument that the 'covenant of redemption' is the same as the covenant of grace. 'Church Covenants' are said to 'add nothing to this Grand Covenant', but as 'an accomplishment of the promise' they are an occasion for the believer to 'enter personally into this Covenant', 'embracing' and 'laying hold of it'. On God's part the church covenant can be understood as 'renewings of the same Covenant without changing the Covenant'.[51] The author (quoted and warmly approved by Keach) thus places the covenant of the local church in a line of succession of renewings of the one Covenant of grace with 'Adam, Noah, Abraham, Isaac and Jacob etc.' In another sermon in the collection, Keach finds baptism and the Lord's Supper to be other places where the taking of the sinner into the Covenant of Grace is 'renewed and confirmed' by the Spirit.[52]

In a moment we shall consider the implication of this theology of covenant renewal for the nature of salvation, but we should note that the later high Calvinism of John Gill shows no interest in linking the 'covenant of grace' with the church covenant. Gill's locking up of God's covenant-making within the persons of the Trinity results in a view of the local church covenant which is modelled thoroughly on a secular

---

50   Keach, *Glory of a True Church,* p. 71.
51   Keach, *Display of Glorious Grace,* p. 211.
52   Keach, *Display of Glorious Grace,* p. 285.

contract of mutual human obligations; 'like all civil societies' the union between members is made by 'voluntary consent and agreement' in which they 'propose themselves to a church'.[53] Gill, notably, refrains from using the traditional phrase 'give themselves up to God' in this discussion, urging only that members 'give themselves up to the church.'

By contrast, Smyth and Keach, at two ends of a century, offer a dynamic account of participation in God's covenant of grace through mutual covenant-making. There is also the theological potential here for developing a link with the second meaning of covenant explored above, the covenant within the very life of God, and for releasing it from the narrow confines of a kind of legal bargain about atonement. That is, we might conceive of the local fellowship of believers as participating within the inner communion of the triune God. In our time this kind of development of the theme of covenant has been made by the theologian Karl Barth, who stands in the tradition of Calvin and yet makes the doctrine of electing grace more dynamic than in the thought of the great Reformer.

In the first place, Barth does not envisage the eternal covenant-decision of God as an 'absolute decree', but as identical with the actual working of God's word in history;[54] so God's sovereign election happens *here and now* in interaction with persons who hear the word, which is nothing less than 'the Person of God speaking'. This means that God's election is understood as a grace that enables the human response of 'yes' to God's 'yes' to us, rather than as a static 'double decree' in which some are destined for salvation and others for damnation. In the second place, Barth envisages a 'primal decree' in which God's making of covenant with created sons and daughters eternally shapes the relationships of love within God's own triune being. The covenant of grace is thus *integral* to communion between Father, Son and Holy Spirit; in the primary decision for covenant with humanity, God determines God's own being throughout eternity, ordaining 'who God is' as 'God for us'.[55] This for Barth is not speculation; we know this because the human person of Jesus of Nazareth is inseparable, by God's free choice, from the person of the eternal Son or Logos. The election of Jesus Christ, representative for all human beings, is a 'double decree' at the 'beginning of all God's ways and works', in which God has elected *humanity* for divine fellowship, and has elected *God's own self* as covenant partner with humanity.[56] 'What a

---

53   Gill, *Body of Divinity*, II, bk. 4, pp. 566–7.
54   Barth, *Church Dogmatics*, II/2, pp. 175–94.
55   Barth, *Church Dogmatics*, II/2, pp. 79-80, 168-9; IV/1, pp. 6-7, 36–8.
56   Barth, *Church Dogmatics*, II/2, pp. 123–5, 161–5, cf. pp. 6–9, 26; IV/1, pp. 45–6.

risk God ran!' marvels Barth, in which only God could lose and creatures could only gain.[57]

The logical conclusion of this uniting of covenant with Trinity in the election of Jesus Christ is that the eternal relationships within the Trinity may themselves be envisaged as a kind of covenant relationship. Barth, however, avoids explicitly speaking of the inner-trinitarian relations as a covenant, while he does speak of them in terms of election. This is because he objects to the traditional picture, characteristic of Calvinistic 'federal theology',[58] of two subjects having legal dealings with each other in a transaction about atonement. Among other problems with this concept, Barth considers that 'since God would not be God if he were not God in [the] unity' of the eternal covenant, there is no need for any subsequent pact or decree to unite God with humanity.[59] Barth is especially critical of any notion that a covenant of grace abrogates a previous 'covenant of works'. From all eternity, God has determined God's own *being* by the covenant of grace.[60] We can thus take Barth's critique and use it as a way of *redefining* an inner-divine covenant in Barth's own spirit; we might say that as God the Father makes covenant of love eternally with the Son in the fellowship of the Spirit, so simultaneously God makes covenant in history with human beings. In one movement of utter self-giving God elects both the divine Son and human children as covenant partners.

This is the kind of theological depth to the concept of covenant that should be particularly congenial to the Baptist tradition of a church gathered by covenant. It has, indeed, recently been employed in some British Baptist writing[61] and been adduced in aid of resisting any

---

57   Barth, *Church Dogmatics*, II/2, pp. 163–4.

58   The major figure is John Coccejus, *Summa doctrinae de foedere et testamento Dei* (Leiden, 1648). See Barth, *Church Dogmatics*, IV/1, 54–9.

59   Barth, *Church Dogmatics*, IV/1, pp. 64–6.

60   Bruce McCormack coins the phrase 'covenant ontology' for this theme in Barth; see McCormack, 'Grace and Being. The role of God's gracious election in Karl Barth's theological ontology' in John Webster (ed.), *The Cambridge Companion to Karl Barth* (Cambridge: Cambridge University Press, 2000), pp. 92–109.

61   See Paul S. Fiddes, 'Church, Trinity and Covenant: an Ecclesiology of Participation' in E. Brandt, P.S. Fiddes and J. Molthagen (eds.), *Gemeinschaft am Evangelium. Festschrift für Wiard Popkes* (Leipzig: Evangelische Verlag-Anstalt, 1996), pp. 37–55; this essay is reproduced, in a slightly revised form, as chapter 4 below. Several of the essays in Anthony Clarke (ed.), *Bound for Glory? God, Church and World in Covenant* (Oxford: Whitley Publications, 2002) rely on this kind of covenant ontology; see especially Anthony Clarke, 'The Covenantal Basis of God's Trinitarian Life', pp. 9–19, Marcus Bull, 'Divine Complexity and Human Community', pp. 45–58, Robert Ellis, 'Covenant and Creation', pp. 20–33. Earlier, similar ideas are found in Hazel Sherman, 'Baptized in the Name of the Father, the Son and the Holy Spirit', in Paul S. Fiddes (ed.) *Reflections on the Water* (Oxford: Regent's Park College/ Macon: Smyth

reduction of a covenant bond to a mere 'strategic alliance', a union only for the sake of performing certain tasks, or making economies, or providing resources.[62] It draws attention to the 'ontological' element in covenant, that is the dimension of sheer being which underlies any doing. Thus our mission to the world shares in the mission of the Father who eternally 'sends forth' the Son.

The Covenant and Salvation

Church covenant making, we have observed, uses at least the *language* of conditionality. That God's covenant might be conditional on human obedience is obviously a modification of Calvin's thought, where God's covenant with his elect must be one of unconditional grace, and thus based on a 'limited' atonement in which only the elect are included. But a powerful motivation for a conditional approach to covenant thinking was the issue of assurance that haunted the Puritan mind, prone to despair in the face of a predestinarian God; how could a believer be sure that he or she was indeed one of the elect and part of God's covenant? Calvin himself had simply appealed to the existence of faith as assurance enough, but English Puritan theology followed the trend that sought to find more visible evidence of election, that is in the living of a life that was obedient to the commandments of God recorded in the scriptures.[63]

This stress on personal obedience, often called 'experimental Calvinism', converged with an interpretation of the second commandment that identified idolatry with any humanly devised worship and ministry, and with a portrayal of Christ as the new Moses, giving rules for the government of his church. As the earliest systematic theologian of Puritanism, Dudley Fenner, expressed it, faithful obedience to the commandments of Christ about the ordering of his church brings God's people 'into a covenant of life and blessedness'.[64] Into this constellation of ideas the Separatist added one further belief; the covenant of God with the church meant that each local congregation was under the direct rule of the covenant-mediator, Christ, without any external ecclesiastical authority. The result of this conjunction of beliefs and anxieties was that

---

& Helwys, 1996), pp. 110–14, and *Transforming Superintendency. The Report of the General Superintendency Review Group presented to the Baptist Union of Great Britain Council* (London: Baptist Union, 1996), pp. 9–13.

62   See Kidd (ed.), *On the Way of Trust*, pp. 22–7.

63   This trend was notably promoted by Theodore Beza. R.T. Kendall, in his *Calvin and English Calvinism*, considers whether the form it took in Puritan England was in accord with Calvin's own theology.

64   Dudley Fenner, *A briefe treatise upon the first table of the lawe* (Middelburg, 1587), D.1.; cit. Brachlow, *Communion of Saints*, p. 36.

discipline of members and true church order was regarded as a mark of salvation, assuring the believer of election within the covenant.

By contrast, those who wanted to stress the unconditional nature of the covenant developed a scheme of biblical history in which a 'covenant of works' had been replaced by the 'covenant of grace'.[65] The original covenant of works made with Adam and Moses was indeed conditional, they asserted, but because it had been broken it had been replaced by a new unconditional covenant of grace, first made with Abraham. This sequence could be appealed to in the cause of maintaining that God's covenant with the national church in England stood firm, while those who wanted to introduce a conditional aspect into God's covenant were accused of falling back into the old 'covenant of works', and as trying to establish salvation by their works.

A conditional view of the covenant, dependent on human obedience for its continuance, was certainly conducive to emerging Arminianism, with its stress on human free will and the possibility of refusing the grace of God. It is not surprising to find these elements in John Smyth's later thought, and then in the ensuing General Baptist tradition. Strictly speaking, from a Calvinist – and a Particular Baptist – perspective, good church order was necessary for salvation only in the sense that having it demonstrated one's already existing election. But there were already signs of convergence between the two approaches in Baptist thinking of the seventeenth century, in the commonly held convictions that (a) the initiative of God's grace was necessary to get any human response started (though for Arminians it could be declined), and (b) that a visible response of faith was necessary to actualize the covenant relationship here and now. With regard to the first, the General Baptist *An Orthodox Creed* of 1679 affirms that:

> justifying faith is a grace, or habit, wrought in the soul by the holy ghost, through preaching the word of God, whereby we are enabled to believe.... and wholly and only to rest upon Christ.[66]

With regard to the second aspect, we find the Particular Baptist theologian Benjamin Keach arguing that while a covenant agreement exists between God and the elect by eternal decree, it is only when by the Spirit we 'choose Jesus Christ as the only Object of our Affection' that 'we enter into an *actual* Covenant with God', and 'the Reconciliation becomes mutual'.[67]

---

65   First propounded by the Heidelberg Calvinist theologians, Ursinus, Olevianus and Zanchius.

66   Art. XXIII, in Lumpkin, *Baptist Confessions,* p. 314.

67   Keach, *Display of Glorious Grace*, p. 282.

I suggest that the very act of making or assenting to the church covenant constantly moved participants towards a *blend* of Calvinist insistence upon the enabling grace of God and Arminian affirmation of 'choosing' Christ. The act surely reminded them of the initiative that God takes in making covenant, as well as requiring them to make their own personal response. The two sides of this mystery of divine grace and human freedom were also, of course, kept in balance by the act of believers' baptism. On the one hand this was a 'seal' of the covenant given to the church by God; on the other, the Separatist insistence on the assent of the congregation to 'the covenant betwixt God and the Faithful made in baptisme'[68] led for Baptists to the unsuitability of infants for baptism since they were – in the words of John Smyth – 'unable to enter into the New Testament by sealing back the covenant unto the Lord, & consenting unto the contract.'[69]

There was then a trajectory already in place which Andrew Fuller took up towards the end of the eighteenth century in his brand of 'evangelical Calvinism', which liberated many Particular Baptist churches for an era of mission. A belief in limited atonement had not extinguished a concern for evangelism altogether, but it had certainly had a dampening effect. Now Fuller's theology provided a spark for the re-igniting of a passion for proclaiming the gospel, by proposing that while only some people were elected to salvation, all people had the positive *duty* to turn to Christ in faith. His theological justification for holding this, by means of a fairly complex doctrine of atonement (which we will be exploring later)[70] was surely not what provided the motivation for mission. Rather, people were gripped by the twin truths that God's grace alone *enabled* response, and that human beings were *obliged* to make that response. The word 'duty' picks up all the echoes of a conditional covenant, and it is not surprising that Fuller had to devote a section in his book, *A Gospel Worthy of All Acceptation*, to refuting the charge that duty belonged to a 'covenant of works' which had nothing to do with salvation.[71]

But the practice of church covenant-making did not only preserve the mystery of grace and freedom. I suggest that it imprinted on Baptist minds the sense that salvation was not merely a point but a process or a story.[72] In the terms used by Benjamin Keach, the eternal covenant is 'actualized' when someone 'embraces' or 'lays hold' of Christ ('when God gives Christ to a Sinner, the whole Covenant is performed to that

68   John Smyth, *The Character of the Beast* (1609), in *Works*, II, p. 645.
69   Smyth, *The Character of the Beast* (1609), in *Works*, II, p. 645.
70   See below, ch. 11, pp. 255–8.
71   Andrew Fuller, *The Gospel Worthy of All Acceptation*, 2nd edition (London, 1801), pp. 112–14.
72   For further exploration of this idea, see below, ch. 10, pp. 240–2.

Person')[73], and this actualizing of the covenant in conversion is then 'renewed' in the event of church covenant-making, as it is also in the acts of baptism and the Lord's Supper. This story of eternal purpose, temporal actualization and renewal is a story of 'Pilgrim's Progress'; in John Bunyan's allegory, the Pilgrim enters the earthly journey of faith through the narrow gate of conversion, but it is only later by a wayside cross that 'his burden loosed from off his shoulders and fell from off his back'.[74] This reflects the typical Calvinist stage of inner assurance, but it also fits with the Baptist placing of assurance in the context of covenant-making and baptism.

Embedded in a covenant theology is therefore a theology of renewal of salvation, which is of course also a strong Old Testament (and especially Deuteronomic) concept. Perhaps this is why in our modern age the movement of charismatic renewal, with its emphasis upon further stages of filling with the Holy Spirit beyond conversion, has had such a powerful influence on Baptist life in England. The idea that salvation is a story or journey should also help Baptists to enter ecumenical conversations where questions of salvation, faith and sacraments are at issue; for instance, the recent report of a working party of Churches Together in England on the nature of baptism, written with strong Baptist representation, found common ground in conceiving Christian initiation as a process, within which baptism has a place.[75]

The Covenant and Voluntary Societies

The mutual and conditional nature of covenant has often been underlined in Baptist history by comparing it with various kinds of contracts in society which require free consent, and the covenanted community has often been designated as a 'voluntary society'. The most influential definition of the church as a voluntary society was offered by John Locke, in the context of his view of human society as bound by a voluntary 'social contract', or by a series of interlocking contracts. In his *Letter on Toleration* (1689), he writes that:

> [A Church] is a free and voluntary Society... no Man is bound by nature to any particular Church or Sect, but he joins himself voluntarily to that Society in which

---

73   Keach, *Display of Glorious Grace*, p. 296

74   John Bunyan, *The Pilgrim's Progress*, ed. R. Sharrock (Harmondsworth: Penguin, 1965), p. 70. Further, see below, ch. 10, pp. 228, 240.

75   *Baptism and Church Membership, with particular reference to Local Ecumenical Partnerships*. A Report of a Working Party to Churches Together in England (London: Churches Together in England, 1997), pp. 13, 17–19, 29.

he believes he has found that Profession and Worship which is truly acceptable to God....[76]

William Brackney, who has written extensively on voluntarism as the basis of Free Church life, believes that in offering this definition Locke was already 'well immersed in the Nonconformist theory of the church as a voluntary society' and was 'reflecting fourscore years of evolution of churchmanship and dissent'.[77] Secular models for voluntary societies, Brackney points out, were available from 1550 onwards with the development of Joint Stock Companies for trading, and from these emerged in 1649 the 'New England Corporation' which was a company for the solely religious purpose of mission among the Indian population. This lasted only for the period of the Protectorate, but the Nonconformist 'New England Company' existed from 1660 to 1776 as a royal chartered corporation combining trade and evangelism.

It might then be argued that the covenant principle in the local church was essentially the principle of voluntarism, developed from both the mutualist aspects of the biblical covenant and from secular models of contract. Not only the language of voluntary consent found from Browne onwards, but explicit analogies drawn between covenant and voluntary societies, might be brought in support of this view. Smyth, for instance, compared the local church covenant with the kind of corporation referred to above:

> as the charter of a corporation is from the King & al the offices have powre from the corporation, so the Church hath powre from Christ, & the Eldership from the church...[78]

In the expanded version of Keach's *Baptist Catechism* made by Benjamin Beddome (1752), the church is called 'a voluntary society', to which is attached the scripture reference 2 Corinthians 8:5, containing the phrase often employed in church covenants: 'they gave themselves to the Lord and to us by the will of God.'[79] We have already noted that Gill stressed that the union between church members is 'like all civil societies, founded... by consent and covenant.' In the nineteenth century Joseph Angus wrote a prize essay on *The Voluntary System* in which he quotes

---

76   John Locke, *A Letter Concerning Toleration* (London, 1689), p. 10.

77   William Brackney, *Voluntarism. The Dynamic Principle of the Free Church* (Wolfville: Acadia University, 1992), p. 16. In *his Christian Voluntarism. Theology and Praxis* (Grand Rapids: Eerdmans, 1997), pp. 33–49, Brackney asserts that voluntarism is a gift of God and so does not diminish the church's dependence upon God's sovereignty and grace.

78   Smyth, *Paralleles*, in *Works*, II, p. 391.

79   Benjamin Beddome, *A Scriptural Exegesis of the Baptist Catechism* (London, 1752), p. 162.

Locke's definition of a church with approval, urges the analogy of free trade, and describes believers gathering together as 'form[ing] a voluntary religious society for the double purpose of obtaining mutual instruction and comfort and of propagating their faith'.[80]

But for all this, voluntarism can only be one dimension of relationships in the local church when they are conceived in *covenant* terms. The link, mysterious as it is, between the church covenant and the covenant of grace means that human consent is inseparable from the initiative of God in making the covenant in the first place, and in offering to re-make it when it is broken. Thus Baptist confessions of faith have usually held together the voluntary 'gathering' of the church with its being 'gathered' or called together by Christ as the covenant-mediator. The Second London Confession (1677/89), for example, describes believers as 'consent[ing] to walk together *according to the appointment of Christ*'; churches, it affirms, are 'gathered by special grace... according to His mind'.[81] The modern English statement, *The Baptist Doctrine of the Church* (1948), declares that 'churches are gathered by the will of Christ and live by the indwelling of his Spirit. They do not have their origin, primarily, in human resolution.'[82]

From a covenantal perspective, it is thus positively misleading to call a local church a 'voluntary society'. According to the covenant theology of the early Separatists, because the local church was under the direct rule of Christ all members shared in that ministry of 'kingship', and so had the right to exercise judgement by 'watching over' the spiritual health of each other and withdrawing from a church where the covenant was broken.[83] This rooting of freedom in the rule of Christ is quite different from Locke's principle of market-place choice, in which a religious person joins with others for worship 'in such a manner as they judge acceptable to [God] and effectual to the Salvation of their Souls.'[84] Similarly, the freedom of a local church from external ecclesiastical government because it is under the rule of Christ differs from Locke's notion that a church as a voluntary society has the freedom to make its own rules and prescribe its own membership qualifications.

---

80   Joseph Angus, *The Voluntary System* (London: Jackson and Walford, 1839), p. 191. Later, however, in *Christian Churches* (London: Ward & Co., 1862), Angus calls the Christian church a 'theocracy'.

81   Arts. XXIX–XXXI, in Lumpkin, *Baptist Confessions*, pp. 318–19.

82   Repr. in Roger Hayden, *Baptist Union Documents 1948–1977* (London: Baptist Historical Society, 1980), p. 6 (my italics).

83   See e.g. Robert Browne, *An Answere to Master Cartwright* (London, n.d.), in *Writings*, pp. 465–6.

84   Locke, *Toleration*, p. 9.

It was essentially the latter view of self-government (also held by Angus)[85] to which Joseph Kinghorn appealed in the nineteenth century dispute over closed and open communion, maintaining that 'if persons ask for admission into any voluntary society they must submit to its terms', in this case believers' baptism as a qualification for coming to the Lord's table.[86] Robert Hall's reply returns to earlier Separatist and Baptist principles, rooting the nature of consent in 'the fundamental laws of Christ's kingdom'; he argues that 'there is little or no analogy' between a church and a 'voluntary society' in the matter of membership, since 'human societies originate solely in the private views and inclinations of those who compose them' whereas 'the church is a society instituted by Heaven'. [87] Although Kinghorn believes that the entrance qualification for communion derives from the 'founder' of the society, Christ, he still stands under Hall's censure of envisaging the church as a voluntary society 'organized with a specific view to the propagation of some particular truth'. For Hall, all Christians are under the rule of Christ in the sense that they belong to the spiritual kingdom which is the body of Christ, and so the table should be open to them.

In what Hall is opposing we can see the heritage of Gill's separation of the local covenant from the eternal covenant of grace. Ironically, although this secularizing of the church covenant as a voluntary society was in the cause of preserving divine sovereignty, it could lead to a demise of the concept of covenant altogether, since it could then be simply *replaced* by voluntarism. In his study of the English Baptists in the nineteenth century, John Briggs judges that the theology and practice of covenanting declined because the image of a community held in covenant seemed too self-enclosed and privatized in an age when churches were working together in mission agencies, associations, alliances for social reform, and inter-church movements for education and health.[88] Here he builds on the insight of W. R. Ward that 'the Sunday School open to all rather than the covenanted meeting of baptized saints was the sign of the times ... the kingdom of God seemed delivered over to associational principles.'[89]

---

85   Angus *Voluntary System*, p. 191.

86   Joseph Kinghorn, *Baptism, a Term of Communion at the Lord's Supper* (Norwich: Bacon, Kinnebrook, 1816), p. 61, cf. pp. 81–2.

87   Robert Hall, A *Reply to the Rev. Joseph Kinghorn*, in Olinthus Gregory (ed.), *The Entire Works of Robert Hall* (6 volumes; London: Holdsworth and Ball, 1831), II, pp. 473–5.

88   J.H.Y. Briggs, *The English Baptists of the Nineteenth Century* (London: Baptist Historical Society, 1994), pp. 15–20.

89   W.R. Ward, 'The Baptists and the Transformation of the Church , 1780–1830', *BQ* 25/4 (1973), p. 172.

Ward thus discerns that there was an 'empirical and pragmatic spirit embodied in the associations'. However, I suggest that the covenant concept, when grounded *theologically*, is itself thoroughly open to the associating of churches together in the widest forms of cooperation. It is true that the voluntary principle of consenting to work together for a particular task was (and indeed remains) the key element in certain larger groupings in which Baptists participated from the seventeenth century onwards, and increasingly in the nineteenth century: examples are centralized funds such as the Particular Baptist Fund, Trusts such as those for theological education, and agencies such as the Baptist Missionary Society, the Bible Society and the Sunday School Union.[90] But there is a danger in supposing that the relating of *churches* together in regional associations and in a national union will *also* be driven by the voluntary principle. This was indeed the view of Angus,[91] who paints a picture of churches coming together under some common direction as a matter of 'expediency' in order to 'extend their usefulness', but the logic of Separatist and early Baptist thought seems to have been more similar to that of Robert Hall. That is, if a local church is under the direct rule of Christ as king then it is necessarily drawn into fellowship with all those who are under Christ's rule and so part of his body. The London Confession of 1644 depicts the associating together of churches in the body of Christ, and while it does not explicitly use the word 'covenant' it follows *A True Confession* of 1596 in applying to congregations the covenant language of 'walking together':

> And although the particular Congregations be distinct and severall Bodies, every one a compact and knit Citie in it selfe; yet are they all to walk by one and the same Rule, and by all meanes convenient to have the counsell and help of one another in all needfull affaires of the Church, as members of one body in the common faith under Christ their onely head.[92]

The freedom of a local church from external ecclesiastical authority is therefore not based in Enlightenment concepts of the freedom of the individual, or in the self-regulation of a voluntary society, but in the lordship of Christ. It follows that whether covenant is an exclusive or inclusive idea depends upon how the rule of Christ in the church and the world is to be understood. In the turmoil following the English

---

90   See William H. Brackney, *Christian Voluntarism in Britain and North America: a Bibliography and Critical Assessment* (Westport: Greenwoods Press, 1995), pp. 27–45.

91   Angus, *Voluntary System*, pp. 191–3.

92   Art. XLVII, in Lumpkin, *Baptist Confessions*, pp. 168–9; this is virtually identical to article 38 of *A True Confession* (1596), in Lumpkin, *Baptist Confessions*, p. 94.

Reformation it was inevitable that Baptists understood the scope of Christ's rule to run in a fairly narrow way, but some recent English Baptist writing has taken up a wider vision of the rule of Christ in reviving the covenant concept; it has urged that if the local church meeting aims to find the mind of Christ for its life and mission, it should be equally anxious to discover how churches in assembly together find his mind. For example, a recent report of the Baptist Union of Great Britain has proposed that British Baptists take a creative step, beyond the explicit definitions of their predecessors, and treat the national union itself as a covenant relationship.[93]

Associations and unions of churches are thus not merely task-orientated, but means of exploring the purpose of God in his world. Further still, Baptist churches and Baptist associations should be eager to discover how assemblies of other denominations, gathering under the same rule, discern the mission of God and their place in it. It is apt that a number of Baptist churches in Wales (though not the Union itself) have been able to participate in the ecumenical 'Covenanted Churches in Wales'; unlike a similar but unsuccessful attempt at covenanting between denominations in England in the mid-1970s,[94] the Welsh Covenant avoided both the language of 'organic union' and the setting of a date for structural unity; instead it declared that 'we do not yet know the form union will take' and echoed earlier covenant documents in expecting that 'God will guide his Church into ways of truth and peace'.[95] This openness in walking together has also been the spirit of the more recent 'Inter-Church Process' or 'Churches Together in Pilgrimage' in Great Britain as a whole, in which the Baptist Union of Great Britain is a partner.[96] The language of covenant was, however, strangely not used in the foundation document for these ecumenical instruments.

Covenants and Confessions

Considerable reference has already been made in this chapter to Confessions of Faith, in which Baptists have sought in the past to explain their beliefs to those outside their own fellowship and to provide a tool for teaching those inside it. Often a church book will contain both a

---

93   *The Nature of the Assembly and the Council of the Baptist Union of Great Britain.* Doctrine and Worship Committee (London: Baptist Union, 1994), pp. 11–17.

94   *Visible Unity: Ten Propositions* (London: Churches' Unity Commission, 1976).

95   Text of the Welsh Covenant in *Not Strangers but Pilgrims. The Next Steps for Churches Together in Pilgrimage* (London: British Council of Churches and Catholic Truth Society, 1989), pp. 74–6. See further Paul Ballard, 'Baptists and Covenanting'.

96   See the 'Swanwick Report', in *Not Strangers but Pilgrims,* pp. 9–15

confession and a form of covenant, adjacent to each other. The confession might be compiled by the minister of the church or, among Calvinistic Baptist churches, the Particular Baptist *Confession* of 1677/89 was frequently used or modified. When Benjamin Keach, for example, published the covenant of the church at Horsley Down, it was bound with a version of the 1689 *Confession*. Sometimes, but it seems not always, the potential member was asked to sign assent to a confession as well as to the covenant.[97]

Appeal has recently been made to this relationship between confession and covenant to propose the adoption of a modern statement of faith by Baptists where one does not exist (for example in Britain). Some have urged that if we are to develop the concept of covenant as a basis for the associating or union of churches together, then a confession of faith is needed as a basis for the covenant; it is said that the 'cooperation' expressed by a covenant requires a 'commitment to shared understanding of the essential Gospel, as expressed in the Confession.'[98] But, as a notable English proponent of this view, Roger Hayden, himself judges about the past situation, 'there was an ambiguity about the link between the Confession of Faith adopted by a church and its covenant document.'[99] While the two might be adjacent, the one was not included in the other. Moreover, the difference in nature between them becomes especially clear when we consider the theological depth of covenant, which is more than an expression of human 'cooperation' or mutual duties; it is nothing less than a participation in the eternal covenant of grace.

Covenant is about relationship and trust, about 'walking together' which is in some mysterious way part of the very journey of salvation. Covenants, as we have seen, pre-dated confessions and were deeply bound up with the nature of the church as existing under the government of Christ. Although some have regretted that the 'basis' of the Baptist Union of Great Britain and Ireland adopted in 1903 (revised 1938) was a simple three-point declaration rather than something like the 1689 Confession, others have recognized in it the character of a covenant.[100] The first clause, which affirms the final authority of Jesus Christ and the liberty of each local church to 'interpret and administer his laws', precisely takes us back to the image of a church agreeing to walk

---

97   So at Alcester, for example, as cited in Hayden, 'Particular Baptist Confession 1689', p. 414.

98   Hayden, 'Particular Baptist Confession 1689', p. 415. The adoption of a Confession has also been urged by G. Beasley-Murray, 'Confessing Baptist Identity', in David Slater (ed.), *A Perspective on Baptist Identity* (Kingsbridge: Mainstream, 1987).

99   Hayden, 'Particular Baptist Confession 1689', p. 414. Cf. Roger Hayden, 'Baptists, Covenants and Confessions' in Fiddes et al., *Bound to Love*, pp. 26–8.

100 See Kidd (ed.), *Something to Declare*, pp. 15–16, 24–5.

together under the rule of Christ. The next two clauses briefly set out the nature of this walking together by affirming believers' baptism and the necessity of world mission, and the three together follow the structure of the commission of the risen Lord in Matthew 28:18-20.

The creation of modern confessions of faith are useful and perhaps essential tools for teaching, communicating our faith to others and ecumenical relationships. But if we are to learn, and yet not be bound by our past, I suggest that a theological and practical distance should be kept between confessions and covenants; confessions should be regarded as the *context* for covenant-making, but never be the *required* basis for 'walking together'. As argued by the authors of a recent study of the *Declaration of Principle*, 'in the making of covenant, be it at Sinai, Calvary or in the present day, the text is always subordinate to the relationship'.[101] In short, there is an openness that belongs to trust which covenant can encourage.

Covenant was an idea that gripped the minds and imaginations of our predecessors in the early days of Baptist life. It belonged to the quest for assurance of salvation in an age of religious anxiety. It provided a sense of identity, claiming continuity with the whole covenant people of God in the universal church. It gave expression to a spirit of renewal, with political and social implications as people looked for the re-making of a broken covenant between God and his church in England. It also gave a sense of empowerment, for people in a covenant relationship with God under the direct rule of Christ were thereby liberated from ecclesiastical authority, free to call their own ministry and celebrate the Gospel sacraments. Covenant aroused enthusiasm because it offered the possibilities of assurance, renewal, continuity and power. The concept declined in the nineteenth century because it could no longer be connected with these aspects; in an age of mission and inter-church ventures it seemed only to denote a community closed in upon itself and upon a narrow definition of its membership.

But, as we have seen, the inner dynamic of covenant is precisely in the direction of openness, towards the goal expressed in the biblical account of the 'everlasting covenant between God and every living creature of all flesh that is upon the earth' (Gen. 8:16). In our age, the making of covenant can accord with a culture which lays stress upon the virtues of openness to others and to the future. At the same time, covenant expresses a necessary closure, in commitment to God and in faithfulness to God's purposes.

---

101 Kidd (ed.), *Something to Declare*, p. 25.

CHAPTER 3

Beginning a New Millennium: Doctrinal Themes of Strategic Significance for Baptists

Enduring Themes: Divine Purpose and Authority

The turn of a century, and even more the swing of a millennium, prompts thought. An artificial boundary of time it may be, but it concentrates the mind wonderfully, providing opportunity for reflection on the past and questions about strategy for the future. As a member of a church in the Baptist Union of Great Britain, I am bound to take a backward glance to two previous moments when British Baptists stood on the threshold of a new century. On the verge of the nineteenth century, a group of Baptist ministers clustered around Andrew Fuller and William Carey found that they could respond to the challenge of God's mission in the world by re-thinking the theme of the sovereign purposes of God. Modifying the strict Calvinism they had inherited, they combined the gracious initiative God takes in salvation with the duty of all people everywhere to respond to God's offer of reconciliation.[1] William Carey's plea, 'Expect great things from God, attempt great things for God'[2] dramatically brings these two aspects together.

Then, on the verge of the twentieth century, the two streams of Baptist life that had flowed separately from the early seventeenth century, Particular and General, were brought together for the sake of mission at home. The New Connexion of General Baptists, many of whose churches were already members of the Baptist Union created by Particular Baptists earlier in the century, abandoned its separate identity to form simply one union of churches. In order to achieve the most inclusive fellowship and so the most effective kind of mission, the newly-strengthened Union decided not to adopt a wide-ranging statement of faith, but rather to

---

1   On this, see further below, ch. 11, pp. 255–8.
2   Sermon to the Northamptonshire Association at Nottingham, 30 May 1792, on the text Isaiah 54:2–3.

create a simple three-point 'Declaration of Principle'.[3] The very first phrase, on which all else rested, was an affirmation of the authority of Jesus Christ:

> That our Lord and Saviour, Jesus Christ, is the sole and absolute authority in all matters relating to faith and practice...[4]

Echoing the claim of Jesus in Matthew 28:18, 'All authority in heaven and earth has been given to me', this theme was to be the basis for all strategies of mission.

Now, trembling on the frontier of the twenty-first century, I believe that these doctrinal themes of divine purpose and authority are still the notes that we need to sound, but with a new orchestration for a new time. This is what I intend to work out in the following four points.

The Final Authority of Jesus Christ

The question of where authority lies must be at the forefront of our theological concerns as we enter a new millennium. In a fast-changing, highly mobile and multi-cultural society (and this is rapidly becoming an accurate description for most parts of the world), two attitudes to religious authority manifest themselves. For convenience, and with apology for jargon, we may call them *legalist* and *post-modernist*. On the one hand there is a desperate search for stability and security by resort to a collection of religious instructions, and this movement can be discerned not only within Christianity but within Islam and Judaism. Though the

---

3   The Declaration, first drawn up in 1883, enlarged in 1904 and slightly revised in 1938 reads:

'1. That our Lord and Saviour Jesus Christ, God manifest in the flesh, is the sole and absolute authority in all matters pertaining to faith and practice, as revealed in the Holy Scriptures, and that each Church has liberty, under the guidance of the Holy Spirit, to interpret and administer His Laws.

'2. That Christian Baptism is the immersion in water into the Name of the Father, the Son, and the Holy Ghost, of those who have professed repentance towards God and faith in our Lord Jesus Christ who "died for our sins according to the Scriptures; was buried, and rose again the third day".

'3. That it is the duty of every disciple to bear personal witness to the Gospel of Jesus Christ, and to take part in the evangelisation of the world.'

Scottish Baptists have a similar Declaration, amplified with some explanatory paragraphs; for the text, see Parker, *Baptists in Europe*, pp. 39–40. There is a detailed discussion of the origins of the Declaration in Kidd (ed), *Something to Declare,* pp. 17–25.

4   This is the version of 1904. The present version, revised in 1938, follows the words 'Jesus Christ' with 'God manifest in the flesh' (see n. 3 above).

term 'fundamentalism' is often used here, this is not really a return to the fundamentals of the faith but a kind of legalistic use of sacred texts that the Apostle Paul once summed up with the phrase, 'the letter kills but the Spirit gives life' (2 Cor. 3:6). Texts are used in a superficial way to bolster up certain inflexible convictions derived from a certain view of the world, rather than listening to the Spirit who breathes through the text and brings it to life in new contexts.

On the other hand, our age shows another reaction to the threat of change, a scepticism that any theories or explanations can be found for the totality of things. There can be small truths for particular circumstances, but no universal Truth. There can be many meaningful stories, but no Grand Story (or 'meta-narrative') which offers the meaning of everything. This mood or movement is often called post-modernism, because it challenges the various confident theories which our modern age has found to explain the natural world and human behaviour. It suspects that economic schemes, psychological and sociological models, scientific theories and political programmes are really concealed ideologies; they may appear to be harmless explanations of the world and society, but they are really concerned to oppress people and subjugate them to a structure of power.[5] This suspicion has in some cases been a healthy one, detecting the kind of dominating systems and forces for which the Apostle Paul had another useful phrase, 'principalities and powers'. But it has also led to a relativism about the nature of truth, and an assault upon Christian explanations of creation and redemption; the Christian understanding of history as 'God's story' is seen as one more ideology concerned to keep people (and often women in particular) in their place and subject to a religious institution. Revelation, it is said, is another word for oppression.[6]

In the face of this two-fold challenge, legalist and post-modernist, we need to recover the truly Christian understanding of ultimate authority. Like the British Baptist Declaration of Principle of 1904 we must begin with Jesus Christ, who is the beginning and the end, the alpha and the omega. That is, our final authority is a person. It is not a book, nor a creed, nor even a basis of faith, but a person in whom God expresses God's self fully. Revelation is not essentially the communication of a message or a list of propositions but (in the words of Karl Barth), 'the Person of God speaking';[7] it is the self-unveiling of God's very self to us, the free offer of divine Being and life, a gift which we find embodied in

---

5   E.g. Jean François Lyotard, *The Postmodern Condition. A Report on Knowledge*, trans. G. Bennington (Theory and History of Literature, 10; Manchester: Manchester University Press, 1984), pp. 27–37.

6   E.g. Mark C. Taylor, *Erring. A Postmodern A/theology* (Chicago and London: University of Chicago Press, 1987), pp. 65–70.

7   Barth, *Church Dogmatics,* I/1, pp. 304–5.

Jesus Christ. This is why revelation is not the oppressive concept that the post-modernist critique claims. In the act of revelation God is not so much telling us what to do as drawing us into the fellowship of a triune life. God is inviting us to share in a network of liberating relationships, to participate in the movements of love that flow between Father, Son and Spirit. As I want to go on to say shortly, this means that God makes 'space' for us to offer our own contribution to the divine project in creation rather than simply demanding that we submit to a pre-existing 'game-plan' for the universe.

If final authority lies in a person, obedience has all the quality of adventure, as personal relationships are open-ended and have room for growth and development. But the nature of this authority also strikes a blow against *legalism*. Absolute authority belongs to Jesus Christ, the incarnate Word of God, and the Bible witnesses to this Word. Baptists certainly do not downgrade the Holy Scriptures; they have always honoured the Bible as the Spirit-inspired gift of God to the people of God. But taking scripture seriously does not mean treating it as a collection of proof texts which are applied to back up a set of rules and regulations; it means finding scripture to be a place of encounter with the Spirit of Christ who conforms our personalities to his. It is the reliable place where we can expect to hear the *living* Word of God, who comes to us with unexpected demands and challenges in our own moment in history and culture. It is the place where we can hear the judgement of Christ upon the reader, and also upon some of the assumptions of the human writers of the text in their own time. Scripture thus always serves the authority of Christ. The Pharisees of Jesus' time prided themselves on being fine Bible students, but Jesus had to rebuke them with the words,

> You search the scriptures, because you think that in them you have eternal life; but they witness to me, and you refuse to come to me that you may have life (John 5:39).

It was in faithfulness to this claim of Jesus that the Confessing Church in Germany in the 1930s wrote its manifesto of resistance to the claims of Hitler to be the mediator of a new revelation. In protest against churches where the Nazi flag stood next to the altar, the Barmen Declaration affirmed: 'Jesus Christ, as he is attested for us in Holy Scripture, is the one Word of God which we have to hear and which we have to obey in life and in death.'[8]

I suggest that the doctrinal theme of Christ's supreme authority as Lord of the cosmos has a particular significance for Baptists as we enter a new millennium. Negatively, there is evidence that some Baptists today

8   The text can be found in Arthur C. Cochrane, *The Church's Confession under Hitler* (Pittsburgh: Pickwick Press, 1976), pp. 239–242.

may be falling into the error of putting Christ and the Bible into the wrong order of authority. Our roots in the Reformation rightly lead us to insist that the church will only be reformed by placing an appeal to scripture above tradition, but our roots in the radical wing of the Reformation should also remind us that the foundation of the church is in *discipleship* to Jesus Christ. We need to recover the Anabaptist emphasis upon the 'following' of Christ.[9] But this theme does not only suggest a timely correction. Positively, our Baptist identity has been forged in an interplay between three sources of authority – Christ, the Bible and the church meeting – and at our best we have understood them to be in that order. The aim of the meeting of the church members for prayer and business is not to make majority decisions, though it is perfectly right to safeguard our freedom through a democratic process. Nor is the aim for one block of voters to oppress and dominate another. The point is to find together the mind of Christ who is present in the midst of his church as the risen Lord to whom 'all authority is given', and to use the scriptures to help us in this search for his purpose in our world today. The British Baptist Declaration of Principle of 1904 brings these three sources of authority together into an almost seamless unity:

> That our Lord and Saviour, Jesus Christ, is the sole and absolute authority in all matters pertaining to faith and practice, as revealed in the Holy Scriptures, and that each church has liberty to interpret and administer His laws.[10]

These three sources can, of course, be found in other Christian traditions. But I suggest that there a distinctively 'Baptist' profile about the way they are blended,[11] and the way they interact with the baptism of a believing disciple into the death and resurrection of Christ. No single element is unique to Baptists, but at different moments in our history they have coinhered in a manner that has made us look 'different' from others, as we have met a particular challenge of the time or a need for service, or a summons to liberty. In an age when the authority of truth is either being abused (by legalism) or under siege (from postmodern attitudes), I believe that there is need for Baptists to explore again the meaning of the personal authority of the risen Christ, and the way this relates to the text which witnesses to him and the group of disciples in which he is embodied. The cosmic Christ, the story and the community – in the interplay of these elements is the response to both legalism and relativism.

---

9   For a modern Mennonite account, see John Howard Yoder, *The Politics of Jesus* (Grand Rapids: Eerdmans, 1972), pp. 115–134.

10   Text in Payne, *The Baptist Union*, p. 162. For the slightly expanded version of 1938, see above, n.3.

11   See McClendon, *Ethics*, 'The Baptist vision', pp. 27–35.

As we engage in mission, since our final authority is the person of the risen Christ, we shall be prepared to find him present in strange and unexpected places (Mt. 25:37–40). The sovereign Lord of the cosmos is not confined within the walls of the church, but is at work on behalf of the rule of God in the world. He is already present wherever there are movements for health and healing or where the oppressed are calling for justice. We are not, with all due respect to John Wesley's phrase, 'taking Christ to the people', but Christ is *with* the people inviting us to join him in service there. The doctrine of the Trinity is not an abstract theory but an expression of the mission of God; the Father who eternally pours forth the Son from his womb is sending forth (*missio*) the Son into the world in the power of the Spirit, in order to draw human persons into reconciliation in the circle of his own relational life.[12] Christ bids us share in this mission of his father, to be sent as he is being sent into the lives of others. The theme of the final authority of Christ therefore gives a certain flavour to evangelism; it is not based in a desperate struggle to make Christ relevant to people, but in a confidence in his transforming presence in different cultures.

At the same time, mission is not complete without the other two aspects of text and community, that is of openly telling the story of Christ in scripture to others, and of being the particular people who are alert to what God is doing in the world, and cooperating with God in faithful discipleship. For Baptists, 'strategy' of mission will thus flow from this understanding of the nature of authority.

A Covenant-making God

The authority of Christ naturally leads us to the biblical concept of covenant, for in the death and resurrection of Jesus Christ God has made a new agreement with the creation, and opened up new possibilities of partnership. The covenant therefore has a 'vertical' dimension between God and humanity, and it was this aspect that Reformation theology stressed. But a 'horizontal' dimension is also implied, especially in the covenant meal of the Lord's Supper. The breaking of the body of Jesus and the shedding of his blood which seal the new covenant are also the basis for making the new community, the body of Christ which is the church. People who are joined in a new agreement to God through the offering of divine sacrificial love are also covenanted together with each other. The two dimensions of covenant are inseparable, and God takes the initiative in both. The biblical concept of covenant is not one of bargain-

---

12   See Leonardo Boff, *The Trinity and Society* (London: Burns and Oates, 1988), pp. 147–54.

making, but a bond in which one partner takes the first step and summons the other into relationship; so the covenant-making God calls us to God's own self and into fellowship with each other.

We have seen, in the last chapter, that it was a highly creative step in early Baptist thinking to bring these two dimensions of covenant more closely together than other Reformation groups had done. Members of congregations living under the pressure of persecution expressed their trust in each other and their mutual dependence through a 'church covenant', in which they promised typically to 'walk together and watch over' each other. These communities understood that they were covenanting with each other and with God in a single pledge of faithfulness. Further, we find in the thought of the early Baptist John Smyth a striking implication for the nature of authority; the authority of the risen Lord, his mind and purpose for his community, is made known in the church meeting when two or more believers covenanted together were present.[13] Believers are bound in covenant relationship with Christ in God's gift of salvation, but what this means for the actualities of daily life is made manifest when believers are committed in covenant bonds to each other.

I believe that this is the second major doctrinal theme of 'strategic significance' for Baptists as they enter a new millennium. There is a need to regain a theology of covenant which fired the imagination of ancestors in the faith. This opens up a strategy for mission in at least three ways. First, it will bind Baptist congregations together in a commitment to mutuality and sharing of resources. The 'autonomy' of the local church is not, I suggest, a truly Baptist concept. From their earliest days, Baptists did not insist on the 'independence' of the local church, but rather the direct dependence of the local church on the authority of Christ. Nothing could be *imposed* upon a local church meeting by other churches or assemblies of churches because it had the freedom and the responsibility to find the mind of Christ. But on the other hand, the primary authority for the local church was the person of Christ, and the whole church universal is his body in the world (Eph.1:22–23). The body is the church in every time and place, its members in glory and on earth, the whole company of Apostles and Saints. So local churches gladly affirmed that they *needed* the counsel and insight of other Christian congregations to find the mind of Christ. Because the local congregation makes the body of Christ visible in one place, it is under the direct authority of Christ and cannot be dictated to by human agencies; but just because its aim is to find the mind of Christ it will seek fellowship, guidance and counsel from as much of *the whole body of Christ* as it can relate to. It will associate

---

13   Whitley (ed.), *Works of John Smyth*, I, p. 252. See also White, *The English Separatist Tradition*, p. 129.

and unite with others, not just for the convenience of getting a job done, but because Christ is calling it to covenant with others.

Baptist churches have therefore always lived together in spiritual interdependence with each other in associations. This was the understanding of the London Confession of 1644, as it held the balance between the privileges of the local church on the one hand, and on the other the necessity to seek the guidance of God from others: 'yet are they all to walk by the same rule and by all means convenient to have the counsel and help of one another in all needful affairs of the church, as members of the one body in the common faith under Christ their only head'.[14] It often seems daring in the English-speaking world to propose that a Union of churches is bound together in covenant. It is less startling in Germany and Sweden where 'union' and 'covenant' are the same word – *Bund* or *Förbundet*. But in the latter countries, perhaps the *theological* meaning of covenant needs to be recovered. Taking a taxi from the Seminary of the Swedish 'Covenant Church', after a visit there, I found that the driver had a sticker on the windscreen proclaiming himself to be a member of the 'Taxi Covenant' (*Taxiförbundet*). But unlike a trade association or trades union, the union of churches is drawn together by the initiative of God under the authority of Christ. While covenant will of course take different forms at local, regional and national level, there will be the same possibility of helping each other to find the purpose of Christ for life and mission.

Recovering a theology of covenant thus means more than the practical matter of stronger churches helping the weaker to finance ministry, important though this is. A second compelling reason for gathering in covenant together is to help each other *discover* the shape and the form of the mission of God in our world today. However large and well-resourced a local church may be, it needs to listen to others to understand its mission. It needs to hear how poor Christians in a Latin American *favella* understand their mission, how black Christians in a South African township understand justice, how Christians in an eastern European church understand the meaning of freedom. In association with local churches closer home, the word from Christ will often come from the small fellowship that may seem the weakest and the most in need of help.

A theology of covenant is thus of strategic importance, in identifying the mission of God and sharing in it. This is also why the Baptist doctrine of the local church should lead it to be thoroughly ecumenical. In direct dependence on the authority of Christ, it can covenant with other parts of the Christian family without losing its liberty. In its church meeting it will want to hear voices from as wide a representation of the body of Christ as it can; it will want to know how wider circles of fellowship, synods and

---

14   Lumpkin, *Baptist Confessions of Faith*, pp. 168–9.

even colleges of bishops, discern the purpose of Christ. It will want to be
drawn into the mission of God alongside others. Indeed, a theology of
covenant is 'ecumenical' in the strongest sense; it takes in the whole
'household' (*oikos*) of the natural world.

Third then, a theology of covenant opens up a wide view of mission.
According to the Old Testament, God makes covenant not only with
human beings but with 'every living creature – the birds, the cattle, the
beasts of the earth' (Gen. 9:8). God relates to all creatures in their own
way, and not only humans but the world of nature sings praises: God is
with the wild hinds as they calve, releases the wild asses to roam freely,
and teaches the hawk and eagle to soar in the sky; the waves roar before
God, the heavens pour forth speech, the trees of the field sing and clap
their hands as the divine king comes.[15] According to Paul the whole
universe is groaning as in childbirth, waiting for God to set it free, its
destiny deeply bound up with the redemption of God's human children
(Rom. 8:21). Of course these are poetic images, but they surely bear
testimony to some kind of response which the natural world can make or
fail to make to the purposes of God, a response which in some way is
connected to the human response. It is a theological challenge for our
age to try and describe this relationship between God and the whole
world, a covenantal relationship between human beings and their natural
environment, in a way that truly expresses mutual dependence rather than
domination. Finding this language will help with our evangelism, in the
telling of the Christian story, and will motivate our concern for peace and
justice in all creation. The vision of God as Trinity will encourage a view
of the world as an inter-related society, interconnected in ways that are
sometimes mysterious and hidden. The world is not a complicated
machine but a complicated family.

The 'New Age' movement of our time has insight into the
connectedness of all living things, but tends to turn the earth itself into a
goddess (*Gaia*). A theology of covenant resists such confusion, making
clear that God always takes the gracious initiative as covenant partner. It
should also make us sensitive to hear the cry for liberation within the
natural as well as the human world. We shall catch a glimpse of the way
that human and natural suffering is taken up into the pain in the heart of
God as the Creator sympathizes with a struggling creation. And so we
come to our third strategic theme.

---

15   Psalms 19:1–4; 29:5–9; 96:12–13; 98:7–9; 104:26; Job 39:1–6, 26–7; Isa.
55:12–13.

The Suffering of God

This theme may seem at first to be not so immediately related to Baptist life as the first two, but it arises directly from the theology of a covenant-making God. A God who opens the divine life to make a new agreement will not remain unaffected by covenant partners, since true partnership involves being open to the impact of the other upon one's own life and being. Love is always a painful process. The one who loves will feel the suffering of another in empathy, and will know the vulnerability of being open to being rejected by the other. We see this kind of alienation and agonizing identification entering the heart of God in the cross of Jesus, as God takes upon God's own self the experience of the forsaken.

For centuries the Christian church resisted the idea that suffering touched the very being of God, instead isolating suffering to a separate human nature of Jesus and not allowing it to break through into his divine personality. The love of God was seen simply as a charitable 'doing good' to creation, rather than as an emotion that brought any disturbance to God's eternal peace and bliss. The reasons for this assertion of the impassibility of God have been well-traced by a number of modern theologians, and there is no need to rehearse them in detail here. Suffice it to say that Christian thinkers confused the denial that God owed existence to anything else with the belief that God could not be conditioned by anything outside God's being. A self-existent God must, they thought, be self-sufficient and invulnerable.[16] Moreover, the picture of a non-suffering God could easily develop into the picture of a God who inflicted suffering on others. This was how divine sovereignty was defined: in the worldly image of a human sovereign, authority was seen as the power to escape suffering and to make others suffer. But as Jürgen Moltmann has rightly pointed out, a God who suffers protests against suffering; a suffering God is on the side of the victims and so cannot be the *cause* of suffering.[17]

It is of considerable interest that Baptist writers and thinkers have been in the very forefront of those who have overturned the concept of the impassibility of God in recent years.[18] Notable among them was the Old Testament scholar Henry Wheeler Robinson, and this perhaps gives one

---

16   For an exposition of this point, see Paul S. Fiddes, *The Creative Suffering of God* (Oxford: Clarendon Press, 1988), pp. 66–8.

17   Jürgen Moltmann, *The Crucified God. The Cross of Christ as the Foundation and Criticism of Modern Theology*, trans. M. Kohl (London: SCM Press, 1974), pp. 25–4.

18   Examples are: James Hinton, *The Mystery of Pain* (London: H.R. Allenson, 1866); H. Wheeler Robinson, *Suffering Human and Divine* (London: SCM Press, 1940); Warren McWilliams, *The Passion of God. Divine Suffering in Contemporary Protestant Theology* (Macon: Mercer University Press, 1985); Fiddes, *The Creative Suffering of God*.

clue as to why this has been a Baptist theme. Baptists have always taken scripture seriously as a source of authority (see my second point above), and Wheeler Robinson found divine suffering to be a truly biblical theme, as the Old Testament prophets unfold the picture of a God who enters with empathy into the grief and pain of his people in exile. There was a revelatory moment, for example, in the response of God to the complaint of Baruch that the life of the people had been laid waste; through Jeremiah God exclaims, 'But on me the waste lies (Jer. 12:11).'[19] For Baptist biblical scholars the witness of scripture was to be preferred to church tradition influenced by a philosophy of an unconditioned Absolute. Moreover, the Baptist conviction that ultimate authority is to be defined in terms of a person was surely also significant; that the power of God was revealed in the crucified Jesus overturns all human ideas of power and authority and shows us that there is – in Wheeler Robinson's words - 'an eternal cross in the heart of God.'[20] Finally, I like to think that the experience of Baptist Christians as a persecuted and oppressed minority in the religious life of Europe over the centuries has given Baptists a particular insight into the nature of God, who cannot be easily identified with the image of rulers who deny religious freedom to their subjects and inflict severe punishments on them when they will not conform.

Whether or not this doctrinal theme can be claimed to be of *historic* interest to Baptists, I believe it should certainly concern us as we enter a new century. It is of 'strategic significance' for at least two reasons. First, anyone who wants to communicate the Christian message today will find the problem of human suffering to be a huge blockage to faith in the minds of many people who are conscious of the agonies of two world wars, the holocaust, Hiroshima, and the killing fields of Vietnam, Rwanda and the former Jugoslavia. Moreover, I suspect that the problem of suffering will grow more acute as the television brings flood, famine and war even closer into the living room, as the situation in the Middle East eludes resolution and as parts of Europe, recently liberated, may well go on tearing themselves apart in ethnic struggle. Baptists who are committed to evangelism will need an apologetic which will not, of course, pretend to answer all the hard questions (or else we would be no better than Job's comforters) but which will at least be able to speak a word of faith into the situation. It may be that the only word that can be said is the assurance that God is not immune from suffering but *sharing* people's pain, that they are not left alone as they enter the dark valley. Perhaps in the end this kind of 'practical theodicy' will sustain people in

---

19   See H. Wheeler Robinson, *The Cross of Jeremiah* (1925), repr. in *The Cross in the Old Testament* (London: SCM Press, 1955), p. 184.
20   Wheeler Robinson, *The Cross in the Old Testament*, p. 185.

their suffering more than any argument can. But there is a place for the development of doctrine in teaching even if it is not appropriate in the actual crisis of pastoral care, and I believe that a faith for the new century needs a vision of a God of creative suffering.

Perhaps the least inadequate explanation of human suffering is the so-called 'free-will defence', which affirms that God's purpose in creating the universe was to make a world of personal beings with whom God could enter into relationship.[21] The argument runs that for them to be real persons they must have been created free to do either good or evil; the only other option was a world of puppets or robots. This does not mean that those who suffer are directly reaping the results of their *own* free choices. Jesus himself warned us against such cruel and judgemental conclusions.[22] But human suffering is seen as the result of a long drift of creation away from the purposes of God, so that people are victims of a distorted universe which has mis-used its freedom. The advantage with this kind of explanation is that it does not pretend that 'suffering is good for you', or that God has designed suffering into the universe as a kind of moral stiffener or educational process. This is why I suggest it is the 'least inadequate' argument. But I believe that Christian preachers and apologists should hesitate to use it without setting it alongside the affirmation that God suffers with us in God's own self. The free-will defence is virtually useless without this context.[23]

Among several reasons for this, I want to mention two. In the first place, even if all suffering is the result of human beings turning away from God's purposes for the world, God has set the whole situation up in the first place. God has created a world with the possibility of evil within it, even though not directly causing evil. God thus carries a kind of final responsibility, even if not an immediate one. It is fitting that a God who exposes creation to the risks of suffering that come from freedom should share the consequences with creatures. In fact the cross of Jesus *does* tell us that God takes responsibility, taking suffering upon God's own self in order finally to overcome the evil that spoils creation. The protest of suffering people against God must not therefore be suppressed or criticized. Even when we have developed an argument about human free-will, the question still remains: 'is it worth it'? As Dostoievsky puts it through the mouth of one of his characters,[24] 'Is the whole universe

---

21 For a defence of this argument, see Alvin Plantinga, *The Nature of Necessity* (New York: Oxford University Press, 1982), pp. 173–89. For philosophical objections, see J.L. Mackie, *The Miracle of Theism* (Oxford: Clarendon Press, 1982), pp. 162–76.

22 Jn. 9:1–3.

23 I have given a longer explanation of this assertion in my *Participating in God*, pp. 164–70.

24 F. Dostoyevsky, *The Brothers Karamazov*, transl. D. Magarshack (Harmondsworth: Penguin, 1962), p. 283.

worth the tears of one tortured child?' Suppose that God cannot make real persons without the risk of evil and suffering. Suppose that God suffers with us and takes the consequences. Nevertheless, is the project worth it? Is it worth making persons at this cost? When all argument has fallen silent, only faith can leap this abyss and say 'Yes, it is worth it. Personal fellowship with God and each other is worth it all.' But because the gap has to be leapt by faith, we can understand anger against God. A certain amount may even be a healthy thing, as in the case of a Christian social worker in a hospice for the dying, writing some time ago in a national newspaper; she wrote that she was glad she believed in God because 'that means I've got somebody to be flaming mad with.'[25]

A second reason for affirming the suffering of God is the impact upon God of giving freedom to the creation. If God is to give created persons a genuine freedom to make real choices, then God must limit God's self. If persons are to be allowed to grow and develop, they must be given room to be themselves. God cannot control but only guide and persuade. This is not a limitation imposed on God from outside; it belongs to the divine sovereign will, because God freely chooses to be this kind of God. Now, such humble self-limitation must mean suffering for God. It will mean some frustration of God's purposes and desires, at least in the short term. This is a painful experience that the Old Testament prophets describe in colourful terms. As Hosea paints the picture, for example, God is like a husband suffering the agony of having an unfaithful wife; his purpose was that Israel should love him and enjoy fellowship with him, but this has been frustrated as she has gone her own way and taken other lovers. Hosea also uses the picture of a disappointed parent – a mother, perhaps:

> When Israel was a child I loved him
> And out of Egypt I called my son....
> But the more I called him, the more he went from me. (Hos. 11:1–2)

There is the pain of God's frustrated purpose in every line of this poem. A covenant relationship allows freedom to the other, and therefore involves pain. In our time, who can doubt that God was frustrated in the divine aims by such an offence as Auschwitz, that God suffered there all the pain of parents who see their children hurting not only themselves but inflicting terrible damage on others?

In a moment I want to draw the implications from this picture of divine self-limitation for a general belief about how God acts in the world, which will be my final doctrinal theme. But before that, there is another 'strategic' reason for proposing the doctrine of divine suffering. As we share with God in mission, we find ourselves in a world where people

---

25   *The Guardian* Newspaper, 17 August 1979.

seem to have a strong feeling about the absence of God. We are entering a millennium in which there is interest in all kinds of spiritual experiences, but in which there is less sense of the presence of a personal God than in past ages. Yet, as I suggested earlier, the triune God is not absent from the world, and Christ as the cosmic Lord is present in many places. We need to develop a theological understanding of how God can be *hidden* without being absent, and this is quite largely connected with the theme of God's suffering. The cry of forsakenness on the cross, our own cries of protest and anger ('Is it worth it?') are spoken to a God who has limited God's own self, anu who chooses to go about anonymous in the world in poor apparel rather than dazzling us with glory. God is hidden in suffering, but is not absent; God has not left the scene, and one witness to this is that we still find ourselves having conversation with God in prayer. A theology of the absence of God, a God who is effectively dead to the world, will not meet the needs of the coming age. A theology for the millennium will be one which explores the hiddenness of God, and which will therefore challenge 'theologies of success' or 'theologies of prosperity' to which Baptists are sometimes prone. As a nameless Jew wrote on the walls of the Warsaw ghetto during the time of genocide:

I believe in the sun even when it does not shine;
I believe in love, even when I cannot feel it.
I believe in God, even when I do not see him.

I suspect that we shall need the help of Jewish believers really to understand this.

Promise and Fulfilment

So far we have been exploring the enduring theological themes of the sovereign purposes and the gracious initiative of God. Expressed by Calvin in a form appropriate for his own age, they have taken new forms in critical moments of Baptist life. From the perspective of our present age, just over the verge of a new century, they have strategic significance for mission as they take on new forms once again: the authority of Christ in relation to text and community, the initiative of God in making covenant as wide as the world, and the self-limitation of the suffering God. Underlying all these is another theme, which Baptists need to reflect upon: the way that God acts in the world.

Baptists have a high expectation of divine action in the world and society, and this can be positive in mission. Baptists expect the Holy Spirit of God to work in people's lives, bringing repentance, spiritual and sometimes physical healing. They have a strong sense of special as well as general providence, and they expect to receive guidance in the making of personal and corporate decisions. They make intercessions and supplications with a high expectation that God will answer prayer. In Carey's words, they 'expect great things from God.' But there are also negative aspects to this; there can be an over-reliance upon 'signs and wonders', a trivializing of divine action in which God provides special favours for those who ask (at its worst, parking spaces when attending meetings), a stress upon 'submission' to the will of God and a passivity to being taken over by emotion and feelings which are sometimes uncritically identified with the Holy Spirit. It is clear that convictions about the nature of God's action in the world are of strategic significance as we seek to share in the mission of God.

I suggest that our thought so far leads us to a view of divine action which is persuasive rather than coercive, which invites human cooperation rather than being unilateral from God's side, and which works from the inside of creation rather than being 'interventionist'. Actually, the notion of 'intervention' is not a biblical but a philosophical concept, as it implies that God is absent from the world until 'breaking in' or 'coming on the scene' (*intervenio*). The biblical conviction, by contrast, is that the God who continuously sustains a relation with the world has the freedom to *do new things* within it. Above all the resurrection of Jesus tells us that God can open up new possibilities when things seem dead (see also Rom. 4:17). These possibilities are not trapped in the conditions of the present, and we may find them to be of three kinds.[26] First there are the possibilities that God knows from all eternity, and from which God has chosen some to actualize in the world in the course of history. Second there are possibilities that God creates from the richness of the divine imagination as creation and history proceed. But third (and this is my main concern here), there are possibilities that emerge from the interaction between God and created beings. We can see from our previous reflections on divine suffering that, in God's humility and sovereign self-limitation, God chooses to allow new possibilities to develop in partnership with human persons. In technical terms, such a theological statement overturns a whole philosophical tradition stemming from Aquinas (and behind him to Aristotle) that for God all possibilities are identical with actualities.[27] But such a concept belonged to the notion

---

26   I have given a longer account of kinds of possibility in my *The Promised End*, pp. 166–75. For the idea that possibility is prior to actuality, see Paul Ricoeur, *Freedom and Nature. The Voluntary and the Involuntary*, trans. E.V. Kohak (Evanston: Northwestern University Press), pp. 48–54, and Eberhard Jüngel, 'The World as Possibility and Actuality. The Ontology of the Doctrine of Justification', in John Webster (trans. and ed.), *Eberhard Jüngel, Theological Essays* (Edinburgh: T. & T. Clark, 1989), pp. 95–123.

27   Further see Fiddes, *The Creative Suffering of God*, pp. 55–6.

of a God who was unmoving and un-suffering. Instead, this is the image of a God who in humility allows a gap between possibility and actuality, a gap in which God can make new choices and in which we can contribute to the project of creation.

Perhaps a picture will assist doctrine here. An artist sets out to paint a picture with a preconceived image of it in her mind; she sees all kinds of possibilities for it, and perhaps has already embodied these in a sketch or a drawing. But as she begins to paint, the materials she is working with begin to make their own contribution as she turns possibility into actuality. The thick swirls of the paint, the texture of the canvas, the feel of the brush, the exact tinctures of the colour she mixes and the shades of light available all make their effect upon the painting. The finished product is a partnership between the artist and her materials, with all their potential and even their resistance to her. This kind of illustration is in fact entirely biblical. Jeremiah perceived that the potter has an intention to carry out, but the way he could do so would be limited by his materials. Quite against his purpose, the clay might be 'marred' in his hands, and he would have to begin again with a new initiative (Jer. 18:4). When this illustration is applied to human persons 'in the hand of the divine potter', we can see how much more the purposes of God are open to the response of created beings. God is not making an assembly-line product in a factory.

This is why the scriptural pattern for describing the acts of God is that of *promise* and fulfilment. It is not *prediction* and fulfilment. God promises to brings about a certain purpose, and always fulfils this promise, but (as an Old Testament scholar has put it)[28] God 'fulfils his promise in unexpected ways'. God promises to give a land to Abraham, but this only comes about through a life in slavery in Egypt. God promises that there will always be a Davidic king with whom to have special relationship, but later, when the kingship has been lost, a prophet declares that the whole nation corporately has now become like a David to God (Isa. 55:3–5). Jesus fulfils Messianic hopes and expectations in such a surprising way that most of the Jewish nation fails to recognize him. There is always this element of surprise and the unexpected because God leaves room for both divine freedom of action and our own. The power of God's loving persuasion is such that God's purposes will surely be fulfilled, but this is not the same as a divine blueprint, an exact set of plans down to the last detail, a script with all the words written in.

This doctrinal perspective is of strategic significance especially for Baptists, because it is essential for those who have a strong conviction about the special as well as the general activity of God. The more

---

28   Walther Zimmerli, 'Promise and Fulfilment' in C. Westermann (ed.), *Essays on Old Testament Interpretation*, trans. J.L. Mays (London: SCM Press, 1963), p. 107.

particular a view of divine activity is, the more it can fall into a kind of passivity or even fatalism. It was this that Fuller and Carey had to confront on the verge of the nineteenth century with their re-thinking of the sovereignty of God, and I suggest that we need to make similar moves of thought today. Among most of our churches there is probably not the need now to modify a strict Calvinism (though there is a resurgence of this tradition in the Southern States of America at the moment), but there is a need to recognize the human contribution that God graciously allows for in the working out of purposes. I mean taking culture and context seriously, as seriously as God does in accommodating God's self to the world.

We will therefore resist attempting to impose grand strategies for mission on various parts of the world, regardless of the cultural setting. We will not think that because a strategy has been successful in one context, it can simply be duplicated in a completely different one. We will not confuse the reality of what is 'spiritual' with certain cultural forms of faith, and we will be alert to the temptation of judging others because they do not express their worship or practice their faith in the same way. We will not attempt to pressurize fellow believers into a certain form of action, conditioned in fact by our own context, by accusing them otherwise of hindering the mission of God. This openness and flexibility in strategy is not a modern relativism (such as I mentioned in earlier in this chapter), but takes the element of *promise* seriously.

At the beginning of a new century what is of strategic importance, as in the past, is the way that we understand the themes of divine purpose, power and authority, and allow these to form our actions. What is 'strategic' is the way we work out the implications of the old baptismal confession: 'Jesus is Lord'.

CHAPTER 4

Church and Trinity: A Baptist Ecclesiology of Participation

A British national newspaper once asked several leading advertising agencies how they would design advertising campaigns for the church, and specifically 'to swell the Church of England's congregations'.[1] The agencies produced a range of posters, with images that they thought would make the church attractive to the present age. One agency focused on the way the church provides a good experience; their poster showed a wooden pew with the message, 'No armchair in the world provides as much comfort'. Another thought the church should be seen as a place of refreshment; a poster showed a busy young mother pictured on a video screen with the message, 'Wouldn't it be wonderful if life had a pause button?'. Yet another presented the church as a place where moral problems could be solved; one of their adverts declared, 'Why are children mugging grandmothers? God only knows. The Church... You'll never really know until you go'.[2]

These images are highly revealing about the ethos of the market place. The journalist who wrote the article made a telling critique when she commented that 'these advertisements end up promoting the church as a break from the rest of one's lifestyle and not an integral part of it.'[3] They offer one product among others. They may *seem* religious in holding out the promise of divine blessings for those who buy into the church, but they miss the truly 'theological' dimension, in the sense of the grounding of the church in the life of God. What is absent is indicated by a German Baptist New Testament scholar, Wiard Popkes, in his study of the Christian congregation, when he asserts that 'The church

---

1   Suzanne Moore, 'Ad Gloriam', *The Guardian Weekend*, 10 April 1993, pp. 6–11.

2   These images came respectively from the agencies of Grey (London), McCann-Erickson and TBWA-Homes Knight Ritchie.

3   Moore, 'Ad Gloriam', p. 11.

is before everything the planting of God'[4], and so 'the church which does not understand itself primarily in a *theo*logical way loses the ground in which it is rooted.'[5] We need, then, to explore some of the implications of what this rooting of the church in God might mean, beginning from some New Testament images but then expanding into a more doctrinal and trinitarian reflection.

What does it really mean, in both exegesis and practice, this *theo*logical dimension? In this chapter I want to argue that it is not simply the activity of God *through the church*, but the sharing of the church *in God*. True ecclesiology is an ecclesiology of participation, and this tells us as much about the nature of God who lives in communion as about the church as a social unit.

Three New Testament Images

We begin with the Pauline image of the church as the 'body of Christ' (e.g. 1 Cor. 12:12, 27). New Testament study in the twentieth century succeeded in awakening us to the power of what had often become a dead metaphor, alerting us to the startling and even shocking impact that the image made when it was first used.[6] Paul was not simply employing the classical trope of picturing a human society as being *like a body* with many limbs, drawing a moralistic application that every member has his or her part to play in the whole.[7] He dares to identify this human social group with the body of a particular person, the Christ who was crucified and is risen to new life. The church is *the body of this Christ*; its members participate in his death and so in his resurrection. Scholars such as John Robinson have in fact proposed that in Paul's view the resurrection body of Christ is nothing more or less than the church as the fellowship of his followers. There is a simple and absolute identity; the bodily form of the risen Jesus is the church. Paul, he suggests, discovered this truth when he

---

4   Wiard Popkes, *Gemeinde: Raum des Vertrauens. Neutestamentliche Beobachtungen und freikirchliche Perspectiven.* (Wuppertal: Oncken Verlag, 1984), p. 42. I have translated *Setzung Gottes* as 'planting of God', but given Wiard Popkes' love of music it might well be translated '*composition* of God'. The present chapter, in its original version, was an essay in honour of Wiard Popkes.

5   Popkes, *Gemeinde*, p. 44. The italics are Popkes'.

6   See John A.T. Robinson, *The Body. A Study in Pauline Theology* (Studies in Biblical Theology 5; London: SCM, 1952); Ernest Best, *One Body in Christ. A Study in the Relationship of the Church to Christ in the Epistles of the Apostle Paul* (London: SPCK, 1955); C.F.D. Moule, *The Origin of Christology* (Cambridge: Cambridge University Press, 1977).

7   For example, Livy, II.32, ascribes the metaphor to the fable of Menenius Agrippa.

persecuted members of the church and was then confronted by a vision of the risen Christ demanding, 'Why are you persecuting me?'[8]

In my view we are not doing justice to Paul's thought if we totally exhaust the transformed bodily existence of the risen Christ into the church. The complementary images of Christ as the head of the body and as the integrating power of the cosmos[9] introduce a corrective here, making clear that the church always stands under the direction and judgement of a Christ who cannot be confined in the church. But the image of the body does make clear that the risen Jesus is identified in a more intimate way with the life of his disciples than in his earthly ministry, that he now has a more inter-personal existence,[10] and that he calls his followers into a corporate life that can never be separated from him. The body of the church, the body of the communion bread and Jesus' own body of resurrection are overlapping and interpenetrating realities that can never be torn apart. Though we have no opportunity to explore it here, this also has an important bearing upon our hope that we will wear the 'body of resurrection', which we often interpret far too individualistically.[11]

The point of the image that we are 'all members of one body' is therefore not just that we 'all have a contribution to make'. The affirmation that all the members are gifted by the Spirit and have need of each other is not just that we share our *charismata* together. The point is that the members join to make the whole body visible, that is to allow *Christ* to manifest himself in the world, to make himself knowable and tangible through all his members. Everyone has a *charisma*, not to fulfill himself or herself, not for mutual satisfaction and good experiences (as the adverts we began with imply), but in order to make Christ visible in ministry to the world around. Like a computer-generated picture of a face, the many features of Christ come together to allow his face to stand out.

A second New Testament image, found in the thought of both Paul and the post-Pauline period, is the church as a temple indwelt by the Spirit of God. While the individual believer can be said to be a temple of the Holy Spirit (1 Cor. 6:19), believers corporately as the church are also 'God's building', God's temple in whom God's spirit dwells (1 Cor. 3:9–17). In line with this I translate Ephesians 2:22 as 'a dwelling-place for God in

---

8   Robinson, *The Body*, pp. 57–8.
9   Col. 1:17–18, which I take to be Pauline.
10   So Moule, *Origin of Christology*, pp. 47–54.
11   I have explored the corporate nature of resurrection elsewhere, in my *The Promised End*, pp. 96–109.

the Spirit'[12] rather than 'a spiritual dwelling-place for God.'[13] The Spirit of God is portrayed as filling the community of believers gathered together as the Shekinah cloud filled the temple of Ancient Israel. We recall that at their best the Old Testament psalmists and prophets knew that this 'dwelling' of God was not the kind of residence in which God would be trapped within the Jerusalem temple as an inviolable guarantee of their security; rather, Yahweh faithfully 'came to dwell' with his people, taking the gracious initiative in coming to encounter his people at the chosen meeting-place.

The images of body and temple are not simply interchangeable, so that the church might be said to be 'the temple of Christ' or the building where Christ dwells. Rather, in Ephesians 2 one image is laid on top of the other, like a palimpsest of manuscripts or (to use a more modern image) like transparencies laid over the other on an overhead projector. The two races who were once hostile and alienated from each other, Jew and Gentile, rooted in totally different cultures, have been reconciled in the *body* of Christ at the cross (Eph. 2:16). This body, in whom strangers have been united, is like a temple indwelt by the Spirit of God. The overlaying of images is vividly present in the description of the structure as 'growing' into a holy temple in the Lord. This is not a building made of inert blocks, but a structure that is alive like a body.

There are several significant consequences in the overlaying but not replacing of one image by another. First, the fact that the building is not simply said to be indwelt by Christ emphasizes (as John Robinson points out)[14] that believers are joined 'organically' to Christ like limbs to a body; the union is much more intimate than even an indwelling might be. Second, the reader is invited to make a connection which is not brought out explicitly in the text: the same Spirit who indwelt the body of the earthly Jesus like a temple[15], and gave him power for ministry, now indwells his body the church. In this sense the church might be called an 'extension of the incarnation'. This is a point to which we must return in re-viewing these images from a trinitarian perspective. Third, the building in which the Spirit dwells is composed of unlike people, not a homogeneous mass but people quite different from each other in culture and tradition who are reconciled in the body of Christ. The diversity of the members is here made the very principle of the indwelling of the Spirit. We might say imaginatively that when God builds a temple God chooses a colourful mosaic of different building blocks, like a Byzantine

---

12   Here I follow Andrew T. Lincoln, *Word Biblical Commentary. Ephesians* (Dallas: Word Books, 1990), p. 158: 'The Spirit is seen as the means by which God dwells in the Church.' Also Robinson, *The Body*, p. 64

13   So RSV, RNEB versions.

14   Robinson, *The Body*, p. 65.

15   Jn. 3:21

basilica. The image of church as temple stresses the catholicity of the church no less than the body with its different members.

This idea of a 'new humanity' (Eph. 2:15) gains further expression in a third image for the church, found in the Petrine correspondence: that of 'the people of God' (1 Pet. 2:9). The overcoming of all exclusiveness in relation to God portrayed in the Ephesian passage is celebrated here by taking the designations restricted to Israel in the Old Testament and applying them to the church. In the parallel epithets, 'a chosen race, a royal priesthood, a holy nation, God's own people' there is a deliberate echo of Exodus 19:6,[16] and the link in both texts between the idea of being the 'people of God' and a 'royal priesthood' is especially significant. It is a people which is close to God, enjoying the intimacy of the divine presence as a 'holy nation', that is called to be a priestly mediator of this blessing to others, and to intercede with God for others. A close relationship with a God who is on mission in the world is never for the sake of one's own satisfaction or privilege but for the sake of service to all nations. The Old Testament writings bear witness to the fact that Israel knew this to be the case, but sometimes forgot it.[17]

The phrase *basileon hierateuma* does present some difficulties in translation, as it appears in the LXX at Exodus 19:6 as a translation of the Hebrew phrase 'kingdom of priests'. The natural rendering of the Greek as 'royal priesthood' stresses the corporate nature of this priesthood;[18] the priesthood belongs to the church as a whole, rather than to any individual within it, or to any office of ministry. It also perhaps evokes the figure of the Davidic king, who in Israel's traditions had a priestly function as mediator of divine blessing in the nation; it is as if this royal priestly function has been 'democratized' from one individual to the whole nation, as Second Isaiah had already suggested (Isa. 55:3–5). These echoes may be present because the preceding part of the passage has pointed to Christ as 'cornerstone in Zion', which may well be a Messianic ascription.[19]

The whole passage thus presents us with an overlaying of the images of the church as temple and as the People of God. The members of the church are 'living stones' in a spiritual temple of which Christ is the cornerstone (as in Eph. 2:22), but they are also a priestly nation offering spiritual sacrifices in dependence upon Christ. Although the passage does

---

16   There is also a conflation with Is. 43:20-21 (quoted from the LXX)

17   See H.H. Rowley, *The Missionary Message of the Old Testament* (London: Carey Press, 1944), pp. 40–2, 67–9.

18   In his study, *The Elect and the Holy. An Exegetical Examination of 1 Peter 2:4–10* (Leiden: Brill, 1966), John H. Elliot therefore prefers the translation 'body of priests'.

19   The Targumim and Rabbinic literature tend to interpret the 'stone' texts of Isa. 28:16 and Ps. 118:22 in a messianic way. See Elliot, *Elect and the Holy*, p. 27.

not explictly refer to the priestly ministry of Christ before God as does
the Letter to the Hebrews, the phrase 'offer sacrifices.... through Jesus
Christ' must imply the function of Christ as mediator and so priest
himself.[20] From being the structure of the temple the metaphor shifts to
their being the priests within the temple, and the images perhaps converge
in the use of the word *oikos* (house) for temple which can also mean
'household'. Nor is the metaphor of the body entirely absent; though the
word itself is not spoken, the new converts are portrayed as 'growing up'
into salvation through receiving 'spiritual milk' or 'life mediated
through the Logos'.[21] It is this concept of vital union with Christ that
enables the writer to portray the temple as something organic, as
composed of 'living stones' in a further echo of Ephesians 2:20–22.

The Expansion of Images: A Trinitarian Perspective

The meaning of any metaphor cannot be trapped within the intention of
its author. Significance will expand as the two terms of the metaphor set
up new resonances and draw readers in to make fresh meaning for new
contexts through their own responses. Theologically, one may say that we
meet the ever-new Word of God within the expansive space of the
metaphor. So it is with these three images in which the church is
compared with a body, a temple and a people. The images open up new
horizons of meaning as we come to them from the further side of the
development of church doctrine about God as Trinity.

Of course, I freely accept that the seeds of a doctrine of Trinity are
already present in the metaphors themselves, as we have seen that they
cannot be understood without reference to God as Father, Son and Spirit.
In fact, we can discern a 'leading profile' of one person which belongs to
each image. The metaphor of body begins with the Son, as the church is
identified with Christ. The image of the temple directs our attention first
to the Spirit, indwelling the church. The image of the people of God
begins from a relationship to God the Father, Father now not of one
nation alone but of all humankind. Moreover, the more that one image
overlays the other, the less possible it is to understand one divine person
without relationship to the others. The members of the body are endowed
with the gifts of the Spirit; the Spirit indwells the body; the priestly
function of the nation before God the Father depends upon the Son as
mediator. In this way, the ecclesiology of the New Testament makes
playful and experimental forays towards a concept of Trinity no less than

---

20   So Francis W. Beare, *The First Epistle of Peter*, Second Edition (Oxford:
Blackwell, 1961), p. 98.

21   So Beare, *First Epistle of Peter*, p. 89.

does its Christology, with its images of Logos and Wisdom. In the interaction of the metaphors for church there is a hint of the complex interaction within the life of God.

However, the horizon of interpretation from which I am coming to the text is the developed concept of a triune God achieved by the Church Fathers in *continuity* with the New Testament, yet also with new insights and new language. I mean the vision of God as three persons, each hypostasis a distinct reality because of its relationships to the other two, and united in a communion *(koinonia)* of life so intimate that we are confronted by one Lord. I do nut mean a kind of mathematical puzzle in which God is supposedly one individual and three individuals at the same time. This was never the understanding of Trinity among the Fathers. They are trying to express the nature of God as complex personality, as an interweaving *(perichoresis)* of relationships, as movements of a giving and receiving within the life of God which is love. We cannot objectify such a communion of relationships; we cannot paint it or schematize it as a diagram. Language of God as Trinity is not a language of observation in which we say 'so that's what God looks like!' It is a language of participation in which we say: 'so that's why we can share in God!'

If we come to the New Testament text with this perspective, then in the first place the *activity* of the triune God through the church is immediately apparent. In the traditional terms of Trinitarian theology, this is the work of the 'economic' Trinity, the self-revelation and the acts of God in his *oikonomia* (or 'household management') in the world. Through his body, Christ makes himself visible and serves the world. The Spirit presences himself in the household of faith as power for new life. The Father bestows his blessings on humankind through the church as his people.

Each of these images can be aligned with a particular form of sociality which the church exhibits. The image of the 'body' points to a sociality which is formed by the coinherence of Christ and believers, and which is established by the being and presence of Christ; this community pre-exists any particular believers in so far as it simply is Christ.[22] The image of the temple is more sociological, pointing to the organization of a gathered community which is the means for hearing the word and receiving the sacraments, and which has a structure which persists through periods of time. The image of the 'people of God' is political in so far as the members of this new nation are bound together by common experiences and by agreed common aims. In the politics of the ancient world, a nation was often defined on the basis of common religious

---

22   A major advocate of this position is Dietrich Bonhoeffer's thesis of 1927, *Sanctorum Communio. A Dogmatic Enquiry into the Sociology of the Church* (London: Collins, 1963), pp. 106–14.

observance rather than biologically, and so Christians came to be regarded as a 'third race'. The image of the body thus seems to deal with the essence of the church, while images of temple and nation apparently concern its form in history; yet we have seen that the images interact so that essence and structure are indissoluble. We cannot separate out a 'pure church' of a fellowship of believers from its social organization. Moreover, all three images are 'theological', not just the first; the church is constituted by the initiative and action of God. In Barth's phrase, 'The Church is when it takes place',[23] and it 'happens' in the works of faith and love which are the events of the Spirit.

However, a trinitarian perspective on these three images of the church does not stop with the 'economic Trinity'. It pushes back into a vision of the 'immanent Trinity', moving from the functional to the ontological. God's actions correspond to God's being, because the self-unveiling of God is a faithful self-interpretation; in free self-giving, God is 'already ours in advance'.[24] There can be no other God than the one we know in the experience of salvation. The economic Trinity leads us to speak, however hesitantly, about the immanent Trinity. So we may say that the church participates in the external activity of God *because* it shares in the inner life of God. To take the first image, the earthly 'body' is identified with the Son who is not only sent into the world in history, but who is eternally sent out by the Father in expressive and ecstatic love ('eternal generation'). In Barth's words, the church 'is the body, and its members are members of this body, in Jesus Christ, in his election from all eternity.'[25] This is the context of meaning in which we can hear the words of the Johannine Christ: 'As the Father has sent me, so I am sending you.'[26] Taking the third image, as the priestly people of God the church shares in the movement of love as the Son offers glory to the Father, and draws in the whole of creation to make its varied sacrifice of praise in dependence on his eternal intercession.[27]

The image of the church as a temple indwelt by the Spirit brings us to ponder the mystery of the identity of the Holy Spirit within the triune being of God. There has been a reluctance in Christian theology to see the indwelling of Christ *by* the Spirit and his birth *from* Spirit in his earthly life as corresponding to anything in the eternal life of God. Instead, stress has been laid upon Jesus' breathing forth of the Spirit

---

23   Barth, *Church Dogmatics*, IV/1, p. 652.

24   The phrase is from Karl Barth, *Church Dogmatics* I/1, p. 383.

25   Barth, *Church Dogmatics*, IV/1 p. 667.

26   Jn. 20:21. Jürgen Moltmann has developed this concept of the 'Trinity of Sending', especially in *The Church in the Power of the Spirit*, pp. 53–56.

27   Cf. Catherine M. LaCugna, *God for Us. The Trinity and Christian Life* (San Francisco: Harper, 1991), pp. 350–6.

upon his disciples, and so a sharing by the Son in some way[28] in the eternal sending forth of the Spirit by the Father. But the traditional belief that the Spirit is the ineffable and mutual love *in* the Father and the Son enables us to see that the church can share with the Son in his receiving of an eternal indwelling of the Spirit, a pouring out of the Spirit of love into the Son by the Father. Recent theology from some Catholic theologians has, I believe rightly, been exploring the interweaving (or *perichoresis*) of the persons even more adventurously, so that the Son may be said to be eternally 'begotten by the Father in the Holy Spirit'[29] or 'in the maternal womb of the Spirit'.[30] Thus the church, born from Spirit and indwelt by the Spirit, shares in a reality which is eternal, and not only a phase in time and space.

All this may be dismissed as highly speculative thinking, but it is actually to do with *praxis*. The church which acts as body, temple and priestly people in practical ways in the world has the power to serve, to focus the presence of the Spirit and to mediate blessing *only* because it is caught up in the life of the triune God. It does not have its own mission, but shares in the mission of God towards the world, God's ecstatic movement of love which draws the creation into fellowship with God's own self. This movement outwards is an expression of the movements and missions of love within God, in which the church astonishingly is called to share.

It is not surprising that the theologian who has in recent years thought most profoundly about this kind of engagement in God, John Zizioulas, is from the Orthodox Church with its tradition of *theosis* or 'divinization' of humanity in God; we must, of course, hasten to add that *theosis* does not mean 'becoming' God but 'participating' in the divine energies. Zizioulas writes about the transformation that is possible from having 'biological existence' to 'ecclesial existence'.[31] As persons, we have a 'biological hypostasis' deriving from our birth as created beings. We have the capacity to open ourselves to others in love, but this is distorted by the ways in which we are bound by the necessities of our natures. In the face of the threat of death, for instance, our body becomes a fortress of individualism. But the persons in the triune God are not bound by any kind of nature, affirms Zizioulas. The *person* is the primary reality, because the person of the Father is the source and origin of the

28   In the Western tradition, the Spirit proceeds 'also from the Son' (*filioque*); in the Eastern tradition only from the Father, and – according to some theologians – *through* the Son.

29   So Thomas Weinandy, *The Father's Spirit of Sonship. Reconceiving the Trinity* (Edinburgh: T. & T. Clark, 1996), pp. 65–77.

30   Boff, *Trinity and Society*, p. 147.

31   John Zizioulas, *Being as Communion. Studies in Personhood and the Church* (London: Darton, Longman and Todd, 1985), pp. 49–65.

communion of the Trinity. The nature or essence of God is the result of the relationships of love in which the persons live. Person determines nature, not the other way around. In saving identification with the uncreated hypostasis of Christ, our persons can therefore also be freed from the bonds of our natures. We are released into a new kind of existence, into open relations of love with others. We have been given a new hypostasis (or personal reality), an 'ecclesial hypostasis'.

Oddly, however, despite Zizioulas' stress that true 'being' is 'communion' with others, his theological account is based on the participating of the *individual* person in the hypostasis of the Son. Zizioulas calls this redeemed person 'ecclesial person', since the result of redemption is certainly a new way of existing in relationship, and the church is the assembly where this happens. Human beings are born again as a new hypostasis in the church; she is the womb, the Mother.[32] But I venture to say that we must also think of the way that the church as a *community* participates in God. What is added to our understanding of sharing in God when this is a corporate as well as an individual sharing? I believe that to answer this question, we must turn to another biblical concept, that of *covenant*. This is an idea, as we have already seen in the first three chapters, that has a long history within the English Nonconformist tradition and particularly in Baptist life. Through the years a distinctive contribution has been made to the catholicity of the church by the use of this image of covenant, and it is perhaps in our time that we can see the possibilities of integrating it with the Orthodox understanding of *theosis*.

Relationship as Covenant

The idea of covenant is most obviously associated with the third image of church, as 'the people of God'. Indeed, the declaration in Exodus 19:6 that Israel is a 'holy nation and a kingdom of priests', recalled in 1 Peter 2:9, is in the context of covenant-making between Yahweh and his people. We must recognize, however, that the idea of covenant in the Old Testament is not a simple one. In Israel's faith, there is a whole variety of understandings of a covenant relationship with God. 'Covenant' points to an agreement Yahweh makes with his people, a relationship to which the partners have bound themselves, in which God says, 'I will be your God and you will be my people'. But there were different types of covenant, the two most distinctive being associated with the names of David and Moses.

---

32   Zizioulas, *Being as Communion*, p. 56.

First, Israel thought of God's offering a covenant which was essentially a *promise* to his people, granting them life and well-being unilaterally from his side. So they celebrated a covenant of God with King David, as the representative leader of the people. In this covenant God promises to establish David's royal house and line of succession for ever (2 Sam. 7), and so to give the whole people health and a good life through God's special relationship with the Davidic king. Although the human partner is called to be obedient to God, this obedience is not presented as a condition for the continuance of the covenant. The sons of David who err from God's way will certainly be disciplined and punished, but the covenant itself is not cancelled; it remains as sheer gift from God, everlasting (2 Sam. 7:14–15). God is certain to fulfill his promises. While the covenant with David is the most outstanding example of a *covenant of promise* in the Old Testament, there are other instances – such as God's covenants with Abraham and Noah (Gen. 9; 17).

But on the other hand, Israel also thought of the mighty act of God in delivering the nation from slavery in Egypt, and at the heart of this story they placed another covenant – one made through Moses at Mount Sinai. This is made with the whole people of Israel, but through Moses as mediator. And this type of covenant stresses definite obligations which are owed by the human partners in the covenant (e.g. Ex. 20:1–17). The survival of the covenant is conditional upon human response to God's demands, to God's commandments; if the people fail in obedience, then the covenant is broken, null and void.

At first sight there seems much difference between these two kinds of covenant. The one appears to be a covenant of promise; the other a covenant of obligation. One seems *unconditional*, the other *conditional*. As Old Testament faith grows and matures it wrestles with the way these two sorts of covenant might be related to each other.[33] But the basis of both of them is the initiative that God takes. The Davidic covenant stresses that God takes the first step, by making a promise of sheer grace to take this people to himself. But the Mosaic covenant is only there because God has made the first move in saving his people from bondage and slavery. The first word here too is God's grace: 'I am Yahweh your God, who brought you out of the land of Egypt … [therefore] you shall have no other gods before me' (Ex. 20:2–3). Moreover, when the covenant is broken from the human side, God will find new ways to make it again. If his people are disobedient, the covenant is smashed, ended. But God will go on searching for his lost people and will again call them into covenant with himself, finding new ways to re-make the covenant

---

33 For example, the Deuteronomists bring together the Sinai covenant together with the Abrahamic; see Ronald Clements, *Abraham and David* (London: SCM Press, 1967), pp. 64–69.

relationship; God will even take the initiative in re-making the hearts of
people so that they will be able to love and obey him (Deut. 30:5–6; Jer.
31:31).

So the difference between these two understandings of covenant is real,
but a matter of emphasis. It is as if God knows that people need
sometimes to hear the word of *promise* more loudly, while at another time
it is the word of *obligation* and responsibility that needs to be stressed.
But behind all the forms of covenant there is the initiative God takes to
call people to God's self. And this is at the heart of the new covenant
celebrated in the New Testament. In Christ, the true Son of David, the new
Moses, God calls people into fellowship. Because of human rebellion a
new covenant has to be made, and the making of it costs not less than
everything, a pain that enters into the very heart of God. In Christ, God
fulfills all the divine *promises* and deals with the results of human failure
to keep our *obligations*.

At the time of the Reformation, stress was laid upon the church as the
new covenant community, brought into being through the blood of the
new covenant in the cross of Christ. That is, the vector line of the
covenant was vertical, between God and humanity. But in the wake of the
Reformation, radical Separatists in early seventeenth-century England
were beginning to use the word 'covenant' in another sense as well, to
denote the agreement that members of a congregation made between
themselves. Often under the pressure of persecution, they made a church
covenant in which they promised to 'walk together and watch over each
other.' It was an early Baptist, John Smyth, who made the creative
theological step of linking this 'horizontal' covenant and the 'vertical'
covenant together; so in 1607 he defined the church as a visible
community of saints where 'two, three or more saints join together by
covenant with God and with themselves'.[34] This was undeniably a creative
development of New Testament thought, in thus making an inseparable
connection between the horizontal and the vertical lines of covenant. The
move was eased, however, because the Old Testament concept of covenant
contained the elements, as we have seen, of both grace and obligation. We
also notice that in the covenant-making of Israel a horizontal dimension
was at least implied, especially as people are urged to imitate the nature of
God in showing *hesed*, covenant faithfulness, to each other. The New
Testament concept of *koinonia* implicitly joins both dimensions. But the
tradition of the Radical Reformation makes the horizontal vector *explicit*
in a mutual human promise-making.

Such groups of believers might be called 'intentional communities', in
the sense that 'people find their identity and give mutual support to one

---

34   Smith, *Principles and Inferences*, in *Works*, I, p. 252; cf. White, *The English
Separatist Tradition*, p. 129.

another in working towards a common goal' (A. Kreider).[35] However, as Edmund Husserl suggests,[36] all societies are in fact 'intentional' to the extent that their members have objects of shared memory which they do not perceive as objects 'out there', but which they 'intend' to be the centre of their identity.[37] Moreover, the members 'intend' each other to be linked to these objects and so 'mean' each other as participants in a shared experience and aim. They have an 'inter-subjectivity of intention', or 'co-intention'. In his book *Ecclesial Man*,[38] Edward Farley finds some value in applying this phenomenological approach of Husserl to the church, but points out that the church differs from other societies in the *kind* of intentional community it is. Its members 'co-intend' each other as existing in a life-world redeemed in Christ, in which they have been freed from the need to establish their own security, and they place their future hope for salvation in each other's hands. Further, this co-intention has the unique feature of being open to the non-participant, to the stranger and the outsider. This is a community that has its identity in drawing others in rather than excluding them, because it can 'intend' or envisage others as sharing a redeemed existence.[39] Such an openness is, we may say, already implied in the New Testament images of body, temple and people.

An intentional community like this is not just a 'voluntary' society which people choose to join or not. As Daniel Turner, a Particular Baptist minister of the eighteenth century put it, calling the church a voluntary society does not mean that 'it is a matter of indifference, whether (having embraced the gospel as divine revelation) [people] join themselves to any Christian society', but rather that 'connecting ourselves with some christian society in particular, should be .... the effect of inward convictions, and not outward violence'.[40] We have already seen that early Baptists spoke of the local church as a 'gathered community', a phrase

---

35   Alan Kreider, 'Lessons from Intentional Communities. Mennonite Perspectives', *Theology Themes*, 4/1 (1995) (Northern Baptist College, Manchester), p. 19.

36   See Hans-Georg Gadamer, *Truth and Method*, trans. G. Barden and J. Cumming (London: Sheed and Ward, 1975), pp. 215–230; Gadamer reflects on Husserl's *Ideas II*, contained in *Husserliana IV* (1952).

37   We need not accept Husserl's belief that there is no objective reality beyond objects of the consciousness to see some point in this observation about a 'horizon of interpretation'.

38   Edward Farley, *Ecclesial Man. A Social Phenomenology of Faith and Reality* (Philadelphia: Fortress Press, 1975), chs. 4–5.

39   Farley, *Ecclesial Man*, pp. 169–74.

40   Daniel Turner, *A Compendium of Social Religion*, Second edition (London: John Ward, 1778), p. 15.

with a double meaning.[41] Its members certainly agree to gather; there is 'inward conviction' involved here, the dynamic of an intentional community. But they are also *gathered* by God. They gather in response to the 'appointment' of Christ,[42] the Lord of the church, who is already gathering them into his one body. Whatever the diversity of the concept of covenant in the Hebrew scriptures, there is the common theme that God takes the initiative in making covenant. This means that when Christians make covenant with each other, when they come to agreement with each other to live together in fellowship and mission, God is still taking the initiative. They are not just *drawing* together, but *being drawn* together.

The Church: Community in God

The concept of covenant thus offers us a rich matrix for thinking of the participation in God that the New Testament images for church point us towards. Using the language of trinitarian theology, we might say that this covenant is both 'economic' and 'immanent', shaping both the inner being of God and God's activity in the world.

In an earlier chapter I suggested that here we might draw upon some insights of Karl Barth about the eternal covenant of grace and – further – that we might extend his 'covenant ontology' in a way which is consistent with his thought.[43] For Barth, the covenant which becomes visible at one moment in human history is in fact the expression of an eternal decision which has a twofold aspect. At the heart of the covenant with all human beings is Jesus Christ, in whom God has elected *both* humanity and God's own self for mutual fellowship.[44] The God who makes this 'double decree' is thus eternally committed to union with human life, a situation which can be stated dramatically by saying that Jesus Christ is not only the elect man but 'the electing God'.[45] How, then, Barth asks, can we speak of election and covenant 'without speaking of the concrete life of the very being of God?' To affirm that God is the living God means that 'this triune being does not exist and cannot be known as a being which rests or moves purely within itself', but 'God is … the triune God … with a definite purpose and reference',[46] which is a

---

41   See above, ch. 2, pp. 42–5.

42   The Second London Confession, ch. XXVI.6, in Lumpkin, *Baptist Confessions of Faith,* p. 286.

43   See above, ch. 2, pp. 35–6.

44   Barth, *Church Dogmatics,* II/2, pp. 162–3; IV/1, pp. 45–7.

45   Barth, *Church Dogmatics,* II/2, pp. 95–101.

46   Barth, *Church Dogmatics,* II/2, p. 79.

self-giving in partnership with the world. The will for covenant with us is 'God's very being'.[47]

Now, as I suggested earlier, if covenant with humanity shapes the inner communion of the Trinity like this, it seems to follow that these relationships too can be envisaged as a kind of covenant. Barth declines to take this step himself because he associates an inner-divine covenant with the 'legal transaction' of Calvinist federal theology, rather than with the 'very being' of God. But for Barth the covenant with humanity runs deep within the triune currents of the divine life. As Bruce McCormack has proposed, it makes most sense of Barth's thought on this subject to understand the making of covenant with Jesus Christ, the representative human son, as being 'given in' the eternal generation of the divine Son from the Father.[48] It is as if, in a single eternal moment, God determines 'to be God again a second time',[49] *and* chooses Jesus of Nazareth to be identified with this second mode of divine being.

Such simultaneous events in God should lead us, I suggest, to think not only of a 'double election', but of a 'double covenant' of love. As Barth himself affirms, the speaking forth of the divine Logos is nothing other than the word of covenant promise, and it seems impossible in thinking about God to detach the expression of God's word from the sending forth of the Son.[50] Again, Barth asserts that the obedience and humility we see revealed in the incarnate Christ is not less than fully divine, and is the appropriate eternal response of the one who is begotten to the one who begets;[51] it is also, we notice, a proper response of a covenant partner.

Following these clues of Barth, we may conclude that our covenant with God, freely given in grace, is bound up with that 'covenant' in God's own communion of life in which God freely determines to be God. If we think of the covenant in Christ like this, then it becomes even more astonishing that our 'horizontal' human dynamic of covenant-making should be taken into the 'vertical' dimension of God's covenant. We are participating not only in God's covenant with us, but in the inner covenant-making in God. Church is what happens when these vectors

---

47   Barth, *Church Dogmatics*, II/2, p. 26f; IV/1, pp. 65–6.

48   Bruce McCormack, 'Grace and Being. The role of God's gracious election in Karl Barth's theological ontology' in Webster (ed.), *The Cambridge Companion to Karl Barth,* p. 103. McCormack, however, goes too far in proposing that the election of the man Jesus is the 'ground' of the triune differentiation of God, so that the triunity of God is 'logically a function of the divine election'... p. 103. Neither self-differentiation nor election are logically prior to the other, but rather simultaneous.

49   Barth, *Church Dogmatics*, I/1, pp. 316, 324.

50   Barth, *Church Dogmatics*, II/2, pp. 99–101, 116; IV/1, pp. 52–4.

51   Barth, *Church Dogmatics*, IV/1, pp. 200–204, 208–10.

intersect, and God in humility opens God's own self to the richness of the intercourse.

To grasp something of this, we need to add the subjective intention of Farley's 'ecclesial man' (or rather, 'ecclesial person') to the objective status of Zizioulas' 'ecclesial hypostasis', and set both in the corporate dimension of covenant. When a *community* is identified with the person of the Son within the triune God, the human dynamics of relationship are transformed. We can readily think of a community as engaging in the covenant bond of God's being, as this inward covenant is precisely *not* a legal transaction or bargain between two subjects, a 'mythological' scene to which Karl Barth rightly objects.[52] If by 'persons' in God we mean not individual beings, but a movements of love which are like the relationship between a Father and a Son in the expectation and openness of Spirit, then a whole community can be immersed into a current of divine life. There are in God movements of giving and receiving which are like the sending out of a child on mission by a parent, like the responding of a child to a parent in obedience and joy, and like the opening up of this relationship to new depths of love and a surprising future. We cannot know such a triune God as we do an object in the world, though in the human confidence that was awoken at the Enlightenment, we *would* like everything to be controlled by the knowing of the human subject. We can only know such a God by participating in the interweaving movements of the divine dance of love, by saying our 'yes' to the Father within the 'yes' of the Son.[53]

In conclusion then, I want to attempt some practical account of what this participation might mean for the life of the church. In the first place, we notice that the individual person often finds it hard to live at ease with the roles he or she assumes in relating to others; there can be a conflict between the true person and the 'mask' which is assumed. But when a community participates in the movement of mission within God, as the Father who sends out the Son eternally from the womb of his being sends the Son into the world, it finds the way that it in turn is being sent out into the world. So the community discovers its vocation as a whole, and those within it discover the individual roles that are really needed by the communal life and find the courage to resist false expectations and type-casting.

Again, there can be a tension between the integrity of the individual self and openness to others, between proper self-centring and destructive self-centredness. But the self can find itself in a community which is aligned with the willing response of the Son to the Father, participating in

---

52   Barth, *Church Dogmatics*, IV/1, p. 65.

53   I have worked out this epistemology of participation in more detail in my book, *Participating in God*, pp. 34–51. In what follows, I follow quite closely *Participating in God*, pp. 51–55.

the movement of the Son's will in saying 'Yes, Amen' to the will of the Father. Openness to others then means not conformity to the *other*, which would be a loss of one's own will, but conformity to *Christ* whom we meet in and through the other. The self is properly centred by being directed outwards to others, and having its own will conformed to the relation of Christ to the Father. This may then mean resistance to what another wants, unless this is also conformed to the Son-Father movement of will. In this way, there can be what Alistair McFadyen calls a 'mutual formation of the will' in society which does not simply swamp the individual's ethical responsibility.[54]

A further need for balance in any community is between diversity and unity. The images of body, temple and nation all express, as we have seen, a diversity within the church. There is only truly church when the assembly is made up of the old and the young, employed and unemployed, male and female, black and white, healthy and handicapped. It should also be made up of those who have quite different tastes in music, sport, films, television programmes and clothes (and these are sometimes the hardest differences to live with). Yet there can be a tension between recognizing the distinctiveness of another and achieving unity of fellowship. Engagement in the life of God means an experience of 'otherness', not only the otherness of God from humanity, the otherness of the Creator from the created; it is to participate in the otherness of the divine persons. It was Aquinas who pointed out that since there is a difference in God between begetting, being begotten and proceeding – or between sending and being sent – there is an infinite difference between the persons,[55] more complete than anything we know in the world where senders are also sent and begetters are also begotten. To be part of a community which participates in the relationships in God means that we are brought up against the challenge of the alien, the radically different, the unlike; but at the same time we have the security of experiencing a fellowship more intimate than anything we can otherwise know.

Finally, there needs to be a balance between dependence and independence in any human relationship, and the maturity to achieve this usually comes from being part of a wider context of relations, beyond the immediate people involved. Healthy particular relationships are always part of a wider sphere, a network of relationships whose edges we can never calculate. The engagement of a community in the triune God places its members in a context of relations which is as wide as the world,

54   Alistair McFadyen, *The Call to Personhood: A Christian Theory of the Individual in Social Relationships* (Cambridge: Cambridge University Press, 1990), pp. 185–6.
55   Thomas Aquinas, *Summa Theologiae* (Blackfriars Edition; London: Eyre & Spottiswoode, 1964–), Ia. 31.2.

as God opens the divine life to include all creation. The Trinity is – in a phrase used by Wolfhart Pannenberg[56] – a 'field of force'. Moreover, the width of this force-field of relations is not just spatial but temporal. The Spirit of hope is continually opening it up towards the future, giving our relations a place in the movement of God towards a new creation. This is what it means for the church not only to *understand* itself theologically but to *live* in God.

---

56   While Pannenberg tends to use this phrase of the Holy Spirit alone, he also (I believe more accurately) applies it to the whole triune life of God as Spirit: see Wolfhart Pannenberg, *Systematic Theology*, trans. G. Bromiley (3 volumes; Grand Rapids: Eerdmans, 1991–98), I, p. 383.

CHAPTER 5

Authority in Relations between Pastor and People: A Baptist Doctrine of Ministry

I have to confess that my heart sinks when students reading out their papers in theology, or preachers in the middle of a sermon, announce that they have consulted a dictionary to help them define some aspect of the Christian faith. 'What can this mean?' they ask rhetorically, and answer triumphantly, 'The dictionary tells us...' But the revelation of the saving acts of God overturns the dictionary, even the Oxford one (the 'Authorised Version' of dictionaries, though perhaps I am partial). What God has done in the cross of Christ upsets human understanding, and breaks open human language. It stretches our everyday usage of words, which is what dictionaries are designed to record, and makes them strange in order to catch just a glimpse of what God is like; 'The foolishness of God', comments the Apostle Paul, 'is wiser than human wisdom' (1 Cor. 1:25). Nowhere is this revolution in language more startling than in questions of *authority* within the community of faith. In his revolutionary manifesto, Paul continues, 'The weakness of God is stronger than human strength.'

The dictionary entry for 'authority' needs, then, to be confronted by a theology of divine authority. We find that the first two meanings given in the *Oxford English Dictionary* are: (1) the power to enforce obedience; and (2) delegated power. Overturning the first definition is all about our vision of God, and transforming the second definition concerns a Baptist view of the church. With regard to the first we shall see that the power of God cannot be characterized by enforcing people to submit to God's self; with regard to the second, I want to argue that the pastor does not hold a power delegated from God. I strongly suspect, moreover, that the second point will never carry conviction unless first we have a proper vision of God. What we think God is like, and the way we understand

divine power, will determine all our understanding of power and
authority in relationships between pastor and people.[1]

Authority and Finding the Mind of Christ

The second dictionary definition of authority directs our attention to the
source of human authority. The secular model of authority is that power
is delegated from above, descending through a chain of command from
the most powerful to the least. Even in democratic societies, where appeal
is made to the 'authority of the people', the same system holds.
Although the final source of power is not a single ruler but a
representative parliament or congress elected by the will of the people, a
particular person's authority still comes by delegation from a superior
power.

Taking over this pattern within the church leads to the concept of an
'order of submission'. The theory is that Christ the King delegates power
downwards, in a kind of pyramid of authority. While in the past this has
taken form in various ecclesiastical hierarchies, there is a modern-day
form which is more charismatic in mood. According to this view of
delegated power, while everyone submits to the Spirit of God, the leaders
in a congregation are to submit directly to Christ, the other men also
submit to the leaders, the women are to submit to the men in spiritual
matters, and children are to submit to their parents.

The shape of this pyramid of power differs, I believe, on different
Baptist scenes. On the British scene, there has been a powerful influence
from what is often called 'Restorationism' or the 'Community Church'
movement, and here the leadership in a church is conceived in terms of
elders, among whom the 'minister' is the first among equals. The leaders
are pictured as 'under-shepherds' to Christ as the 'Chief Shepherd', and
appeal is made to the figure of David in the Old Testament who was both
a shepherd and a king, in order to promote the idea of a shepherd who
also rules. In this pyramid of powerful shepherds, the father as shepherd
in the family unit submits to the shepherd who is his house-group leader,
who in turn submits to the shepherds who are the elders of the church.
The minister makes decisions in consultation with his team of elders, and
he in turn submits to an over-shepherd or 'apostle' with an inter-church
ministry. The 'apostle' finally submits directly to the rule of Christ. Thus
power is delegated downwards; submission is yielded upwards.

---

1   I have worked this out at more length in my book *A Leading Question: The
Structure and Authority of Leadership in the Local Church* (London: Baptist Union
Publications, 1983). Material from that study is drawn upon in the present paper.

Community-church leaders such as Ron Trudinger[2] urge that the church will never be healthy unless it restores this pattern of divine government, as he believes it to be.

The fact that this view of authority is secular rather than biblical can only be properly seen, not by merely quoting texts, but by grasping the picture of God presented by the Bible as a whole. A key passage to which authoritarian accounts of leadership typically appeal, however, is Paul's statement on 'headship' in 1 Corinthians 11:3, and so it is worth pointing out that this text does not in fact present a chain of subordination stretching from God the Father at the top to woman at the bottom. As Karl Barth observes, the apparently untidy order in which man, Christ, woman and God are mentioned makes clear that they are not being arranged in a scale: 'they contain neither deduction from above downwards nor induction from below upwards.'[3] Barth makes clear, in a fine piece of exegesis, that Paul is not depicting a hierarchy or pyramid of power but a series of sets of relationships – God with Christ, Christ with humankind, man with woman. The principle underlying this passage is that there are different covenant relationships, divine and human, which should mirror each other. While there is analogy between them, there is bound to be an openness about the way that this works out in different situations.[4]

Very few Baptist churches in Britain have adopted the pyramid of powerful shepherds in its totality, but the influence is there in a weakened form; there is a general mood of submitting to the spiritual insight of elders, and this can – and does – undermine the place of the church meeting. In other parts of the world, including the United States, there has not been the development of this plural leadership of elders, and the old pattern of minister and deacons persists. However, the idea that authority means delegation from above is still present in other forms, such as the strong pastor who virtually rules the church. In face of these lapses, we should recall the early Baptist conviction that authority finally lies with the rule of the risen Jesus Christ, who is present in the local congregation. This rule is not shared in the sense of being delegated to other individuals from above. There is no chain of command, no pyramid of power. Christ alone rules, and the task of the local church gathered in covenant

---

2   Ron Trudinger, *Built to Last: Biblical Principles for Church Restoration* (Eastbourne: Kingsway, 1982). Andrew Walker, *Restoring the Kingdom. The Radical Christianity of the House Church Movement* (London: Hodder & Stoughton, 1985), pp. 145–54, 169–80, notes that Restorationist Christians prefer to think of shepherding as 'paternal' rather than hierarchical, but also judges that the shepherding system results in a 'level of social control ... far greater than the average Christian church'.

3   Barth, *Church Dogmatics*, III/2, p. 311.

4   For a longer exposition of this point, see Paul S. Fiddes, '"Woman's Head is Man": A Doctrinal Reflection upon a Pauline Theme', *BQ* 31/8 (1986), pp. 370–383.

community together is to find the mind of Christ. It must find his purpose for it as it comes together in church meeting.

So the authority of pastor and church meeting comes from the various parts they play in discovering the mind of Christ who holds the final authority. Upon the whole people in covenant there lies the responsibility of finding a common mind, of coming to an agreement about the way of Christ for them in life, worship and mission. But they cannot do so unless they use the resources that God has given them, and among those resources are the pastor, the deacons and (if they have them) the elders. The church meeting is not 'people power' in the sense of simply counting votes and canvassing a majority: in such a strategy, power blocks can strive with each other to gain a popular vote, with the result that the minority may feel excluded. The aim is to search for consent about the mind of Christ, and so people should be sensitive to the voices behind the votes, listening to them according to the weight of their experience and insight. As B. R. White puts it, 'One vote is not as good as another in church meeting',[5] even though it has the same strictly numerical value.

In all this, the pastor's voice is one that carries weight. The church meeting as the body of Christ looks to those whom it can trust to guide it. Leaders will create trust when they give themselves away for the life of the church, and so have the authority of servants. I want to say more later about the nature of true authority as service which wins trust, but I want to pursue further for a moment the question of delegated power. If the exclusive rule of Christ prevents authority being delegated downwards, would it be more correct to say that power is delegated *upwards* from the church meeting? Some would want to urge that the authority of the pastor comes simply 'from below', in being set aside by the people to fulfill certain functions – to preach (not less or more than twenty minutes), visit, evangelize and generally increase the membership – with an explicit threat of being dispensed with if he or she fails to satisfy those who pay the salary. Baptist churches have certainly behaved in the past as if the minister were employed by the church to carry out its mandates (even though in the UK, legally, a minister is self-employed), and it is perhaps in reaction against this business-model that there has been the desire to recover a view of the ministry established 'from above'.

I believe that the notion of delegation 'from below' can become no less secular than the pyramid of power descending from above. The *offering of trust* in leadership has a very different flavour from *delegating power* to it. On the one hand, the idea of delegation from below can actually conceal a hidden assent to power from *above*; the people can

---

5   B.R. White, *Authority. A Baptist View* (London: Baptist Publications, 1976), p. 28.

delegate or pass over so much authority that they abdicate any responsibility for themselves. We may end in the situation of one church in Northamptonshire in the 1970s, where the church meeting voted itself out of existence in passing over authority to the eldership (and which was consequently removed from the list of churches in the Baptist Union). On the other hand, the notion that the church meeting is simply delegating certain jobs to the minister may lose the whole sense that the risen Christ has actually called this person to the office of spiritual oversight (*episkope*) in the congregation. Though rule has not been passed down from above, the office of pastor has certainly been *created* from above. Here I suggest that John Macquarrie, usually sensitive to the nature of church life, is mistaken in suggesting that when ordination is entrusted either 'in whole *or in part*' to the congregation, the resulting ministry originates 'from below upwards'.[6] The Standard Confession of General Baptists in 1660 was typical in speaking of the 'Elders or Pastors which God hath appointed to oversee and feed his Church'.[7]

Appointment from above and below does not therefore imply a *delegation* of power either from above (hierarchical model) or from below (employment model). It results in a dynamic view of authority in the community, in which oversight flows to and fro between the personal and the communal, since the responsibility of 'watching over' the church belongs both to *all* the members gathered in church meeting and to the pastor. The London Confession of 1644 (Particular Baptist) expresses this balance without any apparent sense of strain; while all members enter into covenant to 'watch over' (oversee) each other spiritually, they also recognize that Christ has called some to an office in which they have a special responsibility for oversight:

> And as Christ for the keeping of this Church in holy and orderly Communion, placeth some special men (*sic*) over the Church, who by their office are to govern, oversee, visit, watch; so likewise for the better keeping thereof in all places, by all the members, he hath given authority, and laid duty upon all, to watch over one another.[8]

The theological basis of this notion of oversight is in the 'rule' of Christ. It is rooted in the authority of Christ as 'prophet, priest and king'. The

---

6   John Macquarrie, *Principles of Christian Theology*. Revised Edition (London: SCM Press, 1977), pp. 425–7. My italics.

7   *A Brief Confession or Declaration of Faith, Set forth by many of us, who are (falsely) called Anabaptists* (London: printed for F. Smith, 1660), hereafter called the 'Standard Confession', in Lumpkin, *Baptist Confessions*, art. XV, p. 229.

8   The London Confession (1644), art. XLIV, in Lumpkin, *Baptist Confessions*, p.168; this wording is virtually identical to article 26 in the Separatist *A True Confession* (1596), in Lumpkin, *Baptist Confessions*, p. 90.

direct presence of Christ as covenant-maker in the midst of the
congregation means that as the gathered disciples find his mind for them,
they share in his rule (kingship) as well as in his priestly and prophetic
offices. Thus they have the power to exercise church disciple in
'watching over' each other. The congregation also has the responsibility
of recognizing whether someone has been called by Christ to embody
this oversight in a personal way, and whether this calling has come to an
end.

The Call of Christ and the Apostolic Office

Authority, I have been suggesting, is about playing particular parts in the
discovery of the mind of Christ and so participating in his rule. To
understand the particular part played by the pastor, we need a New
Testament perspective on ministerial office. In the Apostle Paul's view of
the church, all its members, as limbs of the body of Christ, were expected
to exercise spiritual gifts of ministry; these *charismata* might appear to be
unusual (such as healing and prophecy) or quite ordinary (such as
hospitality and generous giving) but all were gifts of the Spirit for
building up the church in its mission to the world.[9] However, we can see
from various situations reflected in the New Testament documents that, in
addition to these gifts exercised by all, the communities also began to
appoint spiritual leaders called 'elders' (a Jewish title) or 'overseers' (a
Greek title); they also appointed 'deacons' to help them.[10] From the
human point of view we could say that the churches found the need to
have a stable leadership, beyond the spontaneous exercise of gifts; but it
is also clear that they believed Christ was actually calling people to this
episkope (oversight) and *diakonia* (pastoral service). To use a term
frequently used in early Baptist confessions,[11] Christ was creating
'offices' in the church.

These offices of leadership were thus established by the call of Christ
and the recognizing of that call by the body of Christ on earth, the
Christian community. The offices focused and summed up the ministry
of the community, and so must be set aside by it. But at the same time
they had been raised up by an act of divine grace to challenge the

9   Rom. 12:2–8; Eph. 4:11–13, 1 Cor. 12:28, 1 Pet. 4:9–11. See J.D.G. Dunn,
Unity and Diversity in the New Testament (London; SCM Press), pp. 109–114.

10   We catch a glimpse of this situation in Phil. 1:1 and (later) in the Pastoral
Epistles: 1 Tim. 3:1, 8–9; 5:17; Tit. 1:5–7.

11   E.g. The London Confession (1644), art. XXXVI, in Lumpkin, *Baptist
Confessions of Faith*, p. 212; the Standard Confession (1600), art. XV, p. 229; the
Second London Confession (1677), ch. XXVI.9, pp. 287–8; the *Orthodox Creed* (1679),
art. XXXI, pp. 319–20.

community with the Word of the risen Lord. They received their *appointment* (which is not the same thing as *power*) both 'from above' and 'from below'. Though these leaders, like all the members, exercised certain gifts, they could not take leadership upon themselves just because they possessed any particular gift. They had to be appointed by Christ and their fellow members.

The New Testament also shows that a powerful impetus towards the development of these offices in the local church was the dying out of the generation of the apostles. It seems that those called 'apostles' became a much wider group than the original 'twelve'; their qualification was to have witnessed an appearance of the risen Christ, and they appear to have exercised oversight in the churches which they had founded through their own missionary work.[12] Now, in several places in the New Testament, the local church leaders (called either 'elders' or 'overseers') are presented as inheriting the ministry of the apostles. It is perhaps this situation that is reflected in the story of Paul's farewell to the elders of Ephesus in Acts 20:25–8. Further, the Pastoral Epistles present the *episkopos* as having a special responsibility for guarding and teaching the faith;[13] what the early apostles had done in bearing witness to the gospel of the crucified and risen Christ, the overseers were to do for their churches. Of course, the whole community stood in the apostolic succession because it carried on the apostolic faith. But the leaders in the local congregation were to take special responsibility for passing on the faith, and for guiding the church into *being* the apostolic community.[14]

This witness to the apostolic faith carried by the leaders had two basic dimensions, reflecting the ministry of the apostles themselves; it had, we might say, *length* and *breadth*. Its length was in going back to the earliest days of witness to Christ, and its breadth was in being in contact with the universal church as the whole body of Christ. The apostles were witnesses to the appearances of the risen Christ who had been crucified, and they were in contact with the wider church beyond the local scene; they could guide their own local communities out of this wider perspective, admonishing them as Paul did that 'we recognize no other practice, nor do the churches of God' (1 Cor. 11:16). So as the original apostles passed away, the local church needed someone to stand in the succession of the apostle as a guardian of the faith and as a representative of the universal church which holds the faith.

Every congregation still needs such an apostolic ministry today. It can certainly set leaders aside from its own fellowship on the local scene as

---

12   For example, 1 Cor. 9:1; 15:8–9; cf. Lk. 24:46–48. See J.D.G. Dunn, *Jesus and the Spirit* (London: SCM Press, 1975), pp. 272–5.

13   1 Tim. 4:16, 6:20, 2 Tim. 4:2, Tit. 1:9.

14   So E. Schillebeeckx, *Ministry: A Case for Change*, trans. J. Bowden (London: SCM Press, 1981), pp. 17–19.

pastoral servants or *diakonoi*. But it also needs *episkopoi*, overseers who are set aside by the wider fellowship of churches and who can represent the faith of the universal church in all its length and breadth to the local scene. I referred earlier to the minister as a resource to the church meeting in its seeking to find the mind of Christ. The minister's theological education makes him or her much more than a mere source of information, a kind of walking database. It has given the minister a vision of the church universal. Through study of the Bible, the story of the church through the ages and the thought of the world-wide church today, the minister has come to know the faith of the people of God in all the length and breadth of time and space through which God has led it, and in which God has spoken his word to it. From that perspective the minister can proclaim the word of God into the particular local situation in which the church finds itself, and can call that community to take its place in the wider mission of the church in the world today.

All that the minister does, in teaching or in pastoral care, is from the perspective of the universal church as the whole body of Christ, and so widens the vision of those on the local scene. From this standpoint he or she enables and coordinates the spiritual gifts of others, and leads a team-ministry with the deacons. The *diakonoi* also have a ministry of pastoral care, and some will have a teaching and preaching ministry; they will be serving and teaching out of their experience of the local situation and their daily job in society. The church needs this kind of ministry; it needs to hear the word of God spoken out of that background of secular occupation and local concerns. But it also needs the leadership of someone called to stand in the apostolic tradition of the wider church and the universal faith.

It has thus been characteristic of Baptist understanding to hold to a two-fold rather than three-fold ministry: the pattern has been pastor – otherwise named bishop, elder or minister – and deacon.[15] In the words of the Second London Confession (1677):

> A particular Church gathered, and completely Organized, according to the mind of Christ, consists of Officers, and Members; And the Officers appointed by Christ to be chosen and set apart by the Church ... to be continued to the end of the World, are Bishops or Elders and Deacons.[16]

---

15   See above, n. 10. The structure of a two-fold ministry underlies the whole argument of *Forms of Ministry among Baptists. Towards an Understanding of Spiritual Leadership*. A discussion document by the Doctrine and Worship Committee of the Baptist Union of Great Britain (London: Baptist Union, 1994), esp. pp. 19–27.

16   The Second London Confession (1677/1688), ch. XXVI.9, in Lumpkin, *Baptist Confessions*, p. 287.

Inter-church or trans-local ministries have generally fitted into this pattern as forms of the same pastoral *episkope*, not as a third kind of office.[17] Modern New Testament scholarship has, of course, made clear the diversity of forms of ministry in the early days of the Christian church, including the prominence in churches like Corinth of the exercise of spiritual gifts over appointments to leadership.[18] It can thus no longer be claimed that a two-fold office was universal practice in the early congregations, as Baptists had tended to suppose. Those who want to hold (as I do) to this basic pattern must accept that weight will have to be laid on its firmer establishment in the sub-apostolic period, as one of the 'tracks' of tradition into which the church was guided by the Holy Spirit.

In Baptist practice, a person holding the first kind of office (*diakonia*) is set aside by the local church acting on its own, and a person holding the second (*episkope*) is usually only set aside in the context of fellowship with the wider church. If a minister is to represent the church as a whole, he or she must have the call from Christ to this ministry recognized by as wide a section of the church universal as is appropriate and possible, beyond the local scene. From early days of Baptist life there was a coming together of ministers from a wide area around the local church to share in the act of ordination. In accord with this, the General Baptist Assembly of 1702 held that 'the ordination of Elders by Elders [is] of Divine Institution'.[19] In modern times this has been accompanied (and sometimes replaced) by the involvement of a representative figure from the Baptist Union or Regional Association. The practice of ordination of a minister by other ministers was sometimes justified simply by appeal to instructions about laying on of hands in the Pastoral Epistles,[20] or by the need to control the quality of ministry and to

---

17   There was an exception to this principle among some General Baptists in the latter part of the seventeenth century, for whom the bishop or messenger was a distinct office; see below, ch. 9, p. 223, n. 98.

18   See J.D.G. Dunn, *Unity and Diversity in the New Testament*, pp. 107–15. Dunn himself, however, actually underplays the diversity by finding church office only in the Jewish-Christian churches in the earliest years.

19   Meeting at Horsley Down, 26 May, 1702; in *Minutes of the General Assembly of the General Baptist Churches in England*. Edited by W.T. Whitley for the Baptist Historical Society (2 volumes; London; Kingsgate Press, 1909), I, p. 70. John Gill among Particular Baptists gave theological weight to this practice in his *Body of Divinity*, II, bk.3, p. 265, although he regarded the pastor as commissioned to officiate only in the local church where he was a member. On the issue, see Ernest A. Payne, *The Fellowship of Believers. Baptist Thought and Practice Yesterday and Today*. Enlarged Edition (London: Carey Kingsgate Press, 1952), pp. 46–51; Payne, 'The Ministry in Historical Perspective', *BQ* 17/6 (1958), pp. 256–66.

20   See, for example, the reference to 1 Tim. 4:14 in the Second London Confession, and to Tit. 1:5 in the *Orthodox Creed*: Lumpkin, *Confesssions of Faith*, pp.

safeguard the local church from powerful personalities who might want to abuse it.[21] But we may also see in this practice an expression of the link of the *episkopos* with the church beyond the local scene; as Daniel Turner put it in the eighteenth century, 'a minister of a particular church ... is a minister of the church in general'.[22] In re-thinking patterns of ministry for today, this must be the key issue. Some Baptists, beginning from the early years of the nineteenth century,[23] but with increasing momentum today, have wanted to weaken this pattern of ordination because of a suspicion that it is designed to reinforce 'ministerial power'. My argument has been that ordination of 'pastors by pastors' is not about the receiving of an authority delegated from above downwards through a hierarchy of officials. What it expresses, and ensures, is a continuity with the apostolic faith and the recognition of the call of Christ by the body of Christ which is manifest both in and beyond the local church. As long as other ministers are involved in an ordination, however,[24] it is surely not an inappropriate development of Baptist tradition for some who are not ordained to share in the laying on of hands, especially representatives of those who have called the new minister to his or her first pastoral responsibility; inclusion of these may aptly express the recognition of the new ministry by the whole community.

The appointment of multiple 'elders' (*presbuteroi*) by the local congregation, acting on its own, is a relatively recent phenomenon in many Baptist churches; in early Baptist life, the term 'elder' was synonymous with 'bishop' or pastor. But the development of a group of elders, distinct from the minister, illustrates the fact that there can be no

---

287, 320. Daniel Turner, *Compendium of Social Religion*, pp. 48–50, defends the ordination of pastors by other pastors (rather than by a third order of bishops) on the basis of 1 Tim. 4:14 and Tit. 1:5. In this he echoes Calvin, who set the pattern of ordination of elders by elders for the Reformed churches and other churches too: see Calvin, *Institutes,* II, 4, iii:15–16, pp. 325–6.

21   For example, Andrew Fuller in a letter in the *Baptist Magazine* 7 (1815), pp. 454–5; Robert Hall, letter to P.J. Saffery of Salisbury, 16 January 1826, in *Works*, V, pp. 556–7.

22   Turner, *Compendium of Social Religion*, p. 60. The report, *The Meaning and Practice of Ordination among Baptists* (London: Carey Kingsgate Press, 1957), p. 25, regards ordination as in part the occasion when 'representatives of the wider fellowship' acknowledge that a person is called to exercise ministry which is 'recognised throughout the churches.'

23   Michael Walker, *Baptists at the Table. The Theology of the Lord's Supper among English Baptists in the Nineteenth Century* (London: Baptist Historical Society, 1992), pp. 121–37, shows that doubts about ordination preceded the Baptist reaction to the Catholic Revival.

24   I present the case below for the ordination to be *presided* over by a minister with episcopal scope beyond a local church: ch. 9, pp. 221–5.

absolute boundary between the two dimensions of ministry, *episkope* and *diakonia*. This, indeed, accords with the dynamic concept of oversight in the local church to which I have already drawn attention. The two offices give a focus for *episkope* on the one hand and for *diakonia* on the other, but all those who exercise 'oversight' are of course already 'servants' (*diakonoi*) in the church and world, and those who are deacons share to some extent in oversight. The modern emergence of 'elders' thus belongs within the basic twofold structure, in that they can be regarded as a kind of deacon with strong pastoral gifts who share to a greater extent than other deacons in the oversight (*episkope*) of the minister. Team ministry in the local church, between ministers and between ministers and deacons (and/or elders) gives scope for a collegial dimension of *episkope* on the local scene. Given the fact that others will exercise particular kinds of oversight in the congregation, it might be better then to speak of the minister as exercising a 'general oversight', related to every part of the life and work of the community. Others may have oversight in a particular sphere (for example, in youth work), but the one who is called pastor or minister has a responsibility for the whole. This is well expressed in the report *Forms of Ministry among Baptists* (1994):

> He or she will develop an overall vision of the whole Body and the gifts of all its members, and is entrusted with this general oversight to enable all to grow into the identity of Christ the Servant of humankind, and to help them make visible God's own ministry of reconciliation in the world around.[25]

Such an overall vision and oversight is possible, we may add, because of the perspective brought from the life of the church universal.

The openness of the boundary between *diakonia* and *episkope* gives rise to a variety in the shape that ministry takes in Baptist churches; in recent years, through the influence of charismatic renewal on the English scene, an overlap in areas of ministry has also been due to the different ways in which local congregations perceive and give scope for the exercise of spiritual gifts by all the members. On the continent of Europe the place of 'elders', in distinction from the pastor, is rooted further back, in the nineteenth century, with the founding of Baptist churches outside the British Isles. The primary impulse for this movement came from Germany, led by J. R. Oncken and his co-workers, and the primary theological ethos was that of pietism, shaped by early nineteenth-century revivalism. Questing first to the north into Scandanavia, and then east and west from Germany, as well as establishing new churches these missionaries discovered many small pietistic groups which already existed within Lutheran and Reformed life and linked them together. In such missionary outreach, building on pietistic fellowships already gathered in

---

25   *Forms of Ministry among Baptists*, p. 25.

homes, churches were founded with a 'lay leadership', and elders were – and in many regions still are – appointed for life.[26] Although a trained and ordained ministerial leadership has since been added to the life of the congregations, the elders still offer a kind of continuity and permanence to the ministry of the local church while a pastor may only be called to serve for a limited period. We can see that a basic two-fold pattern, however, underlies all these variations: that is, by whatever name they are known, there is one kind of ministry set aside by the local church alone and one by the wider church.

If there is a variation on the theme of *diakonia*, there is also a variation on the theme of *episkope*. In this connection, I suggest that we can still discern the two-fold shape underlying new emergence of 'locally recognized ministry' among Baptists in Great Britain, somewhat akin to the 'locally ordained ministry' of the Anglican church. Seeking to meet the needs of congregations for ministry, and even their 'right, by grace, to leaders',[27] there has emerged the concept of a pastor whose call to ministry is recognized by one regional association of churches,[28] and who is ordained and commissioned to exercise pastoral oversight in a limited local sphere. He or she receives theological education and pastoral formation appropriate for ministry in one place, and will not normally transfer to serve a church in another area. Theologically, this is a much more adequate concept than that of a 'lay pastor', who may well have been operating in effect as minister of word and sacrament. While the 'locally recognized' pastor's sphere of action and competence is narrower than a minister recognized by the national union of churches, who will be available and commended to *all* the churches, this does not mean a separate order of ministry. Such a local minister should still, as *episkopos*, be making the link with the wider church and bringing a vision of the one church to bear on local concerns. He or she will still be a 'minister of the church in general'. Moreover, the influence also works the other way; as the Roman Catholic scholar Edward Schillebeeckx points out: 'local ministers, as critical spokesmen [sic] of their churches, at the same time concern themselves with the management of the "universal church", the bond of love.'[29]

For 'locally recognized ministers' to be truly *episkopoi*, I urge that their training – however abbreviated it is – should still enable them to

26 In Germany, the spiritual leadership of the elders is only recognized in the local church where they are appointed; in Russia they carry the leadership role with them when they move.

27 Schillebeeckx, *Ministry*, p. 40.

28 The proposal before the Baptist Union Council in 2003 was that this local recognition should be *recorded* nationally, in the 'Register of Covenanted Persons Accredited for Ministry' kept by the Union.

29 Schillebeeckx, *Ministry*, p. 74.

represent the whole church. They must not be merely 'locally-interested ministers'. The scope of *episkope* can thus vary, whether resident in one place only, available for movement to many places, or exercised among many places at once (the 'regional minister'), but the underlying structure or bass rhythm remains: there is one kind of ministry set aside by the local community on its own, and one kind set aside in the bonds of covenant love with other churches. Perhaps it would be better to speak of a two-fold pattern, which can diversify into many orders, or ways of being.

This survey of the call of Christ to pastoral office, drawing both on scripture and the experience of Baptist congregations, should make clear why we should resist the view that a minister's authority is simply delegated from the local church meeting. The minister has been commissioned by Christ, and he or she comes into the local situation from the life of the church world-wide. The moment of ordination has brought into one focus the call from Christ, and the recognition of the community which is the body of Christ, gathered together from more than a single locality. Members in the local church meeting must therefore trust the minister to initiate actions they have never thought about, and to interpret the Word of God in scripture in ways that will often challenge their assumptions. It retains the right to recognize whether this person *has* been commissioned by Christ and called to general oversight in this particular place; but as long as it does offer this recognition it also promises to take the risk of trusting the minister, along with its diaconal leaders, in many ways.

Serving and Trust

I have been arguing that, while appointment and recognition are the necessary basis for authority, there is no straight line from one to the other labelled 'delegation', either in the model of hierarchy or employment. The authority of a pastor comes partly from usefulness as a source for discovering the mind of Christ – what we might call being 'authoritative' rather than 'authoritarian'. This, by the way, is akin to the role of 'facilitator' given to the priest or pastor in the base communities of the Latin American churches.[30] The role played by the pastor here is intimately associated with being 'a minister of the church in general', representing the church universal. But this kind of authority also depends upon being trusted, and this I now want to spell out more clearly.

---

30   But there is still always the danger of slipping into clericalism: see Andrew Dawson, 'The Origins and Character of the Base Ecclesial Community: a Brazilian Perspective', in Christopher Rowland (ed.), *The Cambridge Companion to Liberation Theology* (Cambridge: Cambridge University Press, 1999), pp. 109–28.

I return therefore to the first definition of authority given by the *Oxford English Dictionary*, which I suggested has been overturned by the scandalous self-unveiling of God in the cross of Jesus. The first meaning offered is 'the power to enforce obedience', and that would obviously fit in well with the kind of hierarchy of submission (delegation from above) I was describing earlier. But all such notions are projecting human ideas of power and authority onto God. The worldly idea of authority is being able to *make* people do what the authority-figure wants, and so we extend this to God and produce a picture of an absolute monarch who dominates his creation, wanting only subjects who submit blindly to him. We think then that such a God sanctions a whole chain of command below him, a pyramid of submission. But this picture ignores the biblical witness to the God who calls human beings into a partnership of friends, and who shares human tensions and pains in order to bring us into the full growth of personhood. Of course we are to be humble before God, as creatures before their creator; but God also shows an amazing humility towards the creation, out of an infinite love. We speak rightly of submitting to God, but we learn also from scripture about God's submission of God's own self to the conditions of this world. We learn of a God who is humble and patient in love for Israel, open to being spurned and rejected, suffering the frustration of God's plans for the covenant people, and still winning them back by opening the divine heart to them anew. The New Testament shows us the same God, one who becomes flesh and treads the path of weakness to the exposure and isolation of the cross.

I have already explored such a theology of a compassionate God in chapter 3 above. We see from the biblical picture that God does not manipulate us with an irresistible power, but seeks to persuade and influence us to follow the divine purpose through the power of suffering love. In the end, indeed, the ability to change minds and hearts is a much greater power than the authority of a dictator to force obedience. In George Orwell's novel *1984*, the dictator who rules the western world is able to compel people to do whatever he requires; he can make them say 2+2=5, if that is what he decrees. He regulates their lives to the last minute, with monitor screens in every room. But he is unhappy because he cannot force people to *love* him, and he wants to be loved; that is why he calls himself, tragically as well as ominously, 'Big Brother'. The greatest authority is the power to win hearts and minds, to evoke love and trust in another. All other kinds of authority can be defeated; the slave who carries out a master's orders finally defeats his master when he does so with an inner attitude of defiance.

God is not defeated, because suffering love wins through without compulsion. This vision of God must undermine any view of a hierarchy of submission within the church, and it also shows us the central place of serving within authority. We learn from the key passage in Mark 10:42–5 that the only authority lies in serving. This does not merely mean that those who exercise authority should *also* remember that they serve; we all know the fiction of so-called 'public servants', who write letters in the most bureaucratic and pompous style and then conclude with the flourish that we 'it is our mission to serve the community' (a modern cliché which has replaced the older style, 'I remain your humble servant'). This saying of Jesus about himself is far more radical than that; it declares that those who give themselves away in serving have an authority *in so far as* they do so. Their serving *makes* their authority. This is authority as a blend of influence on the part of one, and trust on the part of others.

Jesus is Lord of the cosmos because his self-giving love has the power of utter persuasion, awakening complete trust. In this self-surrender he makes visible the truth about the lordship of God, for the cross tells us that God is never more fully the divine sovereign than in humility and sacrifice.[31] Within the Christian community, its leaders can begin to share in that spiritual authority. Others trust them and are influenced or guided by them, because they give themselves away in service. They have no power to compel others, and those whom they serve have the freedom to reject their service, however hurtful that might be.[32]

Obedience to the Spirit of God as the personal energy in human lives is thus a matter of being *persuaded* by the Spirit of the humble Father and the crucified Son. It is not a matter of being simply 'taken over' or 'swamped' or 'invaded' by a superior power. This again undermines any hierarchy of submission within the church which is based upon the mistaken linking of spiritual gifts to authority. It is sometimes thought that certain people must be submitted to because they possess powerful gifts of the Spirit. They are revered as possessing spiritual powers, and submission to them is seen as submission to the Spirit who has given the gifts. Thus leaders become Gurus.

The New Testament, however, shows us that the *charismata* are not possessions or faculties of those who exercise them. Gifts of the Spirit are in fact always the Spirit's own acts of giving through us. They are not abilities of a believer, but energies of the Spirit. As the New Testament scholar James Dunn puts it, '*Charisma* is always an event, the gracious activity of God through a person. It is the actual healing, the miracle

---

31   Karl Barth stresses this reversal of human expectations about God: see *Church Dogmatics*, IV/1, pp. 158–60, 193–5.

32   Even business management has discovered the effectiveness of servant leadership: see, for example, Larry Spears and Michele Lawrence (eds), *Focus on Leadership. Servant-Leadership for the Twenty-First Century* (New York: John Wiley, 2002).

itself.... it is the particular act of healing as it is performed.'[33] The wind of the Spirit blows, as it were, through the landscape of human life, taking a natural human faculty as a place through which to breathe divine energy. So no spiritual gifting can confer status or authority upon the person who exercises it; it does not belong to him. A corollary is that when a *charisma* apparently happens, it must be tested to discover whether in fact it is an act of the Spirit, or whether it is simply the human faculty which the Spirit can take and use. What occurs may sound like a deep spiritual insight, a word of prophecy and inspiration for the church today, but it may simply be a human opinion or hunch. The whole church as the body of Christ thus retains the responsibility to test whether a particular event is in fact a *charisma*.

One mark of recognition is whether the exercise of a so-called gift has a liberating effect. The way that we think God works in us will affect the way we think of leadership in the church. As I suggested at the beginning of this chapter, no account of church and ministry will convince unless it is grounded in a vision of God. Now, if we think that the Spirit of God manipulates our minds, simply using them as blank screens or unresisting instruments, then we shall tend to carry this notion over into spiritual leadership. But the acts of the spirit are persuasive love. To use another New Testament concept, the rule of Christ means liberation. Once again, a dictionary definition is challenged by the divine crisis in human life. The image of the 'kingdom' or rule of God, as brought by Christ, is that of an open space in which people can experience freedom from the violence and pressure of the powers of this world age, liberation from the forces that spoil life and stop us developing as the full persons God intends us to be. 'He is the head of all rule and authority.... he disarmed the principalities and powers, and made a public example of them, triumphing over them in the cross' (Col. 2:8). Thus the rule of Christ in the community of faith frees the members from oppression of every kind, including their oppression of each other. Discrimination is lifted; the strong do not exploit the weak; the healthy do not despise the sick; the place of women in ministerial leadership is recognized as being fully equal to that of men (Gal. 3:8). The church at the same time looks for signs of the rule of Christ in the world and seeks to cooperate with it, in the ministry of liberation from all kinds of oppression, structural evils and social injustice.

In his rule, Christ takes the risk of calling upon our trust rather than coercing us. In his rule he aims to liberate. In calling people to roles of

---

33   Dunn, *Jesus and the Spirit*, p. 254. Similarly, Eduard Schweizer, *Church Order in the New Testament*, trans. F. Clarke (London: SCM Press, 1961), p. 180; Ernst Käsemann, 'Ministry and Community in the New Testament', in Käsemann, *Essays on New Testament Themes*, trans. J. Montague (Studies in Biblical Theology 41; London: SCM Press, 1964), pp. 65–66.

leadership, as *episkopos* or *diakonos*, he calls them to take those risks too. They must take the risk of serving, of having their gifts tested. At the same time, when the church recognizes the call of Christ to them, it promises for its part to take the risk of trusting them in many ways. As long as it extends recognition, it gives trust.

Authority in Personality

Authority in pastor-people relationships can, therefore, only consist in a servanthood which creates trust. In practical terms, this means that as members of the covenant community seek for the mind of Christ in church meeting, they will draw upon the resource of their pastor or bishop. While each member has, in strictly democratic terms, one vote (and this includes the pastor), they will give *weight* to this particular voice. They will expect to be made uncomfortable by the prophetic word of rebuke and challenge that the pastor is called to speak, out of a vision of the faith and mission of the church universal. Though they have the right to debate and approve all decisions made by the pastoral team of the minister (or ministers) and deacons, they will not always want to do so. Sometimes they will simply trust the leaders they have recognized as called by Christ. They must always test the leaders and test the spiritual gifts they exercise, but this testing need not always be an explicit examination, as the church gradually grows in recognition of the spiritual authority of people who share the divine spirit of service.

In this picture of serving on the one hand, and trusting on the other, we can find two further dimensions of the authority of the pastor – the authority of personality and of truth. By the first aspect I do not mean the force of a powerful and colourful personality, an up-front showman, but an authority won by the pastor because he or she *is* a servant. There is a kind of authority that comes from *being* as well as *doing*. Christ calls people to a particular *way of being* that we may call *episkope* and *diakonia*. By speaking of the usefulness of the pastor as a source for discovering the purpose of Christ, and of the part that the pastor plays, I have not all intended to reduce the meaning of ministry to a functional concept. The terms 'office' and 'ordination' both point to the idea of a way of being which must come before all doing. As Jesus says to his disciples, 'Dwell in me, for apart from me you can *do* nothing.' (Jn. 15:4–5).

It is true that during the history of the church the idea of an 'order' or 'office' of minister has been understood as carrying privileged status or rank. In reaction against this there has been a swing towards stressing the functions which a pastor performs, and this fits in with our modern concerns with the learning of skills and techniques. A pastor might therefore be defined as someone set aside from other occupations to practise skills such as counselling, teaching and even person-management. But, while the learning of skills is important, we make a bad mistake if we think that 'doing' can be separated from 'being'. We become the kind of person we are through what we do, and conversely the kind of person we are shapes our doing. The idea of an 'office' or 'order' alerts us to the dimension of sheer being. The minister's personality will become what it is through seeking to interpret the Word of God in the scriptures, through presiding at the Lord's Table, through intercessory prayer, through thinking through the meaning of the mission of God in the contemporary world, and through sharing in the most intimate moments of people's lives at birth, marriage and death; all this and more will make the pastor who he or she is. Some are called by Christ to be the sort of person to whom others can relate, with whom they can share their deepest fears and hopes, and it is this ministerial character that people value.

This description should make clear that the 'way of being' is not an individualistic mode of the self, but the identity of the self in relation to others. The idea is not to focus on the 'being' of the self, augmenting the solidity of its substance and so increasing the weight of its domination over the objects it deals with. This view of the substantiality of the self and the authority of its presence in the world has rightly come under critique in the postmodern mood of today.[34] Rather, we can understand the very concept of 'being' as the mediation *between* the self and other, so that we become more truly and intensely what we *are* through self-emptying in service to others and suffering with others.[35] In this way the self need be neither authoritarian nor fragmented and lost. We follow our way of being through participating in the interweaving relationships in the triune God, which are a constant movement of giving and receiving in love, a self-giving of Father, Son and Holy Spirit, each to the other and beyond each other to the world.[36] When a patient in a mental-health trust hospital in Oxford referred affectionately to the chaplain not as a 'clergyman' but as 'the prayer-man', it was evident to me that the kind of prayer he had in mind was not 'the flight of the alone to the alone' but compassionate prayer for residents in the hospital, entering into the world (sometimes the strange and alien world) of which they were the centre.

There are, of course, many 'ways of being' for Christian disciples. To have a way of being is not exclusive to Christian ministers. But there are

34   E.g. Jacques Derrida, *Writing and Difference*, trans. A. Bass (London: Routledge, 1993), pp. 229–30.

35   See Oliver Davies, *A Theology of Compassion. Metaphysics of Difference and the Renewal of Tradition* (London: SCM Press, 2001), pp. xx–xxii, 1–8.

36   See above, ch. 4, pp. 78–82.

important implications for a Christian minister. To say that Christ has established a way of life to which this person has been called means that there is bound to be something open-ended about it. A way of life is more than a mere job description; all its functions cannot be neatly defined ahead of time, and what it fully means to 'be' a minister will emerge in new circumstances and in new times. This is the advantage of the word 'office': it indicates a place to be. To paraphrase a word of Jesus in Matthew 11:29, it is if Christ says, 'Take this role upon you and learn from me.' To have an office means that the position of leadership is there: pastors do not have to strive for it by exerting their personality, winning acclaim or being successful in the eyes of the congregation at the cost of enormous stress to themselves. They have been called into it, and can learn humbly what it means to live and work within it. There is a dimension of life here that we might call 'priestly' as distinct from 'prophetic', and Baptists have always been stronger in the latter than the former.

Ordination plays a key part in the development of this way of being. Ordination is the act in which the church, under the guidance of the Holy Spirit, both recognizes a person's call to ministry and commissions him or her for this work. Though taking place in one single moment, it sums up a whole *process* of calling, testing and mutual commitment between candidate and churches. It is thus a moment in which God freely acts, to meet someone with divine grace, to give him or her a new filling of the Holy Spirit to meet the needs of a new stage of life and ministry. The interweaving of the act of the church in commissioning, and the act of God in blessing, is fittingly symbolized by the laying on of hands. It follows from our discussion of authority that the act of ordination does not in itself grant or delegate authority to the person ordained; but it plays a central part in the forming of a person who will *have* authority because of his or her way of being. Ordination is a moment of special encounter with the triune God in which, like baptism, there is grace to help to shape heart, mind and character.

Such a concept of the ministerial vocation does not, I suggest, mean that ordination bestows on someone an 'indelible' order of ministry, so that once people are ordained they must always hold the office of *episkope*.[37] Ordination is a key moment – perhaps the central moment –

---

37   Here I regretfully take a different view from Baptist scholars who think that the nature of ministry as a way of being should lead to the conclusion of 'indelible orders': so John Colwell, 'The Sacramental Nature of Ordination. An Attempt to Re-engage a Catholic Understanding and Practice', in Anthony R. Cross and Philip E. Thompson (eds.), *Baptist Sacramentalism* (Studies in Baptist History and Thought 5; Carlisle: Paternoster, 2003 forthcoming), pp. 244–5; cf. Stephen R. Holmes, 'Towards a Baptist Theology of Ordained Ministry', in Cross and Thompson (eds.), *Baptist Sacramentalism*, pp. 260–2. On the other hand, I also disagree with the basing of the non-indelibility of

in shaping a particular way of being, and what God has done through it cannot be cancelled out, any more than the sacrament of baptism or the Lord's Supper once effective can be made of no effect.[38] But Christ may cease at some stage in the minister's life to issue a call to this particular kind of ministry; the person's way of being may be about to take a radically new direction. What has been is not reversed, but taken up into a new way of being. That a call is coming to an end may well be felt by the individual himself or herself, but it is also discerned by the community of the church (local and trans-local) which has tested and recognized the call in the first place.

Needless to say, those who are called to this task of discernment should be imaginative in looking for new forms that *episkope* itself may take. Given the open-endedness of a way of being, it may be that a person is being called to a new direction *within* the office. Oversight in the Christian community, involving the ministry of word and sacrament, and being a faithful guardian and interpreter of the apostolic tradition in the modern world, can take many other forms than pastoral charge of a local congregation. Suppose that someone was once called and ordained to the pastoral care of a local church, and is now being called to teach Religious Education in school, or to be a social worker, or to be an ecumenical officer, or to be a counsellor in industry, or an administrator in a charitable organization, yet believes that he or she is still called to be a minister. The relevant question to be asked is not, 'is this the kind of job that qualifies someone to be a minister?', or even 'does one have to be a minister to do this job?' Nor should the minister ask, 'Will being a minister give me added authority in this role?' The question is this: can and should the church of Christ commission this person to express his or her way of being as *episkopos* within this new context? It does not matter that others who are not ordained can work as Christian disciples in the same job. The point is that *this* person has already heard the call of Christ on his or her life to be a pastor, and the call has been recognized and marked by ordination. The church is under an obligation – a responsibility that comes from covenant relation with the minister – to ask whether that same call is now taking a new and unexpected form. With all alertness to the surprises of the Spirit, it may be apparent that a person is no longer being called to live in the office of *episkope*. However, what the idea of ordination to an office means is that those coming to ordination themselves set no limits on their offer of service, and do not enter upon this way of being in a conditional manner, saying

orders on a functional view of ministry: see Paul Beasley-Murray, 'The Ministry of All and the Leadership of Some: a Baptist Perspective', in P. Beasley-Murray (ed.), *Anyone for Ordination?* (Tunbridge Wells: Marc, 1993), p. 166.

38   Here I anticipate a later argument, that many events in life may be regarded as sacramental, by extension from the two dominical sacraments; see ch. 8, pp. 187-92.

(under their breath, as it were), 'I'll give this three years and if it doesn't work out I'll try something else'

Baptists then ought not to be embarrassed about an 'order' of ministers (and, indeed, an 'order' of deacons),[39] to which ordination points. There is a 'way of being' which is bound to carry authority with it, though it will be the authority of influence and persuasion that I have described, not one of coercion. The simple distinction between 'clergy' and 'laity' is, however, unfortunate since it contracts the 'ways of being' within the church into two basic classes, which is bound to result in ideas of rank. Here the church was perhaps unduly influenced by the distinction in Roman society between the *ordo* and the *plebs* (those with an 'order' in society, and the rest), which Tertullian first popularized within church life.[40] We must surely affirm that all are the people (*plebs, laos*) of God, but that within the people there are different ways of life and being, of which the pastor's is one.

Authority in Truth

The authority won through serving is expressed in personality, or personal formation in a way of life. It is also a matter of the power of truth. We recognize authority when we hear the word of truth about our lives, our future possibilities, our relationship with God. In real authority there is no question of being compelled to accept what certain powerful people consider to be the truth. The word of truth has an authority inherent within itself; we follow it freely because we recognize it as true (cf. Jn. 8:26–32). It confronts us with a challenge we cannot ignore. Supremely, this Word of truth is Jesus himself. He is our authority because we see in his life, death and resurrection the truth about God and about humanity, and because we perceive this truth in the context of his serving. Truth and serving belong together in Jesus. In the servant saying of Mark 10:45 Jesus proclaims himself as the pattern of proper authority; we trust him absolutely as revealing the true purpose for our lives because he gives himself away for us absolutely. His self-giving love has the power of utter persuasion. Because of the influence of his self-giving we recognize his authority as the true Word of God.

Within the Christian community, pastors can begin to share in that spiritual authority. Others trust them and are influenced by them because

---

39   Among both Particular and General Baptists, deacons were ordained with laying on of hands until the early nineteenth century; see the Standard Confession (1600), Second London Confession (1677), *Orthodox Creed* (1679), in Lumpkin, *Baptist Confessions*, pp. 229, 287, 320. *Forms of Ministry among Baptists*, pp. 44–5, proposed that this practice should be restored.

40   See Schillebeeckx, *Ministry*, p. 38–41.

they give themselves away in service, as at the same time they bear witness to the truth of the Word of God. I have already argued that the *episkopos* in the local church has a special responsibility to guard and interpret the apostolic faith, and when this is combined with humble serving what is true within his witness will carry its own weight of authority.[41] It is in this context that we may say that the ministry of the episkopos is *characterized* by being a ministry of word and sacrament. I have preferred not to *define* it in this way, as what is primary is the call to the office of *episkope*, and there is always – as I have suggested – something open-ended about what this will mean. But oversight will certainly be exercised in the ministry of word and sacrament.[42] While the whole church shares in the ministry of Christ who is the Word of God, to the minister is assigned the primary responsibility for witnessing to the Word in proclamation and in teaching, interpreting in each age the written word of scripture. Other members of the church who have been given the gift of teaching can certainly share in this ministry of the word; but to the minister is given the responsibility for training, overseeing and coordinating all teaching and preaching that happens within the congregation. The *episkopos* is called to stand in the shoes of the apostles, in ensuring that the story of salvation is faithfully transmitted, in new words for new times, and this will at times mean standing over against the congregation with the Word of challenge. It is this ministry which enables the whole church to be 'apostolic' in witnessing to the good news of Christ and the forgiveness of sins as the apostles did.

As the Word of God himself became flesh in history, so the word which is spoken must also be embodied in the drama and the physical materials of the Lord's Supper and baptism. This is one reason why the one who is minister of the word is also minister of the sacraments, and *normally* presides at the Lord's Table and baptizes new disciples. It seems that in most Baptist churches from the seventeenth to the early nineteenth century, *only* the ordained minister was authorized to administer the sacraments by the church meeting.[43] In the development of Baptist

---

41   Nigel G. Wright, 'Inclusive Representation: Towards a Doctrine of Christian Ministry', *BQ*, 39/4 (2001), p. 171, writes of authority as 'the weight of testimony', which is 'weighty to the extent that we bear the Word of God'.

42   In the following two paragraphs I draw quite closely on the text which I drafted for *Forms of Ministry among Baptists*, p. 29.

43   Among many statements of this principle, see: the Second London Confession (1677), ch. XXVIII.2, in Lumpkin, *Baptist Confessions*, p. 290; Thomas Grantham, *Christianismus Primitivus: or, The Ancient Christian Religion* (London: Francis Smith, 1678), 2.2.7, p. 93; Hercules Collins, *The Temple Repair'd* (London: 1702), p. 51; Daniel Turner, *Compendium*, pp. 49–50; Gill, *Body of Divinity*, II, bk. 3, pp. 276–7. E.P. Winter has, however, shown that *some* church meetings – both General and Particular Baptist – would appoint a deacon to preside if the minister were unavoidably

tradition since then, other members may on occasion, by decision of the church meeting, preside at the table. But it is still 'good order' for the minister of the congregation to do so when he or she is present, since the breaking of bread and the pouring of the wine is a visible passing on of the Gospel story which belongs to the guardianship of the tradition. There is also a second reason for the minister to preside: the table is that of the whole church, not just the local congregation, and the minister represents the whole church on the local scene.

Truth, then, is spoken and lived. It cannot be imposed, assent cannot be demanded, because it is the character of truth to liberate.[44] It produces conviction, but it also produces a community life which is notably more liberated than the world around. J. Miguez Bonino tells the story of a local Christian leader in a Latin American country, an uneducated peasant, being interrogated by the police. The officer asks, 'Where did you get these ideas about the rights of the poor?' and the man answers, 'I got them from my teacher.' 'Who is your teacher – name and address?', commands the officer, and the man replies, 'The name is Jesus Christ; the address I don't know; but you will find the teaching in the gospels.'[45]

Some may protest that a few passages in the New Testament (and they are few) urge obedience and submission to spiritual leaders in a much more direct way than the kind of 'trust through serving' that I have been commending. I believe, however, that a study of these passages will show that the context of leadership in the New Testament church was one of the servanthood of leaders,[46] trust awakened in the congregation towards its leaders,[47] a mutual humility[48] and a liberated community life.[49] These radical characteristics were worked out in ways that were suitable for the culture of the time, and were revolutionary for their age. We cannot simply transplant into today's church the exact forms of authority within the New Testament church. We need to ask how the Spirit of God works with us now to express the same trust and liberation within leadership. The place given to women within church leadership was, for instance, revolutionary and even scandalous within the view of first century

---

absent, through illness or imprisonment, anticipating the more widespread modern practice: Winter, 'Who May Administer the Lord's Supper?', *BQ* 16/3 (1955), pp. 128–33.

44   See Hans Urs Von Balthasar, *Theo-logic. Theological Logical Theory. Vol. I. Truth of the World*, transl. A.J. Walker (San Francisco: Ignatius Press, 2000), pp. 120–30.

45   J. Miguez Bonino, *Towards a Christian Political Ethics* (London: SCM Press, 1983), p.101.

46   1 Thes. 2:4–8, Heb. 13:17, 1 Pet. 5:1–3

47   1 Thes. 5:12–13, Rom. 16:1–2, Heb. 13:7

48   2 Cor. 11:20, Eph. 4:21, 1 Pet. 5:5–6

49   Gal. 3:1–5, 4:7–20.

society; but Paul's principle of the new humanity in Christ (Gal. 3:28) must today take a form that is even more liberating to women than the practical forms it was able to take then. We must see how the Spirit of God in our day is fulfilling the promise that 'in Christ there is neither male nor female' by calling women and men to the office of pastor.[50]

The issue of authority in relations between pastor and people is, then, nothing less than a vision of God. The question is this: how shall we imitate today the self-giving humility of God the Father, Son and Holy Spirit? In a servanthood that awakens trust in the truth lies the only possible authority of the pastor.

---

50   See Ruth M.B. Gouldbourne, *Reinventing the Wheel. Women and Ministry in English Baptist Life* (The Whitley Lecture 1997–1998; Oxford: Whitley Publications, 1997), p. 37, 'to talk about women and ministry is immediately to define women as other ... We can only talk about women and men and ministry, because it is together that we give and receive ministry'.

CHAPTER 6

Baptism and Creation

Lovers lie around in it
Broken glass is found in it
Grass
I like that stuff...

Elephants get sprayed with it
Scotch is made with it
Water
I like that stuff

Clergy are dumbfounded by it
Bones are surrounded by it
Flesh
I like that stuff...

Well I like that stuff
Yes I like that stuff
The earth
Is made of earth
And I like that stuff

So a modern poet, Adrian Mitchell, celebrates the materials of the natural world.[1] In some instances he may be right that 'clergy are dumbfounded by it', but we should also recall C. S. Lewis' happy phrase that 'God likes matter; after all, he made it.' Indeed, within the Christian tradition the sacraments are pieces of matter that God takes and uses as special places of encounter with God's own self; grace transforms nature, and grace is nothing less than God's gracious coming to us and to the world. The personal, triune God who is always present to influence and change

---

1   Adrian Mitchell, 'Stufferation', from *Adrian Mitchell's Greatest Hits – The Top Forty* (Newcastle upon Tyne: Bloodaxe Books, 1991), verses 1, 4, 5, 12.

human personalities takes on a deeper presence with us through water, bread and wine. In the sacraments, God's action in creation *and* redemption thus fuses into a particular focus.

Now, with regard to baptism, those in other Christian traditions might suppose that among Baptists there would be the richest expression of the link between redemption and creation. Total immersion, and the involvement of persons who have conscious faith, means that there is the greater opportunity for sacred drama involving substantial contact with the element of water. There is potential for a multi-media drama that will involve the person and the community at every level. As a matter of fact, however, Baptists have to confess that there has been a flight from the 'stuff' of creation. There has been, let it be admitted, a concealing of baptisteries under the floor, an underplaying of the use of the water and the emphasizing of the 'testimony' part, a lack of a sense of drama and (though this is fortunately fast passing) an insulation of the minister from the water by the use of incongruous waders.

Despite this tendency, I want to affirm that the Baptist practice of believers' baptism *does* make possible a recovery of the sense of the baptismal water as an actual element of the *natural* world, as well as a metaphor of God's redemptive activity. This location of baptism in creation also relates, I want to show, to wider issues of Baptist self-identity and to the Baptist contribution to the ecumenical scene.

The symbol of water touches human experience at many points; descent into water, sprinkling with water and passing through water have been part not only of religious rituals but key images in the written and visual arts. We may here conveniently identify five motifs connected with water which have been important for the Judaeo-Christian tradition: birth, cleansing, conflict, refreshment and journey. These, I believe, all have a foundation in natural life and thus arouse deep-laid associations in the unconscious as well as lay hold of our conscious memories. In his book *Christianity and Symbolism*, F. W. Dillistone maintains that 'to find a way of allowing Baptism to exercise its power within the Christian community at the deepest level of the human psyche is one of the most urgent tasks of our day', and he finds the urgency to stem from the fact that these natural images are so powerful that if they are not sanctified within a Christian context 'they will almost certainly present themselves in demonic forms'.[2] This present chapter is an attempt to suggest ways to meet the challenge of a scholar who was my former teacher, and I am glad to acknowledge that my review of the motifs connected with water owes not a little to Dillistone's own pioneering discussion.

In addition, however, to the *natural* context of these primordial images of water, they have been central images as the people of God have

---

2   F.W. Dillistone, *Christianity and Symbolism* (London: Collins, 1955), p. 187.

reflected upon their past experience in *history*, and as they have formed convictions about the way that God acted redemptively for them in that public arena. Thus the symbols are rich in reference to both creation and redemption, and in particular they have been grounded in history through the life, death and resurrection of Jesus. The power of the baptismal event lies in its drawing upon experiences of both nature and history, and its uniting of them in worship.

Birth

In the first place, the descent into water within a religious ceremony has often been associated with a return to the womb, and so with regeneration and the renewal of life. There is an immediate reference here to the fact that the unborn foetus lives in water within the womb, and perhaps a more distant recollection of the ancient concept that the waters of the underworld were the place whence life issued. The latter picture is no doubt connected with the former, especially where rivers are portrayed in ancient texts as issuing from the 'womb' or the 'vagina' of the earth.[3] Conversely then, the vagina of a woman was often described poetically as a 'well' or 'fountain' of life (cf. Prov. 5:15). Woven into the whole complex of imagery is also the *breaking* of the waters in the process of birth; the child is nurtured in the life-giving waters and is then born 'through water'. It is hardly surprising in the light of all this that Carl Jung interpreted mythical expressions of descent into water as a descent into the womb of the unconscious mind, which must be penetrated before new life and creativity can be born.[4] We may trace then, in the human psyche, a deeply embedded urge to return to the waters whence we have come and from there to make a new beginning.

The direct connection of water with birth and regeneration is actually rather rare in the Old Testament. Perhaps Genesis 1:2 presents the Spirit of God 'brooding' over the waters of chaos, bringing creation to birth as if from a cosmic womb (cf. Job 38:8 – 'the sea ... burst in flood from the womb'). Birth imagery is more often used as a way of expressing redemptive experience in history, as Israel is addressed in prophetic oracle as having been a child born and brought to adulthood through such experiences as slavery in Egypt, exodus and wilderness wandering.[5] In his purpose to bring about a *new* exodus for his people, Yahweh is also

---

3   E.g. The Sumerian Paradise Myth of Enki and Ninhursag; in James B. Pritchard, *Ancient Near Eastern Texts Relating to the Old Testament*, Second Edition (New Jersey: Princeton University Press, 1955), pp. 38–9.

4   C.G. Jung, *Symbols of Transformation,* Collected Works of C.G. Jung, transl. R.F.C. Hull, vol. 5 (London: Routledge and Kegan Paul, 1956), pp. 218–19.

5   E.g. Ezek. 16:1–7, Hos. 11:1–4, Isa. 1:1–3; 63:8–10

described as being like a woman in the pains of childbirth.[6] Nevertheless, any association of passing through the *waters* of the Red Sea with images of *birth* is left implicit, while (as we shall see shortly) images of conflict are highly explicit.

The historicizing of birth imagery, however, comes to a remarkable fusion with the water of baptism in the gospel accounts of the baptism of Jesus in the Jordan river, when he is greeted by the heavenly voice with the words 'You are my Son' (Mt. 3:17, Mk. 1:11, Lk. 3:22). To make clear the reminiscence of Psalm 2:7, other ancient versions of Luke's account add, 'today I have begotten you.' This psalm appears to contain a liturgy in which kings of Ancient Israel would be greeted by Yahweh as having been adopted as his sons, and so 'brought to birth' in their coronation.[7] This affirmation is now applied in a special way to Jesus in his baptism, and the image of birth is underlined by Mark and Matthew since they describe the announcement as happening at the very moment when Jesus 'came up out' of the water. There is, of course, no implication here that Jesus himself is in need of spiritual re-birth (as Matthew makes clear in his account, 3:14–15); rather, he completely identifies himself with an Israel which *is* in need of regeneration, and fully embodies in himself the sonship by which the Israelite kings had failed to live, despite all the hopes expressed for them.

The Fourth Gospel carries on the association of water with birth, probably relating this to baptism in the expression 'born of water and the Spirit' (John 3:5). Already, it has been argued, the primary meaning of Jewish baptism of Gentile proselytes had become that of re-birth.[8] Early Christian theologians certainly have no hesitation in comparing the baptismal pool to a womb; Cyril of Jerusalem affirms, 'this wholesome water has become for you both a tomb and a mother..',[9] and Ephraem the Syrian exclaims: 'O womb which daily brings forth without pain the sons of the kingdom of heaven! They descend indeed with their faults and their stains, but they rise up pure as infants. For Baptism becomes a second womb for them.....'[10]

The natural association between baptism and birth has, in fact, been most strongly felt in recent times by women Christian ministers in administering baptism. I heard one woman, for example, speaking movingly of her experience of baptizing her own son as being 'like giving birth to him for a second time.' In the dramatic setting of

6   Isa. 42:14, cf. Isa. 45:10; 66:7–9.
7   See Aubrey R. Johnson, *Sacral Kingship in Ancient Israel*, Second Edition (Cardiff: University of Wales Press, 1967), pp. 128–32.
8   See G. R. Beasley-Murray, *Baptism in the New Testament* (London: Macmillan, 1963), p. 26.
9   Cyril of Jerusalem, *Mystagogical Catacheses*, II (*Catachetical Lectures*, 20), 4.
10   Cit. Dillistone, *Christianity and Symbolism*, p. 186.

believers' baptism, as she raised him from the waters which had enclosed him, the words of Nicodemus about the paradox of re-birth took on a special poignance: 'can a man enter his mother's womb a second time and be born?'

Cleansing

The second major motif to which I want to draw attention is that of water as a symbol of spiritual cleansing. The sense of a need to be purified at every level of our being is another deeply embedded human feeling; the universal use of water for washing the body provides an image for the 'washing out' of inner taint in the mind and spirit. We notice that after a particularly unpleasant experience a person may say, 'I had to take a bath because I felt unclean all over', and we understand Lady Macbeth's anguish after the bloody murder of Duncan when she complains that 'all the perfumes of Arabia will not sweeten this little hand.'

We find the use of water rituals for purification in every known religion. The Old Testament legal codes have many instructions for purificatory rites, as did the community at Qumran with its multiple baths. The bathings and washing of clothes prescribed in the book of Leviticus are intended to prepare the priests and the people for encounter with the holy presence of God, and such rituals stress the integration of the spiritual and physical dimensions of life in the understanding of Ancient Israel. Positively, they bear witness to the psychosomatic wholeness of the human being, and raise echoes in the modern concern for 'holism' and creation-centred spirituality; negatively, they could lead to what we might diagnose as a *confusion* between physical and spiritual uncleanness, as for example in the instructions for ritual washing following contact with the dead and lepers, and for the so-called 'purification' of women following childbirth. Such an anxiety about purification could lead to the exclusion of people as 'unclean', and to the kind of mechanical rituals of washing of hands and vessels that Jesus later condemns (Mk. 7:1–8). On the whole, however, the Old Testament affirms quite impressively that outward cleansing without a 'clean heart' would not fit people for the experience of the holy:

> Purge me with hyssop, and I shall be clean;
> wash me, and I shall be whiter then snow....
> Create in me a clean heart, O God,
> and put a new and right spirit within me....
> The sacrifice acceptable to God is a broken spirit,
> A broken and contrite heart, O God, you will not despise.
> (Psa. 51:7, 10, 17)

This psalm, with its mention of sacrifices and 'burnt offerings' (vv. 16-17) reminds us that alongside the rites of purifying *through water* there was also the purifying *through blood* in the 'sin-offering' (*hattat*). Here the rituals of cleansing begin to interact with the concerns of 'atonement', that is the 'making at-one' of a holy God and sinful human beings. It seems quite clear that the purpose of the sin-offering was not to propitiate God but to expiate sins, that is to 'wash them away' through the cleansing power of blood;[11] the sacrifice both expiated the sin and purified the sinner.[12] At Qumran, when it was no longer possible to make the atoning sacrifice, they quite naturally understood sacrifice to be *replaced* by rituals of washing and bathing, while at the same time they fully recognized the limitations of an outward ceremony: as the Rule of the community puts it, 'a man ... shall not be cleansed by all the waters of washing ... for as long as he scorns the ordinances of God.'[13]

Whether the cleansing agent is water or blood, the Old Testament rituals are drawing upon a deep human desire for purification. They are also affirming that *God* must act through these natural elements to purge human lives of uncleanness. As with the symbol of birth, Israel also therefore historicized the symbol of cleansing. The prophet Ezekiel portrays Israel as having been washed clean by Yahweh in his adoption of her as a nation in past history (Ezek 16:9), and he and other prophets look forward to a new age when there will be a complete cleansing in a single once-for-all purgation (Zech. 13:1, Mal. 3:1–4, Ezek. 36:25).

All these strands are taken up into the New Testament. For the Fourth Gospel, Israel's hopes for a final 'washing' of human life have been fulfilled in history in the ministry of Jesus (Jn. 9:7; 13:5). Atonement has also been located in one decisive historic moment, and purification is a primary image by means of which New Testament writers understand the experience of reconciliation and forgiveness they have received through the cross of Jesus. They interpret his death as a once-for-all expiating sacrifice, and a purification achieved through the sprinkling of blood. It is true that the image of 'washing' from sin is only applied a few times explicitly to baptism,[14] but this ritual symbolizes and actualizes an atonement which is all about cleansing, and for which the New Testament

---

11   The key text is Leviticus 17:11. For further explanation see Paul S. Fiddes, *Past Event and Present Salvation. The Christian Idea of Atonement* (London: Darton, Longman and Todd, 1989), pp. 61–82.

12   See N. Kiuchi, *The Purification Offering in the Priestly Literature. Its Meaning and Function* (JSOT Supplement Series 56; Sheffield: Sheffield Academic Press, 1987), pp. 65–6.

13   *The Scroll of the Rule*, III.4–6; A. Dupont-Sommer, *The Essene Writings from Qumran*, trans. G. Vermes (Oxford: Blackwell, 1961), pp. 76–7.

14   Tit. 3:5, Eph. 5:26, Heb. 10:22; perhaps Jn. 13:5 cf. Rev. 7:14.

writers use the same complex interaction between the agency of water and blood that we find in more ancient texts. For instance, in Hebrews 10:20-22 the ancient 'Day of Atonement' rites of both sprinkling with blood and washing with water are applied to the effects of the death of Christ, together with an unmistakable reference to baptism through which these benefits are received. Believers are urged to approach God 'with our hearts sprinkled clean from an evil conscience and our bodies washed with pure water'.

As a footnote from recent times, I was personally present at a meeting of the Baptist World Alliance in Seoul in July, 1990, when the South Korean Minister of Culture, a Buddhist, greeted the congress members with a speech constructed entirely around the association of baptism with purification. Noting that there was to be an open-air service of baptism in the River Han which flows through the middle of Seoul, he expressed the hope that this act would be the beginning of the spiritual cleansing of the whole city and society, and that this would lead to a purification of the waters of the river itself from the industrial pollution which was spoiling it. Thus in the context of modern environmental problems, the image of cleansing retains its archetypal power.

Conflict

Third, the symbol of water evokes a sense of conflict and the overcoming of hostile powers. Faced with the tremendous force of a tidal wave, or irresistible floods, or the continuous threat of drowning in storms at sea, it is natural that water should also appear as an enemy in the human consciousness. Early myths in the Ancient Near East conceive of the act of creation as a victory over the chaos monster who either is, or dwells in, the sea. So also in the biblical account, creation cuts a place for human beings to live between the seas; the creator God holds back the unruly disorder of the waters and liberates the land (Job 26:12–13; 38:8–11; cf. Gen. 1:6–10).

In Ancient Israel this theme of conflict and victory in creation rarely, however, stands on its own but is connected to the redemptive acts of God in Israel's life and history. In Psalm 74 the writer recalls God's choice of Israel as his people and Mount Zion as his dwelling-place, and among these 'saving acts' he counts the 'cleaving of the sea monster in two' and the regular coming of summer and winter since then. Similarly, in Psalm 89:9–10 the overcoming of the watery chaos monster and the elevating of David to Kingship merge into one focus. Most notably, Isaiah of Babylon fuses the imagery of the dividing and curbing of the chaotic sea at creation with the dividing of the waters of the Red Sea at the Exodus, and so promises a new Exodus for the people in exile (Isa. 43:16–19;

51:9–11); God will once again 'make the ocean depths a path for the redeemed.'

So, in the overcoming of the waters of death and disaster, creation and redemption merge into one flowing process. In the rainbow sign the Priestly theologians found assurance that God was continuing to hold back the waters of chaos that had broken over the earth in the great flood (Gen. 9:12–17). The Psalms also speak of a continual redemption from death in the life of the individual; when in illness God holds back the forces of death and restores health then he is liberating from the power of the underworld (Sheol), a threat which is depicted like taking a grip on the on the sufferer's throat, like the monster of chaos, stifling him with the weight of a great flood of water (Ps. 18:16).

The association of water with a hostile power, and ultimately with death itself, is the predominant meaning that baptism carries in the New Testament. Jesus in his baptism in the waters of Jordan prefigures his plunging into the waters of death at the cross, and (at least in later Patristic thought) his descent into the waters of Hades. Looking to his death he enquires of his disciples, 'Can you be baptized with the baptism with which I am baptized?' (Mk. 10:38) As the Apostle Paul explains, in passing through these waters Christ overcomes the principalities and powers that hold human life in bondage, unmasking and exposing them for the idols and the tyrants that they are, and showing that they have no authority over him by rising from death. Paul urges that we are identified with Christ in baptism; we share in the passage of Christ through the deep waters of death as we pass through the waters of baptism and so we also share in his victory over the dark powers (Col. 2:12–15; Rom. 6:1–5). Christ participates in the most bitter depths of human death, in order that we might participate in his resurrection. In 1 Peter 3:18–22 this idea is similarly presented, while the writer also finds an apt analogy between baptism and Noah's ark which provided survival in the onslaught of the Great Flood.

In the Baptist tradition, total immersion has always been valued as a vivid portrayal of death and resurrection – a descent into the 'grave' and a being raised with Christ. However, this has too often been interpreted in a merely individualistic fashion as a personal dying to self, and the wider symbolism of a confrontation with the hostile powers has been lost. The powers that hold human beings in oppression must also be understood in terms of political and economic structures and governing authorities, and thus baptism is a 'political act'[15] in exposing their pretentious claims on human life.

---

15   See Brian Haymes, 'Baptism as a Political Act', in Fiddes (ed.), *Reflections on the Water*, pp. 69–84.

Journey

Connected with this image of water as a hostile power to be overcome is the fourth motif of a journey over water. Both involve 'passing through the water' and involve danger. But the journey image is less about the hazards on the way than the leaving behind of one territory or area of life, and the setting out for another. The water is a kind of boundary situation. Since rivers and seas form natural barriers to human travel and conquest, as well as natural markers for the ownership of land, it is hardly surprising that the motif of 'crossing the water' has so rooted a place in human consciousness. In Neo-Platonist imagery the soul at the beginning of life makes its journey across the waters of generation riding a dolphin, or it is depicted like a sea-shell cast up from the waves onto the shore.[16] In fact, through various transformations in the history of Christian art, the sea-shell frequently makes its appearance today in ceremonies of infant baptism as a scoop for the water. At the other end of life, the last frontier of the river of death appears in the ancient world as the Styx, and in Christian art as the Jordan, as for example in the final triumphant chapter of John Bunyan's *Pilgrim's Progress*.

Ancient Israel typically understood its experience in more historic terms, and saw its 'crossing the water' as leaving behind one style of life and entering a new covenant relationship. In crossing the Red Sea they separated from life in Egypt as slaves, and in crossing the River Jordan they separated from the nomadic life of the desert (Josh. 1). Passage through water was a mark of separation for the whole nation, as circumcision was a mark of separation from the other nations for the individual Israelite.

In viewing baptism as a replacement for the rite of circumcision, the New Testament understands baptism to be similarly a mark of separation from past life and the kingdom of darkness, and a passing into new kingdom territory. Baptism is a moment of complete re-evaluation of what really matters in life. With its associations of 'crossing the water', baptism actually fits better than circumcision into the network of concepts concerning leaving and entering phases of life. In fact, it is even possible that the development of Jewish proselyte baptism had already been prompted by the story of deliverance at and through the Red Sea, the rite of baptism portraying even better than circumcision the separation of Gentiles from their past life and their entrance into the

---

16   W.B. Yeats employs the image of the dolphin in his poems 'News for the Delphic Oracle' and 'Byzantium', *Collected Poems* (Macmillan: London, 1967), pp. 280, 376. For the Neo-Platonist imagery, see F.A.C. Wilson, *W.B. Yeats and Tradition* (London: Methuen, 1968), pp. 220–2. The classical source for the image of the sea-journey of the soul is Porphyry, *On the Cave of the Nymphs*.

people of God. Paul's exegesis in 1 Corinthians 10:1–2 may, it is suggested, reflect a Rabbinic justification for such proselyte baptism: 'our ancestors all passed through the Red Sea; and so they all received baptism into the fellowship of Moses in cloud and sea'.

Within the history of the Christian church, the act of receiving baptism has similarly meant a costly separation from one kind of culture, and entrance into the new humanity in Christ. In parts of Africa and Asia today the receiving of Christian baptism carries the cost of expulsion from family, tribal and societal life. In this sense too, baptism is 'a political act'.

Refreshment

Finally, water is a means and a symbol of refreshment. The sprinkling of water that cleanses from taint also produces a renewal of energies. The pouring of water, whether for drinking or for bathing, carries the sense of renewal of life. Especially in a hot country, bathing in water reinvigorates the body just as streams irrigate a dry land.

The natural basis of this symbol needs no further elaboration. However, we notice that once more the Israelite theologians and poets gave it a definitely historical location. The story of the striking of water from a rock by Moses in the desert wilderness placed the gift of water among the redemptive acts of God in history (Num. 20:1–12), and the incident was often recalled.[17] As the prophets lament the exhausting of national energies they also look forward to a renewal by Yahweh, and they identify the future pouring out of life-giving water with the Spirit of Yahweh (e.g. Isa. 44:3; cf. Ezek. 43:1–11).

The 'pouring out' of the Spirit is thus associated closely in the New Testament with baptism (Mk. 1:10; 1 Cor. 12:12–13), together with the image of 'drinking' the Spirit. The Fourth Gospel offers a fusion of these images, as it depicts an invitation that Jesus makes on the last day of the Feast of Tabernacles, when large jars of water were drawn from the fountain of Gihon and poured out on 'he altar; as the water is poured, Jesus invites the spiritually thirsty to drink from the 'living waters' of the Spirit which flow out of his heart (Jn. 7:37–9). The Old Testament motif of water-from-the-rock also probably lies behind the evangelist's account (cf. 1 Cor. 10:4). It is possible (though not certain), as Raymond Brown argues,[18] that the evangelist intends a reference to baptism here, as he may also intend in the earlier story of the Samaritan woman at the well

---

17   Pss. 105:40–1; 94:8; 78:15–16; Isa. 43:20; 44:3; 48:21; Deut. 8:15.

18   Raymond E. Brown, *The Gospel According to John* I–XII (The Anchor Bible; London: Chapman, 1966), pp. 179–80, 327–9.

and Jesus' promise there of 'the water of life' (Jn. 4:14). Both stories and Jesus' sayings within them were frequently connected to baptism by the early church Fathers, and the scene with the woman at the well appears in early catacomb art as a symbol for baptism. There is, of course, no simple *equation* of the 'living water' with the water of baptism; rather, drinking the living water (the Spirit) is *associated* with baptism since the gift of the Spirit is received through it.

The Communication of Grace

All this means that if the drama of baptism is properly arranged, the contact with the element of water should arouse a range of experiences in the person baptized and in the community which shares in the act. Immersion into water, with both its shocking and pleasurable sensations can evoke a sense of descent into the womb, a washing away of what is unclean, an encounter with a hostile force, a passing through a boundary marker, and re-invigoration. In all these aspects, water is a place in the material world that can become a 'rendez-vous'[19] with the crucified and risen Christ.

It may be protested that tracing a kaleidoscope of natural motifs as I have done leads to the bewildering impression that baptism means anything and everything, and therefore nothing in particular. However, just as the Old Testament writers appeal to the natural symbol of water to express their experience of God's acts in history, so the various aspects of the baptismal water enable us to participate in the death and resurrection of Jesus. This is the controlling event, and to it all the motifs relate, although (as I have suggested) the third motif of conflict makes the most obvious reference. Immersion into water conveys the 'shock' of dying, of being overwhelmed by alien powers; coming out from water conveys resurrection, an emergence to new life in which the hostile powers have not been left behind but in which there is new energy to deal with them.

Now, I want to stress here that the water in baptism is not merely a *visual aid* to help us understand various spiritual concepts; in its sheer materiality or 'stuffness' it actually *communicates* the presence of the transcendent God. A created thing provides places and opportunities for a transforming encounter. From an Old Testament perspective we can understand this as based in God's nature as both Creator and Redeemer, as Lord of both the cosmos and history. But we can gain a deeper appreciation of the rooting of sacrament in creation if we follow through the Apostle Paul's insight that through baptism we participate in the

---

19   Beasley-Murray, in *Baptism in the New Testament*, speaks similarly of baptism as a 'trysting place': p. 305.

'body' of Christ. In Jesus Christ God is committed to the utmost extent to materiality, to human flesh. But with the eternal decision of God to be identified totally (in act and being) with a human son, and with the eternal decree that this son should be the means of creating a new human community, God is also committed to taking on the whole body of the universe. Human flesh is after all entangled with the entire organic structure of the cosmos; it could not exist without this context and community in which it is embedded.

Both creation and incarnation therefore tell us that the God who relates God's self to human beings also has a *kind* of relation, and evokes a *kind* of response, within created reality at every level. We hardly yet have a language to describe this reciprocation between God and the natural creation, but the Scriptures provide a poetic portrayal of it, with images such as the seas roaring the praise of God, the rivers clapping their hands, the trees and hills singing for joy, the oaks whirling in adoration, the skies speaking words of witness, the sea monsters playing with Yahweh and the whole universe groaning as if in the pangs of child birth, longing for God to set it free.[20] Thus God makes covenant not only with people, but with 'every living creature that is upon the earth' (Gen. 9:10). In our time, the movement of thought called 'process theology' has depicted nature at every level, including that of sub-atomic particles, as responding to God's 'aims' and desiring 'satisfaction' in a cosmic community of relationships.[21] Even if we do not want to accept this synthesis of science and religion literally, we may at least find it to be a helpful contemporary myth which tries to find words for the mutual influence between God and the world.

Creation is thus a redemptive act, as God lures on all reality to correspond to divine purposes, to reflect the harmony of the vision that pleases God. Following one of the motifs mentioned above, creation is redemption in the sense of overcoming the waters of chaos. But at the same time the particular redemptive acts of God in human *history* will have an effect upon *creation* itself. Whatever relation there may be between God and other parts of the creation, human persons have certainly been given a unique capacity to be sons and daughters of God; so we may believe with the Apostle Paul that when human response to God through faith in the Word incarnate in history is complete, this will have a decisive impact upon the redemption of the natural world. When human beings reach the destiny for which they are intended in Christ, the 'universe itself will enter upon the liberty and splendour of the children of God' (Rom. 8:19).

---

20   Pss. 19:1–4; 29:9; 96:11–12; 98:7–8; 104:26; Rom. 8:19–22. For other relevant scriptural images, see above, ch. 3, p. 56.

21   See e.g. J.B. Cobb and D.R. Griffin, *Process Theology: an Introductory Exposition* (Belfast: Christian Journals, 1977), pp. 63–80.

This brief theological sketch should make clear why the symbolism of water has resonance on both the level of creation and redemption, concerning both natural phenomena and human history. There is no merely random collection of images here – they refer to the activity and self-disclosure of the God who relates to every dimension of the life of the universe. Baptism into the body of Christ means a new depth of relationship between the believer and Christ; it must also involve a new relationship between the individual believer and the whole community of those who are consciously in covenant partnership with God in Christ (the church – 1 Cor. 12:13). But further still, in the light of the commitment of the triune God to the body of the cosmos, baptism means a new relation of believers to as yet unredeemed humanity, and to our whole natural environment.

Thus, in baptism a person becomes involved in a deeper and new way with the web of loving relationships that God weaves with the whole creation. As John Macquarrie puts it, a sacrament 'focuses' the presence of God which we can find elsewhere; God's presence is not limited to the signs of water, bread and wine, but we can discern it most clearly there.[22] This means that when the baptismal candidate, or the community which witnesses the baptism, encounters God anew through this particular water, they will be the more aware of the presence of God in other situations where water is involved in birth, conflict, cleansing, journey or refreshment.

The Scope of Grace

The conveying of grace through created things in baptism, as I have been describing it, has considerable implications for the Baptist claim that baptism has its fullest meaning when *believers* are involved rather than very young infants. Discussion between those who practise infant baptism and those who practice believers' baptism often seems to get stuck in a dispute about the place of grace on the one hand and faith on the other. One often hears it said that infant baptism recognizes the *grace* of God, while believers' baptism stresses the *faith* of the person. I hope to have given a rather different slant on this question by approaching it from the viewpoint of the rooting of baptism in creation.

Baptists should in fact be quite willing to recognize that there are elements of *both* faith and divine grace in the act which is called infant baptism. There is the prevenient grace of God, already at work deep in the being of the child, giving life and wholeness, and enticing it towards a personal response of faith in due time. There is the faith of parents and

---

22   John Macquarrie, *Principles of Christian Theology*, p. 449.

the Christian community, supporting and nurturing the child as it grows. Many Baptists will also recognize that the completed sequence of infant baptism *and* later personal faith in Christ sealed in confirmation constitutes initiation into the church as the body of Christ, and most Baptist churches in England do not therefore require baptism of believers in this situation.[23] When salvation is seen as a process or a journey, as the report *Baptism, Eucharist and Ministry* urges,[24] many Baptists can readily perceive different combinations of grace and faith at different stages of the journey, and can find various ceremonies appropriate to mark the stages.

But for all this, Baptists will find important dimensions of baptism missing in the rite as applied to infants, so that it is hard to use the word baptism with a fullness of meaning. A Baptist will certainly find something lacking in the *faith* expressed there, as the infant himself or herself can vow no personal allegiance to Christ as Lord. But it is not only faith that lacks fullness. It needs to be understood in ecumenical conversations that a Baptist will also want to say that the scope of *grace* in such a baptism is narrower than in the baptism of believers.

After all, grace is not a kind of supernatural substance that is impartially poured out in different circumstances. It is the gracious coming of God, as supremely personal, into relationship with created beings, an encounter in which God is also – in astonishing humility – open to being affected by them and their response. If we understand salvation to be not a momentary event, but a journey of growth, then baptism provides a point within the process when God draws near to transform persons in a special way. Salvation cannot be isolated within the act of baptism (as the variety of Christian experience of conversion testifies), but it can be 'focused' there in the moment when the Christian believer is made part of the covenant community of Christ's disciples. Using an element of creation, water, God offers an opportunity in baptism for a gracious encounter which is rich in experience and associations.

The five water-motifs I have surveyed indicate some of the range of experiences through which God enters into relationship with us in life – experiences of new beginning, cleansing, conflict, crossing boundaries and refreshment of spirit. These experiences which come from living in God's creation are 'focused' in the event of baptism. Moreover, if that encounter is characterized by love then it will be reciprocal, and in coming graciously God will be open to empathy and shared feeling with the believer who is offering himself or herself for radical discipleship. It

---

23   For details, see below, ch. 7, p. 140.

24   *Baptism, Eucharist and Ministry* (Faith and Order Paper 111; Geneva: World Council of Churches, 1982), 'Baptism', paras. 8–10, pp. 3–4.

is an event which *opens meaning* for all who participate in it, and which is therefore truly initiatory. Some meaning is grasped by the person being baptized in the moment of the event; much more is grasped in retrospect as the believer looks back to this moment of decisive meeting with the crucified and risen Christ; meaning expands in those who share in the act of baptism as part of the church community. In the case of the baptism of infants, however, there will inevitably be some *foreclosing* of meaning; because the main participant is a very young infant, the meaning of the grace of God will be mainly limited to the idea (important though it is) of prevenient grace.

Indeed, it is fairly easy to see how the Christian church has continually narrowed the meaning of baptism. Different traditions have tended to overstress one of the five motifs mentioned above, at the expense of others. For example, the Roman Catholic Church has placed major emphasis upon the second motif, the imagery of cleansing; infant baptism has been defined as a washing away of original sin and (in Augustine's influential view), of original guilt. This has enabled the development of a theology in which infants can be the 'proper' subjects of baptism. At the opposite extreme, Baptists have tended to emphasize the aspect of baptism as a boundary marker for believers; they have stressed the fifth motif, a moment of separation from past life and commitment to new kingdom values. Despite the potential of believers' baptism for a richness of meaning, they have sometimes narrowed it to that of 'following Christ through the waters of baptism', a mere phase of obedience on the pilgrim journey.

Protestant churches in the Puritan tradition who baptize infants have usually, following Calvin, seen baptism mainly as a sign of the covenant.[25] Unlike a Baptist picture of the covenant community, this concept of sign is used to justify the baptism of infants as a means of bringing families within the scope of the covenant promises.[26] F.W. Dillistone has argued that this Puritan theology also belongs in the area of 'separation' imagery (what I have designated as the fifth motif), and that it has narrowed the New Testament concept of 'the seal of the Spirit' in baptism to a mere sign which is too closely equivalent to the Jewish sign of circumcision, so losing the dynamic of the presence of the life-giving Spirit.[27]

A Baptist may argue (as I have done above), that only the baptism of believers at a responsible age can adequately draw upon the whole range of water-symbolism, and enable the baptismal pool to be the focus for God's creative-redemptive process. However, in this case, Baptists should

---

25   See Calvin, *Institutes*, II, 4, xiv:5–7, pp. 494–6; xvi:1–5, pp. 529–34.

26   For a Baptist view of the relation of children to the covenant community, see below, ch. 7, pp. 131–9.

27   Dillistone, *Christianity and Symbolism*, pp. 202–6.

be more alert than they have been to the width of the range of significance. Exploration of such imagery as 'descent into the womb' may well help Baptists to understand and value the prevenient grace of God that is involved in the whole nurture of a child in the Christian community before it comes to 'birth' as a morally responsible being, and this may lead them to affirm some of those aspects which are vividly presented in the practice of infant baptism.

In considering the narrowing of the significance of baptism, perhaps the extreme case is those who are suspicious of any 'sacramentalism' at all, and who argue that baptism is merely an *optional* outward ceremony symbolizing an inward grace. They view baptism as just one way of bearing witness to having received salvation. Some may argue here that ritual washings were simply part of Jewish culture, and so the baptism of Jesus should not be given normative status within the life of the church thereafter; after all, it may be pointed out, Jesus himself apparently never baptized. In reply, we may suggest that the whole of the Pauline insight into salvation, being identified with the body of Christ in death and resurrection, relies upon the baptismal metaphor (e.g. Rom. 6:1–6) and it is hard to see how one could be meaningful without the other. However, we may also point to the location of baptism within the whole scene of creation as we have been considering it. This surely confirms the centrality of the rite to human renewal. The character of baptism as a 'creation symbol' gives it a universality; the archetypal symbols of immersion, sprinkling and washing with water are embedded so deeply within the human consciousness that there is something 'given' about a water-ritual, and a worshipping community is bound to be impoverished if it attempts to do without this creation-redemption sacrament.

Baptism, Authority and the Purpose of God

Sacraments can, however, carry overtones of power with them. Baptists cannot help but notice that at times in past history the practice of infant baptism has been misused to support hierarchical structures of authority in church and state. When it was thought that infants must be baptized to grant them salvation and entrance to heaven, then those who had the right of baptizing naturally had a powerful sanction to exercise, and a means of control over people. Believers' baptism underlines a final allegiance to Christ alone, though also affirming that this allegiance is not worked out as a private individual, but within the whole *polis* or human community. Those baptized as believers enter upon a form of church membership which among Baptists (and other dissenting groups arising from the Radical Reformation) is understood to carry responsibilities of active discipleship. The final authority in a local church is the rule of Christ among his disciples, the presence of the risen Lord who has the 'crown rights of the redeemer.' Human authority consists in the responsibility of all the church members, gathered in church meeting, to find the mind and purpose of Christ for their life and mission.

In coming to their consensus the members of the church will draw upon such resources as their spiritual gifts, the counsel of other churches and the insights of a trusted leadership; but they retain the responsibility of making a decision together about what they believe to be the will of Christ. Though Baptists might be surprised to have it so described, their view of the church meeting is therefore quite sacramental,[28] and is rooted in a conviction about grace in creation. They expect the Spirit of God to take material and earthy things – their own bodies, gathered together – and use them for a divine-human encounter, for a means of grace. As in the communion bread, the participants in this meeting expect to 'discern the body of Christ' (1 Cor. 11:29). The initiation into the body of Christ received in baptism is continued in Lord's Supper *and* church meeting. Immersion into the death and resurrection of Christ in baptism is to be renewed in eucharistic celebration and in corporate decision-making about community life-style and service in the world.

Placing the church meeting of the baptized within the perspective of creation also brings a further insight, about the way that decisions are arrived at. While freedom is safeguarded by the mechanism of a democratic vote, the point is not for one block of voters to defeat another, or for a majority to oppress a minority voice. It is to perceive the purpose of Christ among the members of his body. But the question then arises as to what it really means to 'find the mind of Christ' in his body, and here a theology of identification with the 'body' of Christ through baptism in the whole context of creation can help.

All too often, and not only among Baptists, the purpose of God for people is understood to be a fixed programme like a kind of pre-existing divine 'blueprint' or game-plan. In the particular context of a Baptist church meeting, the result may be that when members believe they have found the divine 'plan', those who have not voted for a certain course of action may feel effectively excluded; it seems their views are of no account. It is certainly not only those who practise *infant* baptism who can, as mentioned above, misuse authority in the baptized community. But baptism should point us towards a deeper kind of involvement with the God who has taken on the cosmos as a body, and who has therefore opened God's self to include the responsiveness and creativity of all the members of the body. If God is involved, by free desire, in an organic process of growth with the human and natural community of the world, then while we must seek for the *purposes* of God as expressed in the

28   See further below, ch. 8, pp. 170–4.

incarnate Word of Christ, there is bound to be something open-ended about those purposes. They cannot have the closure of a detailed plan. This God involves the creation in the forming of divine purposes, and to *seek* the mind of God also means to *contribute* to the vision of God.

In practical terms, even when a decision has been made in a Baptist church meeting, the members will want to go on listening to those who have opposed it or been unhappy with it, to gain something from their insights as the decision is worked out in detail in changing circumstances. It also means that while a local meeting of the baptized in Christ cannot be imposed upon by any external authority, it will always be open to listen to the voices of others, aware that it is dependent upon their help in finding the mind of Christ, whether the voices come from wider groupings of churches or from society outside the church.

In baptism, then, the candidate *and* the community find themselves involved in a deeper way in God's relationships with church, human community and cosmos. The water as an element of creation actually enables that participation to take place, evoking such experiences as birth, cleansing, conflict, journey and renewal. These motifs are planted deeply in the human awareness of the natural world, but they also belong to the story of God's pilgrimage with people through history, and are finally focused in the life, death and resurrection of Jesus Christ.

Through this participation, human persons are enabled not only to discern the purposes of God for the universe, but to take a part in shaping them. There is a hint of this in Adrian Mitchell's poem, selected verses from which I began with, for the 'stuff' he celebrates is not only the resources of nature, but what human beings create from it:

> Dankworth's alto is made of it, most of it,
> Scoobdedoo is composed of it
> Plastic
> I like that stuff
>
> Man made fibres and raw materials
> Old rolled gold and breakfast cereals
> Platinum linoleum
> I like that stuff.[29]

This too is the world which God is humble enough to take and use. This is the world into which God was content to be immersed for our sake.

---

29   Adrian Mitchell, 'Stufferation', verses 9–10.

CHAPTER 7

Believers' Baptism: An Act of Inclusion or Exclusion?

The Boundary-marker of Baptism

Here is an instructive story. The old Baptist Chapel in Tewkesbury, Gloucestershire, which dates from the first half of the seventeenth century, gradually fell into disuse as a place of worship over the years. Until quite recently it had been converted into two cottages, and was lived in by a succession of families. Then it was decided to restore it to its former appearance, and workmen set about demolishing and rebuilding. They were puzzled, however, by what appeared to be one odd feature of these cottages: why, they asked, did they have only one coal-hole between them, and why was it so huge? Gently the Baptists explained that this was not a receptacle for keeping coal in, but the baptistery.

I wonder what reactions among Baptists might be to this story, and to the ignorance of the workmen. A typical response might be: 'Well of course they didn't understand – they weren't part of the church fellowship'. The workmen were 'outsiders' – why should they know any better? In our age, many things in a church building are going to be baffling to the average woman or man in the street, but a huge tank for baptism rather than a small font is likely to be more baffling than most. So I suggest we have a parable here: the walls of the baptistery can be a kind of fence, shutting the fellowship of believers into its familiar ways, making it feel at home and secure in its own identity, but shutting others out. Believers' baptism can be a kind of boundary between cultures, a marker between the sub-culture of Baptist Christians and the wider culture of our secular society. It divides the insiders from the outsiders.[1]

The baptism of believers is a door into the gathered community of believers, an act which *includes* someone who professes Christ within the group of his disciples. In the words of the Apostle Paul, we are 'baptized into the body of Christ'. Baptism is not a private, individual act of

---

1   For this idea, see Richard Kidd, 'Baptism and the Identity of Christian Communities' in Fiddes (ed.), *Reflections on the Water*, pp. 87–91.

devotion, but an event in the midst of the congregation: and so it is properly followed by a reception into membership of the church, usually at the Lord's Table. A recent survey of the worship practices of churches in the Baptist Union of Great Britain has shown that this is usually the case in about 70% of its churches, who receive into membership those whom it baptizes, either at the same service or at a later communion service. (It should give us pause for thought, however, that apparently some 24% of the churches surveyed do not link baptism and church membership in any way).[2]

Believers' baptism is thus an act which includes and embraces the professing disciple in fellowship life. But there are critical voices who suggest that in other ways it excludes. In this chapter I want to consider four groups whom the practice is often accused of shutting out: these are (a) half-believers, or those who may be on the way to faith, of whatever age; (b) believing children; (c) members of churches which practise infant baptism; (d) people either with learning disabilities or a mental illness. I want to ask whether these are indeed excluded and made to feel unwelcome by the boundary marker of believers' baptism among Baptists, and if so what can be done about it. After all, together they make up a vast number of people. Here is a significant challenge to Baptists: how to be an open and hospitable people while keeping baptism for believers only.

Welcoming Those on the Way to Faith

Many churches that practise the baptism of infants think of this in terms of offering God's own generous hospitality, widely and freely. I have in mind here not so much paedobaptist Free Churches – notably the United Reformed Church and Methodists – but the Church of England, the Roman Catholic and Orthodox Churches. Their picture is that of a mission field *inside* the borders of the church, as well as outside it. Putting it another way, the church and society around have blurred edges. Inside a parish there will be many people who are half-way to faith, or on a journey towards a saving relationship with God in Christ. They have, as it were, the first stirrings of faith within them, and these need to be fostered and nurtured.

---

2   Christopher J. Ellis, *Baptist Worship Today. A report of two worship surveys undertaken by the Doctrine and Worship Committee of the Baptist Union of Great Britain* (London: Baptist Union, 1999), pp. 21–22. Of those responding, 15% received into membership at the same service as baptism; 47% received into membership at the same or the next convenient communion service; a further 7% received into membership some time later.

It is urged that people may show this longing to know God, and so a desire to discover the true meaning of life, when they bring a baby for baptism. It may of course just be a piece of folk-religion, mere social custom: the christening gown has been handed down in the family from great-grandfather onwards and the new baby just has to wear it. Or the family may fear that something dreadful may happen to the child if it is not 'done'. But the parents may really be on a quest for God at the heart of life, and are beginning to realize this at this wonderful moment of birth. They are at least half-believing, full of wistfulness. By baptizing the child, the church first accepts and welcomes the parents in God's name, and has a reason for going back to them on pastoral visits in future months and years with the aim of bringing them nearer to God. At a crucial moment when their hearts are more open to God than ever before, they are not rejected. Of course, there will also be Christian parents bringing their children into the household of faith, but here we are concerned with those on the edges of the church.

Further, in baptism (it is said) the church proclaims that the grace of God has already been poured out for this child in the life, death and resurrection of Jesus. 'While we were still sinners, Christ died for us' (Rom. 5:8). The believers gathered in the service of baptism declare that God's grace is already at work by the Holy Spirit in this new human life, desiring to bring her or him into a transforming relationship with God's self. This 'prevenient' grace of God is what will make faith possible in future years. The child is thus signed with the sign of God's grace, in hope and expectation that she will make the gifts of God her own in due time. Moreover, as well as the many mysterious ways in which God will surround her by the influences of grace, she has been brought within the borders of the church where God's salvation is known and openly received, and so she will be helped towards her own response of faith by the community of faith, by its prayers and its love. The child may of course refuse God's offer of grace when she grows older and is able to decide for herself: but meanwhile God has already acted in baptism to set her on a path towards salvation.

This account is bound to present Baptists with a strong challenge, as it has many elements of truth in it. This is a picture in which the baptizing of infants and the accepting of their parents creates a field for mission *inside* the boundaries of the church itself. Parents and children are prepared to hear the good news of Christ through an act in which God's gracious welcome is embodied. As a former Archbishop of York, John Habgood, puts it:

A Church which deliberately chooses an open policy [for baptism], which welcomes those whose beliefs may seem inadequate, without patronizing them, and which is not offended by those who seem merely to want to use it for their own convenience, is not thereby saying that its beliefs do not matter.[3]

For all this, Baptists will generally decline to agree that baptism is the most appropriate means to express this open hospitality of God. One aspect of the argument is the characteristic Baptist protest that a very young infant cannot himself or herself have the kind of faith which is required for baptism; the predominant impression given by the New Testament is that baptism is for those who have made repentance towards God and can consciously profess their personal faith in Christ as their Saviour and Lord. It is a powerful moment of testimony to what Christ has achieved in a person's life, and a step of obedience for a disciple following in the footsteps of Christ. As several Baptist writers have stressed, baptism is thus 'an acted creed'.[4] But, as I have already argued in considering the relation of baptism to the created world,[5] this is only part of the case that Baptists can make to the wider church. An equally important question is whether the baptism of infants can express the richness of the grace of God which is promised in the event of baptism, and doubts about this are highlighted by the use of baptism as a means of hospitality. This practice certainly makes clear the *prevenient* grace of God, the gracious work of the Holy Spirit that goes ahead of us, preparing human minds and emotions, and drawing people into the fellowship of God's life. But the New Testament witness is to more than a welcoming grace in baptism, more than an invitation; it speaks of a *transforming* grace.

The baptismal pool may be pictured as a meeting-place between the believer and the triune God. Emil Brunner envisaged baptism as a place of 'divine-human encounter', a 'two-sided happening' involving 'personal correspondence'.[6] The Baptist New Testament scholar George Beasley-Murray uses the term 'trysting-place';[7] although a somewhat archaic form of expression (I have previously used *rendez-vous* myself),[8] it does catch an essential dimension of what the meeting is about. It is

---

3   John Habgood, *Church and Nation in a Secular Age* (London: Darton, Longman and Todd, London, 1983), p. 91.

4   H. Wheeler Robinson, *Baptist Principles* (London: Kingsgate Press, 4th edn, 1945), p. 30; Robinson, *The Life and Faith of the Baptists* (London: Kingsgate Press, 2nd edn, 1946), p. 80; Gilbert Laws, 'Vital Forces of the Baptist Movement', in J.H. Rushbrooke (ed.), *The Faith of the Baptists* (London: Kingsgate Press, 1926), p. 14.

5   See above, ch. 6, pp. 117–22.

6   Emil Brunner, *The Divine-Human Encounter*, trans. A. Loos (London: SCM Press, 1944), pp. 128–35. Brunner's criticism of infant baptism, voiced as it was by a paedobaptist in the Reformed tradition, was enthusiastically received by R. Birch Hoyle in 'Emil Brunner Vindicates the Baptist Position', *Baptist Times*, 30 June 1938, p. 508.

7   Beasley-Murray, *Baptism in the New Testament*, p. 305.

8   See above, ch. 6, p. 117.

about love and faithfulness; it is like a 'tryst' between two lovers. The term has its limits, however, in that this meeting is never entirely private but always in the context of the community; it is in the company of others that the believer comes to meet God – Father, Son and Holy Spirit – with her trusting love, however weak it is. God meets her in everlasting love, to transform her life. The New Testament thus speaks of this meeting with a profusion of pictures of God's grace; it is a moment of new birth (Jn. 3:5, Tit. 3:5), forgiveness and cleansing from sin (Acts 2:38, 1 Cor. 6:11, Heb. 10:22), immersion in the Holy Spirit and the receiving of spiritual gifts (1 Cor. 12:13, Acts 2:38; 10:47), deliverance from evil powers (Col. 1:13), union with Christ (Gal. 3:27), adoption as a child of God (Gal. 3:26), and membership in the body of Christ (1 Cor. 12:13, Gal. 3:27–28).[9]

The act of immersion into water and rising from it pictures death, burial and resurrection with Christ. It plunges the whole person into a multi-media event, engaging both the mind and all the bodily senses, especially seeing and feeling. But according to the New Testament it is more than a visual aid: it is a moment when we actually share with Christ in his death and resurrection (Rom. 6:1–11, Col. 2:11, 1 Pet. 3:21). Christ has shared to the uttermost in our sinful death of judgement and estrangement from God, so that when we die to ourselves with him, we might rise with him to newness of life. The London Confession of Particular Baptists in 1644 states that baptism by immersion 'being a signe, must answer the thing signified', which it defines as:

> first, the washing of the whole soule in the blood of Christ: Secondly, that interest the Saints have in the death, buriall, and resurrection; thirdly, together with a confirmation of our faith, that as certainly as the body is buried under water, and riseth againe, so certainly shall the bodies of the Saints be raised by the power of Christ, in the day of the resurrection...[10]

While Baptist confessions such as this have been anxious not to *confuse* the 'sign' with the 'thing signified', they do look for some real correspondence and *connection* ('answer') between the two. There are, of course, Baptists who think of baptism essentially as a profession of faith and act of obedience, and are suspicious of any 'sacramentalism'. They are too ready to claim their understanding as 'the Baptist position', and are often too unaware of the tradition in Baptist life, going back right

---

9   This and the next paragraph follow closely two paragraphs which I wrote for *Believing and Being Baptized. Baptism, so-called re-baptism, and children in the church. A discussion document by the Doctrine and Worship Committee of the Baptist Union of Great Britain* (Baptist Union, London, 1996), p. 10.

10   Art. XL, Lumpkin, *Baptist Confessions*, p. 167.

to its beginnings, of valuing baptism as a means of God's grace.[11] But I
invite such as these to think back to their own baptism. As they waited to
enter the water, what was in their minds? No doubt there were some
passing thoughts about whether the water would be the right temperature,
some rehearsing of words they might speak if they were to give their
testimony, perhaps some worries about whether the friend with the towel
would be there at the strategic moment. But I suggest that, however
slightly-formed the thought, there was also a real resolve to surrender
themselves anew to Christ, and a desire that they might be 'blessed' in
some way through the event. With regard to worship-acts, Baptists are
sometimes happier with the language of blessing than of 'grace'. In a
recent booklet produced by the Baptist World Alliance, titled *We Baptists*,
there was resistance from some Southern Baptist members of the editorial
group to speaking of 'means of grace' in connection with baptism, while
they agreed on the phrase 'a moment for divine activity (that is, when
God freely meets us anew *with his gracious blessing*)'.[12] A theology of
blessing, however, ought to be explored in the light of the biblical idea
that a blessing is a real and powerful communication of the grace of God.

'Something happens' when a blessing is spoken or acted out, not
because it is a 'magical' formula that forces God's hand, but because
God takes the opportunity to be graciously present and to transform
people by a personal coming to them. It belongs to the class of actions
sometimes called 'prophetic symbolism', and it seems to have been

---

11   Baptist interest in a sacramental approach to baptism was renewed in the
twentieth century by such writers as H. Wheeler Robinson, *Baptist Principles*, pp. 26–
31; Neville Clark, *An Approach to the Theology of the Sacraments* (Studies in Biblical
Theology 17; London: SCM Press, 1956), pp. 29–35; Clark, 'The Theology of
Baptism', in A. Gilmore (ed.), *Christian Baptism* (London: Lutterworth Press, 1959), pp.
306–26; R.E.O. White, *The Biblical Doctrine of Initiation* (London: Hodder and
Stoughton, 1960), pp. 270–317; and G.R. Beasley-Murray, *Baptism in the New
Testament*, pp. 263–305. This has been explored by Anthony R. Cross, *Baptism and the
Baptists. Theology and Practice in Twentieth-Century Britain* (Studies in Baptist History
and Thought 3; Carlisle: Paternoster Press, 2000). However, this twentieth-century
movement only revived a long-standing strand in Baptist thinking, as has been shown
by Anthony R. Cross, 'Dispelling the Myth of English Baptist Baptismal
Sacramentalism', *BQ* 38/8 (2000), pp. 367–91; Stanley K. Fowler, *More than a Symbol:
The British Baptist Recovery of Baptist Sacramentalism* (Studies in Baptist History and
Thought 2; Carlisle: Paternoster, 2002), pp. 10–155; P.E. Thompson, 'A New Question
in Baptist History: Seeking a Catholic Spirit Among Early Baptists', *Pro Ecclesia* 8/1
(1999), pp. 66–72. A significant declaration of baptism as 'a means of grace to all who
receive [it] in faith' was made in the 'Reply of the Churches in Membership with the
Baptist Union to the "Appeal to all Christian People" issued by the Lambeth Conference
of 1920', in Rushbrooke (ed.), *The Faith of the Baptists*, p. 88.

12   *We Baptists*. Study and Research Division, Baptist World Alliance (Franklin,
Providence House, 1999), p. 27; my italics.

reflection on the place of these in the faith of the Old Testament, and the coming of the Holy Spirit through them, that prompted H. Wheeler Robinson to re-emphasize the sacramental nature of baptism.[13] A significant New Testament instance of blessing is the story of Jesus' meeting his disciples behind their locked doors after his resurrection, blessing them with the words 'Peace be with you', and breathing out into them the gift of the Holy Spirit to empower them for mission (Jn. 20:19–23, cf. Lk. 24:49–51).

I suggest that the particular blessings of baptism cannot all be received by an infant who cannot bring his or her own faith to the encounter with God. But there *is* a blessing to be given and received, that of the 'prevenient' grace of God and the prayers of the church. There is a blessing of welcome and acceptance. The Gospel writers seem aware of this as they record the story of Jesus taking young children up in his arms and blessing them (Mk. 10:13–16). This is indeed the story that is usually read at acts of 'infant presentation' in Baptist churches,[14] and it is usual for the minister to follow the example of Jesus in laying hands on the infant's head and pronouncing a blessing such as the words given to Aaron (Num. 6:24–6). This is also an occasion for the acceptance of parents into the church community, even when they seem to have little faith or to come with mixed motives and attitudes. Child and parents are welcomed. If the parents are already members of the church then of course they can join the congregation in making promises to surround the child with Christian nurture, and make special promises of their own as Christian parents; if not, they still have an opportunity for expressing thanksgiving for the birth of the child, and dedicating themselves in general to the responsibilities of being a good parent. The promises will differ according to the faith of the parents, but the blessing of the child will be exactly the same, for it is the blessing of a God who is extravagant in generosity and self-giving love.

As R. L. Child insisted more than fifty years ago, this is not a service of 'infant dedication', as Baptists have sometimes called it, wrongly placing

---

13   See, for example, H. Wheeler Robinson, *The Christian Experience of the Holy Spirit* (Library of Constructive Theology; London: Nisbet & Co., 1928), pp. 192–4; Robinson, *The Life and Faith of the Baptists*, pp. 177–8.

14   See, for example, *Patterns and Prayers for Christian Worship. A Guidebook for Worship Leaders*. Baptist Union of Great Britain (Oxford: Oxford University Press), pp. 110–111. Grantham, *Christianismus Primitivus* (1678) 2.2.1, p. 6, urges those practising infant baptism to follow the bidding of Jesus in presenting children to him and praying for them instead. For a historical account of the service of infant presentation and blessing, see W.M.S. West, 'The Child and the Church: A Baptist Perspective' in William H. Brackney, Paul S. Fiddes and John H.Y. Briggs (eds.), *Pilgrim Pathways. Essays in Baptist History in Honour of B.R. White* (Macon: Mercer University Press, 1999), pp. 75–110.

weight on the story of the infant Samuel, but 'blessing of infants and dedication of parents'.[15] In the blessing there is (at least) a proclamation of the gospel, prayer for the child which 'provides a channel for the grace of God to work'[16] in his or her life, and an acceptance of the child into the sphere of God's gracious influence in the community. A recent discussion document received by the council of the Baptist Union of Great Britain expresses the effect of blessing like this:

> It can be said that the child's relationship to God is 'affected' through this blessing, not in any mechanical or magical way, but in so far as a new relationship is being made with the community of the church in which God is at work through his grace. The love of God towards the child has not of course changed, as if it were not present before; the child is already within the orbit of the love of God through living in his world, but he or she needs to be positively accepted by the Church into the 'embrace of the Body' to deepen this influence.[17]

I am not proposing here that the rite of infant blessing is exactly the same as infant baptism; as I intend to make clear later, baptism in water at whatever age is freighted with a symbolism that makes it a unique 'focal point of the initiation experience'.[18] Here I am simply addressing any who may be worried that restricting baptism to adult believers offers no welcome to those 'on the way' to faith. The point is surely that we need two pictures of mission to those around us. The first is that familiar to those who speak of a 'gathered church': the mission field of those who need wholeness of life seems to lie outside the sharply-drawn boundaries of the church, and baptism is a means of commissioning disciples to be missionaries or servants to this area 'outside'. But there is another picture, in which the sphere of mission lies at least partly inside the blurred boundaries of the community of the church, as it overlaps with society as a whole. In baptizing infants, the 'established churches' begin their care of those among whom mission takes place, both children and their parents. In the first picture, the baptized are *agents* of mission; in the second they are *recipients*. By offering the blessing of infants, I suggest that Baptists too can create a whole field of mission that lies at least partly inside the church.

So the boundary of the fellowship of baptized believers is there, but it is an open boundary, with plenty of room for hospitality and for travellers passing in and out. Of course, Baptist churches have other ways

---

15   R.L. Child, *The Blessing of Infants and the Dedication of Parents* (London: Carey Kingsgate, 1946).

16   *Believing and Being Baptized*, p. 46.

17   *Believing and Being Baptized*, p. 47.

18   A. Gilmore, *Baptism and Christian Unity* (London: Lutterworth, 1966), pp. 63-4.

of opening the fences around the community: through – for example – Sunday Schools, mother and toddler groups, care for the aged, unemployment and business enterprise clubs, and uniformed organizations for young people (less usual now). The very holding of services of 'public worship' makes it possible for people who are 'on the way' to faith to express their sense of thanksgiving for life, their concern for those they love, their worries about the state of the world, and their hopes for the future. They can be helped to begin to speak to God about these issues and feelings, through sharing in hymns, scripture and prayers. We should, then, ask ourselves from time to time whether our worship has become so intense and subjective, so reflective of the total commitment of the baptized, so full of pious catch-phrases, so much an entertainment of the in-group, that it excludes those who simply want to say thank-you to God.

These are not yet members of the body of Christ, not yet limbs and features which as they come together enable Christ to become visible in the world. We might say, however, that they belong in the sense that they are *embraced* by the body, like a child enfolded in its mother's arms.[19] Another New Testament image that has the capacity for expressing different kinds of belonging is the 'household of faith', as a space in which people can dwell in various ways. Those who are 'half-believers' or on the way to faith are like guests or friends in a household, and sometimes such people can become so close to a family that they 'share its tears and laughter',[20] and contribute so deeply to its life that they may not think of themselves as 'outsiders' at all. Yet, in the household of the church, they still need to face the challenge of becoming committed disciples of Christ.

In this new century we are part of a culture that has reacted against the extreme individualism of the Victorian age (and back beyond that, to the Enlightenment). If we are to minister to society as a whole, and to its various social groupings that can no longer be confined to a nuclear family, then we must learn to 'open up space' within the boundaries of the gathered church. We must learn hospitality which is not patronizing and which values people for whom they are. We must let our living space overlap with that of others.

---

19   This image is used in *Believing and Being Baptized*, p. 42. There, however, it is applied to *all* children in the church, including believing children; this is a view that I am modifying in this present chapter.

20   Here I am quoting from Paul Martin, 'Towards a Baptist Ecclesiology Inclusive of Children', *Theology in Context* 1 (2000), p. 50.

Integrating Believing Children

Again, a story. Some while ago there was a special Harvest Festival day at Swindon Central Church, a Local Ecumenical Partnership including Baptists;[21] the theme of the day was water, and several imaginative events were arranged. For example, a woman member of the church walked three miles to the church from her nearby village with a jar of water on her head, as many African women still fetch water today. She spoke about what it felt like to do this heavy task, so that everyone gained an understanding of what countless women are required to do in our world. The water was then poured into communion glasses, and everyone shared in the fruits of her exhausting labour. The baptistery also became a focus of attention. Children filled it with water – brought from closer at hand! Fish were added, and some water plants. The children began to understand that water brings life, and that the waters of baptism bring the most important life of all.

I am sure that this day of shared experience helped the children to feel that the communion table and the baptistery were not strange objects that had nothing to do with them, but in some way belonged to them as well. *Yet*, of course, none of them had actually been baptized in that baptistery, and the children of Baptist parents would not have been baptized at all; many of them had not shared in the Lord's Supper. So the criticism may be made that those practising believers' baptism exclude children from membership of the church. It may be said that they shut out the very persons whom Jesus urged us to become like, if we want to enter the kingdom of God. He put the children in the midst, giving them an honoured place; do we put them on the margins of church life?

This topic overlaps with that of the previous section, but is not quite the same, as here we are concerned with *believing* children rather than 'half-believers'. Earlier I suggested that children who have not yet come to faith may, like adults in the same position, be 'embraced' within the body. This embrace may aptly begin with hands laid on in blessing, and prayer that in due time the child may become a member of the body of Christ. Because, in the Baptist view, baptism is not appropriate for very young children, the words used in the act of blessing will not use baptismal language which declares them *to be* 'members of the body of Christ', as is the case in churches that practice infant baptism. The church prays that they may come to faith in Christ for themselves, be baptized, and so become members of the body in due time. Until they have come to a living faith, they belong by being held within the body, as friends in the household, part of the fellowship (*koinonia*). Although they are

---

21   The church brings together what used to be five congregations – Baptist, United Reformed Church and Methodist – in a single-congregation LEP.

dependent on others in ways that adult believers are not, this does not mean that the whole body cannot learn from them. Indeed, the faith of all cannot grow without listening to their witness.

This is true even of very young children, and worship can be enriched by truly integrating them within it. I do not just mean 'having a talk for children', which may be quite inappropriate for any but the older ones. I mean listening to their contribution to worship. For one period of the worship at least, it is good to have the whole fellowship together. As the youngest children cry in frustration or anger or tiredness, we can take this into our prayers: we can hear through them the crying of children throughout the world, many of whom are crying through hunger, or because they have lost their parents in war, or because they are being abused. It is a loss to the prayer-life of the whole congregation when parents have to take crying children out, or feel under pressure to do so. For ten or fifteen minutes at least their cries can become our prayers of intercession. As young children laugh or giggle, let us listen and try to re-capture the sheer unspoilt enjoyment they take in the world, and its absurdities – even those of the minister. Let their laughter help us to laugh before God. As slightly older children ask questions, or make comments in loud voices, let us not hush them, but think about what they have said: let their questions, asked without the slightest worry of appearing foolish, become our questions to God in prayer, for God showed the greatest truth through a cross which seemed to the wise to be sheer foolishness.

These are just some examples of the way that children *on the way to faith* can deepen our worship of God, as they are embraced in the fellowship of the body. Children do not need to be baptized to be welcomed and included. We do not have to follow the argument that goes like this: children should belong to the church; baptism is the way to belong; therefore infants should be baptized. Rather, there are *different ways of belonging.*[22] Children belong because of the grace of God that goes ahead of us.[23] But a more difficult criticism remains. What about the

---

22   This is the point made by *Believing and Being Baptized*, pp. 44–5.

23   Thomas Helwys, *A short and plaine proofe ... that all men are redeamed by Christ. As also, that no infants are condemned* (Amsterdam?: 1611) maintains that 'by grace Christ hath freed Adam, and in him all mankind, from that sin of Adam', and so infants are within salvation until they consent, responsibly, to sin. Grantham, *Christianismus Primitivus*, 2.2.1, pp. 3–4, argues that all young children, having no personal guilt of their own, are 'within the verge of this vast Body' (i.e. the church universal), and may 'by the grace of God' be heirs of the salvation achieved by Christ. Particular Baptists took a more restricted view of those covered by redemption, but still stressed that children of believers belonged in the church; John Tombes, *Examen of the Sermon of Mr Stephen Marshall about Infant Baptism* (London: 1645), pp. 32–3, describes them as 'born in the bosom of the Church, of Godly parents who ... will

136

Tracks and Traces

children who *have* come to a real faith in Christ for themselves? Perhaps they are children of Christian families, and are gradually growing up within faith, making their own response to God as they hear the story of Jesus. It will obviously not be the same kind of response that an adult will make, but will have its own reality and value within the particular experience of a child.

Paul Martin makes the point that children like this are not, like others, on the way *towards* faith but they are making a journey *within* faith. Appealing to studies in faith development, he suggests that they may indeed be 'moving towards an expression of faith that is appropriate for adults, but their journey may nevertheless be one *in* Christian faith.'[24] Even if the journey towards an adolescent and an adult faith is a rough one, involving crisis, trauma, doubt and confusion, it is still a journey marked by a basic trust in God. Not all children in the church are thus making the same journey. Only some are journeying on the road of faith, but for those who are it seems both proper and important to affirm that they are members of the body of Christ. They are more than embraced in the body; they *form* part of the body that embraces others. They are members in the sense of helping to make up the identity of the covenant community in which Christ takes bodily, material form.[25]

Why then, it may be asked, should they not be baptized? Is it excluding such believing children from a means of grace if baptism is not offered to them until the age of – say – thirteen or fourteen? Baptist churches in the Southern United States baptize regularly at the age of eight, and in some congregations children have been baptized as early as four. If children can believe, why cannot they receive the baptism of believers? Here I believe that the tradition of English Baptist church life is right to ask children to wait until later. Baptism is not simply believers' baptism, but a 'disciples' baptism'. It is a moment for taking up the responsibilities of carrying our cross, suffering opposition for the sake of Christ, and sharing in the mission of God in the world. It is an occasion when the Spirit gives gifts for ministry, and calls us to use them in some vocation in life. It is not right to impose these demands and burdens on a child, for whom the playfulness of childhood is something which anyway passes too quickly away. There is something about the Victorian phrase

---

undoubtedly educate them in the true faith of Christ.' On the whole matter, see Michael Walker, 'The Relation of Infants to Church, Baptism and Gospel in Seventeenth Century Baptist Theology', *BQ* 21/6 (1966), pp. 242–62.

24   Martin, 'Towards a Baptist Ecclesiology Inclusive of Children', pp. 7–8; similarly, Anne Dunkley, *Seen and Heard. Reflections on Children and Baptist Tradition* (The Whitley Lecture 1999–2000; Oxford: Whitley Publications, 1999), pp. 34–7. Cf. James Fowler, *Stages of Faith* (Harper and Row, San Francisco, 1981), pp. 91–114, 274–81.

25   See below, ch. 8, pp. 184–5.

'little soldiers of Christ' that ignores the particular experience of being a child and thrusts adult duties upon them.[26] I have to confess that I find the American custom of 'child-preachers' and 'child-healers' closer to the ethos of child film-stars than ministry to the world. Jesus himself seems to have waited until he was thirty to begin a preaching ministry.

For some children there will thus be a considerable gap of time between believing and being baptized. How then can we apply the rich and profuse New Testament language of salvation to the event of baptism itself? Are such children not already 'saved', sharing in the benefits of Christ's redemption? Indeed they are, but then the same gap appears in adult life. The very notion of 'believers' baptism', which requires someone already to profess faith before being baptized means that there will always be a gap between entering upon salvation (conversion) and baptism. For some this will be a short space of time, especially for those coming from outside the church who have experienced a sudden, radical change of life. For others it may be a period of some years, as was not unusual in the life of the church in the first four centuries. Baptists must then reckon with a process of initiation, or beginning the Christian life. The first directing of conscious faith towards Christ will be initiated by the grace of God, and must be accompanied by an act of the Holy Spirit bringing the believer into fellowship with Christ. As James D.G. Dunn notes, in the thought of the Apostle Paul 'the Spirit is the beginning of the salvation process'; whatever relation this had in temporal sequence to water-baptism, 'it was by receiving the Spirit that one became a Christian'.[27] If we also want to affirm that believers are 'incorporated into Christ' through water-baptism, the 'beginning' of Christian life must therefore be an extended process not a single moment.

We can understand the relation of coming-to-faith and baptism with the help once again of the picture of a journey, a 'Pilgrim's Progress'. This is indeed true of the New Testament presentation of salvation, which is not a single point, but a process or a journey in life. Different writings give us three senses or tenses for salvation. Christians *have been saved* through the once-for all event of the cross of Jesus (e.g. Eph. 2:8); we are *being saved* as we are grow day by day in our healing relationship with God and are gradually made more like Christ (e.g. 1 Cor. 1:18); we *shall be saved* at the final appearing of Christ in glory (e.g. Rom. 5:9–10). We cannot know the mysterious beginning of our salvation, far back in the

---

26   Similarly, Grantham, *Christianismus Primitivus*, 2.2.1, p. 6, argued that children of believers were 'related to the visible church', but that they should not be 'brought to particular duties of the New Covenant' in baptism; unlike my present argument, he did not however regard them as 'visible members' of the local church.

27   James D.G. Dunn, 'Baptism and the Unity of the Church in the New Testament', in Michael Root and Risto Saarinen (eds.), *Baptism and the Unity of the Church* (Grand Rapids: Eerdmans Publishing/ Geneva: WCC Publications, 1998), pp. 82–3.

secret purposes of God, who begins a work of 'prevenient' grace in
drawing human hearts to God's self. We cannot fully know what the end
will be like, what it will really mean to have a 'body of glory' and live a
new creation. Whenever the process of salvation actually began for us,
baptism can be a decisive moment, a high point in the whole process of
'being saved'. This is a meeting-place provided for us, to which God
promises to come in order to meet our faith with divine grace, although
we also meet God in many other times and places in life.

Shortly I want to apply this insight to the question of the openness of
Baptists to adult believers who have received infant baptism. But for the
moment let us continue to think about the place of believing children in
the church. For children growing in faith, baptism will mark a decisive
point within their whole journey of salvation. They will have passed
through various stages of trusting Christ, as more and more of Christian
truth dawns upon them (and, if experts in child development are to be
believed, their way of thinking becomes more conceptual). Emerging
from childhood to young adulthood, ready to take on a range of
responsibilities in life, they reaffirm their faith in Christ and willingly
embrace discipleship with all its duties and privileges. They covenant with
fellow believers and with God in baptism, and God bestows the Spirit
graciously upon them in a new way to equip them for a life of ministry.

At first sight it may seem that the words of the Apostle Paul in 1
Corinthians 12:12–14 stand against the naming of not-as-yet-baptized,
but believing, children as 'members' of the body of Christ:

> For just as the body is one and has many members, and all the members of the body,
> though many, are one body, so it is with Christ. For in the one Spirit we were all
> baptized into one body... Indeed, the body does not consist of one member but of
> many.

The exegetical problem is, of course, solved if we understand the baptism
in view here *only* as baptism in the Spirit, with no direct reference to
water-baptism.[28] But with Romans 6:1–4 in mind, it seems most likely
that Paul is speaking here about baptism in Spirit *and* water. The point of
the passage, however, is not to define who are, and who are not, members
of the body of Christ. Paul's aim is to describe the *unity* of the body. As
one commentator puts it, 'Indeed, despite the considerable literature on
this text suggesting otherwise, Paul's present concern is not to delineate
how an individual becomes a believer, but to explain how they, though
many, are one body.'[29] What makes them one in their diversity is the

28   So Dunn, *Jesus and the Spirit*, pp. 261–2. I consider the relation between
baptism in Spirit and water below, pp. 148–50.
29   Gordon D. Fee, *The First Epistle to the Corinthians* (New International
Commentary on the New Testament; Grand Rapids: Eerdmans, 1987), p. 603.

reception of the one Spirit. Paul, then, is writing to those who have been baptized, to urge them to use the gifts they have been given by the Spirit on that occasion for the sake of the one body of which they are individually members, and to value the gifts of others. It is clear that nobody can be baptized without either becoming a member of the body of Christ or being immersed more deeply into the body.[30] But we need not deduce from this text that those who are on the way to baptism in water, and so as yet unbaptized, are not already members of Christ through the Spirit, nor that they have no contribution to make to the body.

If we are not to exclude believing children in our fellowship we thus need to think in a more open way about what 'membership' means. Believing children are already members of the body of Christ, but they have not yet covenanted with other members; they are not yet on the roll of disciples available for service. They are members of the body, but not yet commissioned. What has been regarded as reception into church membership in Baptist tradition is actually, for them, this moment of commissioning. Before this, children do not have a vote in church meeting, but they do have *voices* to which we need to listen as we think about the meaning of the life and mission of the church. As members of the body of Christ, they supply some of the limbs through which Christ will become visible. The face of Christ will have empty patches if the features they supply are missing. Outside the church children are increasingly being listened to as they speak about their experience of being educated, or receiving medical care, or (alas) suffering abuse. They are no longer expected to be seen but not heard. We need to listen to the stories of *all* children; and among these we need to discover the way that children experience salvation in their own way, and know the presence of Christ with them. Christ wants to show himself to us through them, not through 'child-preachers' but through their simply being children.

Being Hospitable to Other Christians

In the ecumenical church of 'Christ the Cornerstone' in Milton Keynes, there is both a font and an open baptistery. This is not unusual in churches that combine Baptist congregations with those that practise infant baptism. What is more unusual about this new building is that water flows constantly from font to baptistery, and back from baptistery to font.[31] Here is a sign of hope that churches now divided by baptismal

---

30   I spell out the idea of a process of incorporation below, pp. 150–2.

31   A similar arrangement was, however, already also part of the design of Swindon Central Church. The Church of 'Christ the Cornerstone' brings together Baptist,

practice may one day be fully united. The one water runs between two pools, and as you enter the building you hear immediately the sound of gentle, rushing water. When I preached there one Sunday I was disappointed to find that the water pump was turned off for the hour of worship; I would have liked the sound of flowing water to have formed a background for at least the prayers of intercession for our world.

In an age when all Christian churches are being urged to recognize each others' baptism, and to affirm a 'common baptism',[32] Baptists appear to be exclusive. In the UK, for example, they do not share in the common baptismal certificate that is used by some other members of the 'Churches Together...' ecumenical process. It seems that believers' baptism is a boundary that shuts other Christians out, in so far as those practising it as the only form of baptism cannot simply and straightforwardly affirm the baptism of others as infants. Of course, there are ways of showing hospitality, of opening out fellowship to welcome others. In the recent survey of 'Baptist Worship Today', it became apparent that only 17% of churches in the Baptist Union of Great Britain require believers' baptism for people to be members in any way; 51% admit to full membership on profession of faith alone, and another 24% admit to a kind of associate membership without believers' baptism.[33] But we should notice that this is an openness which is based on recognizing people's faith as Christian believers, as true disciples of Christ, and in itself does not imply any theological view of their baptism as infants. It can lead to people becoming members without any kind of baptism at all, which is a curious situation for a church called 'Baptist'. Pain can also be caused on all sides when the question of so-called 're-baptism' arises, especially in Local Ecumenical Partnerships where there

---

Anglican, Methodist, United Reformed Church and Roman Catholic congregations in a Local Ecumenical Partnership.

32   For example, in the recent discussions about the meaning of *koinonia*: see Thomas F. Best and Günther Gassmann (eds.), *On the Way to Fuller Koinonia* (Faith and Order Paper 166; Geneva: WCC Publications, 1994), pp. 268–77.

33   Ellis, *Baptist Worship Today*, p. 23. Elsewhere in Europe some form of 'associate membership' is widespread; sometimes in post-communist Eastern Europe this is driven by the need for Christians to register with the state as members of a particular church (e.g. Croatia). Fully 'open membership' is less usual, but some churches in Germany, Sweden and Denmark practise it. Furthermore, a number of Baptist churches in the Nordic countries have adopted a form of 'transferred membership' (the 'Aarhus model') by which believers who have been baptized in infancy and are in good standing in their own denomination will be received as members by transfer letter; similarly, most churches in Italy will not require believers' baptism of those baptised as infants in Protestant denominations (mainly Waldensian and Methodist). Outside Europe, churches tracing their roots to the Southern Baptists of the USA tend to insist on closed membership, while churches in partnership with British Baptists or the American Baptist Churches USA are more likely to allow for open membership.

is an attempt being made to live together without boundaries and partitions. When someone already baptized as an infant asks for believers' baptism, this will cause offence to infant-baptizer partners, but to believer-baptists raises questions of freedom of conscience before God.[34] Whatever happens, it seems there will be hurt somewhere.

A way forward which will avoid excluding each other may lie in regarding baptism as one moment in a larger process of initiation, or the beginning of the Christian life. In the past Baptists have compared the events of one baptism with another; the question has been, 'is infant baptism true Christian baptism'? But in thinking about the place of children, I offered the image of a journey of salvation in which baptism played a part. If we are not to use baptism as a means of exclusion, we must begin to compare not single moments but *journeys*, and this means listening to others' stories of their journey.[35] One journey, a Baptist experience, may be from infant blessing through Christian nurture in childhood to believers' baptism, laying on of hands for gifts of the Spirit, and then increasing use of those gifts in ministry in the world. An Anglican or Reformed journey might be from infant baptism, through Christian nurture in childhood, to public profession of faith, laying on of hands in confirmation for gifts of the Spirit, to be used in ministry in the world. Another journey that can be found in all churches would be from hearing the story of Jesus for the first time as an adult, repentance and conversion, believers' baptism, laying on of hands and consequent serving.

We are in a broken situation where churches have different beliefs about baptism, due to different interpretations of scripture and different paths they have taken in history. Without abandoning their convictions, Baptists might be able to value and affirm someone's *whole* journey of experience, and not just the moment of public profession of faith on which attention is usually fixed; they might be able gladly to recognize how God has used every stage of the journey, including baptism in infancy, for saving purposes. Correspondingly, those who baptize infants as well as believers (since all churches practise believers' baptism in the case of older converts) might feel more free to offer *some* parents the option of delaying the baptism of their child until a later age, with the alternative of a service of infant blessing.

The often-quoted report *Baptism, Eucharist and Ministry (BEM)* did in fact propose that churches should seek mutually to recognize whole

---

34   Agreements on the process by which candidates baptized as infants may, after careful counselling, be baptized as believers, have been concluded with the Methodist Church and the United Reformed Church. These agreements have been reprinted in *Baptism and Church Membership*, pp. 48–53.

35   This is essentially the approach taken by *Baptism and Church Membership*, p. 13.

patterns of initiation. While its phrase 'common baptism' has become a touchstone for ecumenical discussion, the report was realistic in seeing that the mere fact that all churches practised some form of baptism would not in itself achieve the mutual recognition of each other's baptism as 'a sign and seal of our common discipleship'. It suggested that:

> Churches are increasingly recognizing one another's baptism as the one baptism into Christ when Jesus Christ has been confessed as Lord by the candidate or, in the case of infant baptism, when confession has been made by the church (parents, guardians, godparents and congregation) *and affirmed later by personal faith and commitment.*[36]

The phrase 'and affirmed later' is attached clearly to the clause beginning 'when'. This is how, it suggests, mutual recognition is possible, *when* baptism is part of a whole journey into faith. What can be recognized by those practising believers' baptism, it suggests, is infant baptism plus a confession of personal faith. The commentary to clause 12 also spells out this mutual recognition of whole patterns or processes of initiation, stressing that both forms of baptism (infant and believers') require to be set in the context of Christian nurture, in which the baptized person – at any age – needs to grow in an understanding of faith:

> In some churches which unite both infant-baptist and believer-baptist traditions, it has been possible to regard as equivalent alternatives for entry into the church both a pattern whereby baptism in infancy is followed by a later profession of faith and a pattern whereby believers' baptism follows upon a presentation and blessing in infancy.

The article then urges all churches to consider whether they, too, cannot 'recognize equivalent alternatives in their reciprocal relationships'. That these equivalent alternatives are not simply the different forms of baptism but whole patterns of initiation is made clear by the 'clarification' of this clause offered by the official report on the responses made to *BEM* (1990):

> Some churches ask what is meant by 'equivalent alternatives'... It is not the act of "infant baptism" and the act of "believers'/adult baptism" in themselves that are there proposed as "equivalent alternatives", but rather two total processes of initiation which the text recognizes.[37]

---

36   *Baptism, Eucharist and Ministry*, 'Baptism', para. 15, p. 6, under the heading 'Towards mutual recognition of baptism.' My italics.

37   *Baptism , Eucharist and Ministry 1982–1990. Report on the Process and Responses* (Faith and Order Paper 149; Geneva: WCC Publications, 1990), p. 109.

That this had been intended all along was understood by the Baptist Union of Great Britain in its original response to *BEM*, when it commented that 'It has long been clear that a total process of Christian initiation wherein, at some point, all the necessary elements – including responsible faith-commitment – find a place offers the most promising way forward to mutual recognition on the baptismal issue.'[38] Other Baptist statements since then have underlined the desirability of comparing, not one isolated moment of baptism with another, but the whole sequence of events which mark the beginning of the Christian life and discipleship.[39] The Baptist view will be that the process of initiation has not come to an end until a baptismal candidate exercises his or her own faith in Christ. If this cannot be found within the event of baptism itself, as in the case of the baptism of infants, then initiation will have to be 'stretched' in some way to accommodate it. Traditionally this moment has been located in western churches within confirmation, but whether or not it takes this particular form, Baptists will expect personal faith (arising from divine grace) to be a part of Christian *beginnings*.

However, appeal to a common *process* of Christian beginnings, or a common *journey* into faith and salvation runs somewhat against the stream of another momentum of thought which has swelled larger since the publication of *BEM*. There is a widely-held view among churches practising infant baptism that there should be a 'unified rite' of initiation, bringing the aspects which have been variously signified by baptism, chrismation/confirmation and first communion as close together as possible.[40] The influence of the baptismal theology of the Orthodox Church here has been pervasive, but among western Protestant paedobaptist churches it has not led to a sequence of rites closely linked in time, but rather to a different kind of 'integration'. In this approach, the gift of the Spirit and incorporation into Christ is located entirely in the event of water-baptism itself. Baptism is regarded as 'complete sacramental initiation'. Any act of anointing or laying on of hands that

---

38   Max Thurian (ed.), *Churches Respond to BEM: Official Responses to the 'Baptism, Eucharist and Ministry' Text* (6 volumes; Geneva: WCC Publications, 1986–88), 1, p. 71.
39   E.g. *Believing and Being Baptized*, pp. 28–33; Paul S. Fiddes, *Believers' Baptism: an Act of Inclusion or Exclusion?* (Hertfordshire Baptist Association, 1999), pp. 14–15; S. Mark Heim, 'Baptismal Recognition and the Baptist Churches', in Root and Saarinen (eds.), *Baptism and the Unity of the Church*, pp. 156–9, 162–3; George R. Beasley-Murray, 'The Problem of Infant Baptism: An Exercise in Possibilities', in *Festschrift Günter Wagner*, ed. Faculty of Baptist Theological Seminary, Rüschlikon (Bern: Peter Lang, 1994), pp. 12–13.
40   See, for example, a Lutheran view by Eugene L. Brand, 'Rites of Initiation as Signs of Unity' in Root and Saarinen (eds.), *Baptism and the Unity of the Church*, pp. 134–6.

follows baptism, whether at the time (Orthodox chrismation) or later on (western 'confirmation') cannot be seen as part of sacramental initiation, though they certainly are part of Christian growth.

Traditionally among western paedobaptist churches, there has been a kind of 'two-stage' view of initiation or Christian beginnings. Despite the fact that confirmation was a late development in the west (ninth century), and despite ambiguity about whether candidates were confirming their faith or whether God was confirming (establishing) their salvation, some view of an extended process prevailed. The two rites might be understood as two sacramental acts in sequence, or two parts of the same sacrament divided in time.[41] In the Reformed tradition, *completion* of initiation in confirmation was thus seen to be necessary to leave place for the confession of personal faith. By contrast, however, the recent Toronto Statement on Christian initiation in the Anglican Communion, 'Walk in Newness of Life' (1991) makes the unequivocal claim that 'Baptism is *complete sacramental initiation* and leads to participation in the eucharist'.[42] The rite of confirmation is affirmed as having a continuing pastoral role as a means of 'renewal of faith' among the baptized, or a reaffirmation of the baptismal covenant, but it is not to be seen in any way as a completion of initiation.[43]

This example shows the tensions that arise, however, with this approach. The authors of the report do not seem to be able to avoid the image of a process of initiation entirely, since they approve 'the recovery of the earlier tradition of the church that eucharist is in fact the fulfilment and sacramental completion of the initiatory process.'[44] This is despite the insistence elsewhere in the report that baptism alone is 'complete sacramental initiation'. If *eucharist* is after all needed to complete the

---

41   See, for example, *Baptism and Confirmation*. A report submitted by the Church of England Liturgical Commission to the Archbishops of Canterbury and York in November 1958 (London: SPCK, 1959), pp. xii–xiii.

42   David R. Holeton (ed.), *Christian Initiation in the Anglican Communion. The Toronto Statement 'Walk in Newness of Life'*. The Findings of the Fourth International Anglican Liturgical Consultation, Toronto 1991 (Grove Worship Series 118; Bramcote: Grove Books, 1991), 'Principles of Christian Initiation' c, p. 5.

43   'Walk in Newness of Life', section 3:19–20, pp. 17–18. The later Anglican report *On The Way. Towards an Integrated Approach to Christian Initiation* (London: Church House Publishing, 1995) makes an attempt to find a way between 'sacramental completeness' of baptism and 'initiatory process'. Deliberately building on the Toronto statement, this works out the principles stated there into practical arrangements for 'the welcome and nurture of new Christians' in the Christian community. In the case of those baptized in infancy, it regards their journey into active faith as a 'process of initiation'; but in order not to undermine the sacramental completeness of baptism, this journey is called '*Christian* initiation' rather than the 'sacramental initiation' which begins the journey: see pp. 37–8, 93.

44   'Walk in Newness of Life', section 3:6, p. 15.

process, then why not *confirmation* or some similar occasion for a
personal confession of faith? What perhaps is needed is a sacramental
theology in which baptism, at whatever age, is not incomplete as *baptism*,
but is incomplete as *initiation*. If the practice of believers' baptism is not
to exclude, we must thus attempt an account of initiation which, while
recognizing the integrity of two practices of baptism, is as inclusive as
possible.[45]

Initiation: A Theology of Inclusion

If we are to speak of a process of initiation in which baptism may stand
either near the beginning (infant baptism) or near the end (believers'
baptism), we need constructively to develop a theology of initiatory
process. This must support any attempt to compare 'equivalent
processes', as *Baptism, Eucharist and Ministry* proposes. What we need is
a theology, and not just a practice, of inclusion. Here I suggest that there
are three dynamics which may help us, each being an interplay of
balancing factors, and all depending on a theological view of baptism as
immersion into the threefold fellowship of God who is Trinity.

An Interplay of Grace and Faith

Christian initiation as a process or journey is, first, characterized by an
interplay of divine grace and human faith at all stages. The journey
begins in the hidden depths of prevenient grace, at work beneath the
surface of human life and consciousness, originating in the eternal desire
of God for fellowship with human persons. We are called to respond to
God's project in creation with trust and obedience, and initiation into this
partnership for any person ends with his or her conscious and responsible
response. At any stage in this process of making a partnership (or
covenant), baptism can be a meeting-place between grace and faith and
so can focus the two realities. We need to abandon the stereotypes that
infant baptism only expresses divine grace, and that believers' baptism
only witnesses to human faith.

However, we must recognize that the *nature* of 'grace' and 'faith' will
be different at different stages of the journey, or at different phases of

---

45   The next section follows closely a section in my article, 'Baptism and the
Process of Christian Initiation' in Stanley E. Porter and Anthony R. Cross (eds.),
Dimensions of Baptism. Biblical and Theological Studies (JSNT Supplement Series 234;
Sheffield: Sheffield Academic Press, 2002), pp. 295–303, used by kind permission of the
publishers.

Christian nurture. 'Grace' and 'faith' are not blank counters. They indicate movements of *relationship* between God and human life – the self-giving movement of God towards creation and the trustful movement of human beings towards God. Grace and faith are aspects of participation in God, of being drawn into the interweaving movements of relationship in the triune life, which are like relations between a Father and Son, ever renewed and opened to the future by a life-giving Spirit.[46] In the baptism or the blessing of an infant, the nature of faith is the corporate faith of the community and the vicarious faith of sponsors, full of hope for what this child can be. It is not the trusting response of the child himself or herself. The nature of grace is essentially prevenient, a surrounding of the child with the gracious presence of God, in and outside the church community, grace taking every opportunity to draw this child deeper into the life of God and God's mission in the world as he or she grows up. Faith will then show different characteristics at different stages of human development, sometimes defined as 'experienced', 'affiliative', 'searching' and 'mature' faith;[47] in a manner suitable for the stage in the journey, faith will be 'owned' by a person during the last two of these phases.[48] In the baptism of a believer of responsible age or in some rite of commitment like confirmation, there will be the faith of the community *and* the 'owned faith' of the individual. In turn this faith will be responding to grace which is not only prevenient but transformative, empowering the believer to share in God's own ministry of reconciliation. Since grace and faith are interwoven in relationship, the nature of God's gracious approach to a person is bound to differ according to the nature of human faith which is possible. For those who practise infant baptism and some later rite of renewal and commitment there are then not 'two stages' of initiation but a continuum with at least two focal points within it.

The statement of the influential 'Ely Report' of the Church of England that after baptism 'there can be no place for further degrees of initiation' or 'no place for any degrees of being "in Christ" or "in the Spirit"'[49] therefore seems to reflect too static view of the relation

---

46   For this dynamic view of Trinity, see David Cunningham, *These Three are One. The Practice of Trinitarian Theology* (Oxford: Blackwell, 1998), pp. 58–74; Fiddes, *Participating in God*, pp. 28–50.

47   So John H. Westerhoff in John H. Westerhoff and Gwen N. Kennedy, *Learning Through Liturgy* (New York: Seabury Press, 1978), pp. 163–9. Fowler, *Stages of Faith*, pp. 119–211, proposes six stages: undifferentiated, intuitive-projective, mythic-literal, synthetic-conventional, individuative-reflective, conjunctive and universalizing.

48   Cf. Westerhoff, *Learning Through Liturgy*, pp. 167–8, 175, recommending 'a covenant to assume responsibility for their own faith' at about the age of thirteen.

49   *Christian Initiation. Birth and Growth in the Christian Society* (Westminster: Church of England Board of Education, 1971), pp. 27–31.

between God and human persons. There is, of course, an interplay between grace and faith throughout the whole of life as a 'baptismal process', a daily journey of dying and rising with Christ.[50] But I am suggesting that there is a specific range of interplay that belongs to the period of initiation, extending over one section of the journey, a phase that we call 'the beginning'. How then shall we demarcate the ending of this section, and say that initiation has come to end? It cannot be a matter of salvation having been finished, since salvation must be a life-long (possibly an eternal) process of 'being saved', being transformed into the image of God which is visible in Christ. The 'baptismal process' of life is also a journey of salvation. Questions such as 'is Baptism sufficient for salvation, or is some other rite needed?' are altogether then on the wrong track. I suggest that the section of the journey of salvation which is called 'initiation' is about becoming a disciple, about responding to the call to be a disciple and taking up the responsibilities of a disciple. Faith must become an ethical response before the beginning has come to an end. Thus far Karl Barth is surely right when he insists that the beginning of Christian life involves 'the grateful Yes of man to God's grace... [which] must become at once the Yes of a grateful work... to the foundation of the Christian life belongs the ready doing of this work.'[51] Though Barth adds immediately that this first step is 'empowered' by grace, he unfortunately divides the human 'Yes' from the divine 'Yes', baptism in water from baptism in Spirit, as two different moments. Baptists will agree with Barth that the 'grateful Yes' is most appropriately located in believers' baptism,[52] but unlike Barth many will also want to locate *God's* Yes in this event; Barth makes it purely a human act of obedience, responding to a prior baptism with the Holy Spirit.[53]

Those who practise believers' or disciples' baptism will find it disclosing the particular kind of interplay of grace and faith that happens towards the end of the process; those practising infant baptism will have a focus of the particular interplay that happens near the beginning. Baptism, in this view, is always 'complete' for what it is: there is nothing defective about the presence of the kind of grace and faith *appropriate* to

50   See Gordon Lathrop, 'The Water that Speaks: the *Ordo* of Baptism and its Ecumenical Implications', in Best, Thomas F. and Heller, Dagmar (eds.), *Becoming a Christian. The Ecumenical Implications of Our Common Baptism* (Faith and Order Paper 184; Geneva: WCC Publications, 1999), pp. 24–8.

51   Barth, *Church Dogmatics*, IV/4, p. 42.

52   For the link between baptism and morality, or a kind of 'ethical sacramentalism', see Robinson, *Baptist Principles*, p. 13; Beasley-Murray, *Baptism in the New Testament*, pp. 284–5; White, *Biblical Doctrine of Initiation*, p. 271.

53   This is strangely at odds with his earlier insistence that all divine self-revelation is mediated 'sacramentally' through secular objects: see *Church Dogmatics*, II/1, pp. 50–62.

the point in the process where it happens. Barth's polemical reference to infant baptism as 'half-baptism' misses the point here. But in no case can baptism be complete *initiation*. In the case of infant baptism the later moment of freely accepted discipleship will belong to the foundation or beginning of Christian life; eucharist and confirmation (or some other rite of laying on hands) will not complete baptism, but they will complete initiation. In the case of believers' baptism, the apprehending of the person by God's grace before baptism, prior faith and first communion are all part of the process. Baptism in the triune Name is a sort of 'snapshot' or 'freeze frame' of a flowing movement, a moment symbolizing the whole but not containing the whole. Advocates of believers' baptism may regret that the picture is taken so early with the baptism of infants; they will prefer that the particular interplay of grace and faith in the life of the young child be expressed in the rite of infant blessing. However, there is a good case for saying that the symbol will be undermined if the picture is taken more than once.

An Interplay of Spirit and Water

There has been a long dispute in the history of the church about the relation of the Spirit to water-baptism. Especially relevant to our concerns is the Pauline concept of the 'seal of the spirit' which has been a storm-centre of different interpretations. The majority of New Testament scholars locate the 'seal' in water-baptism, as the primary endowment of the Spirit, enabling and accompanying the participation of the believer in the death and resurrection of Jesus, and giving the believer a foretaste of the reality of the new creation.[54] It is thus a parallel concept to 'baptism in the Spirit' and coincides with baptism in water. Others detach the 'seal' from water baptism, placing it either before or afterwards. James Dunn argues, like Karl Barth, that the action of being 'stamped' (sealed) with the Spirit or 'immersed' (baptized) in the Spirit is the gift of God which begins the process of salvation, and is separate in New Testament thinking from water baptism. He is concerned that the church has given water baptism the prominence that is really due to the Spirit.[55] By contrast, Orthodox exegesis has followed the practice of the third century

---

54   See G.W.H. Lampe, *The Seal of the Spirit: A Study of the Doctrine of Baptism and Confirmation in the New Testament and the Fathers* (London: Longmans, Green, 1951), pp. 53–63; Beasley-Murray, *Baptism in the New Testament*, pp. 174–7 understands it to be a sealing with the name of Jesus in baptism, and so a mark of ownership. Pauline texts are 2 Cor. 1:22; Eph. 1:13; 4.30; cf. 1 Cor. 6:11; 12:13.

55   Dunn, 'Baptism and the Unity of the Church in the New Testament', pp. 85, 97–8; cf. James D.G. Dunn, *Baptism in the Holy Spirit* (London: SCM Press, 1970), pp. 131–4.

church and located the 'seal' in an immediate post-baptismal rite of anointing, first recorded in the account of baptism by Hippolytus.[56] In this 'sacrament of the Holy Spirit' there is a 'personal coming of the Holy Spirit' as a 'gift' to the one baptized.[57] It was perhaps this rite of anointing that the western church extended into the later rite of confirmation; but whatever the historic development, it was certainly in support of the practice of confirmation that older scholars in the Tractarian tradition wanted to read a post-baptismal rite of 'sealing' into the New Testament accounts.[58] We should also observe that Pentecostalism has placed 'baptism in the Spirit' after water baptism as a 'second blessing', and that this has been followed in a more flexible way by the modern charismatic movement. We might wonder whether this is a parallel development, or an after-echo, of the tradition of a post-baptismal anointing.

From this tradition of interpretation we might draw two conclusions. First, on the basis of New Testament exegesis, it is certainly proper to reserve the metaphors of 'sealing' and 'baptism' to express the activity of God's Spirit within water-baptism. But second, the diversity of experience of the church through the years shows that the activity of the Spirit cannot be *confined* within the moment of baptism. The Pauline writings witness to many operations, promptings and fillings of the Spirit in Christian experience;[59] Aquinas speaks of many 'sendings' of the Spirit;[60] Karl Barth remarks that the Spirit makes 'many new beginnings.'[61] This should make us cautious about appealing to 'the seal of the Spirit' to support a notion of 'completed initiation' in baptism. We may say that there are different comings of the Spirit appropriate to various stages of the process of initiation, as well as to the whole life-long journey of Christian growth. Just as baptism provides a focus for grace and faith, so it also offers a focus for the coming of the Spirit; however, the Spirit actually comes to persons before and after the rite, at whatever

---

56   See The Apostolic Tradition of Hippolytus, XXII (reconstructed by Gregory Dix), in Max Thurian and Geoffrey Wainwright (eds.), *Baptism and Eucharist. Ecumenical Convergence in Celebration* (Geneva: WCC/ Grand Rapids: Eerdmans, 1983), p.8; cf. The Service of Holy Baptism in the Greek Orthodox Church, ibid., p. 15.

57   Alexander Schmeman, *Of Water and the Spirit* (London: SPCK, 1976), pp. 78–9, 103–4.

58   E.g. Dom Gregory Dix, *The Shape of the Liturgy* (London: Dacre Press/ A. & C. Black, 19642), p. 260. However, Aidan Kavanagh, *Confirmation. Origins and Reform* (New York: Pueblo, 1988), believes the origin of confirmation to be in the laying on of hands for blessing in dismissal.

59   See Dunn, *Jesus and the Spirit*, pp. 201–2

60   Aquinas, *Summa Theologiae*, 1a.43.5–7. Cf. Francis A. Sullivan, *Charisms and Charismatic Renewal* (Dublin: Gill & Macmillan, 1982), pp. 69–75.

61   Barth, *Church Dogmatics*, IV/4, pp. 39–40.

age it is performed. The process of Christian growth is that of being
drawn more deeply into the triune life of God, and the metaphor of
'coming' is one way of pointing to this increasing participation.

Baptists will be inclined to argue that the metaphor of 'sealing' makes
full sense in the context of believers' baptism; but just as grace and faith
have a *particular* nature within the two kinds of baptism, we might say the
same of 'sealing with the Spirit'. With infant baptism it is bound to have
more a sense of a 'stamp of ownership' and 'foretaste', while with
believers' baptism it will be more strongly associated with the giving of
spiritual gifts (*charismata*) for ministry in the church and world. It is
difficult to conceive of infants receiving *charismata*, since according to
the New Testament understanding these are not gifts in the sense of
permanent possessions, but dynamic acts of the Spirit here and now
through a believer. As James Dunn puts it:

> Charisma is always an event, the gracious activity of God through a man [sic]. It is
> the actual healing, the miracle itself ... it is the particular act of service as it is
> performed ... the exercise of a spiritual gift is itself the charisma.[62]

This in itself is an argument for the extension of the period of initiation
to the point when the Spirit can manifest *charismata* in human persons
and commission them for responsible service in the world. Whether this is
a laying on of hands within the occasion of the baptism of a believer, or
in a rite many years after infant baptism, it is still part of beginnings. Just
as in baptism the Spirit takes an element in the natural world – water –
and uses it as a place of encounter with God for renewal of life, so the
Spirit takes natural human faculties and opens them up as a place to
manifest spiritual gifts. When this begins to happen it is the end of *the*
beginning, the end of laying foundations. A woman or man has become
a disciple.

An Interplay of Christ's Body and Church

In the New Testament writings, the phrase 'body of Christ' has three
meanings – the risen and glorious body of Jesus who was crucified, the
community of the church, and the eucharistic bread in which the
community shares.[63] While some scholars make a total identity between at

---

62   Dunn, *Jesus and the Spirit*, p. 254.
63   E.g. (i) Rom. 7:4; Phil. 3:21; Jn. 2:21; (ii) 1 Cor. 6:15; 12: 4–31; Rom. 12:3–
8; Eph. 4:1–16; Col. 1:18; (iii) 1 Cor. 10:17, 24, 27, 29.

least the first two senses,[64] and others separate them out,[65] we should probably regard these realities as interweaving, overlapping and conditioning each other rather than being simply the same thing. In this overlap there is room for process and development in Christian nurture.

By envisaging a 'process' of incorporation, I am not proposing that it is possible to be a member of the body of Christ in one sense and not at all in another. Nor am I advocating a movement from 'partial membership' (as a young child, or new convert) to 'full membership' (as a believer come of age), a view that has been rejected in recent thought among paedobaptist churches.[66] Nor am I suggesting that we should see some sort of progression from membership in the 'universal, invisible church' to membership in the local institution of the church.[67] I am suggesting that, at different stages of the journey of initiation, a person may be related to *each* of the senses of 'the body of Christ' in a way *appropriate to that stage*. This is only possible to envisage because Christian nurture is about being drawn more deeply into the interweaving movements of the triune life, rather than being on one side or another of a single gate called 'membership'. We are concerned with organic relationships in a community, with a 'belonging' which takes diverse forms. 'Incorporation' should then be conceived as a journey or process of entering more deeply into the reality of the body, just as we have been thinking of grace, faith and the gifting of the Spirit.

So, with regard to the second sense of the 'body of Christ' – the church – we have seen that Baptists hesitate to attribute 'membership', in Paul's use of the image (1 Cor. 12:12–13), to very young infants before they have exercised any faith for themselves.[68] Baptists might, however, consent to the pronouncement by others that infants who are baptized become a member of the body, in so far as they are welcomed and embraced by the church, and immersed into its prayers and ongoing pastoral care. Until a young child exercises his or her own trust in Christ, Baptists will regard this as 'membership' in the general sense of *belonging* within the community which is called 'the body of Christ'; they are not yet members in the organic sense of themselves being a limb of the mystical body, through which Christ becomes material, tangible

---

64   Robinson, *The Body*, pp. 51, 79; L.S. Thornton, *The Common Life in the Body of Christ* (Westminster: Dacre Press, 1944), p. 298.

65   Best, *One Body in Christ*, pp. 111–14.

66   See Brand, 'Rites of Initiation as Signs of Unity', p. 135, 'Baptized members can only mean full members'. However, Beasley-Murray, *The Problem of Infant Baptism*, p. 12, still writes of 'growth... towards full membership'.

67   E.g. Barth, *Church Dogmatics*, IV/4, pp. 37–8; Susan Wood, 'Baptism and the Foundations of Communion', in Root and Saarinen (eds.), *Baptism and the Unity of the Church*, pp. 38–41.

68   See above, pp. 128–9, 133.

and visible in the world. This latter kind of membership is declared as a promise for the child, to be fulfilled in due time.

With regard to the first sense of the body of Christ – incarnate and glorified – relating to the body means belonging to the *person* of the risen Christ who has continuity of identity with Jesus of Nazareth; it means being conformed to the movement of relationship in God which is like a Son relating to a Father, characterized by a self-giving (dying) and a newness of life (resurrection). By their human existence all persons participate in some way in God, in whom 'they live and move and have their being'; God makes room for the world in the fellowship of the divine life, and 'all things hold together' in Christ.[69] Through welcome into the church which makes the dying and rising of Christ visible in the world, the infant will be drawn more deeply into the life of God, and so be shaped by the body of Christ in the first sense as well as the second. There is, then, a *kind* of incorporation which belongs to the stage of infancy – though Baptists will want to mark this by the blessing of an infant rather than by baptism.

At the end of the process of initiation – whether it has begun in infancy or in later life – a person relates to the body of Christ as a disciple, commissioned for service. The disciple is in covenanted relation with other disciples in the community of the church, and exercises the spiritual gifts that characterize being a distinct 'limb' or member of Christ, conformed to the person of Christ through an 'owned' faith. This is not 'full' membership as contrasted with an earlier 'partial' membership; it is the kind of membership *appropriate* to being a disciple of Christ on active service in the world, sharing in the mission of God. Between the beginning and the end of the phase of initiation, membership may be manifested in a variety of ways. A growing child, for instance, exercising a trust in Christ which is appropriate to being a child, will be an essential part of making the body of Christ visible. He or she is not yet commissioned as a disciple to work in the world (by believer's baptism or some kind of confirmation), but is still a member of the body, contributing a feature to the face of Christ which stands out in the community. Moreover, all who are members in this way may share in the 'body of Christ' in the third sense, the eucharistic bread. The point is not that baptism qualifies for admission to the Lord's Table, but that all who are members of the body may nourish their lives through feeding spiritually on the body of the crucified and risen Christ.[70]

---

69   Col. 1:18. Behind the redaction of this song, the notion of the whole universe as the body of Christ is still visible; see Ralph P. Martin, *Colossians and Philemon* (New Century Bible; London: Oliphants, 1974, pp. 59, 63–5.

70   The implications of this for the participation of children in the eucharist I leave for the next chapter: see below, ch. 8, pp. 183–5.

Accepting Those with Special Needs

The last groups of people I want to think about are very varied, and I certainly do *not* want to suggest that they fall into a single category. However, different as they are, they have one thing in common: they might appear to be excluded by an act of baptism that places stress upon personal confession of faith, *if* that is taken to mean a strong ability to understand and communicate concepts. I am thinking about people with learning disabilities, people with certain mental illnesses, and those with forms of dementia such as Alzheimer's disease.

If the practice of believers' baptism demands of those to be baptized an ability to give a logical account of their beliefs, and if it requires an intellectual grasp of the doctrine of atonement, then it will of course prove a high barrier that some will never be able to get over. One can see then the attraction of an act of baptism that places all the emphasis on God's accepting love, such that it can be administered even to unconscious infants. Now, the picture of baptism I have been developing so far does have some demands that need to be met from the side of the candidate, as he or she comes to the meeting-place of the waters. We have seen that there are at least two requirements. First, there must be a response of trust in God, as God is manifest in the face of Jesus Christ. Second, baptism involves discipleship, or a commitment to serve God and take part in God's mission in the world. Trust and discipleship: these may be accompanied by varying degrees of understanding, and sometimes they can be most effective when understanding is very weak.

We have also seen that people, whether adults or children, within the community life of the church may be following one of two paths: they may be on a journey *towards* faith, or they may be on a journey *within* faith. None are rejected; all are included within the community of Christ, but they will belong in different ways. Some will belong by being embraced within the body, surrounded and wrapped around by the love of the members; others will be members of the body themselves. We should not, of course, be too certain that we know exactly where people are on their journey of life. Now, I suggest that exactly the same principle applies to those who have a low or a disturbed understanding. It will take spiritual discernment, a gift of the Spirit, to detect the journey which they are making. It will need insight that penetrates beyond the surface appearance, beyond skill with words, to responses that are expressed in the simplest of words, in 'cries too deep for words', in the movement of the body, and the look in the eyes. When response and discipleship are discerned, it is right to baptize. But all, let us remember, are accepted; there are different ways of belonging, of which baptism is one.

In some with learning disabilities, such as Down's Syndrome, there seems to be a very high potential for both trust in God and discipleship.

If any should doubt this, let them read the book by a Baptist historian, Faith Bowers, on mentally handicapped people in the church, titled *Who's This Sitting in My Pew?* Herself the mother of a Down's Syndrome son, she writes of the gifts that the handicapped bring to the church: in their simplicity of approach, in their direct and uninhibited manner, in their authentic joy and uncalculating love, they cut through the defences that people build around themselves. They feel beneath the surface, she suggests, and 'encounter the real person beneath.'[71] She gives as an example one man in the church whom others found stern and intimidating, but whom her son Richard made a friend of easily. The handicapped are not just recipients, as his mother makes clear; she speaks of the service they give, even in small, menial tasks, as having a rich quality of discipleship. Her son has recorded his own joyful account of his baptism,[72] news of which he had spread widely among all those whom he came into contact with, and many of whom attended. Another person in Faith Bowers' book writes of his friend, John, quite severely handicapped, his speech difficult to understand, who simply said to the minister at a baptismal service 'me next'; John's friend, with insight, writes that 'this was not put as a question, more as a statement of his faith,' and adds that those present at his baptism 'will not easily forget his singing of "Jesus loves me, this I know" before he was baptized.'[73]

With those who are more cut off from communication, there is more need for sensitive, spiritual discernment of trust and discipleship. One hospital chaplain recalls talking to a group of mentally handicapped children about light, and one of her visual aids was a picture of a candle. Suddenly, one of them, Andrew, got up from his place and struggled forward. He wanted, insistently, the large candlestick from the altar; she helped him get it and he firmly held it at the front during the rest of the talk. She could not tell what, if anything, he had understood, as his disability was a severe one. But she felt, intuitively, that something was going on between him and God deep beneath the surface. Another time, later, she was talking to the congregation about prayer, and asked "Do you talk to God each day?" It was Andrew's voice that surprised her with a confident "Yes!".[74]

There is also need for discernment with those who have, not a learning disability, but a mental illness such as schizophrenia, who may experience the world around in a quite different way from those who are not ill. But even those who live in a world which is real to them but unreal to the rest of us, may learn to trust Christ to be their Lord in *that* world. God is not

---

71   Faith Bowers, *Who's This Sitting in My Pew? Mentally handicapped people in the Church* (London: SPCK, 1988), p. 106.
72   This may be read in Fiddes (ed), *Reflections on the Water*, pp. 16–17.
73   Bowers, *Who's This Sitting in my Pew?*, p. 118.
74   Quoted in Bowers, *Who's This Sitting in my Pew?*, p. 81.

absent there either; Christ walks its unfamiliar roads and is incarnate in all worlds that there are. There is, I believe, no disability or illness that means someone must be excluded from believers' baptism.[75] The boundary of baptism includes only those who trust and are committed to discipleship, but we will constantly be surprised by those who fulfill those conditions, and whom God deeply desires to meet with grace in the waters of death and resurrection.

The Witness of Baptism

I began this chapter with the observation that there is a boundary between church and world which is set up by believers' baptism. It was the setting up of such boundaries that Ernst Troeltsch, in a classic work of religious sociology, regarded as the mark of a sect in contrast to a church.[76] But the boundary of baptism, I have suggested, creates a space in which many different people can live. It excludes none from fellowship, while it does mean that people will belong to the Christian community in different ways; not all will belong as disciples through baptism, but may belong as those who are 'on the way towards faith' and who are embraced by the body.

The boundary then does not seal off the community of the baptized from others. It even means that what is done in the church may have an impact on people's lives far beyond the community itself. The event of baptism, for example, a picture of plunging into waters and rising to new life, an image of cleansing and refreshing, can be a powerful one for those who do not belong to the Christian community in any way at all. It can still awaken a sense that there is something more to life than materialism, that there is a Creator who offers the possibility of new life.[77] Just one example of this comes from what may seem an unlikely source, the singer Madonna talking about her album, *Ray of Light*.[78] The interviewer remarked that there were many images of water on the record, and Madonna responded:

> Well, there's water in birth and there's water in baptism, and when you go into the bath or the ocean there's a feeling of cleansing, a feeling of starting all over again. Being new, being healed. That's sort of what's going on in my life.

---

75   Also see Michael Taylor, 'Include Them Out?', in Faith Bowers (ed.), *Let Love Be Genuine. Mental Handicap and the Church* (London: Baptist Union, 1985), pp. 46–50.

76   Ernst Troeltsch, trans. O. Wyon, *The Social Teaching of the Christian Churches* (2 volumes; London: Allen & Unwin, 1931), 1, pp.331–2.

77   See above, ch. 6, pp. 111–13.

78   *The Guardian* Newspaper, 6 February 1998.

Baptism is indeed a boundary, but it is also a witness that crosses all boundaries.

CHAPTER 8

The Church as a Eucharistic Community: A Baptist Contribution

In documents of the ecumenical movement, such as *Baptism, Eucharist and Ministry*, it is usual to find the church described as a 'eucharistic community'.[1] At first glance, this may seem to be a phrase altogether alien to the Baptist ethos, in which language such as 'fellowship of believers' is more familiar. To speak of the church as a 'eucharistic community' implies that the celebration of the eucharist or Lord's Supper in some way *constitutes* the church, or defines its nature, though not necessarily as the sole factor. The phrase affirms a great deal more than the truth that believers, gathered together, *express* their faith and common life through table fellowship. Such a merely expressive view has been widespread among Baptists since the mid-nineteenth century, largely prompted by a reaction against the Tractarian sacramentalism of that time,[2] but I want to argue that it neither represents earlier Baptist thought, nor is characteristic of the underlying trend of Baptist thinking about church and sacraments. Despite all the diversity of Baptist tradition that we shall need to explore, there is a particular Baptist contribution to the idea that the celebration of the Lord's Supper is actually one of the events that *constitute* the church.

We may say that the Lord's Supper or eucharist (the latter term has occasionally been used by Baptists since the seventeenth century)[3] constitutes the church as community, *if* two truths can be affirmed within a Baptist perspective. These are: that the sacrament is a means of enabling the presence of Christ with his people, and that sharing in the table identifies the membership of the church of Christ. I suggest that there is

---

1   E.g. *Baptism, Eucharist and Ministry*, 'Eucharist', para. 26, cf. 19–21, pp. 14–15.

2   See Walker, *Baptists at the Table*, pp. 91–7.

3   E.g. Benjamin Keach, *Tropologia. A Key to Open Scripture-Metaphors* (London: Enoch Prosser, 1683), IV, p. 44, 'Who ought to partake of the holy Eucharist?' Books I–III were published together in 1681 and 1682 (Book I by Thomas de Laune), and Book IV by Keach was added in 1683. Cf. John Gill, *Body of Divinity*, II, bk. 4, p. 648.

indeed a Baptist contribution to be made to both of these truths, but that
they raise issues about the relation between three meanings of 'the body
of Christ' as found in the New Testament – communion bread, church
and the glorified person of the resurrected Jesus.[4] Resolving these will
require us to move beyond exploring the tracks of past tradition, to a
tracing out of a doctrine of God for the present and the future.

The Lord's Supper and the Presence of Christ

Deeply rooted in the Baptist story is the conviction that the church is
constituted by the presence of Christ. For Baptists, a key text for the
nature of the gathered congregation has been Matthew 18:20: 'where two
or three are gathered together in my name, there am I in the midst of
them'. Every congregation, confessed the English Baptists at Amsterdam
in 1611, 'though they be but two or three have Christ given them'.[5] The
aphorism of Ignatius, *ubi Christus, ibi ecclesia* ('where Christ is, there is
the church'),[6] echoing the dominical promise, has been often quoted, but
the idea took on particular force in the situation of a movement of dissent
from the established church. Faced by the claims of ecclesiastical
authority, the early Separatists claimed that it was the risen Christ, present
in the midst of the congregation in the authority of his threefold office as
prophet, priest and king of the household of God, who gave his people
the seals of the covenant, and so the right to celebrate the sacraments (as
priests), to call some to the ministry of the word (as prophets) and to
exercise a mutual discipline among each other (so sharing the kingly role
of Christ).[7] Later we shall need to reflect theologically, in a way that early
Baptists did not, on how this presence might be related to the presence of
Christ in the world, outside the community of faith. But for the moment,
it is enough to note that the church may be called a 'eucharistic
community' if the Lord's Supper is a central (though not the only)
means through which Christ *becomes present*, or *more deeply present* to

---

4 See above, ch. 4, pp. 66–7.
5 *A Declaration of Faith of English People Remaining at Amsterdam in Holland*
(Amsterdam: 1611), written largely by Thomas Helwys, art. 11, in Lumpkin, *Baptist
Confessions of Faith*, p. 120; cf. the London Confession (1644), art. XXXIII, in
Lumpkin, *Baptist Confessions*, p. 165; see Payne, *Fellowship of Believers,* p. 23.
6 Ignatius, *To the Smyrnans,* 8.2; cf. Barmen Declaration, art. III: 'The Christian
church is the community ... in which Jesus Christ acts as Lord in the present, in word and
sacrament, through the Holy Spirit' (see above, ch. 3, fn. 8).
7 See, for example *A Declaration of Faith* (1611), art. 9, in Lumpkin, *Baptist
Confessions*, p.119; the London Confession (1644), arts. X, XIII, in Lumpkin, *Baptist
Confessions,* pp. 159–60, 166; the Second London Confession (1677), ch. VIII.1, in
Lumpkin, *Baptist Confessions*, p. 260.

the fellowship of believers; more correctly we might say, if Christ uses the eucharist *to presence himself.*

Discussion about the sense in which Christ is believed among Baptists to be present to his people in the Lord's Supper cannot proceed by distinguishing between the terms 'ordinance' and 'sacrament'. This is a misunderstanding that should be cleared away at the outset. To be sure, in modern times, those who have taken a purely memorialist view of the Supper and have rejected anything resembling 'real presence' have preferred the term 'ordinance', thus stressing in their own mind that the Supper is celebrated as an act of obedience to the command of Christ.[8] Baptist confessional and theological writings of the seventeenth and eighteenth centuries show, however, that the matter is not as simple as this. Both terms – sacrament and ordinance – are used, and often in the very same sentence, as in the (General Baptist) *Orthodox Creed* of 1679: 'Those two sacraments, viz. Baptism, and the Lord's-supper, are ordinances of positive, sovereign and holy institution, appointed by the Lord Jesus Christ, the only lawgiver...'.[9] Moreover, the terms in themselves do not indicate the degree to which the elements are considered to be a means of grace, or what has popularly, since the mid-nineteenth century, been dubbed 'sacramentality'. The terms cannot indicate the *way* in which (to use a phrase from the London Confession of 1644) 'a sign must answer the thing signified.'[10] General Baptist writings, for instance, leaning more towards Zwingli than to Calvin, may use *sacramentum* in Zwingli's sense of a pledge of mutual love (a soldier's oath). Particular Baptist writings, while reflecting Calvinist ideas of a 'spiritual eating and drinking' of the body and blood of Christ, often prefer 'ordinance' to affirm the origin of the Supper as a gift of Christ and its necessary place in properly ordered worship.

Both General and Particular Baptist theologies in the first two centuries of Baptist life witness to the Supper as an occasion for 'communion' with Christ, for receiving the 'benefits' of his atoning work on the cross, and

---

8   For example, among English Baptists, John Clifford, *The Ordinances of Jesus and the Sacraments of the Church* (London: n.p., 1888), pp. 18–20; among American Baptists, Augustus Hopkins Strong, *Systematic Theology* (3 vols; Philadelphia: Griffin and Rowland, 1909), pp. 930–5.

9   *Orthodox Creed* (1678), art. XXVII, in Lumpkin, *Baptist Confessions*, p. 317. Other examples of both words being used together are: *A Short Confession of Faith* (Amsterdam, 1610), art. 23, in Lumpkin, *Baptist Confessions*, p. 108; Grantham (General Baptist), *Christianismus Primitivus*, 2.2.7, pp. 96–8; Hercules Collins (Particular Baptist), *An Orthodox Catechism: Being the Sum of Christian Religion, Contained in the Law and Gospel* (London: 1680), pp. 25, 44; Keach, *Tropologia*, IV, pp.42–5; Keach, *The Child's Delight: Or Instructions for Children and Youth* (London: William and Joseph Marshall, 1702), p. 38.

10   London Confession (1644), art. XL, in Lumpkin, *Baptist Confessions*, p. 167.

for spiritual feeding and nourishment of the soul. In some sense they all regard the meal as a 'means of grace', and lack the intense suspicion of this phrase that was generated in the debates of the nineteenth century.[11] Their communion hymns, in particular, evidence a deep gratitude to Christ that 'Thy Flesh is Meat indeed/ Thy Blood the richest wine.'[12] It is a travesty, then, to regard the General Baptist approach as being an extreme form of Zwinglianism in which the memorial of the supper is a cerebral exercise of memory unaccompanied by spiritual benefit in the present, and in which the *sacramentum* is only the pledge of the disciples' faithfulness to each other, unaccompanied by the fulfilment of God's pledge of love to us. It is unlikely that Zwingli himself held such a bare memorialism.[13]

Of course, there are differences between the General and Particular Baptist traditions here, and different nuances within each, but we need to use the proper tool for laying bare this diversity. I suggest that what we need to explore is the *kind of relation* that is being expressed between the bread and wine and the 'body' of the now risen and glorified Christ.[14] This begins from a Reformation perspective, but will take us into the realm of modern doctrine, since it is enquiring about the nature of the presence of the triune God in the world. The Reformation question which forms our point of departure is this: given that the earthly body of Christ now exists, after the resurrection, in a glorified state in heaven, what kind of presence can Christ have with his church through the eucharist?

A Localized Presence of the Body in the Elements

Early Baptists, in company with all other children of the Reformation apart from Lutherans, rejected one answer given to this question. That is, in the words of Calvin, that the risen body of Christ has a 'local presence'

---

11   For examples, see discussion below, pp. 164–6. As the Second London Confession makes clear, faith is a grace, and so the sacraments which strengthen it are a means of grace: ch. XIV, in Lumpkin, *Baptist Confessions*, p. 268.

12   Joseph Stennett, *Hymns in Commemoration of the Sufferings of our Blessed SaviourJesus Christ, Compos'd for the Celebration of His Holy Supper* (London: 17093), p. 35. Walker, *Baptists at the Table*, pp. 17–30 aptly quotes from other hymns by Samuel Stennett, Benjamin Beddome and Anne Steele.

13   For a recent re-assessment of Zwingli's sacramental theology, see H. Wayne Pipkin, *Zwingli: the Positive Religious Values of his Eucharistic Writings* (Leeds: Yorkshire Baptist Association, 1986) and Gottfried W. Locher, *Zwingli's Thought: New Perspectives* (Leiden: Brill, 1981).

14   Though the bread signifies 'body' as distinct from 'blood', all sacramental theologians are clear that the risen body of Christ includes body and blood.

in the bread and wine.[15] This type of eucharistic theology centres upon ideas of substance, and finds that the 'substance' of the transformed humanity in Christ either replaces the substance of the bread (scholastic transubstantiation, leaving the 'accidents' of the bread untouched), or exists alongside the substance of the bread (consubstantiation) or is 'hidden under' it in divine humility (Luther). In a desire to prevent worship of the elements and a 'carnal eating', Baptists followed both Calvin and Zwingli, against Luther, in asserting that the body of Christ could not be omnipresent and so could not be present within the many consecrated hosts and chalices of Christendom at the same time as in the heavenly sanctuary.[16] The argument ran that the risen body of Christ, although transformed, must still share the characteristics of human bodies, including dimension, location, unity and visibility. Omnipresence and invisibility of body would be 'against reason',[17] as well as denying the real union of the divine Logos with humanity and thus the incarnation. The second person of the Trinity, united with a human body and soul, exists in heaven at the right hand of God the Father, awaiting a return to earth in the final coming: 'his Body cannot be in two places at one and the same time'.[18]

From a modern theological viewpoint, we may judge that the denial of a localized containment of the body within the bread and wine helps to avoid a static notion of presence, and allows for a more dynamic kind of presence-as-encounter throughout the whole drama of the Supper. Indeed, modern ecumenical consensus on the eucharist has moved in this direction, away from a restriction of presence within the substance of bread and wine to encounter with Christ through the whole action of the rite.[19] Early Baptist thought on this matter insisted that the body of Christ was in heaven in the interests of affirming, positively, that spiritual

---

15   Calvin, *Institutes,* II, 4, xvii:14, p. 566.

16   Zwingli, *On the Lord's Supper* (1526), in G.W. Bromiley (trans. & ed.), *Zwingli and Bullinger* (Library of Christian Classics 24; London: SCM Press, 1953), Second Article, pp. 214–22; Calvin, *Institutes*, II, 4, xvii:26, 29–30, pp. 579, 583–6; Grantham, *Christianismus Primitivus*, 2.2.7, pp. 97–8; Keach, *Tropologia*, IV, pp. 39–41; Gill, *Body of Divinity*, II, bk. 4, p. 651. The argument persists into the nineteenth century: see Benjamin Godwin, *An Examination of the Principles and Tendencies of Dr Pusey's Sermon on the Eucharist* (London: Jackson & Walford, 1843), p.11; John H. Hinton, 'Anglican Ritualism, III. The Miracle of the Altar', *Baptist Magazine* 59 (1867), p. 217.

17   E.g. Keach, *Tropologia*, Bk. 4, p. 40; cf. Hinton, 'Anglican Ritualism, II. The Real Presence', *Baptist Magazine* 59 (1867), p. 154, 'an established maxim of physical philosophy that no substance can exist in more than one place at the same time'.

18   Keach, *Tropologia*, IV, p. 40, citing as was usual Matt. 28:6, 'He is not here, for he is risen'.

19   E.g. *Agreed Statement on the Eucharist* (Windsor 1971), Anglican-Roman Catholic International Commission (London: SPCK/Catholic Truth Society, 1972).

nourishment flows from the exalted person of Christ, and that this was offered in some way through the communion of the Lord's Supper. But the *form* of the argument does seem to place human rationality above divine mysteries. It also claims a literality for the scriptural description 'at the right hand of the Father' that it denies to the scriptural declaration 'this is my body'. Moreover, it opens up the vital theological question of the way that Christ can be present at all in the church and the world before his final appearing. As we have seen, Baptist ecclesiology has centred on the presence of Christ in the midst of his people, and to the promise in Matthew 18 it has added the promise of the risen Lord, 'Behold, I am with you always, to the end of the world (Mt. 28:20).' If the risen body of Christ is located only in heaven, understood as a separate sphere of reality from earth, then some other manner of presence must be found. As Grantham puts it, 'his Body which was raised [does] not fill all places at once.'[20] If the risen body of Jesus cannot be present under the species of bread and wine, then by the terms of the argument used, it seems that neither can it be present in the midst of a church meeting.

It is at this point that reformed theologians have appealed to a doctrine of the Holy Spirit, as the one who makes Christ present.[21] This can be understood, according to Calvin, in a kind of two-way movement. The Spirit enables the members of the church to 'ascend' to enjoy fellowship with the embodied Christ in the heavenly places. Those who want to include the body of Christ under the substance of the bread, Calvin complains, 'do not understand the mode of descent by which he raises us up to himself.'[22] Correspondingly, Christ descends in the Spirit to his church, but not in the body. With regard to this latter presence, Calvin comments that 'although the whole Christ is everywhere, yet everything which is in him is not everywhere.... there are different kinds of presence'.[23] We notice, however, that this argument rests on his belief that in the incarnation the Logos remained in heaven while at the same time being united with a body on earth (the so-called extra-Calvinisticum in the history of dogma); according to Calvin, just as the divine Logos could remain ruling the universe without a body in heaven during the earthly life of Jesus, so after his resurrection, the Logos can be present unembodied on the earth. In recent years Karl Barth has rightly objected that an existence of the Logos 'outside' the incarnation hardly takes seriously the eternal covenant of grace in which God commits God's self without any reserve to be identified with the human Jesus of Nazareth.[24]

20   Grantham, *Christianismus Primitivus*, 2.2.7, p. 97.
21   Calvin, *Institutes*, II, 4, xvii:10, p. 563; xvii:31, pp. 586–7.
22   Calvin, *Institutes*, II, 4, xvii:16, p. 569.
23   Calvin, *Institutes*, II, 4, xvii:30, p. 586.
24   Barth, *Church Dogmatics*, IV/1, pp. 179–83; see above, ch. 4, pp. 78–80.

This must have implications for the ongoing presence of the risen Christ in the world, though Barth himself does not pursue them. Presence without body seems to deny the assumption of humanity by the Word of God no less than the notion of an omnipresent individual body. It must be admitted that Baptist theologians in the past have not approached these questions with the rigour of Calvin himself, even when relying on him for arguments against transubstantiation. They have often been content simply to affirm a presence of Christ in the congregation 'through the Holy Spirit', which has matched an emphasis on 'worship in Spirit and in truth', offered in sincerity of heart. There are inconsistencies here which need to be exposed, not only about the meaning of incarnation, but about the presence of the whole fellowship of the triune God in the world; at the same time, we shall see that other elements of Baptist understanding of the 'body of Christ' offer the possibility of resolving them.

Though united in rejecting the view that the transformed body of Christ has a 'local presence' in the substance of bread and wine, non-Lutheran reformed thinkers show a spectrum of views on the character of the presence that are hard to categorize. I have already suggested that there is no simple polarity between Calvin and Zwingli, or between Particular and General Baptists on the English scene. All affirm a communion with Christ which gives blessing, and which makes the Supper – in some sense – a 'feast on which our souls feed'.[25] Perhaps the distinctions can best be seen when we ask how the metaphor of 'feeding' is being employed; while it remains a metaphor, the question is how reducible, expendable or replaceable it is.

Participation in the Body Closely Connected with the Elements

Calvin offers a theology of the presence of Christ in the eucharist in which the metaphor of 'eating the flesh' and 'drinking the blood' of Christ is inseparably connected with consuming the elements, and which is essential for expressing 'full communion with Christ'. He is, he declares, 'not satisfied with the view of those who, while acknowledging that we have some kind of communion with Christ, only make us partakers of the Spirit, omitting all mention of flesh and blood.'[26] For our human nature to be transformed through fellowship with Christ, we must share in the glorified body of Christ which is 'pervaded with

---

25   The phrase is from Calvin, *Institutes*, II, 4, xvii:1, p. 557. Cf. Anne Dutton, *Thoughts on the Lord's Supper, Relating to the Nature, Subjects, and Right Partaking of this Solemn Ordinance* (London: 1748), p. 33, 'His Soul-refreshing presence'.

26   Calvin, *Institutes*, II, 4, xvii:7, p. 561.

fullness of life' and which is like 'an inexhaustible fountain'.[27] While the bread is 'the symbol, not the reality' of the sacred communion of flesh and blood', we must not think that God will 'hold forth an empty symbol.' The flesh and blood of Christ which belong to his glorified body in heaven feed our souls 'just as bread and wine maintain and support our corporeal life'. While this body is not spatially located in the elements, and is at an enormous distance from us in heaven, through the 'secret virtue of the Holy Spirit' we are raised to the heavenly sanctuary to be united with 'things separated by space'.[28] Thus, while Christ as mediator is 'always present with his people', in the Lord's Supper he 'exhibits his presence in a special manner.'[29]

Calvin is well aware that to speak of a consuming of the flesh of Christ is a metaphor of a spiritual reality, and cannot be 'agreeable to reason',[30] but the mystery of the penetration of our human life by the transformed humanity of Christ cannot be articulated without it. An English Particular Baptist of the late seventeenth century, Hercules Collins, echoes this indispensable quality of the image when he says that 'as the Bread and Wine sustain the Life of the Body, so also his crucified Body, and Blood shed, are indeed the Meat and drink of our souls'[31] so that 'by the Holy Ghost... though [Christ] be in Heaven, and we on Earth, yet nevertheless we are Flesh of his Flesh, and Bone of his Bones.'[32] Such a testimony to 'spiritual eating' is well represented among Baptists from the seventeenth century to the present day, who in prose and hymn have found the substance of the elements to be (as C.H. Spurgeon put it), 'an ordinance of grace' through which we pass, as through a veil, 'into Christ's own arms',[33] so that he 'feeds us with his body and blood ... to enter into us for food'.[34]

While this approach to the presence of Christ through – but not as – the elements of bread and wine was characteristic among Baptists of the Particular/Calvinist tradition, it was also similarly expressed among many General Baptists. The difference we find is that Particular Baptist writings tend to treat the physical eating (in faith) as an act which is simply simultaneous with spiritual nourishment, while General Baptist writings tend to regard the physical partaking as an act which leads on in some way to such nourishment. In the latter case, there is a kind of gap between

27   Calvin, *Institutes*, II, 4, xvii:9, p. 563.
28   Calvin, *Institutes*, II, 4, xvii:10, pp. 563–4.
29   Calvin, *Institutes*, II, 4, xvii:30, p. 586.
30   Calvin, *Institutes*, II, 4, xvii:24, p. 577.
31   Collins, *Orthodox Catechism,* pp. 41–2.
32   Collins, *Orthodox Catechism,* p. 39.
33   Charles Haddon Spurgeon, *Till He Come* (1894; repr. Pasadena: Pilgrim Publications, 1971), p. 251.
34   Spurgeon, *Till He Come*, pp. 69, 353.

the exhibiting of the sign and reception of the benefits signified, in which there is space for the worshipper to enter the heavenly sanctuary. An early General Baptist Confession expresses this sequence by regarding the bread and wine as prompting a kind of plea or supplication, to 'mount upwards with the heart in holy prayer, to beg at Christ's hands the true signified food'.[35] This last phrase comes from the *Short Confession* of 1610, a slightly emended form of the Mennonite Waterlanders' Confession of 1580, signed by the English congregation of John Smyth.[36] It is clear, nevertheless, that the elements are more than a witness or teaching aid about the saving work of Christ; in a manner which echoes Calvin, these earliest General Baptists confess that Christ, 'glorified in his heavenly being [as] the alive-making bread' constitutes a 'spiritual supper', and that Christ makes the faithful disciple 'partaker of the life-giving food and drink of the soul'.[37]

Similarly, the later *Orthodox Creed* of 1679, a General Baptist document with some Particular Baptist influence in it, echoes the (Particular Baptist) Second London Confession in attributing a 'spiritual nourishment and growth in Christ' to participation in the Supper, and adds the phrase 'sealing unto them their continuance in the covenant of grace.'[38] But it does not include the explanation of this nourishment offered by the earlier confession, which makes it simultaneous with the very act of eating and drinking:

> Worthy receivers, outwardly partaking ... do then also inwardly by faith, really and indeed, yet not carnally and corporally, but spiritual receive, and feed upon Christ crucified and all the benefits of his death...[39]

Again, the General Baptist writer Thomas Grantham speaks of 'Gods presence in his Ordinances', and affirms that in the Supper by faith 'we herein eat the Flesh of the Son of God and drink his blood';[40] at the same time the whole tone of his discussion is that Christ crucified is 'held forth' and 'offered' in the elements in a way that calls for us to make an 'approach nigh to God'.[41] By contrast, and it is just a contrast of

---

35   A Short Confession (1610), art. 32, in Lumpkin, *Baptist Confessions*, p. 110.

36   The idea of spiritual feeding in the Lord's Supper is not contained in two other major Mennonite confessions – the Schlechtheim Confession of 1527 and the later Dordrecht Confession of 1632.

37   A Short Confession (1610), art. 32, in Lumpkin, *Baptist Confessions*, p. 110; *Propositions and Conclusions* (1612), art. 72, in Lumpkin, *Baptist Confessions*, p. 137.

38   *Orthodox Creed*, art. XXXIII, in Lumpkin, *Baptist Confessions*, p. 321.

39   Second London Confession, ch. XXX.7, in Lumpkin, *Baptist Confessions*, p. 293.

40   Grantham, *Christianismus Primitivus*, 2.2.7, pp. 91, 93.

41   Grantham, *Christianismus Primitivus*, 2.2.7, pp. 87–8, 92.

emphasis, Benjamin Keach (a Particular Baptist) lessens the gap between the holding forth and the receiving of Christ:

> There is a mystical Conveyance or Communication of all Christ's blessed Merits to our Souls through Faith held forth hereby, and in a glorious manner received, in the right participation of it.[42]

In the next century the Particular Baptist theologian, John Gill, affirms the simultaneity of eating and being nourished by Christ: 'to eat of this bread spiritually is no other than the communion of the body of Christ, or a having fellowship with him while feeding on it ... as bread taken into the mouth and chewed is received into the stomach ... so Christ being received and fed upon by faith, believers are one body and spirit with him ... they are one bread.'[43] A century more later, another Calvinistic Baptist, Spurgeon, urges us to 'pass beyond the outward signs into the closest intimacy' with Christ; so he can say that: 'He calls upon us to eat bread with Him; yea, to partake of himself, by eating his flesh and drinking his blood.'[44]

Benefits of the Body Loosely Connected with the Elements

Despite the differences in emphasis, we notice that for much of their history, Baptists of both a Particular and General persuasion associated the spiritual nourishment of the presence of Christ in the closest way with the elements of bread and wine. For them, the metaphors of eating and drinking cannot be replaced, as they indicate an aspect of receiving the mystery of grace which cannot be otherwise expressed. It seems to have been in reaction against the perceived 'sacerdotalism' of the Oxford Movement and renascent Catholicism in the nineteenth century that, for some Baptists, the benefits of the presence of Christ become more loosely connected with the eucharist. The change of mood is characterized by Alexander Maclaren, who declares that:

> the purpose of the Lord's Supper is simply the commemoration, and therein the proclamation of His death. There is no magic, no mystery, no 'sacrament' about it. It blesses us when it makes us remember Him. It does the same thing for us which any other means of bringing Him to mind does. It does that through a different vehicle. A sermon does it by words, the Communion does it by symbols.[45]

---

42   Keach, *Tropologia*, IV, p. 45.
43   Gill, *Body of Divinity*, II, bk. 4, p. 655.
44   Charles Spurgeon, *Till He Come*, p. 99.
45   Alexander Maclaren, *Expositions. Paul's Epistles to the Corinthians* (London: Hodder & Stoughton, 1909), p.173.

While, however, Maclaren admits that this view might be called 'a poor, bald Zwinglianism', it is not as slender as the radical successors to Zwingli made the Reformer's thought. It is clear that Maclaren regards both the preached word in the sermon and the visible symbol in communion as a means through which Christ 'is to be incorporated within us by our own act', for 'the true life of the believer is just the feeding of our souls upon him ... our hearts feeding upon the love which is so tender, warm, stooping and close'.[46] Where Maclaren differs from an earlier General Baptist like Grantham, or a contemporary Particular Baptist like Spurgeon, is that there is nothing distinctive about the operation of grace through the Supper as compared with the sermon. The implication follows that the latter can be substituted for the former with no loss.

This way of thinking is encouraged when the physical sign is entirely disconnected from the spiritual meaning. For John Clifford, the sacraments 'of themselves do not bring the soul into living union with the Saviour', just because they are material substances – 'of the earth, earthy'. They are symbols which reveal truth, and the 'real presence of the Christ is the Divine answer to the penitence, trust and worship of the humble and devout soul'.[47] The bread and the wine, as symbolic proclamation, do have the power to awaken spiritual response, so that Christ becomes 'more real to us as our Redeemer' when we eat and drink.[48] But while this has some resonance with the earlier General Baptist conviction that the sacraments prompt our supplication to God for the benefits of Christ, the looseness of connection between the elements and the benefits is seen when Clifford writes in the same context of an outright opposition or 'battle' between the material and the spiritual, between ceremony and the religion of the spirit, between the external and inwardness.[49] For Clifford, as for many modern Baptists, it seems that the 'cold symbols'[50] communicate divine truth despite their unsuitable nature.

The Presence of Christ in the Body of the Congregation

Both the tighter and looser connection of the presence of Christ with the sacraments can be combined with a further idea of presence, which has a distinctively Baptist flavour to it. This stresses the overlap between the

46   Maclaren, *Corinthians*, p. 174. Similarly, Benjamin Godwin, *Examination of ... Dr Pusey's Sermon*, pp. 71–3.
47   Clifford, *Ordinances of Jesus*, p. 19
48   Clifford, *Ordinances of Jesus*, p. 23
49   Clifford, *Ordinances of Jesus*, p. 25.
50   Clifford, *Ordinances of Jesus*, p. 7.

'body of Christ' as held forth in bread, and the 'body of Christ' lived as the congregation. In some way, sharing in the Lord's Supper deepens not only the relationship of Christ with the individual believer, but the presence of Christ in his gathered people. The real presence of Christ is manifested in the community of the church, as it becomes more truly the body of Christ broken for the life of the world. This was an insight firmly grasped by Zwingli, despite the popular view that he held to a 'mere memorialism'; commenting on the words of Paul in 1 Cor. 10:17 that 'we who are many are one body because we all eat of the same bread', he affirmed that 'We eat bread so that we are made into one bread ... What we become by this eating ... is the body of Christ.'[51]

One way of expressing this is to play on the double meaning of the word 'communion'. Baptist writings on the Lord's Supper commonly slide from the meaning 'communion with Christ' to 'communion with each other',[52] and the term 'fellowship' works in the same way. Now, this might be used to undermine any tight connection between the presence of Christ and the physical elements, and to a large extent this has been true of Baptist beliefs over the last 150 years. Both John Clifford and, earlier, Charles Williams, find a key meaning of the Supper to lie in the enhancement of the fellowship of love among believers. While stating that the elements of the Lord's Supper are 'neither the cause nor the vehicle of grace', Williams affirms that Christ is to be located in the gathered congregation, where his body can be 'discerned' (1 Cor. 11:29). Christ is truly present among a 'company of believers ... thinking of what the Lord Jesus did and suffered for them, and opening their minds and hearts to His all-conquering love.'[53] For John Clifford, the Lord's Supper is a celebration of the central fact of love in the Christian experience, 'promoting the special grace of brotherly love [and] fostering the 'communion of saints'.[54] But it is clear that the double meaning of communion, and the most embracing sense of fellowship (*koinonia*) also has the potential for linking the presence of Christ in the congregation to the presence of Christ through the elements.

---

51 Zwingli, *Letter to Matthew Alber*, 16 November 1524, trans. in H. Wayne Pipkin (ed.), *Huldrych Zwingli. Writings* (2 volumes; Allison Park: Pickwick, 1984), 2, p. 141.

52 E.g. The *Orthodox Creed*, art. XXXIII, in Lumpkin, *Baptist Confessions*, p. 321: 'pledge of communion with him, as also of our communion and union each with other, in the participation of this holy sacrament.'

53 Charles Williams, *The Principles and Practices of the Baptists* (London: Baptist Tract Society, 1879), p. 41.

54 John Clifford, *The True Use of the Lord's Supper* (London: Marlborough & Co., n.d., ?1878), p.4.

Similarly, the modern idea that a community is formed by the stories that it tells[55] can be allied with various understandings of presence. As the community shares together in recalling the narrative of the Lord's Supper, it does not only rediscover its identity; it enters imaginatively into the saving events of the story of Jesus which have made it what it is. So the group takes its place, through its ritual practices, in the narratives that constitute it. This socio-linguistic approach to the nature of a community makes clear that participation in the Lord's Supper is a corporate event rather than a piece of individualistic spirituality, but it could be invoked to support an understanding of the supper as a 'bare memorial'. It might be said that when communities recall their stories and are shaped by them, however imaginatively they enter into the tale, this is finally a matter of the power of memory. Alongside the 'sacred' story of the exodus from Egypt, one might for example set the 'non-sacred' story of the migration of a whole community into the UK from the West Indies. Each community, British-Jewish and British-Caribbean, lives by its story; if the latter is a matter of memory, it might be urged, then so is the former. But if one believes that God takes the words, symbols and actions of the biblical story as a means of making God's self present with us, then remembering the story (*anamnesis*) allows us to encounter the same God who was present in the community in the past, in exodus, crucifixion and resurrection. In telling the story we encounter the crucified and risen Lord anew, and this forms the community as the representative of this Lord in the world.[56] Out of the telling of the biblical story, it may then also be possible to notice the surprising presence of the triune God in stories that we tend to regard as secular, and to encounter God anew through recounting them as well.

It is here that the Baptist way of celebrating the Lord's Supper perhaps makes a fundamental contribution to the eucharistic liturgy of the world-wide church. Without a prayer-book, and simply taking the account of the Apostle Paul in 1 Corinthians 11 as their liturgy, Baptists have always told the words of institution as a story which has been 'handed on' to the community. Usually, a prayer of thanksgiving follows the story, or is interleaved in the narrative without breaking the story-line. This stands in contrast to those churches which have followed the Roman Catholic and Orthodox tradition, incorporating the words of 1 Corinthians 11:23–6

---

55 See e.g. George W. Stroup, *The Promise of Narrative Theology* (Atlanta: John Knox, 1981), pp. 101–98; Stanley Hauerwas, *The Peaceable Kingdom. A Primer in Christian Ethics* (Notre Dame: University of Notre Dame Press, 1983), pp. 96–102; George A. Lindbeck, *The Nature of Doctrine. Religion and Theology in a Postliberal Age* (London: SPCK, 1984), pp. 116–24.

56 For a Baptist exposition of this idea, see Stanley Grenz, *The Social God and the Relational Self. A Trinitarian Theology of the Imago Dei* (Louisville, KY: Westminster, John Knox, 2001).

into a prayer of consecration addressed to God the Father; in this syntax ('Jesus gave you thanks') the story is being told directly to God, and only being overheard by the community.

I suggest, however, that the identifying of the body of Christ with the community gathered at the eucharist goes beyond even ideas of communion and story. It means that as the members of the church share in bread and wine, Christ takes hold more firmly of their own bodies and uses them as a means of his presence in the world. Just as Christ uses the physical stuff of bread and wine as a meeting-place between himself and his disciples, so he uses their bodies as a means of encountering them through each other, and as a meeting-place with those outside the church.[57] If we understand the sacraments as doorways into the fellowship of God's triune life, then the community itself is being made an entrance, for its members and for all others.[58] This understanding depends upon a close connection between the presence of Christ and the elements, at least as place of encounter; the taking of created body in bread and wine is extended into the taking of human bodies in the meeting of the church. So the church itself becomes a sacrament, and participates bodily in the mission of God in the world. In some sense (which I intend to explore shortly), it also becomes an extension of the incarnation.

What evidence is there for calling this vision of the church a Baptist one? We can certainly find the language of the church as sacrament in modern ecumenical discussion, which often refers to the Dogmatic Constitution *Lumen Gentium* of Vatican II: 'The Church, in Christ, is in the nature of sacrament – a sign and instrument, that is, of communion with God and of unity among all men'.[59] The Orthodox theologian Alexander Schmeman in his reflections on the eucharist employs a maxim of Feuerbach, 'Man is what he eats', to new effect.[60] This echoes,

---

57   Gerhard Lohfink, *Does God Need the Church? Toward a Theology of the People of God*, trans. L. Maloney (Collegeville: Liturgical Press, 1999), p. 259, writes of the 'Church as the real and physical presence of Christ in history'; earlier, see Robinson, *The Body*, pp. 51–55, and John Knox, *The Church and the Reality of Christ* (London: Collins, 1963), pp. 84–90.

58   See Fiddes, *Participating in God*, pp. 281–3, 294–9.

59   *Lumen Gentium* (21 November, 1964), I.1, in Austin Flannery (ed.), *Vatican Council II. The Conciliar and Post Conciliar Documents* (Dublin: Dominican Publications, 1975), p. 350. See Günther Gassmann, 'The Church as Sacrament, Sign and Instrument' in Gennadias Limouris (ed.), *Church, Kingdom, World: The Church as Mystery and Prophetic Sign* (Faith and Order Paper 130; Geneva: WCC, 1986), pp. 1–17.

60   Alexander Schmeman, *For the Life of the World* (Crestwood: St Vladimir's Seminary Press, 1963), p. 11. Also Schmeman, *Church, World, Mission. Reflections on Orthodoxy in the West* (Crestwood: St Vladimir's Seminary Press, 1979), pp. 136–7, 'the raison d'être of the church is to be the sacrament of the new creation'.

curiously, the sentiment of Zwingli to which I have already referred, that we become the body of Christ by eating the bread. In the Baptist tradition this kind of language is also not unknown. Among the General Baptists, Grantham weaves together the supper, the church and the body of Christ:

> Yea, here Christ gathers his People together at his own Table, as one Family. And it is that Table, to which all Saints are to approach with such preparation as may render them fit for communion in that Mystical Body, the Church; which is also called Christ, because of that unity they have with him, and one another in him.[61]

Among the Particular Baptists, Hercules Collins answers the question, 'What is it to eat the Body of Christ'? by bringing together the glorified body of Christ in heaven and the church as the body of Christ on earth into the closest identity:

> It is ... more and more to be united to his sacred Body, that though he be in Heaven and we on Earth, yet nevertheless we are Flesh of his Flesh, and Bone of his Bones: and as all the Members of the Body are quickened by one Soul; so are we also quickend and guided by one and the same Spirit.[62]

But, rather than isolated quotations, the strongest reasons for regarding the church as a sacrament in Baptist tradition are two fundamental elements of its praxis. First, the very concept of the church meeting, in which the members gather together to seek for the mind of Christ, assumes that the presence of Christ can be known through the bodies (and voices) of fellow-believers. I have already made this point in thinking about baptism as a sacrament of creation.[63] Members vote on issues, not to impose a majority view but to find the purpose of the risen Lord for their life and mission. Because Christ is embodied among them through the meeting of their bodies, they expect to be able to discern his mind for them. In the seventeenth century it was common practice for members to hold the church meeting either immediately before or after the Lord's Supper. So the church book, which recorded the names of the members, the church covenant and all the decisions taken in the church meeting was kept in a drawer in the bench behind the Lord's table, or in the 'table pew'. Here is a symbol of the sacramental significance of the coming together of human bodies into the body of Christ – table and church book together.

A second aspect of praxis concerns Baptist opposition to establishment of the church, and the Baptist vision of a new kind of politics. The significance of this for a sacramental theology has recently

---

61   Grantham, *Christianismus Primitivus*, 2.2.7, p. 89.
62   Collins, *Orthodox Catechism*, p. 39.
63   See above, ch. 6, pp. 122–4.

been urged by two Baptist theologians, Philip Thompson followed by
Barry Harvey. Though their thesis is a contentious one, I believe that it is
basically correct, although we shall see that it raises a problem they do
not seem to deal with. These authors recall that Baptists were asserting the
freedom of the local congregation to order its life under Christ in
opposition to a state church; in the local fellowship of believers Baptists
found a renewed *polis* in the practices and politics of the body of Christ.
Drawing on Peter Berger's theory that ritual as something external and
objective legitimates social arrangements,[64] Thompson argues that the
sacraments had been employed to legitimate a confusion of the church
with the state. Accordingly, sacrament among Baptists was also to
legitimate the new *polis*: as Thompson puts it, 'Christ had to be truly
present in true [Baptist] sacramental practice, otherwise Baptist criticism
of the state church's idolatrous practices would flounder....'[65] The
sacramental practices of the state church were regarded as idolatrous,
argues Thompson, because they made the state itself the mediator of
salvation, usurping the prerogative of God and making the state itself
sacramental: so 'Christ had to take form in the politics of the community
of faith, or else the Baptists' claim lost its sure foundation.'

Harvey adds that the sacramental embodiment of Christ in the new
polis of the community of believers restored the intimate connection
between the sacramental body (*corpus mysticum*) and the ecclesial body
(*corpus verum*) which had been emphasized in the patristic era but
obscured in the political theology of the Middle Ages.[66] Baptism was the
grafting of the believer into the body of Christ,[67] and so – as Harvey puts
it – a 're-membering into the body politic of Christ, the *corpus verum* or
the earthly-historical form of the crucified and risen Christ'. Baptism as
sacrament, concludes Harvey, confers proper significance on all bodies,
whether communal or individual, 'thus relativizing all other political
expressions by locating true politics within the church.'

A central belief to which Thompson and Harvey rightly point is the
freedom of God, which it seems had been infringed by binding
sacrament with the worldly authority of the state. But the objection may
be raised: is the identifying of the church, a human community, with

64   Peter Berger, *The Sacred Canopy: Elements of a Sociological Theory of
Religion* (New York: Doubleday, 1967), pp. 32–4.

65   Philip E. Thompson, 'Sacraments and Religious Liberty: From Critical Practice
to Rejected Infringement', in Cross and Thompson (eds.), *Baptist Sacramentalism*, pp.
48–9.

66   Barry Harvey, 'Re-Membering the Body. Baptism, Eucharist and the Politics of
Disestablishment', in Cross and Thompson (eds.), *Baptist Sacramentalism*, pp. 102,
105, 107. Cf. Henri de Lubac, *Corpus Mysticum* (Paris: Aubier, 1948), pp. 160–190.

67   Perhaps neither Thompson nor Harvey take enough account of the fact that this
was a General Baptist emphasis, less common among Particular Baptists.

sacrament a similar restriction on the freedom of God and the lordship of Christ? Moreover, does making the church the 'new *polis* of Christ' mean that Christ is not free to embody himself, as the Lord of the cosmos, in structures of society and culture, and in movements for justice and freedom outside the church? While the church is indeed a model of the kingdom of God, the borders of the actual kingship of God are wider than the church. The question which faces us is whether the rightful Baptist protest against an idolatrous unity of church and state has room for a willingness to see what Dietrich Bonhoeffer called, 'the way in which Jesus Christ takes form in the world'.[68]

Earlier I raised the point that there is a tension between the Reformers' – and early Baptist – denial of the local presence of Christ's body in the world and an understanding of the congregation as the body of Christ. While this was a paradox that early Baptist thinkers failed to resolve (or even to notice), it is intensified by the perception of modern liberation theology that Christ is to be found among the poor, the oppressed and rejected in society.[69] We are unlikely now to hold the Reformation view that an incarnate and glorified body of Christ remains localized in heaven until the *parousia*, and so the issue of the presence of Christ in the world will scarcely take that shape; but a sacramental understanding of the congregation also raises questions about the presence and location of the body of Christ. This makes it the more pressing that we find some way of relating and distinguishing the 'body' of Christ in incarnation, eucharist and community.

Moreover, the sacramental understanding of 'community' must reach beyond the bodies of believers into the whole body of the world. From the focus of the Lord's table, we can discern the presence of God at every meal table, and in the whole process of sustaining life in our complex ecosystem. Every living creature and plant needs food and nourishment in order to survive and grow. We may find here the presence of the generous God who was found at the meal-table of Jesus when he ate with outcasts and sinners during his ministry, and when he shared table-fellowship with his disciples after his resurrection. In the previous chapter I have already suggested that, starting from the focus of baptism, we can find God in the many occasions in the world where water is involved: in the experience of the breaking of waters in birth, in moments of

---

68   Dietrich Bonhoeffer, *Ethics*. Edited by Eberhard Bethge, trans. N. Horton Smith (London: SCM Press, 19712), pp. 66–68; cf. p. 170 (pp. 69–73), 'the reality of Christ assumes reality in the present world, which it has already encompassed, seized and possessed.' Also, Bonhoeffer, *Letters and Papers from Prison. The Enlarged Edition*. Edited by Eberhard Bethge, trans. R. Fuller, F. Clarke and J. Bowden (London: SCM Press, 3rd edn, 1971), pp. 381–2.

69   See Moltmann, *Church in the Power of the Spirit*, pp. 126–130, 'Christ's presence in the poor'.

refreshment, when passing over a boundary river, in the washing away of what is unclean, and in facing the hostile force of great floods.[70] The particular moment of encounter with God through the elements of eucharist and baptism can thus awaken us to the God who can be met through the many bodies of the world. Discerning the body of Christ in the breaking of the bread enables us to discern him through the broken bodies of the prisoners, the thirsty and the hungry. In accord with this perception, Teilhard de Chardin speaks of 'prolongations' and 'extensions' of the eucharist. He writes, 'from the particular cosmic element into which he has entered, the Word goes forth to subdue and to draw into himself all the rest.'[71]

We have seen that, within a Baptist perspective, the church may be regarded as a eucharistic community for the first reason I offered at the beginning of this chapter: sharing in the Lord's Supper enables Christ to be present in the church, through the bodily form of the elements and the community. But this need not narrow the borders of the sacramental community to the church. All bodies in the world have the potential to be sacramental, awakening us to the presence of the creative and redemptive God, becoming doorways into the flowing relationships that we call Father, Son and Holy Spirit, entrances into the dance of their *perichoresis* of love. This leaves us, however, with the question as to how we might still maintain meaningful distinctions between the incarnation of Christ in a particular body, and the sacramental presence of Christ in the stuff of bread and wine, in the congregation and in the cosmos. I intend to attempt an answer after considering a second reason why the church may be considered a eucharistic community; as I proposed earlier, this is because sharing in the table identifies the membership of the church of Christ. This, no less than the first reason, also raises issues about the different forms of the body of Christ.

Sharing in the Eucharist and Membership of the Church

In the catholic tradition, membership of the church is received through a once-for-all baptism 'into the body of Christ', and is renewed constantly through sharing in the body of Christ at the eucharist. So participating in the Lord's Supper identifies someone as a member of the church of Christ through its link back to baptism, integrating the three strands of membership, baptism and eucharist. In the earlier years of Baptist life, the three were held closest together among General Baptists, who emphasized

---

70   See above, ch. 6, pp. 109–17.
71   From Pierre Teilhard de Chardin, *Le Prêtre* (1917) in *Hymn of the Universe*, trans. S. Bartholomew (London: Collins, 1965), p. 14.

baptism as a 'church ordinance', 'ingrafting into Christ, and into the body of Christ, which is his church'.[72] Until the mid-nineteenth century Baptists in this tradition (including, latterly, the New Connexion)[73] thus insisted uniformly on a church order in which believers' baptism had to precede admission to the Lord's Supper. Although, as time has gone on, Baptists have picked these strands apart, we can see that there has been a consistency in wanting to define membership of the church through eucharistic sharing.

Membership at the Table Despite Baptism

While an early Particular Baptist confession declares that by baptism women and men are 'planted in the visible church or body of Christ',[74] among this group of Baptists there always tended to be a theological detachment of baptism from admission to membership of the church. The baptism of a believer was a rite symbolizing death, burial and resurrection with Christ, and its association with membership and the Lord's Supper was usually viewed as a matter of good church order rather than part of the order of salvation. Some Particular Baptists thus appealed to this loose theological connection in order to support the practice of 'mixed communion', or the opening of the table to those who had been baptized as infants but not as believers. For example, John Bunyan and Henry Jessey in the seventeenth century, Robert Robinson in the eighteenth century and Robert Hall in the nineteenth century all regarded those baptized as infants as 'unbaptized' (as regards water-baptism), but still welcomed paedobaptists to the Lord's Table.[75] As Robinson put it: 'We affirm, then, that baptism is not a church ordinance,

---

72   *Orthodox Creed*, art. XXVIII, in Lumpkin, *Baptist Confessions*, p. 317. The Standard Confession (1660), art. XI, in Lumpkin, *Baptist Confessions*, p. 228, regards baptism as 'the new Testament-way of bringing in Members, into the Church by regeneration'; cf. Thomas Grantham, *The Loyal Baptist or An Apology for Baptized Believers. In Two Sermons* (London: T. Grantham, 1684), 2, p. 12.

73   Articles of Religion of the New Connexion of General Baptists (1770), art. 6, in Lumpkin, *Baptist Confessions*, p.344.

74   The 'Somerset Confession' (1656), art. XXIV, in Lumpkin, *Baptist Confessions*, p. 209.

75   John Bunyan, *Differences in Judgment about Water-Baptism No Bar to Communion* (London: John Wilkins, 1673), pp. 32–5; Henry Jessey, Sermon on Rom. 14.1, 'Such as are weak in the Faith, receive you', printed as an appendix to Bunyan's *Differences in Judgment*, p. 121; Robert Robinson, *The General Doctrine of Toleration Applied to the Particular Case of Free Communion* (Cambridge: Francis Hodson, 1781), pp. 2, 24–29; Robert Hall, *On Terms of Communion*, in *Works*, II, pp. 101–3.

that it is not naturally, necessarily and actually connected with church fellowship'.[76]

Open communionists stressed that they should accept fellow-believers with whom they differed on 'inessentials', since 'Christ has accepted them'.[77] The need to live in Christian charity with fellow-disciples who showed the evident marks of faith and holy living outweighed the need to follow 'church order' which had precedent in the history of the church, but which these advocates of mixed communion were not convinced was a matter of strict ordinance by Christ and warranted in scripture. Paedobaptists might be in error about baptism, but this error was less serious than the mistake a church would be making if it turned away disciples whom Jesus himself welcomed by his divine prerogative. General Baptists opposing mixed communion insisted on the sequence of the two sacraments, while Particular Baptist opponents tended to lean on the question of obedience to Christ: disciples who were disobedient to the command of Christ to be baptized should not, they thought, be received at the Table.

It is significant that a strong motivation for open communion was the need felt to maintain the unity of the church in the bonds of love. Thus, sharing in the Lord's Table was a mark of being a member of the church universal. Those who practised open communion and closed membership were bound to make a theological detachment of fellowship at the table from membership of the local congregation,[78] and we may judge that those who offered both open communion and open membership were

---

76   Robinson, *General Doctrine of Toleration*, pp. 29–31, 45. In this he follows the tradition of John Bunyan, *Differences in Judgment*, pp. 28–30 , and is followed by Hall, *A Reply to the Rev. Joseph Kinghorn, Being a Further Vindication of the Practice of Free Communion*, in *Works*, II, pp. 337–8.

77   This relies on a parallel drawn with Romans 14–15: so Bunyan, *Differences in Judgment about Water-Baptism*, p. 43, 'Christ hath received them'; Henry Jessey, 'Such as are weak in the Faith, receive you', p. 105, 'The Lord has received them'; Daniel Turner, *A Modest Plea for Free Communion at the Lord's Table; Particularly between the Baptists and Poedobaptists* (London: J. Johnson, 1772), p.6 'Christ does himself accept of Paedobaptist Christians...'; Robert Hall, *On Terms of Communion*, pp. 93–4, 'all whom Christ has received', p. 104 'those whom we acknowledge Christ to have accepted'.

78   Churches with *open* communion but *closed* membership grew in number during the late eighteenth century among Particular Baptists, and had become the norm among them by the mid-nineteenth century; see Briggs, *English Baptists of the Nineteenth Century*, pp. 135–6. In the second half of the century, C.H. Spurgeon was a notable influence for this position in the churches that were founded under his inspiration in and around London; see Timothy George, 'Controversy and Commmunion: the Limits of Baptist Fellowship from Bunyan to Spurgeon' in D.W. Bebbington (ed.), *The Gospel in the World. International Baptist Studies* (Studies in Baptist History and Thought 1; Carlisle: Paternoster Press, 2002), pp. 55–8.

more consistent.[79] But in either case, eucharistic sharing precisely identified members of the *catholic* (universal) church. In his *Compendium of Social Religion*, for example, Daniel Turner presents the Lord's Supper as a necessary sign of the 'visible' unity of the whole church of Christ 'in the bonds of peace and love'. Though the Christian church is, 'because of the great numbers of its members', dispersed into 'many distinct societies', since these are all under Christ as one head 'they are to be considered but as parts of the same whole; composing one intire spiritual body'.[80] To preserve their unity in love,

it is absolutely necessary, that, however different an independent in some respects, any of these societies may be, they should be all form'd upon the most catholic and uniting principles, upon the whole: and by some common external means or bond of social unity, maintain (if possible) a visible communion one with another....

This visible catholicity, urges Turner, is expressed through the Lord's Supper, which 'was intended, amongst other things, to be a standing, visible, external pledge and means, of that divine union and fellowship, all true christians have with Christ, and one another in ONE BODY...'[81] So it is the duty of all Christian churches, concludes Turner, to lay the table 'as open as possible to the free access of ALL, who appear to love our Lord Jesus Christ in sincerity'.[82] It is important here to see that open communion is not founded essentially upon individualism and private faith, but on a catholic ecclesiology with a clear concept of the relation of

---

79 Today open membership churches are in the majority among churches of the Baptist Union of Great Britain (see above, p. 140), but until the second half of the nineteenth century these were still relatively few. Among Particular Baptists, open membership (with open communion) existed in the seventeenth century mainly in churches that had begun as generally independent and then either included Baptists or became predominantly Baptist: examples are churches pastored by Henry Jessey (London), John Bunyan (Bedford), John Tombes (Leominster), Vavasour Powell (in Wales) and the church at Broadmead, Bristol. In 1780 the church at New Road, Oxford, was re-founded on the basis of open membership, and its covenant document is a notable statement of the principle (see below, pp. 247–8). By 1883, John Clifford claimed that two out of every three of 'the leading churches of the Particular Baptist type' were open membership: see his article 'Conference on the Conditions of Church Membership', *General Baptist Magazine*, 85 (1883), pp. 53–4. General Baptists of the New Connexion remained almost entirely closed, until they joined the Baptist Union in 1891. See B.R. White, 'Open and Closed Membership among English and Welsh Baptists', *BQ* 24/7 (1972), pp. 330–34; Briggs, *English Baptists of the Nineteenth Century*, p. 136.

80 Turner, *Compendium*, p. 119. This echoes the wording of the Particular Baptist 'London' Confession of 1644, art. XLVII, in Lumpkin, *Baptist Confessions*, pp. 168–9. Robert Hall begins his argument, in *Terms of Communion*, pp. 9–14, with the need for the plurality of true churches to be in unity with each other; cf. pp. 105–8.

81 Turner, *Compendium*, p. 120.

82 Turner, *Compendium*, p. 121.

the local church to the whole body of Christ. The sacrament is a visible bond of unity between societies of believers, not only between individual believers.

We might discern a distinctively Baptist concept here of unity through the body of Christ, both locally and universally, rather than unity being made through the president at the eucharist. In many church traditions, it is the celebrant who makes the link at the table with the wider church, either representing or being the bishop of the region, who is the focus of unity; members are one because there is one bishop, one catholic church, one Lord of the church and one triune God. There is an echo of this concept among Baptists, since until the early nineteenth century the celebration of the Supper was reserved to the ordained minister of the congregation, whose ministry had been recognized at more than a local level, by other ministers in the area who shared in the act of ordination.[83] We have, in considering the doctrine of ministry, already seen that an important function of the local minister or *episkopos* is to represent the wider church at the local level.[84] But for Baptists the primary focus of unity in the Lord's Supper is the body, manifested in the bread, and for this reason those advocating open communion urged that the celebration of the supper with an open invitation was a means of creating unity, regardless of beliefs about baptism or the validity of ministries. In this sense, Baptists have a very strong view of the church as a eucharistic community, a community whose members are identified by their breaking of the one bread.

The celebration of the table, by making the unity of the body of Christ visible here and now in this event, also anticipates the final visible unity of the church worldwide. The Supper is held 'until Christ comes' (1 Cor. 11:26), echoing the promise of Christ that he and his disciples will share new table fellowship 'when the kingdom of God comes' (Luke 22:18). While the kingdom is yet to come in its fullness, there are already signs or anticipations of the kingdom in the world, wherever there is liberation and healing; in the same way, there are already signs of the visible unity of the church, although the final manifestation of the one body of Christ awaits the eschaton. It has been a Baptist view to lay stress on the incomplete and fragmentary nature of visible unity here and now, but not to abandon the quest to achieve as much visible unity as is possible.[85] The Supper, shared with all Christians, is both a way of manifesting unity now and a foretaste of the future oneness of the church. Likewise, as Spurgeon pointed out, the use of bread, wine and water in the sacraments

---

83   For details, see above, ch. 5, pp. 91–2, 104–5..
84   See above, ch. 5, pp. 89–90.
85   For details, see below, ch. 9, pp. 202–4.

is an anticipation of the 'lifting up' of matter in the final glorification of the whole creation.[86]

Membership at the Table and Different Forms of Baptism

The drawback with affirming membership at the table 'despite baptism' is that one sacrament, baptism, seems to be downgraded in favour of the other. In the seventeenth century William Kiffin was already levelling this accusation against open communionists; with regard to their treatment of baptism, he quotes approvingly the words of Daniel Rogers (an Independent and paedobaptist minister), that the one who cares not for 'Christ sacramental' cares not for 'Christ God', since Christ draws near in the sacrament.[87] Moreover, as Michael Walker rightly points out, the ironic result of taking baptism lightly is that the sacrament of the Lord's Supper itself is likely to suffer the same fate.[88] Those who regard the one as an inessential outward ceremonial are likely in time to apply the same reasoning to the other. Thus, while Particular Baptist ministers such as Robert Hall had a high, Calvinistic view of the sacrament as spiritual nourishment, their view that baptism was not a necessary prelude to receiving it was bound in the end to make sharing in the Supper optional as well. This indeed happened as General Baptists took up the cause of open communion from the mid-nineteenth century onwards; their change of mind seems to have been due to a combination of a more radical Zwinglianism about the Supper with a more recent Enlightenment exaltation of 'spiritual religion' over its material forms.

Another reason for urging open communion was the need to respect the 'sacred right of private judgement' of paedobaptists who believed that they had been rightly baptized as infants. Though the notion of 'private judgement' has an Enlightenment ring to it, recalling a humanistic confidence in the light of reason and a subjective individualism, it is also rooted in the statement of Paul in Romans 14:5, 'let all be fully persuaded in their own minds'. This in turn is placed in the context of divine judgement: 'for we shall all stand before the judgement seat of Christ' (v. 10). 'Private judgement' thus meant, for open-communion Baptists, that every person's conscience should be respected because, in the last resort, all must answer for their convictions

---

86   Charles Haddon Spurgeon, 'The Double Forget-Me-Not', in *Metropolitan Tabernacle Pulpit,* LIV (London: Passmore and Alabaster, 1908), no. 3,099 (5 July 1874), p. 315.

87   William Kiffin, *A sober discourse of right to church-communion wherein is proved ... that no unbaptized person may be regularly admitted to the Lords Supper* (London: Enoch Prosser, 1681), pp. 42–3.

88   Michael Walker, *Baptists at the Table*, pp. 79–80.

and decisions to their master, Christ:[89] 'Who art thou that judgest another man's servant? To his own master he standeth or falleth' (Rom. 14:4). Now, such an appeal to private judgement *could* be used to support the cutting of the sequence between baptism and the Lord's Supper; Robert Robinson and Robert Hall, for instance, regard the paedobaptist as unbaptized, but as responsible to Christ alone for their error and so not on that account to be excluded from the table by other servants of Christ.[90] However, another group of Particular Baptist ministers invoked the right of private judgement in a rather different way, allowing them to give more weight to church order which placed baptism before sharing in the Supper.

Writers on open communion such as Daniel Turner, his friend John Collett Ryland and John Brown of Kettering lay stress on the fallibility of everyone's private judgement, including that of Baptists. Turner, for instance, dares to state – in the face of some Baptist outrage[91] - that 'it is evident in fact, that the points in Baptism, about which we differ, are not so clearly stated in the Bible (however clear to us) but that even sincere Christians may mistake them. A private opinion therefore, on the one side or the other, can never be justly made an indispensible term of communion at the Lord's Table.'[92] This argument from fallible conscience is a kind of theology of intention. The paedobaptist may be seen as upholding and honouring baptism in his own mind, argues Turner, because he intends to have been baptized, and this intention should be respected until eschatological exposure of the truth. In a pamphlet jointly written with John Collet Ryland, he asserts:

> If my Poedobaptist brother is satisfied in his own mind, that he is rightly baptised, he is so to himself; and, while the answer of a good conscience attends it, God will and does own him in it, to all the ends designed by it; so that while he

---

89   Turner, *A Modest Plea*, pp. 5, 11; Robinson, *General Doctrine of Toleration*, p. 39, arguing the connection between duty and benefit; Hall, *Terms of Communion*, pp. 91, 93, 95; *Reply to Rev. Joseph Kinghorn*, p. 346; John Brown (minister at Kettering), *The House of God Opened and his table free for baptists and pædobaptists, who are saints and faithful in Christ* (London: Joseph Brown, 1777), p. 3.

90   Robinson, *General Doctrine of Toleration*, pp. 23–30; Hall, *Terms of Communion*, pp. 89–93.

91   E.g. Abraham Booth, *An Apology for the Baptists. In which they are Vindicated ... Against the Charge of Bigotry in Refusing Communion at the Lord's Table to Paedobaptists* (London: Dilly, Keith, Johnson, 1778), pp. 82–3; Dan Taylor, *Candidus Examined with Candor. Or, a Modest Inquiry into the Propriety and Force of what is contained in a late Pamphlet; intitled, A Modest Plea for Free Communion at the Lord's Table* (London: G. Keith, 1772), pp. 12–14.

92   Daniel Turner (under the name 'Candidus'), *A Modest Plea for Free Communion at the Lord's Table; Particularly between the Baptists and Poedobaptists* (London: J. Johnson, 1772), p. 7; cf. *Compendium*, p. 125.

considers it as laying him under the same obligations to holiness in heart and life as I consider my baptism to do me, why should he not commune with me at the table of our common Lord?[93]

Similarly, Turner speaks of the Paedobaptist Brother as having 'an equally just Right' to the Lord's Table because he is 'a Believer in CHRIST, answering in a good conscience to what HE thinks true baptism'.[94] The key question, as opponents of Turner gleefully pointed out, is whether a Baptist can give any objective value to this intention, that is to regard the paedobaptist believer as actually baptized, beyond respecting his view that he is baptized.[95] Turner's response depends on a distinction between the 'substance' and the 'form' of faith and practice, combined with the right of private judgement already considered. Consciences can differ about 'non-essentials', which are to do only with form.[96] So conscientious believers may differ about the 'subject and mode' of baptism, i.e. believer or infant, immersion or sprinkling, because there is a 'substance' to baptism which is deeper than the form. John Brown takes a similar line, arguing that 'Believing Paedobaptists have the same spiritual views of the ordinance of Water-Baptism ... as the Baptists ... so that there is an agreement in the substance, though not in the external mode of it'.[97]

Affirming the 'equal title'[98] of all Christians to the privilege of the Lord's Table, Turner thus writes about 'our common union in Christ... as professedly devoted to him by the same baptism, (at least as to what is essential to that purpose)...' This implies that baptists and paedobaptists have 'the same baptism' in essence. Turner roundly criticizes those who 'set up separate communities' based on 'non-essentials' with the result of dividing 'the visible catholic church'.[99] But clearly, baptism itself is not an inessential; he defines one of the essential marks of the gathered church as being 'submission to Christ by the same common sign or token of devotion to God, viz. baptism with water in the name of the Father, Son and Holy Spirit', and regards baptism as the means 'by which we are first formally incorporated into the visible church, or body

---

93 Turner, *A Modest Plea*, p. 10.

94 Turner, *Charity the Bond of Perfection. A Sermon, The Substance of which was Preached at Oxford, November 16, 1780, On Occasion of the Re-establishment of a Christian Church of Protestant Dissenters in that City* (Oxford: 1780), p. 23.

95 E.g. Taylor, *Candidus Examined*, pp. 9, 11; Booth, *Apology for the Baptists*, pp. 59–60; later, Joseph Kinghorn, *Baptism A Term of Communion at the Lord's Table* (Norwich: 1816), p. 88.

96 Turner, *Charity*, p. 17.

97 Brown, *House of God Opened*, p. 7.

98 Turner, *Compendium*, p. 127.

99 Turner, *Compendium*, pp.135–6.

of Christ' and so 'the beginning and foundation of this external communion.'[100]

There are, of course, problems with this approach. In our day we have become rightly uneasy about stripping 'form' away from a supposed 'substance' in religious practices, aware of their inseparable cultural and social conditioning. But we should notice that Turner is not suggesting – as opponents objected[101] – that baptism itself is a mere shadow or disposable sign of another substance such as faith, but that a particular mode and subject is the form which can be distinguished (not separated) from baptism as the substance. This argument is, moreover, always placed in the context of respecting paedobaptists' own judgement that they have been baptized. This allows Turner and others to refrain from calling paedobaptists 'unbaptized', and to give real value to the church order that places baptism before the Lord's Supper, while still not giving it the absolute authority of a dominical ordinance. It also clears them from the earlier accusation of Kiffin that they want a non-sacramental Christ: as Turner writes:

> Our Paedobaptist Brother pleads, 'That he believes that he is rightly baptized – that if he is mistaken, it is an Error of his Head, not of his Heart ... That it ... does not affect the Institution itself, which he reveres, but only the Subject and Mode of it – That he ... feels in his Conscience the same obligations to Holiness of Life, which are the Essentials of Baptism...'[102]

Membership at the Table and a Process of Initiation

The argument from private judgement about 'inessentials' is obviously limited to its time. It is also a pity that Turner and others do not seem to have much more to say theologically about the 'substance' of baptism than devotion to Christ and the call to a holy life. But the intention of the argument is surely worthwhile – from a Baptist perspective, to identify participants in the Lord's Supper as members of the one church while not denying the validity of their mode of baptism. In our time, the way of achieving this intention may well be somewhat different; at least, another approach must be placed alongside the older one.

Several times in this book I have urged the mutual recognition of a 'common pattern of Christian initiation' rather than a 'common baptism'.[103] Rather than simply equating one mode of baptism (infant)

---

100 Turner, *Compendium*, pp. 16, 120n.
101 See e.g. Booth, *Apology for the Baptists*, pp. 135–7, cf. pp. 48–50.
102 Turner, *Charity*, pp. 26–7.
103 See above, pp. 40, 120, 141–5.

with another (believer), an ecumenical way forward would be to place whole journeys of Christian beginnings alongside each other. The process of initiation must include the prevenient grace of God working deep within the human heart, some act of blessing and welcome of infants by the church corporately (where children in the church are on the journey of faith), formation in faith, an obedient 'yes' to God in Christ for oneself, immersion or sprinkling with water in the triune name, a first sharing in the Lord's Table, a moment of making covenant relationship with other Christians and the receiving of spiritual gifts for the ministry of God in the world. These elements of initiation may be either close together (as in the conversion of an adult from outside the church), or be spread out over a number of years (as in the growth of a child into faith within the community of the church), and the act of baptism may come earlier or later as a focus or 'freeze-frame' of the whole process, which involves throughout a working together of divine grace and human faith. Baptists will believe that the sacrament is better kept until the moment when someone takes on the responsibility of discipleship and service in the world, and there can be a convergence of the grace of God with the 'owned' faith of the believer. But if another church tradition places baptism in water earlier in the process, with young infants, we may say with eighteenth-century Baptists that 'Christ has received them', and confess that our own judgement is always fallible. This, I suggest, is a theological basis for the open membership and open table which is operated by the majority of churches within the Baptist Union of Great Britain today, and by many other Baptist churches throughout the world.

I have also suggested that we may discern different ways of belonging to the 'body of Christ', suitable to different stages in the process of initiation. At different points in the journey, a person may be related to each of the senses of 'the body of Christ' – the incarnate and glorified body of Jesus, the eucharistic bread and the community – in a way appropriate to that stage. This is only possible to envisage because Christian nurture is about being drawn more deeply into the interweaving movements of the triune life, rather than being on one side or another of a gate labelled 'membership'. We are concerned with organic relationships in a community, in which belonging takes diverse forms.[104] 'Incorporation' should then be conceived as a journey or process of entering more deeply into the reality of the body. In this context, all may share in the eucharist who are in any way members of the body: 'we who are many are one body because we all share in the one bread.' This centring on the body of Christ, in bread and community, brings some revision to the simple sequence of baptism first, Lord's Supper second. The point is whether someone is a member of the body of Christ, or in

---

104 See above, ch. 7, pp. 133, 135, 151–2.

the process of being initially formed as a member, a journey in which baptism must be included at some point. This, I suggest, honours the tradition of church order in which baptism is the essential foundation for sharing in the Supper, while not in all circumstances holding to a strict chronological sequence.

The sequence may well be modified in the case of children who are growing into faith. In some Anglican churches in the present day, children who have been baptized as infants may receive the eucharist before they are confirmed – that is, before some moment at which they publicly confess their own faith and receive the laying on of hands for the receiving of spiritual gifts. The reason often advanced for this change in established custom is that baptism is 'complete sacramental initiation' and therefore they need not wait for another ritual act before receiving the sacrament of the Lord's table.[105] My argument in the previous chapter has been that baptism, at whatever age, is never complete initiation but part of a whole process of Christian beginnings. It is certainly appropriate for children to share in the eucharist who have been baptized and are an active part of the family of the church, on the way to the completeness of initiation (which will include making the faith of their sponsors their own). But the reason for this is not that 'baptism admits to communion' as a kind of entrance qualification. A theology of the body means that those who are members of the body, on the way to being disciples, may share in the eucharistic body. In this sense the church is truly a eucharistic community.

Between the beginning and the end of the phase of initiation, membership may be manifested in a variety of ways. A growing child, for instance, exercising a trust in Christ which is appropriate to being a child, will be an essential part of making the body of Christ visible. He or she is not yet commissioned as a disciple to work in the world (by believer's baptism or some kind of confirmation), but is still a member of the body, contributing a feature to the face of Christ which stands out in the community, and valued by the other members. In a Baptist church, such children will not have been baptized. But if we think consistently about a theology of the body, and if we allow for a comparability of different patterns of initiation, I suggest that they may be received at the table and share in bread and wine. If they are on the journey of being formed as a member, having a childlike faith and having been welcomed into the community through some act of infant blessing, then they cannot be excluded from the table which identifies members.[106] It is essential that

---

105 See above, ch. 7, pp. 143–4.

106 This argument differs from those who urge admission of the unbaptized to the eucharist either on the grounds of an open invitation to the table, or as a means of leading seekers to faith: for these positions, see the responses of several Methodist Churches in Thurian (ed.), *Churches Respond to BEM*, 4, pp. 169, 178–9; 2, p. 205.

sharing in the table should not be an individual, subjective decision by either the child or the parents; the journey of initiation requires a point when the church as a body receives the child, and exercises faith on his or her behalf, praying that God will work graciously in this young life to bring fullness of salvation. Infant blessing is not a pious wish, but a prophetic symbol in which God acts to bring life to those who are blessed. It is also, we may venture to say, an act instituted by the Lord Jesus himself, who took children up in his arms and blessed them (Mk. 10:13–16). Only those believing children who have previously been received in this way should be received at the table, and they should be enrolled in a group preparing for baptism later as a believer, namely the 'catechumenate'.[107]

Now, this theology of the body makes it the more important to be able to distinguish between ways of being related to 'the body of Christ'. Children in the church who do not yet have faith of their own, and also adult enquirers and those on the 'fringe' of the congregation, will belong to the community without actually being a member of the body of Christ. As I have suggested above, they will be embraced by the body, and will be valued for whom they are, without yet being a limb of the body which is doing the embracing.[108] There can then be a difference between being a member of the body, and being part of a community where Christ is embodied. This is also true of the wider community beyond the church; people may belong to social groups or movements in which Christ takes form in the world, without themselves being members of his body. We may discern the form and presence of Christ, for example, in a group which is working for racial equality, or providing refuge for women who have suffered violence from their husbands, or offering medical care in refugee camps; this does not mean that all those who are members of those groups are also members of the body of Christ, though many will be. We must then finally trace out a theology in which the different dimensions of the body of Christ – incarnate, eucharistic, ecclesial and secular – are envisaged as related but not simply the same.

Identifying the Body

The difficulty that seems to arise in relating the various dimensions of the body of Christ is traceable, I suggest, to a particular model of divine

---

107 The statement *The Child and the Church. A Baptist Discussion* (London; Carey Kingsgate Press, 1966), p. 34, argued that 'at this moment of the Dedication Service what is happening is that the church is adding the child to its catechumenate'; however, the document did not *restrict* membership of the catechumenate to children received through an act of blessing.

108 See ch. 7, pp. 132–5.

presence. A well-established linkage between the different meanings of the term 'body of Christ' is the idea of the indwelling of divine Logos in different bodily forms. The Word dwells in the body of Jesus, the church, the substance of bread, the body of the world. The dynamic image of 'encountering' Christ in and through body is thus reduced to a static concept, and to such questions as: 'how does the Logos indwell the body?' 'Does the Logos indwell these bodies in the same way?' 'Does the Logos indwell all these bodies at the same time'?

This model was best known in the early church in the school of Antioch, where theologians developed Christologies in which the Logos dwelt in a human being, complete with a human soul, 'like a God dwelling in a temple'.[109] The school of Alexandria was more suspicious of this language, wanting to affirm that the Logos did not just 'come into' a man, but 'became man'.[110] But in the Alexandrian shape of Christology the notion of indwelling is just beneath the surface: the Logos takes a body and vitalizes it, as a directing principle, or a kind of driver (*hegemon*) in a vehicle.[111] The body is a part of the cosmos, and so by assuming it the Logos marks out a space in the cosmos for redeeming it. The body is subject to vulnerability and death, and by means of this body the Logos becomes internal to the cosmos in order to overcome corruption. As time went on, mainstream Alexandrian Christology affirmed explicitly that the human body of Christ included a human soul, fulfilling the requirement that 'what has not been assumed cannot be healed',[112] but the Logos remained the governing principle in the body, so that the 'person' of Christ was divine even though Christ had a human nature as well as a divine one.

This is a dualism of imperishable spirit and perishable body, and it has had a remarkable impact on Christian thinking. The church is rightly envisaged as a space marked out in the world where redemption is celebrated, but a dualism can be carried through into this image: then the church is conceived as a social body different from all others because it alone is indwelt by the Logos. To call the church an extension of the incarnation is taken to mean that it is only in this corporate body and its sacraments that Christ dwells in the world. In his earlier study of Christology, even Bonhoeffer seems to fall into this way of thinking; referring to the church, he writes: 'Just as Christ is present as the Word

---

109 E.g. Diodore of Tarsus, *Fragment* 20; Theodore of Mopsuestia, *Homiletical Catachesis*, 8.5 (referring to Jn. 2:19); Theodore makes clear that God's indwelling is 'by good pleasure', or by the divine will: *On the Incarnation*, 7 (fragment 2).

110 E.g. Athanasius, *Against the Arians*, 3.30. However, he still uses the imagery of dwelling in a temple: see *On the Incarnation*, 8; 9; 20.

111 E.g. Athanasius, *Against the Arians*, 3.35. Cf. Cyril of Alexandria, *Against Nestorius*, 5.2.

112 Gregory of Nazianzus, *Letters*, 101.7.

and in the Word, as the sacrament and in the sacrament, so too he is also present as community and in the community ... it means that the Logos of God has extension in space and time in and as the community.'[113] If, on the other hand, we want to speak of the embodiment of Christ in the world beyond the church, and so apply the same dualistic model universally, then it does not seem possible to draw any boundaries at all between the church and the world. The divine Reason or Word pervades all matter, human culture seems simply to be divinized, and there is the danger of absorbing Christian faith into the embrace of folk-religion. There is, moreover, another effect of this dualism which is damaging to church and world alike: in the Enlightenment the divine reason was largely supplanted by the human individual will and intellect, and the results in the domination of nature by the human subject have become all too clear in recent years as we survey the despoiling of the ecosystem.

The question of the relation between the individual body of the risen Christ, the sacrament and the community is evidently more complex than a notion of indwelling the body. Here recent social theory is helpful, in seeing the *individual* human body as an index to the *social* meanings of 'body'; the powers and dangers of social structures are mapped onto the body, or reflected onto it. 'Just as it is true that everything symbolizes the body, so it is equally true that the body symbolizes everything else' (Mary Douglas).[114] Indeed, the 'body' is hard to define just because it is related to infinitely variable social contexts. Bodies are increasingly seen not as the instrument of a subjective consciousness (the mind, soul or spirit), but as the ensemble of a set of techniques for living (*habitus*) in society. Particularly significant is the relation of bodies to space. Bodies, for instance, have often been used to maintain the boundaries between the spaces in which social groups practice their characteristic styles of life: the wearing of uniforms or liturgical garments, or the adoption of a hair style such as Rasta dreadlocks, or the very way that we move in walking or dancing, can all underline that we belong to a social arena that is marked off from others.[115] On the other hand, the body can be employed to challenge such boundaries. Mikhail Bakhtin famously drew attention to the world of carnival, and the grotesque and exaggerated form that the bodies of participants may adopt there, in their fantastic costumes and bizarre behaviour. He suggested that this was a kind of 'open body',

---

113 Dietrich Bonhoeffer, *Christology*, trans. J. Bowden (London: Fontana, 1971), pp. 59–60. Later, Bonhoeffer states that the space of the church is 'something which reaches out far beyond itself'; see *Ethics*, p. 174.

114 Mary Douglas, *Purity and Danger: An Analysis of Concepts of Pollution and Taboo* (London: Routledge & Kegan Paul), p. 122.

115 See Fiona Bowie, *The Anthropology of Religion* (Oxford: Blackwell, 2000), pp. 55–61, 71–2.

breaking down the boundaries between social bodies, and indeed between human and animal bodies in the world.[116]

In our present culture there is a reaction against the definition of self by means of established social spaces, characterized by narrow practices taking place within them and directed by a particular, dominant force. We experience our bodies today in the setting of new configurations of space. We live in a world where space is less the confined space of established social groups, and more the open arenas of global networks of information and communication. This globalization can be seen in the music, fashion, film and travel industries, and most strikingly in the phenomenon of cyberspace. These cultural forms transcend all former social boundaries and create a wide space in which to exist.[117] All this has made us more aware of what has been true all along, that the individual body is shaped not so much by the powerful 'spirit' of a group, as by living in interactive networks. Moreover, the individual body not only reflects the social body in cognitive acts (through what we think) but also in intuitive, aesthetic and 'whole-body' ways. This is strikingly manifest in the way that the music industry today crosses all national and linguistic boundaries.

All this is illuminating for our question. The metaphor of divine indwelling is certainly a useful one, and has good biblical precedent. Yahweh is depicted as dwelling with his people in the Old Testament, and the eschatological hope is for this dwelling to be universal and permanent: 'The dwelling of God is among mortals...'[118] According to the writer of the Fourth Gospel, the Logos dwelt, or 'pitched his tent', 'among us' (Jn. 1:14). The concept of indwelling is especially applied to the presence of the Holy Spirit, in individuals and in the community; we have already seen, in a study of images of the church in the New Testament, that the church is depicted as being indwelt by the Holy Spirit, not by Christ. It *is* the body of Christ, inspired and motivated by the Spirit.[119] All these images are, however, relational in various ways: the metaphor of indwelling (*skenoun*), drawing on the story of the 'tent of meeting' (*mishkan*) in the wilderness wanderings of Israel, expresses the truth that 'God is with us'. The image of dwelling becomes problematic when it ceases to be relational and becomes dualistic, as a powerful, directing agent infusing and mobilizing a material body. Then the activity of the Holy Spirit in the world is envisaged as permeating matter,

---

116 Mikhail Bakhtin, *Rabelais and His World*, trans. Helene Iswolsky (Bloomington: Indiana University Press, 19842), pp. 19, 26–7.

117 See Scott Lash and Jim Urry, *Economies of Signs and Space* (London: Sage Publications, 1994), pp. 13–28, 54–9.

118 Rev. 21:3; cf. Ezek. 37:27–28; Lev.26:11.

119 See above, ch. 4, pp. 67–8.

as the mind in a body.[120] This error is likely to happen when the metaphor of indwelling is not used in a balanced or two-directional way: we need to think not only of God's indwelling the world, but our dwelling in God.

In human culture, we have seen that bodies find their identity in relation to social spaces characterized by activities and relationships. The doctrine of the Trinity depicts a space in God in which created beings can dwell. To speak of God as Father, Son and Spirit is to say that there are relationships in God: there are flowing movements of giving and receiving in love, like a father sending out a son on a mission of reconciliation in the world, a son responding in loving obedience to a father, and a spirit of discovery, always opening up these relations to new depths and a new future.[121] Within these interweaving relations and actions (*perichoresis*), in this eternal dance of love – which can also be pictured as relations between daughter and mother, daughter and father, son and mother – there is room for created beings to move and to dwell.

With this vision of a God who makes room for us, we can begin to see the connection, and difference, between bodies. There is first the body of Jesus of Nazareth, the whole physical being of the Jesus who walked the dusty roads of Galilee, whose feet were washed by the tears and ointment of women, whose body was fixed to a cross and laid in a tomb; the person who was fully embodied in this way offered an obedient response to God his Father which was exactly the same as the movement of responsive love within God's dance of life. The son-father relation that Jesus embodied can be mapped exactly onto the son-father relation in the Trinity, with no remainder, so that the two can never be torn apart. The incarnate and risen Christ is the eternal Son, the only-begotten, the Word (Logos) of God whereas we are always adopted sons and daughters. As we say 'Abba, Father' we lean always on his response of 'yes' to the Father, and so always encounter the risen Christ. Individual believers can occupy this space in God which is shaped like a child's relation to a parent, because the space is Christ-shaped; we are 'in Christ'. Individuals and their bodies, as they share in this movement of saying 'yes' to the Father, are thus limbs and members of the body of Christ, not the body itself. Together in community they make up the whole body; so the life of the community, mapped onto the life in God, is not just 'like' a body – it is the body of Christ. Likewise the actions of breaking of bread and the

---

120 This I judge to be a problem with the way that Process thought employs the image of the world as God's body; it rightly affirms the reciprocity of God with the world, but still thinks in terms of a mind-body relation, with mind as the transcendent aspect of God and body as the divine immanence: see Charles Hartshorne, *Man's Vision of God: and the Logic of Theism* (Hamden: Archon Books, 19642), p. 185.

121 See my *Participating in God*, pp. 36–8.

pouring of wine can fit into the movement of self-breaking and self-outpouring within God, becoming the place where we encounter in an ever deeper way the self-giving of Christ. Covenant, as I have already urged, is about sharing in the covenant which exists eternally within the fellowship of God's life;[122] the eucharist is the meal of the new covenant, enabling the community to enter anew into these relations.

Wherever, too, in the world patterns of human sacrifice and self-giving correspond to the movement in God which is like a son responding to the mission of the father, there we can discern the body of Christ. The whole natural world responds in its own way to the creativity of God, singing God's praises by being what it is (Psalm 19:1–4), and this response too fits in with the giving of glory to the Father by the Son. So different bodies in the world – the individual bodily form of Christ, the sacraments of bread, wine and water, the eucharistic community, groups in society, and all the variety of matter in nature – are all related to a common space. In all of them Christ can be embodied, his form discerned in them; in all of them he can take flesh. Through all of them the gracious presence of God can be experienced. This is not because there is some identical directing principle in all, such as spirit or logos or divine spark, but because they all participate in the space opened up for creation within the relations of the triune God. Thus Christ, as Bonhoeffer puts it in his later work, takes form in the world, and Christians 'allow themselves to be caught up into the way of Jesus Christ, into the messianic event'.[123]

The poet Gerard Manley Hopkins continually celebrates the unique expressiveness of every created thing. In one poem, for instance, he rejoices in the different ways that kingfishers and dragonflies catch the light, and in the quite different sounds of stones falling into water, strings being plucked, bells rung. Everything has its intrinsic reality and value, its 'being indoors' or 'inscape', in his special terminology:

> As kingfishers catch fire, dragonflies draw flame;
> As tumbled over rim in roundy wells
> Stones ring; each tucked string tells, each hung bell's
> Bow swung finds tongue to fling out broad its name;
> Each mortal thing does one thing and the same;
> Deals out that being indoors each one dwells;
> Selves - goes itself; *myself* it speaks and spells;
> Crying, *What I do is me; for that I came.*

Hopkins attributes this unique identity of all things to the presence of Christ, indwelling all inscapes, responding through them to the Father.

---

122   See above, ch. 2, pp. 36–7 and ch. 4, pp. 79–80.
123   Bonhoeffer, *Letters and Papers from Prison*, p. 361.

They are sacramental because they can share in the joyous movement ('playing') of love between the Son and the Father.

– for Christ plays in ten thousand places,
Lovely in limbs and lovely in eyes not his
To the Father through the features of men's faces.[124]

The lives of individuals and communities will occupy space in God, and so manifest the body of Christ, in their own characteristic ways. We can thus discern differences between the embodiments of Christ, his 'playing in ten thousand places'. The life-style of the church will not be simply the same as the culture of the society in which it is placed, and will at times be called to challenge it; this is because the church's life will be shaped by the preached word and the sacrament, which embody the pattern of relationships in God in their own particular ways. Only the church, not the secular society, is a *eucharistic* community. Social groups outside the church, and the coherence of things in the natural world may become, at times, a 'sacramental' community in that they become occasions for Christ to embody himself, and become gateways into the dance of God's life. But only the church is formed by the actions of the two sacraments which recall the story of Jesus, and bring it into the present. Only in the church are bread, wine and water means through which Christ promises to be present, and where he can regularly be expected to meet us.

The church can discover more about the meaning of its story through finding Christ embodied outside its walls· it may, for example, find out more about the meaning of salvation and healing in life as it experiences movements for social justice and liberation. But as the covenant community it has a particular witness to the story, and has an inescapable duty to go on telling it. Thus it seems apt to reserve the name 'body of Christ' for the eucharistic bread and the eucharistic community. The whole world may be called 'the body of God', not because God is the world, but because the triune God takes many bodies in the world to make the divine presence known, and to open entrances – sometimes surprisingly – into the divine dance of life. But the phrase 'the body of Christ' has a specific historical reference, to the story of the earthly and risen Jesus; while Christ embodies himself in many places in the world, it is appropriate to assign 'body of Christ' as a permanent name only to the one who takes bodily form, the sacrament that recalls his story, and the community which takes its place within the story in an act of covenant loyalty. But other persons and objects can at times represent the 'body of

124 Hopkins, 'As Kingfishers catch fire', *Poems of Gerard Manley Hopkins*, ed. W. H. Gardner and N.H. Mackenzie (Oxford: Oxford University Press, 1967), p. 90.

Christ', and the shock value of metaphor can direct us back to the
eucharist and the eucharistic community:

> You are there also
> at the foot of the precipice
> of water that was too steep
> for the drowned: their breath broke
> and they fell. You have made an altar
> out of the deck of the lost
> trawler whose spars
> are your cross. The sand crumbles
> like bread; the wine is
> the light quietly lying
> in its own chalice. There is
> a sacrament there more beauty
> than terror whose ministrant
> you are and the aisles are full
> of the sea shapes coming to its ministration.[125]

---

125 R.S. Thomas, 'In Great Waters', in *Frequencies* (1978), repr. in R.S. Thomas,
Collected Poems 1945–1990 (London: Phoenix Press, 2001), p. 351.

CHAPTER 9

The Church's Ecumenical Calling:
A Baptist Perspective

The Present Form of the Call

Some while ago my predecessor as Principal at my college in Oxford felt the need for a couple of days' spiritual retreat, and booked himself into a house run by the Carmelite Order. He was made to feel very welcome, but during a discussion period on the second day a nun turned to him with an air of anxious enquiry. She knew he was a distinguished Baptist historian, so she thought he could answer a question that had often troubled her: could he please explain why Baptists were followers of John the Baptist rather than Jesus? Such ignorance of the identity of Baptists is, fortunately, not widely shared on the British church scene. But I begin with this story to make clear that I am bound to approach the subject of this chapter in at least a partly 'apologetic' way, wanting to clarify the distinctive Baptist contribution to the ecumenical adventure which may sometimes be overlooked by other ecumenical partners. I also, however, want to identify the particular challenge which I believe is posed to Baptists today by 'the call to be one', and to suggest ways in which Baptists might respond to it. In our day, I believe that we may detect three general trends in the way that churches are hearing God's call to unity.

Unity from the Roots

First, the kind of unity that churches are seeking today is one which begins *from the bottom up* rather than top-down. The story of the Carmelite nun shows perhaps that mutual understanding *has* to begin on the ground. Whatever fine things have been happening in the airy heights of theological commissions, such as the dialogue between the Baptist World Alliance and the Roman Catholic Church,[1] it is another thing for

---

1   *Summons to Witness to Christ in Today's World. A Report on the Baptist-Roman Catholic International Conversations, 1984–1988.* Sponsored by the Vatican

this to trickle down to the roots. It is better for unity to grow at grass-roots level in the first place, in a sharing of resources for worship, witness and social action at local and regional levels. This was a central point in the Swanwick Declaration which led to the creation of 'Churches Together' (in England, Scotland and Wales) and the 'Council of Churches for Britain and Ireland' (now 'Churches Together in Britain and Ireland'). Replacing the former British Council of Churches, the aim was to create lighter ecumenical instruments designed not to join existing church structures together, but to serve the churches in their actually working together *as they are*.[2] The hope was that these new forums and assemblies would assist cooperation to turn into commitment and so enable a growing into unity. This new ecumenical pattern enabled the participation of the Roman Catholic Church in Britain; the approach, and especially an emphasis on working together in mission, also commended itself to the member churches of the Baptist Union of Great Britain, which in 1995 re-affirmed membership of 'Churches Together' by very large majorities.[3]

Not just in the UK but in many places, ecumenism begins with local clusters of churches engaged in theological education, or with mission, or with chaplaincies to hospitals, prisons, education and industry, or with the sharing of buildings, or with a local campaign against injustice, or with a participation in inter-faith dialogue. When in the late 1990s the Council of the Baptist Union of Great Britain set itself to a restructuring of the way that member churches associate together in the regions, it proposed to scrap the old grouping of Baptist churches at 'district' level; it observed that the 'supportive clusters or networks' that had grown up over the last few years 'often cross denominational boundaries' and it aimed to encourage this to continue.[4]

Unity as Full Communion

A second general trend I detect is towards the vision of 'full communion' rather than 'one world church'. The picture of visible unity generally on view is that of a continuing variety of churches, each with

---

Secretariat for Promoting Christian Unity and the Baptist World Alliance (McLean: Baptist World Alliance, 1988); see esp. section E. 'Challenges to Common Witness'.

2   *Not Strangers But Pilgrims*, p. 12.

3   The Baptist Assembly at Plymouth, 6 May 1995, reaffirmed membership of Churches Together in England by 90.21% of those present and voting, and membership of the Council of Churches for Britain and Ireland by 81.27%.

4   *Relating and Resourcing. The Report of the Task Group on Associating*, issued January 1998 for presentation to the Council of the Baptist Union of Great Britain, March 1998: sections 3:4, 3:8 pp. 8–9.

their own heritage, tradition and emphases, but each in full communion with the other. It is this kind of goal of union which was envisioned by the WCC Assembly at Canberra in 1991: 'when all the churches are able to *recognize* in one another the one, holy, catholic and apostolic church in its fullness.' Such a communion, the statement spells out, will be nurtured in a common sacramental life, will confess a common faith, will have a common life in which members and ministries are mutually recognized and reconciled, and will exercise a common mission in the world.[5]

This stress on communion, or fellowship (*koinonia*), is rooted in a theological vision of God who lives in a fellowship of love as Father, Son and Holy Spirit. This has been expounded at length in the basic document of the Fifth World Conference on Faith and Order (1993), called 'Towards Koinonia in Faith, Life and Witness':

> The terms koinonia and communion have a wide reference. Koinonia is used to refer to the life of the Trinity or to that gift God offers in all its fullness to the whole of humanity and creation. They refer to the Church of Jesus Christ and to the way in which Christian communions understand their own life experienced at a local, national or worldwide level.[6]

The abiding of the communion of the church in the communion of God means that in spite of separation the various churches are *already* in communion. This is a new note that has been struck in recent years, a feeling that churches are not 'out of communion' – they *cannot* be if they exist in God's communion. But they can be said to share 'an existing though imperfect communion' or a 'degree of communion'.[7] The document 'Towards Koinonia' admits that it is difficult to find the language to describe this 'growing conviction' and this increasing experience of 'already sharing in one communion of God's own life ... a reality that already binds Christians together.'[8] Those Baptists who affirm only an invisible, *spiritual* unity of all Christians and churches, may feel that they have been vindicated here; but we should not miss the fact that the document goes on to say that this experience should encourage us to

---

5   'The Unity of the Church as Koinonia: Gift and Calling' ('the Canberra Statement'), in Michael Kinnamon (ed.), *Signs of the Spirit. Official Report. Seventh Assembly of the World Council of Churches*. Canberra, Australia, 7–20 February 1991 (Grand Rapids: Eermans/Geneva: WCC Publications, 1991), 2.1, p. 173; cf. Report, para. 66, p. 250.

6   'Towards Koinonia in Faith, Life and Witness', in Best and Gassmann (eds), *On the Way to Fuller Koinonia*, para. 45, p. 276.

7   *The Church, Local and Universal*. A Study Commissioned and Received by the Joint Working Group between the Roman Catholic Church and the World Council of Churches (Faith and Order Paper 150; Geneva: WCC Publications, 1990), p. 10.

8   'Towards Koinonia', para. 45, p. 277.

move forward to overcome the barriers that prevent full and visible communion, for the sake of God's reconciling activity in the world.

Unity in Diversity

A third general trend arises from this stress on full communion – that is the acceptance of diversity in the unity. Again appeal is made to the vision of a triune God: just as God lives in unity and true diversity as three persons in one God, so the church in God's image can and should show *legitimate diversity*. The catchword here is 'reconciled diversity' not uniformity. This does raise the question, however, of what are legitimate and illegitimate diversities. The document 'Towards Koinonia' suggests that diversity is not acceptable where it denies the 'common confession of Jesus Christ as God and Saviour', where it justifies discrimination on the basis of race of gender, where it prevents reconciliation, where it hinders the common mission of the church, and where it endangers the life in *koinonia*.[9]

This is fairly wide-ranging, and while it clearly and properly rules out – for instance – a church based on apartheid, it might also rule out uncomfortable challenges to the status quo which are truly prophetic. Perhaps life in *koinonia* sometimes *needs* to be 'endangered'. The report of the Lambeth Conference of the Anglican Communion (1998) titled 'Called to be One' makes the important point that diversity must include pain. Noting that churches exist in different cultural contexts with particular stories and marked by sin, the report says:

> If visible unity is about living in the world the communion of God's own life, then our portrait of visible unity must show that tension, even conflict, will always be part of life this side of the kingdom. 'Sharp things that divide us can paradoxically turn out to be gift ... the world with all its divisions is not used to such a possibility as this: that those on opposing sides should stay together, should remain in dialogue, bearing each other's burdens, even entering one another's pain.'[10]

These last words about one another's pain take us into the heart of the triune life of God, for there we find brokenness, desolation and loss as communion is open to receive the impact of the cross. In this rich harmony, the wounds of Jesus are not absorbed but remain as a witness to the suffering of the world.

---

9   'Towards Koinonia', para. 57, p. 280.

10   *Called to be One*. Section IV, Lambeth Conference 1998 (London: Morehouse Publishing), p. 24, citing the Response to the Archbishop of Canterbury, Lambeth Conference 1988, p. 292.

So, to summarize where we have come so far, the sense of ecumenical call which is widespread at present is a calling to work from the roots, to work towards full communion, and to live with diversity, painful though it is. I have been using the term 'call' because it echoes the statement of Ephesians 4 that we are *called* to be one, and so reminds us that all true movements for unity have their origin in the desire, initiative and the summons of God (cf. the prayer of Jesus in John 17). The opening verses of this chapter in Ephesians have been often quoted in the dialogues of the modern ecumenical movement, in which the readers are urged to be:

> eager to maintain the unity of the spirit in the bond of peace. There is one body and one Spirit, just as you were *called* to the one hope that belongs to your *call*, one Lord, one faith, one baptism, one God and father of us all, who is above all and through all and in all.

This passage either states or hints at three theological ideas that define the call to unity, and I want now to use them as the framework for the rest of this chapter. First there is the image of the body; second there is an evoking of the fellowship in which God lives, as 'one Spirit ... one Lord (Christ) ... one Father'; and thirdly there is the allusion to covenant with the phrase 'bond of peace.' One body, one fellowship, one covenant. Though these ideas overlap and intertwine, I am going to take them each in turn.

The Call to One Body

A fundamental image of unity is the one on which Paul concentrates in 1 Corinthians 12, that of the church as the body of Christ. The daring manner with which the early Christian community used this title, and the startling claim it makes, has perhaps been dulled by over-familiarity. As we saw in an earlier chapter,[11] the early Christians were not just describing themselves by analogy as a 'body' of people – as we might speak today of soldiers as 'a fine body of men and women'. They were asserting that they were the body of *a particular person* – Jesus Christ, Jesus of Nazareth who was now the risen Lord of the universe. They were venturing to say that people could touch and handle the risen Christ by touching the outstretched hands of the church. As Christ was once to be seen on the streets of Nazareth and Jerusalem, so he is visible in the Christian congregation (1 Jn. 1:1–4). He lives out his life through all his members. *Body is about visibility.*

---

11   Chapter 4, pp. 66–8.

Now, what I want to underline here is that the *primary* meaning of the 'body of Christ' is the whole, universal church. Since Christ is the Lord of the universe, the exalted ruler of the cosmos, his body must be the universal company of all the redeemed. This link is brought out clearly in Ephesians 1:22–23 (cf. Col. 1:24):

> And God has put all things under his feet and has made him the head over all things for the church, which is his body, the fulness of him who fills all in all.

So Paul states in 1 Cor. 12:13 that 'by one Spirit we were all baptized into one body – Jews or Greeks, slaves or free – and all were made to drink of one Spirit.' This 'all' cannot simply mean all in one local community, or Paul would not – for instance – include himself within it, writing to Corinth. This perception ought to shape our understanding of the familiar picture that immediately follows it in verses 14–30, that of the many members making up the body: 'now you are the body of Christ, and individually members of it'. This body too cannot only be the single congregation.[12] Baptists have, of course, insisted that the local company of believers can *also* be called the 'body of Christ'. Wherever two or three are gathered together, wherever the body of the communion bread is broken (1 Cor. 10:16–17), there is the body of Christ.[13] But the local congregation is always a '*manifestation* of the one Church of God on earth and in heaven';[14] it derives from the one body. It not then a question of many small bodies making up one large body, by a kind of spiritual arithmetic; the small bodies exist as an 'outcropping' of the whole body.[15] Separate churches already relate together because the body exists before us, and we are called to enter it.

This sense of the one, trans-local body of Christ is prominent in early Baptist thinking. In considering the bond of covenant existing between local congregations, I have already cited the (Particular Baptist) London Confession of 1644 as asserting that '*although* the particular Congregations be distinct and severall Bodies ... *yet* are they all to walk by one and the same Rule ... as members of the one body in the common

---

12   So *Relating and Resourcing*, 2:6, p. 4: 'The Body of Christ is not confined to local churches but finds expression in the relations between churches as well as within them'; *The Nature of the Assembly and the Council*, pp. 6–7, 9–11.

13   See above, ch. 8, pp. 168–74.

14   *The Baptist Doctrine of the Church* (1948), reprinted in Hayden (ed.), *Baptist Union Documents 1948–1977*, 8.

15   The image comes from the Congregationalist P.T. Forsyth, who wrote of the local church as an 'outcrop' of the universal, because Christ is 'a corporate personality... with all the Church latent in him': Forsyth, *The Church and the Sacraments* (London: Independent Press, 2nd edn, 1947), p. 66.

faith under Christ their onely head.'[16] That was London, but here is another example from the countryside, from the 'Somerset Confession' drawn up in Bridgewater in 1656, which asserts that it is 'the duty of the members of Christ ... *although* in several congregations and assemblies (being one in the head) if occasion be, to communicate each to other in things spiritual and things temporal.'[17] We note in both confessions that the separateness of the congregations is regarded as a matter of 'although'. The London Confession of 1644 even goes so far as to describe this situation as being a matter of simple practical necessity:

> though wee be distinct in respect of our particular bodies, for conveniency sake, being as many as can well meete together in one place, yet are all one in Communion, holding Jesus Christ to be our head and Lord; under whose government wee desire alone to walk...[18]

In the record of the first general meeting of the Abingdon Association (Particular Baptist) in 1652 there is an interesting theological argument advanced for the churches to hold 'a firm communion with each other': that is, there is the same relation between the particular churches as there is between the particular members of one church. The record adds, 'For the churches of Christ doe all make up one body or church in generall under Christ their head.'[19] From the General Baptists, the *Orthodox Creed* (1679) affirms that the 'visible church of Christ on earth is made up of several distinct congregations, which make up that one catholick church, or mystical body of Christ.'[20] In line with this it refers to the representatives to general councils or assemblies of churches as making 'but one church',[21] although it must be said to be unusual among Baptists in using the word 'church' to refer directly to a gathering of churches.

It is not just that the terms 'body' and 'Christ as head' are used in all these examples to *describe* wider assemblies than the local congregation. The point is being made that local churches are therefore under a *necessity* 'to hold communion among themselves for their peace,

---

16   See above, ch. 2, p. 44; art. XLVII, Lumpkin, *Baptist Confessions*, pp. 168–9; my italics.

17   Art. XXVIII, Lumpkin, *Baptist Confessions*, p. 211.

18   London Confession (1644), Introduction, 'To All that Desire', Lumpkin, *Baptist Confessions*, p. 155.

19   B.R. White (ed.), *Association Records of the Particular Baptists of England, Wales and Ireland to 1660*. Part 3. The Abingdon Association (London: Baptist Historical Society, 1974), p. 126; in support, the statement cites Eph. 1:22f., Col. 1.24, Eph. 5:23ff., 2 Cor. 12:13f.

20   *Orthodox Creed*, art. XXX, Lumpkin, *Baptist Confessions*, p. 319.

21   *Orthodox Creed*, art. XXIX, Lumpkin, *Baptist Confessions*, p. 327.

increase of love and mutual edification',[22] just as members in any congregation are called by Christ to gather together. Here the recent report of the Baptist Union of Great Britain, 'Relating and Resourcing', seems just a little uncertain of its aim when it says, 'that as membership of a church is a freely chosen act so churches *might and should* freely choose to join a communion of churches'.[23] The words 'and should' are key here, and are at odds with 'might'. While, of course, membership of both the local and the wider body involves free human choice, this is always in obedient response to a divine imperative; the call is there because the one body is already there. Belonging to a wider association is no more an optional alternative than belonging to Christ. Here an earlier discussion document of the Doctrine and Worship Committee of the Baptist Union of Great Britain speaks more unambiguously when it declares: 'It follows from a biblical understanding of Church as covenant, fellowship and body that there is also no option about local churches being part of a wider fellowship of churches. They are gathered together by Christ.'[24] The distinctive Baptist view has not been that associating is only an option, but that these wider assemblies cannot *impose* their decisions on the local church meeting. The reason for this, as should have become abundantly clear in the progress of argument in this book, is that each church, like the wider church, is under the rule of Christ alone.[25] This has implications for an ecumenical understanding of conciliar forms and reception of decisions, as we shall see in a moment.

Belonging together in one body has implications for 'visible unity'. The one, universal body of Christ cannot be totally invisible, as this would undermine the whole point of the metaphor, which is about visibility and tangibility. Churches have the *duty* to relate together because they are summoned to allow Christ to become manifest through his body. If he is to become visible at every level of human society – local, regional, national and international – and if his word of challenge is to be heard in every human forum, then he will be humble enough to take on the rags and tatters of our human organizations. This is the meaning of incarnation: the divine Word is willing to come among us even in the poverty-stricken form of an association of Baptist churches or a council of Christian churches with all their mixed motives and failures.

One sometimes hears it said among Baptists that there is indeed the local and the universal body of Christ, but only the local body is visible. The universal body is claimed to be completely *invisible*, a purely spiritual reality with no material embodiment. So (it is said) there is no

---

22 Second London Confession, ch. XXVI.14–15, Lumpkin, *Baptist Confessions*, p. 289.
23 *Relating and Resourcing*, 2:5, p. 4.
24 *The Nature of the Assembly and the Council*, p. 8.
25 See above, pp. 6, 42–5, 51–4, 122–3.

need to make this visible through structures of association, or churches together having an ecumenical unity which can be seen by the world.[26] Now, Baptists certainly reflected from their earliest days on the relation between the 'invisible church' and 'visible saints'. They *did* think that there was an invisible church here and now on earth as well as in heaven, but they did not use this concept as a justification for rejecting wider visible structures of the church beyond the local congregation.[27]

Early Baptists understood the 'invisible church' to be the total company of all the redeemed, whether they were inside or outside the visible church, and whether they lived in the past, present or future. Those in the Calvinistic tradition understood the 'invisible church' or the 'spiritual kingdom'[28] simply to be God's elect, those named for salvation from before the beginning of the world and for whom Christ had died. It was the church in the mind of God, and was the universal church in its fullness. Saints became 'visible' when they gathered in 'particular congregations' to live under the covenant rule of Christ, and when their profession of faith and their ethical behaviour gave visible evidence that they were indeed chosen to be sons and daughters of God.[29] Baptists in the Arminian tradition also understood the 'invisible church' to be the whole number of the regenerate, and were usually content to regard this also as the company of the 'elect', as long as it was understood that the effectiveness of the atonement made in Christ was not restricted to a fixed and predetermined number of elect persons. They thus took a more relaxed view of the mysterious interaction between the electing grace of God and human freedom and duty to respond in faith.[30] The congregation of John Smyth affirmed in their *Propositions and Conclusions* (1612) that the 'outward church visible consists of penitent persons only', and is a 'mystical figure outwardly, of the true, spiritual, invisible church; which consisteth of the spirits of…. the regenerate.'[31]

---

26   An influential voice here was Augustus Hopkins Strong, *Systematic Theology* (Philadelphia: Griffith & Rowland, 1909), pp. 887–91.

27   The next few paragraphs rely closely on my argument in 'Church and Salvation: A Comparison of Baptist and Orthodox Thinking', in Anthony R. Cross (ed.), *Ecumenism and History. Studies in Honour of John H.Y. Briggs* (Carlisle, Paternoster Press, 2002), pp. 134–8.

28   The London Confession (1644), art. XXXIII, in Lumpkin, *Baptist Confessions*, p. 165.

29   Ibid. See also The Second London Confession, ch. XXVI.2, in Lumpkin, *Baptist Confessions*, p. 285.

30   See e.g. The *Orthodox Creed*, art. IX, in Lumpkin, *Baptist Confessions*, p. 303: 'a great mystery indeed'.

31   *Propositions and Conclusions concerning True Christian Religion, containing a Confession of Faith of certain English people, living at Amsterdam* (1612–1614), first draft made by John Smyth, art. 64–5 in Lumpkin, *Baptist Confessions*, p. 136.

There were several advantages in making a contrast between an 'invisible' and 'visible' church. First, it stressed the mixed nature of the church as it appeared to human eyes; any congregation was bound to be made up of the regenerate and the unregenerate, and this was explained by the fact that the visible church was not exactly identical with the invisible church. Second, it recognized the freedom of a sovereign God to be in a saving relationship with whomever God wished, regardless of their membership in earthly organizations. These first two points introduced a necessary dose of humility into the hearts of those who regarded themselves as 'visible saints', and also prevented the identifying of the church with any territorial jurisdiction. Third, it laid stress on the importance of the local church as a place where the universal church became visible. The local assembly was not a deficient fragment of a larger structure, but the 'whole church'.

However, the positive affirmation of the local congregation as making the invisible catholic church visible did not imply the negative – that there was no visibility anywhere else. *Wherever* the church was visible, there was always a greater, invisible church; but the contrast between invisible and visible did not exactly match the contrast between wider and local church. We have already seen this exemplified in the affirmation of a larger 'body' of churches in relation, and it is interestingly expressed in the *Orthodox Creed* (General Baptist). This contains an article headed 'Of the invisible catholick Church of Christ' (xxix) which affirms that 'There is one holy catholick church, consisting of, or made up of the whole number of the elect, that have been, are, or shall be gathered by special grace'.[32] The accompanying article on 'Of the catholick Church as visible', already quoted above, then equates 'the visible church of Christ on earth' with 'several distinct congregations', and is careful to place in apposition 'church' (singular) and 'congregations' (plural). It is clear that the body of Christ becomes visible, not only in *each* congregation, but in the gathering of congregations together.[33]

What is at issue here may be illuminated by a comparison and contrast with the approach of the Eastern Orthodox Church. According to Orthodox thought, the 'visible church' is the whole church here on earth, composed of many specific congregations. The title 'invisible church' essentially refers to the church in heaven, the glorified saints and the angels. Orthodoxy strongly insists that there are not two churches but only one. In its theology and in its liturgy, it affirms one communion, one continuous reality. It is thus only in human terms that one speaks of 'the church visible and invisible'. In Orthodox thinking, the phrase 'invisible church' does not indicate some ideal, indivisible church which

---

32   The *Orthodox Creed*, art. XXIX, in Lumpkin, *Baptist Confessions*, p. 318.
33   The *Orthodox Creed*, art. XXIX, in Lumpkin, *Baptist Confessions*, p. 319.

may be contrasted with a divided church as it is on earth. The true church exists here and now on earth as the Orthodox Church, visible and undivided; it must be one because God is one.[34] Some Orthodox thinking still allows for regenerate believers outside the boundaries of the visible church, but these are 'united to her by ties that God has not chosen to reveal to her.'[35] In the words of Kallistos Ware, who takes this view, 'Many people may be members of the church who are not visibly so; invisible bonds may exist despite an outward separation.'[36] Ware is careful *not* to say that such make up an 'invisible church' on earth – it is the *bonds* to the one visible church that are invisible.

Though there is a good deal of overlap here with a Baptist view (and especially that each specific congregation is 'the church in wholeness'[37]), Baptists will want to affirm that the church on earth is always a mixture of the visible and the invisible. Its visibility – whether local, regional or international – is always fragmentary, and will not be complete until the final coming of the kingdom of God. This does not mean, as Miroslav Volf maintains from a confessedly Free Church perspective, that the notion of the church universal is *only* an eschatological reality, and that the only link between local churches at the moment is the presence of the Holy Spirit in the hearts of believers.[38] Of course the church universal will be *partly* invisible, as we shall not see it in its glory until the eschaton; the lordship of Christ over the cosmos is only partially acknowledged at present. It is partly hidden. But this does not mean that Christ does not *want* to be visible and manifest in the world in his whole body, as far as is possible. Such a view would not fit well with 1 Corinthians 12 where the members bring their gifts together to make up the one body. Daniel Turner in the eighteenth century urged 'open communion', as we have seen, because he believed it to be an imperative for the universal body of Christ to come to visible expression in some way.[39] The same sense of necessity is expressed in words from the Confession of Faith of the

---

34   Timothy (Kallistos) Ware, *The Orthodox Church*. New Edition, (Harmondsworth: Penguin, 1997), p. 245.

35   Alexis Khomiakmov, 'The Church is One', in William J. Birkbeck, *Russia and the English Church* (Eastern Churches Association: London, 1895), section 2, adding that these the church 'leaves to the judgement of the great day'. For a similar eschatological perspective on the church, see Dumitru Staniloae, 'The Orthodox Doctrine of Salvation', in Staniloae, *Theology and the Church*, trans. R. Barringer (Crestwood: St. Vladimir's Seminary Press, 1980), pp. 209–11.

36   Ware, *Orthodox Church*, p. 308.

37   See John Zizioulas (Metropolitan John of Pergamon), *Being as Communion*, pp. 147–53, 235–6.

38   Miroslav Volf, *After Our Likeness. The Church as the Image of the Trinity* (Grand Rapids: Eerdmans, 1998), pp. 203, 213, 250.

39   See above, ch. 8, pp. 177–8.

German Baptist Union, that 'It cannot be God's will for denominational
barriers to hinder the visible fellowship of all believers'.[40]
   Where Baptists will take issue with the Orthodox vision of the church
universal is in the equating of *visibility* with *indivisibility*. It is the tragedy
of the church to have been broken through the contingencies and
conflicts of history. It is visible indeed, but in pieces whose fragmentation
is a scandal to the world and which enters the heart of God as a cause of
grief and pain. It is an aspect of the divine humility, we may say, to allow
the church to be divided, and it is a dimension of God's experience of
the cross. The claim of the Eastern Orthodox Churches to be the one and
only indivisible Catholic Church will seem to Baptists to be a too swift
moving on from the Good Friday of history, which must always be held
in tension with the brightness of Easter morning.
   Like the Orthodox Church in the East, the Roman Catholic Church in
the West deduces from the unity of God and the sole lordship of Christ
that the one church *must already exist*, in reality and visibility. A
significant difference is that while the Orthodox understand the unity of
the church to be guaranteed by the bishop in each region in collegial
fellowship with all other bishops, the Roman Catholic Church finds the
final sign and guarantor of unity to be the Bishop of Rome; in the
encyclical *Ut Unum Sint* Pope John Paul II speaks movingly of his
'ministry of unity', and places weight here on Jesus' words to Peter,
'strengthen your brethren.'[41] From this perspective, the conviction that
visible unity must already exist leads to a certain understanding of the
relation of churches to each other. Several recent documents have
followed Vatican II in affirming that 'the One Church of Christ ...
subsists in the Catholic Church, governed by the Successor of Peter and
by the Bishops in communion with him'.[42] This phrase seeks to
harmonize two doctrinal assertions – first, that the church of Christ exists
in its fullness only in the (Roman) Catholic Church, and second, that
outside of her structure, many 'elements of the church' (*elementa
Ecclesiae*) can be found, characterized by sanctification and truth, which
'derive their efficacy from the fullness of grace and truth entrusted to the
Catholic Church.'[43] The document *Dominus Jesus* sets out to clarify the

---

   40   Parker, *Baptists in Europe*, p. 69.
   41   *Ut Unum Sint. Encyclical Letter of the Holy Father John Paul II on Commitment
to Ecumenism* (London: Catholic Truth Society, 1995), paras. 88, 90.
   42   Vatican II, *Lumen Gentium*, 21 Nov. 1964, para. 8, in Flannery (ed), *Vatican
Council II*, p. 357; cf. Vatican II, *Unitatis redintegratio*, 21 Nov. 1964, para. 4, in
Flannery (ed), *Vatican Council II*, p. 457; *Ut Unum Sint*, paras. 10, 86; *Dominus Jesus*,
Congregation for the Doctrine of the Faith, Declaration on the Unicity and Salvific
Universality of Jesus Christ and the Church, August 6, 2000, para. 16: text at
www.vatican.va/roman_curia/congregations.
   43   *Dominus Jesus 17*; *Unitatis redintegratio*, para 3, p. 456.

consequences of this approach. Only the Orthodox Churches of the East, which *Ut Unum Sint* had named as 'Sister Churches',[44] may properly be called 'Church' alongside the Catholic Church; the one Church of Christ is 'present in them' because they stand in true apostolic succession and have retained a valid ministry and celebration of the eucharist, despite not being in full communion with Rome.[45] The non-Catholic Christian communities in the West, stemming from the Reformation, are 'not Churches in the proper sense', but may be called 'ecclesial communities'.[46] They certainly show aspects or elements of the One Church, and those baptized in them are incorporated into Christ and 'are thus in a certain communion, albeit imperfect, with the Church.'

These fine semantic distinctions result partly from a view of apostolic succession and episcopacy, but even more fundamentally from a doctrine of God. If the *unity* of God is the predominant basis for ecclesiology, then we must ask where the one church is *already* visible as a unitary structure. Having established that to our satisfaction, we will then see in others only 'aspects' or 'elements' of that way of being the church. Such a dogma may well recognize (as does *Dominus Jesus*) that 'the lack of unity among Christians is a *wound* for the church',[47] but it will not think that it is deprived of its fundamental visible unity, only that disunity hinders the *completeness* of its catholicity in history.[48] The question, then, is this: how deep are the wounds of the church, and behind these, the wounds of God? If we hold the unity of God in tension with the suffering and brokenness of God, as one who is hurt by lack of love in the world,[49] then we may be able to see the one church of Christ in each other despite our imperfect communion together. The church is broken for two reasons: it shares in the dying of Christ for the world, and so must always be humiliated, being broken like eucharistic bread to nourish others; but it is also divided through its own sin. In both kinds of fragmentation it manifests the suffering which is inflicted upon God, and its lack of wholeness should not prevent us from recognizing it in each other. Indeed, we may be able to recognize it precisely *through* the broken nature of the body, while we seek to heal the wounds that are self-inflicted by its own disobedience and lack of faithfulness.

---

44   *Ut Unum Sint*, paras. 55–7.

45   *Dominus Jesus*, para. 17.

46   Although Vatican II and *Ut Unum Sint* had used the phrase '*Churches* and Ecclesial Communities' to refer to the Western Protestant churches, *Dominus Jesus* is perhaps more consistent here in following through the implications of the underlying ecclesiology.

47   *Dominus Jesus*, para. 17.

48   *Unitatis redintegratio*, para. 4, p. 458.

49   See above, ch. 4, pp. 57–61.

In many ways, recent statements of the Roman Catholic Church, especially *Ut Unum Sint*, have been generous to other Christian communions, and have breathed a true spirit of ecumenicity. Baptists should hesitate to criticize, since at the beginning of their history they could be *very* confident in labelling other communions as 'false churches', especially the newly re-formed Church of England. They found the marks of a true church not only to lie in the true preaching of the word of God and the right administration of the sacraments, but in a form of church discipline based in the congregation; the way that the church was ordered was a matter of obedience to God, and leading an obedient life was a mark of assurance of salvation.[50] They should then not be too hasty in accusing others of making oversight (*episkope*) a determining mark of being the true church. But Baptists, having learnt from their history, will be bound to be impatient at the slowness with which Christian churches recognize the true, apostolic church in each other. They will find difficulties in the recent ecumenical convention of a 'step by step' approach to recognition, and will want to move on quickly from an informal noticing of the marks of church in each other to a formal recognition that the one church of Jesus Christ 'subsists' in the other. They will not think that a certain form of *episkope*, or the intention to create it in the near future, is a necessary sign of apostolic continuity which must be established before this recognition can be offered. On the British scene, for example, they will think that sharing life and mission in the ecumenical process of 'Churches Together' already assumes a recognition that the church of Christ is present in all those in partnership there.

A Baptist view of the visibility of the church universal will therefore be a mixture of realism about broken communion, and determination to overcome the scandal of division. While the church universal can at present be 'glimpsed imperfectly in the total global reality of churches, denominations and Christian networks',[51] we are called to make it more visible. Something of this duality is expressed in another of the 'propositions' of John Smyth (1612). This is an interesting piece for Baptists, as it clearly assumes that the 'outward', that is *visible*, church is far wider than the local church. There is no sense here that the body of Christ is only visible in a particular congregation; indeed, since all those who profess true repentance and faith are 'visible saints', this would make little sense. But what *is* visible is 'rent' asunder; the body is indeed broken:

---

50   See Brachlow, *The Communion of Saints*, pp. 54–5.
51   Response of the Baptist Union of Great Britain to seven questions put to churches by the 'Called to be One' process of Churches Together in England, question 1; unpublished paper approved by the Baptist Union Council, November 1994.

That all penitent and faithful Christians are brethren in the communion of the outward church, wheresoever they live, by what name soever they are known, which in truth and zeal, follow repentance and faith, though compassed with never so many ignorances and infirmities; and we salute them all with a holy kiss, being heartily grieved that we which follow after one faith,and one spirit, one Lord, and one God, one body, and one baptism, should be rent into so many sects and schisms: and that only for matters of less moment.[52]

Making Christ Visible

The language of the 'body' of Christ is about the visibility, the apprehensibility, of Christ. From previous discussion in this book, we may recall three converging theological ideas that concern the form that Christ takes in the church and the world. First, the gathering together of members with gifts bestowed by Christ 'constructs' the body in its fullness, limb joined to limb, feature to feature until the appearance of Christ stands out.[53] Second, human individuals and communities can participate in the movements within God which are like a father sending out a son on a mission of self-surrender and sacrifice, and which are like a son celebrating the goodness of a father; sharing in these currents of relationship, human sons and daughters make the divine Son manifest.[54] Third, in an eternal movement of covenant making within God, human sons and daughters are identified as partners with the Son in a relationship of mutual love and self-offering.[55] In these three ways Christ takes form in human life, and becomes manifest and tangible in the midst of relations between human beings. In particular, I want to set this visibility in the context of two ecumenical concerns, mission and conciliarity.

Visibility in Ecumenical Mission

The aim of the exercise of spiritual gifts as Paul describes it in 1 Corinthians 12, is for Christ to use all his members in order to become reachable and graspable by people today, to draw them into the life and love of the triune God. *Charismata* are not assigned for self-fulfilment, but to fulfil God's ministry of reconciliation. Schisms have happened in churches when people are aggrieved because they feel that they are not

---

52   *Propositions and Conclusions*, art. 69, Lumpkin, *Baptist Confessions*, p. 137.
53   See above, pp. 67–8, 150–2.
54   See above, pp. 53, 56, 72–4, 80–2.
55   See above, pp. 36–7, 78–80, 189–90.

being given proper scope for their gifts, as they believe them to be; if they cannot exercise them where they are they will go and form another church where they can. But the point of the gifts is to allow Christ to become visible, and everything must be subordinated to that.

All this applies to the uniting of churches together. It will mean a gathering together of *charismata*. As I suggested earlier, the picture of the body in 1 Cor 12 applies on the level of churches living and working together: 'the eye cannot say to the hand, I have no need of you.' Referring to the whole Communion of Saints, the (Particular Baptist) Second London Confession of 1677 speaks of 'communion in each others' gifts and graces.'[56] A single local church will be very unlikely to have all the gifts needed for mission in our modern, complex society. Allowing Christ to become visible means a sharing of gifts, and also material resources. It is not charity when a richer church gives assistance to a poorer one; it is a matter of sharing life within one body, for 'if one member suffers, all suffer together.' The report 'Relating and Resourcing', adopted by the Council of the Baptist Union in March 1998, rightly comments that:

> The local church may be competent, but it is scarcely omnicompetent ... no local church is complete of itself and does well to seek for that of Christ which is expressed in the wider body ... To fulfil the mission of Christ, churches have to do it together that they may make up for each other's lacks and set forth the whole Christ.[57]

Concern to fulfil the mission of God in Christ actually motivated the beginning of the modern ecumenical movement. This is usually dated to 1910 with the International Missionary Conference in Edinburgh, the first international meeting of church leaders from all denominations in modern times. As they considered mission strategy it became clear to them that there were wider issues of disunity on the agenda, and especially disagreements about doctrine between the churches; from this discussion there issued the First World Conference on Faith and Order at Lausanne in 1927, to which five Baptist Unions and Conventions sent representatives. These two streams of the ecumenical movement, the International Missionary Council and 'Faith and Order', were eventually brought together with the 'Life and Work' movement of the churches into the formation of the World Council of Churches in 1948; some Baptist Unions were again among the founder members.[58] The letter of

---

56   Second London Confession, ch. XXVII, Lumpkin, *Baptist Confessions*, p. 289.
57   *Relating and Resourcing*, 2:7, p. 4.
58   Baptist founding members were: Baptist Union of Great Britain and Ireland, Baptist Union of Scotland, Baptist Union of Wales and Monmouthshire, National Baptist Convention (USA), Northern Baptist Convention (USA), Baptist Union of New

invitation sent to churches in 1938 to take part in the establishment of a World Council urged the churches to see this move towards unity 'against the background of the Church's primary task of World Evangelisation'.[59] But the link between mission and unity had already been understood by the Baptist William Carey, one of the earliest and major influences on the missionary movement of modern times. In a letter of 1806 to the Secretary of his missionary society, Carey proposed 'a general association of all denominations of Christians, from the four quarters of the world', to meet every ten years or so. Proposing the Cape of Good Hope as a convenient, central venue, he called for the first meeting to be in 1810 or no later than 1812, commenting that 'we could understand each other better, and more entirely enter into one another's views by two or three hours conversation than by two or three years epistolary correspondence.'[60] Carey's vision, dismissed as 'one of bro[r] Carey's pleasing dreams' at the time,[61] had to wait another hundred years before its realization at Edinburgh in 1910.

Making Christ visible together, in wide association, means the sharing of gifts and resources to make Christ known. While there are evident advantages in efficiency, this also means facing a deep challenge to established convictions and practices, calling for risk and trust in each other. The Swanwick Declaration, the founding document of Churches Together in Britain and Ireland, observes that any kind of resource sharing means 'taking holy risks' for the sake of common mission. One risk it suggests is allowing one church or agency to act on behalf of others, whether in evangelism or social service, without everyone feeling *they* have to be there.[62]

Mission will be effective when we act in a way that makes Christ visible in his body. But to do this, we need to be able to make decisions together, to discern the purpose of Christ. Being the body of Christ means receiving the promise of knowing his mind, when members are gathered

---

Zealand, China Baptist Council, and Union of Baptists in Holland. At present, only 22 Baptist Unions or Conventions are members of the WCC (including the Baptist Union of Great Britain), but these represent a membership of about 18,500,000, and so about 44% of Baptists throughout the world.

59   *Documents of the World Council of Churches* (Amsterdam: WCC, 1948), p. 9. M. E. Aubrey, General Secretary of the Baptist Union of Great Britain at the time, was one of the fourteen signatories of the letter of invitation, and a member of the first Central Committee.

60   Letter from William Carey (Calcutta) to Andrew Fuller, 15 May 1806; original at St. Mary's Church, Norwich, copy in the Angus Library, Regent's Park College, E13 (16).

61   Letter from Andrew Fuller to William Ward, 2 December 1806; Angus Library H/1/1.

62   *Not Strangers But Pilgrims*, p. 13.

and Christ becomes manifest among them. On and beyond the local level, this means the development of conciliar forms through which member churches can meet and consult.

Visibility in Conciliar Forms

In an attempt to envisage what it would be like for churches to be in full communion, the Canberra Statement of the WCC (1991) speaks of a common *confession* of the apostolic faith; a common *sacramental* life entered by one baptism and celebrated together in one eucharistic fellowship; a common *life* in which ministries are recognized by all; and a common *mission* witnessing to all people to the Gospel of God's grace and serving the whole of creation. But if this fullness of communion is to be sustained, the statement goes on to say, it must 'be expressed on the local and universal levels through conciliar forms of life and action.'[63] That is, we are urged that communion is only possible if churches take responsible decisions together in some kind of council or assembly ('conciliar forms').

The later Faith and Order document 'Towards Koinonia' makes clear that 'conciliar communion' is not just required for questions of strategy and resources between the churches; more fundamental is the need for churches to meet under the guidance of the Holy Spirit to discuss the nature of the apostolic faith and to discern the ways that it should be discerned and proclaimed in the context of our modern world. 'It is only when churches are in communion with each other that they will be able in conciliar deliberation and decision-making to teach together the one faith in ways that are acceptable to all.'[64] It is essential that churches should hear the way that scripture is read and understood in contexts quite different from their own; a church in the affluent west is not in a position to know that scripture 'means' until it has heard how it is interpreted, for instance, by a church in the poverty of the shanty towns of South Africa or Brazil, or by a church living as a minority faith in the Middle East. However, 'Towards Koinonia' also points out that:

> Decisions taken in such conciliar communion will require reception by the whole church. Such structures and forms of authority should be seen as gifts of God to keep churches faithful to the Apostolic faith and enable them to witness together in evangelical freedom.[65]

---

63   For details of the Canberra Statement, see n. 5 above.
64   'Towards Koinonia', para. 62, pp. 281–2.
65   'Towards Koinonia', para. 61, p. 281.

Baptists have a special contribution to make here, I suggest, in their view that authority is a matter of finding the mind of Christ.[66] It is precisely their convictions about the place of the local church meeting, and the freedom of the local church from outside human constraint, that should make Baptists very open to listening to others. The church meeting is not about preserving independency, or showing how self-sufficient a local church might be, but is about finding the mind of Christ. This is a proper quest for the body of Christ gathered together, wherever it might be. In church meeting members should thus take very seriously the decisions and the advice of their own regional association and national (union or convention) councils and assemblies; this openness is easily, then, extendable to ecumenical councils in which the church has a representative part. The church meeting cannot be *imposed* upon by outside church authorities, but this is because the final authority, according to Baptist understanding, is not the church meeting but Christ himself present in the meeting. And the same Christ is present to make himself visible in his body not only in the local congregation but in wider assemblies.

A concern to find the mind of Christ thus leads to a delicate balance between insights and decisions at conciliar level, and the freedom to test those decisions in the local fellowship. As expressed by the Council of the Baptist Union in its reply to the *Ten Propositions* of the Churches' Council for Covenanting in 1977, the last major effort to create common structures for the churches in the UK:

> Conciliar forms ... may become the means by which the Lord of the Church speaks to the churches. It is however for the churches to recognise his voice ... Authority is not simply a matter of decision making at some appropriate point or level. It is also a matter of recognising and reception of decisions through the whole range of the church's life.

The need for 'reception' of conciliar decisions in the local congregation is, of course, realized by all Christian churches, as is made clear by the 'Towards Koinonia' document quoted above. Among the Orthodox Churches, Vladimir Lossky points out that perception of divine truth in councils of churches involves a 'harmony of two wills', divine and human, appealing to the formula of Acts 15:28, 'It seemed good to the Holy Spirit and to us.' While Lossky here has in mind the mysterious harmony of will between the *bishops* and the Spirit,[67] there is a quite widespread Orthodox opinion (and notably in the school formed by the Russian Orthodox Alexis Khomiakov) that the decisions of councils can

---

66   See above, ch. 5, pp. 84–8.

67   Vladimir Lossky, *The Mystical Theology of the Eastern Church* (London: James Clarke, 1957), p. 188; cf. p. 183.

only be regarded as dogma when there is evidence, over time, that they have been accepted by the whole people of God. This assent is not expressed formally, as in a Baptist church meeting, but 'lived' in the will of the people.[68]

The particular Baptist contribution seems to be to bring together in a dynamic way the discerning of the body and the mind of Christ at both conciliar and local level. The dialectic remains, and cannot be resolved by simply ceding authority in one direction or the other. It is in the midst of the tension, in having to bring two processes of discernment together, that Christ becomes visible. There are, to be sure, Baptist churches which hold fast to what they call their 'autonomy'. There have, in contrast, been proposals among Baptists themselves to surrender the authority of the church meeting upwards, on at least *some* issues, to a synodical form of government on which it is represented. In modern times a report of the Northern Baptist Association *The Way Ahead* (1960) took this approach.[69] In the seventeenth century the *Orthodox Creed* took a similar view, apparently reflecting the practice of the group of General Baptist churches in the Midlands (Buckinghamshire, Hertfordshire, Bedfordshire and Oxfordshire) which formulated it. According to the confession, General Councils or Assemblies 'consisting of Bishops, Elders, and Brethren, of the several churches of Christ ... make but one church, and have lawful right, and suffrage in this general meeting, or assembly, to act in the name of Christ.' Rather similar to the concerns of the modern document 'Towards Koinonia', the article declares that this is 'the best means under heaven to preserve unity, to prevent heresy, and [provide] superintendency among, or in any congregation whatsoever within its own limits.'[70]

There were many other General Baptists of the time, however, who strongly resisted this view of the power of assemblies, and the (Particular Baptist) Second London Confession of the same period makes clear that the meeting of the 'messengers' from 'the many Churches holding communion together' were not entrusted with 'any jurisdiction over the Churches themselves.'[71] This does not mean that Baptists should not be open, in an ecumenical age, to the development of *some kind* of synodical structure; indeed, the Council of the Baptist Union of Great Britain, as distinct from its Assembly, has the representative form, though

---

68   See Ware, *Orthodox Church*, pp. 252–3.

69   *The Way Ahead*. A Report on Baptist Life and Work by the Moderator's Commission of the Northern Baptist Association (Darlington: 1960), pp. 22–4. Cf. Alec Gilmore, 'Baptist Churches Today and Tomorrow', in Gilmore (ed.), *The Pattern of the Church. A Baptist View* (London: Lutterworth, 1963), pp. 149–51.

70   *Orthodox Creed*, art. XXXIX, in Lumpkin, *Baptist Confessions*, p. 327.

71   The Second London Confession (1677), ch. XXVI.15, in Lumpkin, *Baptist Confessions*, p. 289.

not the power, of a synod.[72] But it seems important to preserve the cutting edge of the dialectic between council and church meeting, and even the Anglican solution of three Houses in Synod (Bishops, Clergy and Laity) does not entirely capture the Baptist insight into the rule of Christ both *in* the local church and *among* the churches. This dialectic, however, might take two forms.[73]

In the first, the local church meeting busies itself with testing, and either approving or rejecting, *all* decisions taken at a wider level. This implies a distinction between what might be called 'finding' and 'recognizing' the mind of Christ. While it is freely admitted that the local church is not competent alone to *find* the mind of Christ on some issues, it is claimed that the local church is always alone competent to *recognize* truth once a proposal is put before it. A group of churches claim to have perceived the mind of Christ, and to have come to a decision in association which they could never have reached alone. But it remains for the individual church meeting to test that claim and confirm that decision. This kind of approach believes that we need wider consultation in order that the Lord might speak to his church, although it is for the individual churches to judge whether the Lord *has* spoken – or whether it was just the wind in the tree tops. The association life of Baptist churches might come more alive if church members gathered in their own church meetings really believed that they needed the insight of other churches into their situation, to see things they could not see for themselves. The relation of churches together would not be then be simply about richer churches helping the poorer; it would be about a readiness to hear the prophetic word for a large and affluent church coming from the smallest and least well-endowed fellowship.

A second form the dialectic might take preserves the distinction between 'finding' and 'recognizing', but places more stress upon the way of trust that we have already explored with regard to ministerial leadership.[74] Just as a church might trust the conclusions of its own spiritual leaders (when they have won authority by serving) so a church meeting might normally follow the decisions of association and union assemblies as a matter of mutual trust and without fierce debate. B. R. White judges of the early Baptist churches that 'They seem to have felt that they needed a very good reason for not falling in with the

---

72   This point is made in *The Nature of the Assembly and the Council*, pp. 17–20, suggesting that Council (weighted to representation from Associations) and Assembly (gathering representatives from all local churches) are two complementary ways of expressing covenant relationship and finding the mind of Christ.

73   In the next two paragraphs I follow quote closely my argument in *A Leading Question*, pp. 62–3.

74   See above, ch. 5, pp. 95–9.

programme and advice of their association.'[75] Of course, the church meeting would still be free to recognize, in exceptional circumstances, that there were good reasons *not* to confirm the wider decisions.

The second form of the dialectic between council and church meeting perhaps reflects more clearly the conviction that Christ becomes visible in his body wherever individual members and corporate members (churches) gather together. Trust finally is being exercised not only in each other but in Christ. If it be protested that such an open-ended process could never be incorporated within ecclesial structures, a response might be that structures should carry within themselves the witness that they are always provisional and never ultimate.

The Call to One Fellowship

A second New Testament image for the church is that of a 'fellowship' – *koinonia* – and around this cluster other words like 'sharing', 'participation', 'communion' and the many phrases with 'one another' in them. The ecumenical calling is a call to koinonia. This fellowship certainly has a *local* reality (in Acts 2:42 we read: 'and they devoted themselves to the.... fellowship, the breaking of bread and the prayers.') But once again there is a larger and a wider fellowship to which Christians belong, which is not just an accumulation of warm feelings, as if it were made by adding all local fellowships together into a mega-fellowship.

Like the body of Christ, koinonia is an *existent reality before* us. In the first place, it already exists in God, in the mutual giving and receiving of love between the Father and the Son in the communion of the Spirit; Jesus is portrayed as praying in John 17:21 'that they may all be one, even as you Father are in me, and I in you, so that they may also be in us, so that the world may believe that you have sent me.' The doctrine of the Trinity, as the church developed it, was not a kind of holy mathematical puzzle in which belief was required to demonstrate how spiritual a believer was. Mystery has, however, often been degraded into puzzle, as is well illustrated in one response to a survey by a sociologist on what the doctrine of the Trinity meant to ordinary church members, entitled 'The Triune God in Hackney and Enfield'. This was the contribution by one Baptist church member grappling with the mystery of three persons in one God:

---

75   White, *Authority*, p. 28.

If God was two persons he'd be less than what he is, and if four, more than necessary. [But] if God decides to make another one, it's all right with me.[76]

Despite this opinion, God as Trinity is not a conundrum but a conceptualizing of an experience of fellowship. Several times in this study we have explored the way that we find ourselves embraced in a network of relationships in God, so that we can only speak of God as communion. We share in the Son's obedience to the Father, the Father's sending of the Son, and the sorrow and joy of the Spirit that unites them. This fellowship that God experiences in God's self is what the Creator intends for the whole of creation. God's purpose is to bring the whole universe into koinonia, into reconciled relationships and harmony (Rom. 8:21; Eph. 1:10; Col. 1:19–20). Meanwhile the church bears witness to this fellowship, and shows it as a foretaste of the communion which is to come. Thus we enter a fellowship that is greater than ourselves, greater than the local scene, greater than the present age, greater than the finite world.

Now, if the church is the foretaste of koinonia, an advance advertisement for the koinonia of the whole universe, brokenness of fellowship is a scandal to the world. It means hindrance to mission, because it prevents witness by life to the fellowship that God intends for creation. It prevents the church working for peace and justice, for the renewal of human life and for care of the natural world. Perhaps the key text of the ecumenical movement has been John 17:21, the prayer of Jesus for his disciples 'that they may all be one ... so that the world may believe you have sent me'.

This is not just the argument of the besieged ark – that in a hostile world we all need to keep together in order to fight the opposition. That kind of argument has little regard for the demands of truth, and the need to take seriously the things that separate us. The point is more positive: we cannot witness to koinonia unless we *embody* it. To take just one example, until the churches are more united, it is not possible to rebuke the exclusive nationalism of particular Christian groups. It will not be possible, for instance, to be heard by the world saying that certain Orthodox Serbian groups are failing to reflect the koinonia of Christ in Kosovo, or that certain Protestant groups are falling short of the image of Christ in Northern Ireland. To make such statements seems, in the eyes of the world, to be only one sect of Christianity attacking another sect. Another voice I heard on the BBC news not long ago was equally chilling; it was an Arab Christian in Palestine declaring that from now

76   Geoffrey Ahern, *The Triune God in Hackney and Enfield: 30 Trinitarian Christians and Secularisation*. Unpublished paper presented to The British Council of Churches Study Commission on Trinitarian Doctrine Today (1984), © The C. S. Lewis Centre for the Study of Religion and Modernity, p. 21.

onwards, after Israeli incursions into the West Bank, he was not a Christian who happened to be an Arab, but an Arab who happened to be a Christian. Here again is a nationalism that denies koinonia. All these voices contradict the vision of Ephesians 2:15 that 'Christ has created one new humanity in the place of two'; but it will be hard to maintain that vision against nationalism if the church does not actually witness to it in its own life.

The WCC report from Canberra suggests that 'nationalism is positive when it unites people in the struggle for cultural, religious and political self-determination, but negative when it is used to dominate some and to exclude others.'[77] Negative nationalism, we may say, is a privileging of one's own ethnic story above all others, making one's own particular story into an idol. Fellowship is a rich harmony of stories, a mutual indwelling of stories, a weaving together of the stories of one's own life, church and nation into a greater story. This common story is the drama of God's creative and redemptive acts in the universe; it is told in many ways, including creed and baptism. To return for a moment to our key text from Ephesians 4, the declaration 'one faith and one baptism' is set in the middle of the triune affirmation, 'one Spirit, one Lord, one Father.' The common story we share is God's own story.

Traditionally the one story has been set out in the form of creeds, and especially the Apostles' Creed and the Nicene Creed. The World Council of Churches has in fact asked its members to consider seriously whether they might all adopt the Nicene Creed (in the form agreed by the Eastern and Western churches in 381, the Creed of Nicaea-Constantinople) as a way of confessing their common faith, and so as a way of recognizing in each other the apostolic faith.[78] The document 'Towards Koinonia' appeals to those churches which do not normally use a creed to 'recognize it as a central expression of the apostolic faith and thus to use it on occasion.' Correspondingly, it appeals to credal churches to recognize the substance of the creed in the beliefs of other churches who do not use credal forms.[79]

We have already seen that, while Baptists have characteristically refused to bind themselves to creeds, they have compiled 'confessions' for use in teaching, for making clear the basis on which they covenant together, and for explaining their belief and practice to those outside Baptist communities. In these confessions, the major creeds and statements of the world-wide church have often been explicitly acknowledged.[80]

---

77   Kinammon (ed.), *Signs of the Spirit*, Report, para. 78, p. 253
78   See *Confessing the One Faith. An Ecumenical Exposition of the Apostolic Faith as it is Confessed in the Nicene-Constantinopolitan Creed* (Faith and Order Paper 153; Geneva: WCC Publications, 1991), pp. 3–8.
79   'Towards Koinonia', para. 54, p. 279.
80   For examples, see above, ch. 1, p. 9.

Responding to the appeal that the Creed of Nicaea-Constantinople should be commended and used 'on occasion', the model covenant service recently published by the Baptist Union of Great Britain includes the Creed of Nicaea-Constantinople in its resources; it urges Baptist readers to notice that the Creed is a better vehicle than modern statements of faith for the making of covenant, because it sets out a story of salvation, not a set of principles.[81] It is the great missionary story of the triune God, beginning with the making of heaven and earth and ending with a new creation; it tells of the part played in the drama of creation and redemption by Father, Son and Spirit in the unity of the divine koinonia; it enables those who say the creed to be drawn anew into God's story, and so into God's own fellowship of life.

It is the idea of 'story' to which I also appeal in a previous chapter about baptism and inclusiveness. There I suggest that we should compare *whole stories* of initiation, not just the single moments of baptism. Rather than asking whether infant baptism is equivalent to believers' baptism, we should listen to people's story of their beginning in the Christian life, perhaps stretching over many years, and including several key moments of professing faith and receiving grace; in these journeys baptism of one kind or another would have marked a stage. The potential for the comparison of whole processes of initiation is well expressed in a recent report of Churches Together in England, in which representatives of both believer-baptist and infant-baptist churches participated:

> The water rite of infant baptism on its own would not be considered as baptism by Baptists... but perhaps infant baptism within a believing community, followed by Christian nurture, personal faith and communion [i.e. eucharist] might be regarded as a total process of initiation alternative to the Baptist process of Christian nurture, personal faith, believer's baptism, reception into membership and communion.[82]

It was not only the response of the Baptist Union of Great Britain to *Baptism, Eucharist and Ministry* which noticed that this report offered a way forward along the lines of initiation as a process.[83] The Baptist Convention of Burma – now Myanmar – also did so in its response,[84] and urged all its local churches to set up groups to study *BEM* carefully, to enable Baptist church members to understand the place of baptism in all

---

81   *Covenant 21*, pp. 14–15.

82   *Baptism and Church Membership*, p. 13. A similar view had already been urged in the report of a British Council of Churches Working Party, *Christian Initiation and Church Membership* (London: BCC, 1988), pp. 27–9.

83   For this response, see above, ch. 7, p. 143.

84   *Churches Respond to BEM*, 4, p. 187. However, it did understand the document as speaking of *baptism* as a process, rather than *initiation*.

churches, whether infant-baptist or believer-baptist. The result was an agreement at the level of the Myanmar Council of Churches to refrain from baptizing as believers those already baptized as infants, and the Baptist Convention made clear to its ordained ministers that they were expected to carry through this policy. While there must remain some uncertainty about how far this decision is followed at local level, the ecumenical partners affirm that the very existence of this agreement has made possible the deep and lively partnership in mission between Baptists and paedobaptist churches – especially Anglican – in Myanmar.[85] It is worth recording also that the response to *BEM* of the Baptist Convention began with a statement about 'our motive for responding to BEM':

> We do not respond simply because it is expected of us. We respond because of our commitment to unity and the ongoing mission of the whole church in the whole world. BEM ... is intrinsically related to the life that we are to offer for the whole world.

Myanmar Baptists have led the way here for other Baptist Unions and Conventions. It is a matter of regret that many ecumenical statements following *BEM* have continued simply to emphasize a 'common baptism' alone rather than a common process of Christian beginnings. Placing single moments side by side (infant baptism, believers' baptism) will accentuate differences, but comparing whole journeys of faith and salvation may enable mutual recognition to happen; this will not perhaps at first be 'recognition' in the form of an official formula, but as the flash of insight as people listen to each others' stories and exclaim 'it's the same journey!'.

But if this is to be a way forward for fuller fellowship between Baptist and paedobaptist churches, then those practising infant baptism will have to ensure that they *do* provide for a significant moment of personal confession of faith, and public witness to that faith, during the process of nurture of the Christian disciple. This will mean giving higher profile to the moment of 'confirmation', or something like it, against the trend to downplay confirmation in favour of a single 'unified rite of initiation.[86] The recent Anglican-Methodist covenant in Great Britain gives some sign that this can happen, as the report states that 'In our churches baptism is generally seen as the essential first stage of a process of Christian initiation that includes Confirmation and participation in Communion', and 'Confirmation is regarded by both Churches as a means of grace

---

85   Documentation in 'A Brief Outline of the Anglican History in Myanmar and the contact between the Anglican Church and the Baptist Church in Myanmar', unpublished paper by Archbishop Samuel Mahn San Si Htay and others, presented to Anglican-Baptist International Conversations, Yangon, 18–20 January 2001, p. 6.

86   For details of this trend, see above, ch. 7, pp. 143–4.

within the total process of initiation'.[87] We notice here that baptism is not
only located as a moment within the process of *life-long growth* into
Christ, but within the process of *initiation*, the particular phase within the
life-long journey that is characterized by beginnings.[88]

Let us be clear about the large step it will be for local Baptist churches
to be persuaded (not coerced) to decline baptism to those already
baptized as infants, against the definite request and 'instructed
conscience' of the person concerned, who *wants* to be baptized as part of
his or her growth in discipleship. If such enquirers are to be encouraged
to find the gracious activity of God in their baptism as infants, and to
complete their initiation (if they have not already done so) by laying on
of hands instead of a new baptism, then churches must be able to see that
there are two alternative paths for Christian beginnings which are truly
comparable. The journeys, though placing baptism at different points,
must equally offer opportunities for God's grace, human faith and
human obedience to Christ to be displayed. This means, I suggest, that
paedobaptist churches must be seen to be commending *both* these paths
as well, and not discouraging those parents in their fellowship who want
their new-born children to receive a blessing rather than baptism,
preferring them to wait until a later time of personally-owned faith to be
baptized.

Baptists too must face a challenge to their accustomed ways of
thinking. When they reject infant baptism as 'no baptism at all', they
dismiss too easily the hurt protest of those so baptized that they are
'unchurching' them. They dispose of the charge with an emphatic (and
perhaps amazed) denial that any such thought was in their minds. As I
have suggested above, Baptists will want to recognize the church of Christ
in other Christian communities as soon as they discern there the presence
of the body of Christ. It seems that Baptists can gladly recognize an
infant-baptizing church as a 'true church', while declining to recognize
their practice of the sacrament, by appeal to the argument that it is faith
that makes the church, not baptism. In the last hundred years, many
'open membership' churches in England have admitted those baptized as
infants, less because of a positive theological evaluation of infant baptism,

87   *An Anglican-Methodist Covenant. Common Statement of the Formal
Conversations between the Methodist Church of Great Britain and the Church of England*
(London: Methodist Publishing House and Church House Publishing, 2001), paras. 122,
126, pp. 40–41. The report also refers to 'Baptism ... in the context of full Christian
initiation... (143, p. 45).

88   There is a tendency in recent ecumenical documents to affirm a process of 'life-
long growth into Christ' begun by baptism, but to overlook the nature of *initiation* into
Christ as process also: e.g. the statement of a Faith and Order consultation held at
Faverges, France, in 1996, printed in Best and Heller (eds.) *Becoming a Christian*, pp.
78–81.

than because a profession of personal faith has been considered to be the essential element for membership, *regardless* of baptism. This kind of ambiguity was noted in the Baptist-Lutheran Conversations (1990), and among the recommendations was that 'Lutherans would be grateful if a solution could be found whereby the membership practice does not question the integrity of their baptism.'[89] Can the link between 'true baptism' and 'true church' be dismissed so quickly, when the sensibilities of others need to be respected?

From the seventeenth to the nineteenth centuries, there were of course many Baptists who *did* insist strongly that entrance to the church, according to the scriptures, was through both faith *and* baptism; some of these drew the conclusion that only 'closed' communion and 'closed' membership was therefore valid. In addition, we should give weight to the widespread Baptist acceptance of the Reformers' dictum that a true church is one where the word of God is rightly preached and the *sacraments are rightly administered*.[90] It appears incongruous to other churches, if not to Baptists, to affirm that a community is truly church and at the same time believe that its baptism is invalid. The critical question is this: can there be any way of affirming that all paedobaptist communities are 'church', on the basis of both faith *and* baptism? We have seen that some of those advocating open communion in the eighteenth century resolved this impasse by laying stress on respecting the integrity of others' beliefs about infant baptism.[91] '*They* believe they have been baptized' may be an inadequate argument when it is grounded in an Enlightenment view of *private* judgement, but it becomes stronger when based on leaving the final judgement to Christ on the Day of Judgement. This, perhaps, is one strand of a way through for Baptists. Recognizing 'two integrities' about baptism makes sense, second, when it can be placed in the coherent theological framework of initiation as a whole process. Such a dual approach will, of course, be costly to all traditions; but the priority is Christ's call to unity.

---

89   *Baptists and Lutherans in Conversation. A Message to our Churches*. Report of the Joint Commission of the Baptist World Alliance and the Lutheran World Federation (Geneva, 1990), p. 23.

90   The case of non-sacramental Christian communities is often raised here – especially the Salvation Army and the Society of Friends. I suggest that we can recognize the church in these communities because they are held within the sacramental life of the church universal. It is scarcely credible, however, to think of the church universal living from the sacramental life of Baptists; this, it seems, would have to be the case if the baptism of infants were invalid.

91   See above, ch. 8, pp. 179–82.

The Call to One Covenant

We have been thinking about the ecumenical call as a summons to one body and one fellowship. It is also, I proposed earlier, the call to one covenant. In examining the concept of covenant throughout this volume, we have explored the two images of 'walking together' and 'watching over each other'. If we are to envisage a common covenant in which *all* share in walking together, this has to involve a common understanding of the promise to 'watch over each other'. 'Watching over' is, of course, just old English for the Greek term *episkope* or oversight.

A few years ago I was invited to give a paper on the Baptist understanding of ministry to the Council of the Baptist Union of Great Britain. In the course of this I dared to use the word *episkope*. One minister arose from the floor in a mischievous spirit. He knew, he said, what a telescope was; he knew what a microscope was; but he was baffled by sort of instrument an 'episcope' might be. The collapse of the council into laughter put an end to any serious attention to the paper. If I had been thinking fast enough on my feet I should have said something like: 'a telescope is for far-seeing, a microscope is for near-seeing, and *episkope* is for over-seeing'. This is what it means in the New Testament, for it is a thoroughly biblical word.

Ecumenical documents urge us all to recognize three dimensions of *episkope* – personal, collegial and communal – within and among the churches. That is, oversight should be exercised by the whole community (communal), by individuals with special commissions (personal) and by those commissioned persons working together (collegial). Baptists have in fact always had these dimensions of watching over the people of God. They understand that the basic personal ministry of 'oversight' is given to the minister or pastor in the local church, whom many early Baptists called either 'elder' or 'bishop' without distinction.[92] However, oversight in the community flows to and fro between the personal and the communal, since the responsibility of 'watching over' the church belongs both to *all* the members gathered in church meeting as well as to the pastor.[93] Collegial oversight in the local community may sometimes take the form of several pastors working together in one congregation, but will always include the team ministry of pastor with deacons and 'elders' (in the modern sense).[94]

Although holding that the local minister is a bishop, or an 'overseer', most Baptists do recognize *episkope* at an inter-church level. Oversight is

---

92   See above, ch. 5, pp. 90–1.
93   See the London Confession, art. XLIV, in Lumpkin, *Baptist Confessions*, p.168.
94   On the changing sense of 'elder', see above, ch. 5, pp. 92–4.

exercised communally by a regional association of churches, which in assembly seeks the mind of Christ for the life and mission of the member churches, while having no power to *impose* decisions on the local church meeting. Personal oversight is provided by senior ministers who work among the churches in a region, and who take different forms in different unions or conventions world-wide. In British Baptist life these are now appointed directly by the churches together in assembly in a regional association, just as a local church meeting sets aside its own *episkopos*. Regional associations now have a team of three or four 'regional ministers', between them exercising pastoral care for ministers, giving leadership in mission, assisting churches with settlement of ministers, and supervising lay training.[95] Collegial oversight thus has a good deal of scope, although the dimension of personal oversight may be a little muted in comparison with the earlier situation of one 'General Superintendent' appointed for a wide area. At national level, representatives of churches and representatives of associations meet in an assembly ('union' or 'convention'). Oversight flows freely between the communal and the personal here too, as personal oversight is exercised by officers of the denomination. In England, these work in 'national teams' with the regional ministers to plan and care for various areas of church life, providing collegial oversight.

In some Eastern European Baptist unions (for example, Latvia, Moldova and Georgia), as well as in some African and Asian Baptist unions, senior pastors working among the churches are designated as 'bishops' in distinction from local ministers. However, in virtually all Baptist unions and conventions today this appointment is not regarded as a separate level of ministry; it is understood to be an extension of the episcopal ministry of the local pastor, different in scope but not in kind.[96] The theological principle here is that first the church gathers in fellowship (*koinonia*), whether at local or regional level, and this fellowship calls for oversight (*episkope*). There is no sense that the office of trans-local oversight, however it is expressed, has the special function

---

95   The report, *Transforming Superintendency* 7.5, p. 24, stressed that the pastoral care of ministers should be the primary task of the General Superintendents, an emphasis that was somewhat modified with the creation of a team of 'regional ministers', as proposed by the later report, *Relating and Resourcing*.

96   The same point is made by the Lutheran theologian, Wolfhart Pannenberg, in 'Lutherans and Episcopacy', in Colin Podmore (ed.), *Community – Unity – Communion. Essays in Honour of Mary Tanner* (London: Church House Publishing, 1998), pp. 184–5. However, he locates the main link with the universal church in an episcopal ministry which transcends that of the local church pastor. Schillebeeckx, *Ministry*, p. 69, lays stress on the mediaeval Thomist view that the difference between the presbyterate and episcopate was a difference only of jurisdiction, not consecration.

of *creating* the fellowship and unity of the church.[97] The inter-church minister thus belongs within the basic structure of a twofold office (*episkope* and *diakonia*), as outlined in earlier discussion.[98]

While there is much in all this that Baptists share with other Christian communions, there is a less 'tight' connection between *episkope* and apostolicity in Baptist thinking. There is a general agreement growing on the ecumenical scene that apostolic succession is not in the first place about handing on a particular ministry through the laying on of hands in an unbroken chain from the earliest apostles to today. Continuity is not, in its primary manifestation, about a strict sequence of one bishop ordaining another from the early days of the church to the present. Rather, it is about the succession in faith and life of the *church* as a whole, as the Christian community continues to participate in the mission of Jesus and is faithful to the words and acts of Jesus transmitted by the apostles. Apostolic succession is about the continuing story of the covenant community. This is the kind of emphasis that was made in the document *Baptism, Eucharist and Ministry*, and which the Anglican church made in its agreement with the Lutheran churches of the Nordic and Baltic Countries, at Porvoo.[99]

Baptists will generally be happy with this understanding of what it means to be apostolic. They have a strong sense of continuity in faithfulness of the covenant community. This is expressed in a typical Baptist way in the church book, which records all the deliberations and decisions of the church meetings over the years; in this way the current generation acknowledges that it is part of the story of God's faithful people in that place in the past, who have themselves aimed to stand in the succession of the earliest church. Nor will Baptists have problems with a second aspect of apostolicity identified by the present ecumenical consensus, that this continuity is served by the ministry of word, sacrament and pastoral oversight within the church.[100] However, a third

---

97   This was the view of Cyprian, e.g. *Letters*, 33.1; 66.8.

98   See above, ch. 5, p. 91. An exception to this view is to be found in the (General Baptist) *Orthodox Creed* (1679), art. XXXI, which defines three kinds of officers: 'Bishops, or Messengers; and Elders, or Pastors; and Deacons....' Bishops 'have the government of those churches that had suffrage in their election, and no other ordinarily; as also to preach the word, or gospel, to the world'; Lumpkin, *Baptist Confessions*, pp. 319–20.

99   *Together in Mission and Ministry. The Porvoo Common Statement*. The British and Irish Anglican Churches and the Nordic and Baltic Lutheran Churches (London: Church House Publishing, 1993), para. 40, p. 24; cf. *Baptism, Eucharist and Ministry*, 'Ministry', para. 34, p. 28.

100   *Porvoo Common Statement*, para. 41, p. 24; cf. *Baptism, Eucharist and Ministry*, 'Ministry', para. 35, pp. 28–9. These first two aspects are explicitly affirmed by *Forms of Ministry among Baptists*, p. 29.

aspect will give Baptists more difficulty. This is the affirmation that, while the ordination of bishops is not of the essence of apostolic succession, the bishop is a necessary *sign* of the apostolicity of the community.[101] To have those who watch over God's people ordained continuously in one place is a testimony to the unbroken nature of the covenant. To consecrate a bishop in historic succession, and for that bishop to ordain local presbyters, is a sign of God's continual faithfulness to the church, and a sign of the church's 'determination to manifest the permanent characteristics of the Church of the apostles'.[102]

Baptists believe that it is appropriate that among those who ordain the minister in the local church there should be a representative of the wider church, and this is usually (though not always) a regional minister. As we have seen above, among other reasons for this practice is the fact that the local minister is understood to be a minister of the church universal, opening up the horizons of the local community to the faith and mission of the world-wide church. But at present this is generally a matter of good practice, rather than being essential. Among most early Baptists the participation of other ordained ministers was what was required. When a regional minister, or the president of a Baptist Union presides at the act of ordination, this may certainly be seen as pointing to the ongoing faithfulness of the church to its apostolic foundation. But this is not to say that Baptists in general accept that ordination of a minister requires this particular witness.[103] Moreover, unlike bishops in episcopal churches, regional ministers (or, in the USA, 'executive ministers') among Baptists have no further consecration beyond their original ordination as pastor/minister, which is itself regarded as ordination to the ministry of *episkope*; thus they do not have a separate ordination which could be said to be a special sign of apostolic continuity.

Baptism, Eucharist and Ministry points out that in various churches one of the aspects of *episkope* – communal, personal and collegial – tends to have been overemphasized at the expense of others, and a corrective needs to be applied. 'Each church needs to ask itself in what way its exercise of ordained ministry has suffered in the course of history'.[104] Perhaps such questioning among Baptists might lead to a situation in which the 'induction' of regional ministers always included a

---

101 *Porvoo Common Statement*, paras. 46–51, pp. 26–28.

102 *Porvoo Common Statement*, para. 50, p. 27.

103 There were exceptions in the past, e.g. in the *Orthodox Creed* of General Baptists where the elder (i.e. pastor) in the local church was to be ordained by 'the bishop or messenger God hath placed in the church he hath charge of': art. XXXI, Lumpkin, *Baptist Confessions*, p. 320. There are exceptions in the present, such as the invariable involvement of the president of the Baptist union or convention in ordinations in several Eastern European countries.

104 *Baptism, Eucharist and Ministry*, 'Ministry', Commentary (26), p. 26.

recalling of their original ordination to *episkope*, and an affirming of their ministry as a particular sign of the church's continuity with the apostolic tradition. It would then be no great step beyond present practice to ensure that a regional minister, or a minister with a scope of oversight beyond the local church, was not only included in the group of ministers laying on hands in ordination, but was always the one who presided over the act.

It seems that there will be no real hope of visible unity in the church of Christ without some agreement on this personal sign of being apostolic. Those churches who claim a 'historic episcopate' understand bishops to be a God-given sign and focus of standing in the tradition of the faith. Bishops are a key part of the plot of the story. This seems on the face of it to be a huge difference from the way that Baptists tell the story. But we may hope that all churches will be open to re-thinking, re-visualizing in an imaginative way, what this sign might look like. If those churches which own a historic episcopal succession insist that 'bishops' must always be as they are now, then they are not open to the new forms that covenant can take. Alongside 'watching over each other', covenant requires a 'walking together' in a spirit of adventure.

In a recent series of conversations between the Anglican Communion and the Baptist World Alliance, hosted in Myanmar, the model of unity in the Church of North India was cited as one possible example of a 'local adaptation'[105] of the historic episcopate. The CNI declares in its constitution that 'the Church is not committed to any one particular theological interpretation of episcopacy,' and the Bishop of the Eastern Himalayas Diocese, himself a Baptist minister, stressed that the CNI defines the episcopate as being both 'historic and constitutional'. The 'constitutional' aspect means that in all decisions the bishop has to win the consent of the church council which he immediately serves. This evidently blends personal and communal *episkope* (and so gives a new meaning to collegiality) in a way which builds upon both the Anglican and Baptist tradition, without exactly duplicating either. Bishop Sahu expressed the situation in this way:

> As president of his diocesan Council... [the bishop] has obviously a great deal of influence. If he has earned the trust of his people, there is a great deal of freedom available to him to take initiatives. But in all matters he must carry his Council

---

105 The term comes from the Lambeth Quadrilateral, four principles proposed by the Lambeth Conference of 1888 as the basis for visible unity between the churches. Alongside Holy Scripture, the Apostles' and Nicene Creeds and the two sacraments of Baptism and Eucharist, it placed 'the Historic Episcopate, locally adapted in the methods of its administration to the varying needs of the nations and people called by God into the Unity of His Church.'

with him... Pastoral authority is not a coercive authority. It is based on a leader's servant spirit, which must manifest the compassion of Christ.[106]

Significant too was the declaration of the uniting Baptist churches within the new CNI, who took note that the proposed episcopate would make 'reasonable provision for all believers to share in seeking the mind of Christ in the affairs of the Church as far as they are able'. The Baptist churches also affirmed that they were acting 'in exercise of the liberty that they have always claimed ... to interpret and administer the laws of Christ'.[107] This reflects in a new context the general Baptist understanding of the liberty of the local church; it seems that the Baptists of North India were claiming a freedom to work out the implications of the 'lordship of Christ in his church' in new forms of *episkope*. It must be added, however, that not all Baptist churches in the existing Council of Baptist Churches in North India agreed with them, and not all joined the new CNI.

In that time and place a group of Christians were evidently willing to take risks in 'walking together' and finding new ways of 'watching over each other'. In this they were surely echoing the summons of the John Howard Shakespeare, in his book *The Churches at the Cross-Roads* (1918), who urged that 'The true dimensions of the Church will appear only as we bring together the historic past and the Divine working in the present age.'[108] Shakespeare, General Secretary of the Baptist Union of Great Britain in that period, brought the office of 'General Superintendent' into being in modern times, which has now developed into 'Regional Ministers'. While E.A. Payne has claimed that the creation of superintendents was in effect reviving the seventeenth-century office of 'messenger' among General Baptists,[109] it was clear that Shakespeare also intended the new superintendency to exercise some of the functions

106 Dhirendra Kumar Sahu, 'Episcopacy in the Church of North India', paper presented to Anglican-Baptist International Conversations, Yangon, 18–20 January 2001, pp. 5–6. Cf. Sahu, *The Church of North India. A Historical and Systematic Theological Enquiry into an Ecumenical Ecclesiology* (Frankfurt am Main: Peter Lang, 1994), pp. 167–76.

107 Baptist Declaration of Principle, in *The Constitution of the Church of North India* (Delhi: ISPCK, 2001), p. 15.

108 J.H. Shakespeare, *The Churches at the Cross-Roads. A Study in Church Unity* (London: Williams and Norgate, 1918), p. 84.

109 E.A. Payne, *The Baptist Union*, p. 183. For details of this office among General Baptists, see B.R. White, *The English Baptists of the Seventeenth Century* (London: Baptist Historical Society, 19962), pp. 30–1, 46–7, 117–18. White judges that it was an 'order of inter-church officers which the Calvinistic Baptists were also to come near to using but never to institutionalize' (p. 30).

of a bishop in the episcopal church structure.[110] On the larger scale, and he thought in the largest terms, he hoped to achieve first a union among the Free Churches in England, and then in time to lead this united Free Church into union with the Church of England.

Shakespeare laid stress upon the willingness of many in episcopal churches to accept 'the fact of episcopacy' without insisting on 'any theory as to its character'. To this openness on one side he brought his own openness, asking:

> Do we not feel that we must face the gravest question of all? Is there any reality in the doctrine of the Holy Ghost as the guide and teacher of truth, and if so, can we believe that a form [i.e. episcopacy] which goes back to the beginning of Christian history, and has taken its place 'in the greater part of Christendom as the recognized organ of the unity and continuity of the Church' arose without the guidance of the Spirit?

To this, however, he adds another question: 'Or, on the other hand, can we believe that the guidance of the Spirit has been so completely withheld from the non-episcopal churches that they have gone quite astray?'[111]

The form that *episkope* might take in the future is surely only one instance of allowing tracks from the past to converge with traces of God's movement into the future. The ecumenical calling of the church must be a summons to move on, to tread the pilgrim path in ways known and 'to be known'. God help the church if she gets stuck when she should be walking steadily on, her face turned to the coming kingdom.

---

110 See Peter Shepherd, *The Making of a Modern Denomination. John Howard Shakespeare and the English Baptists, 1898–1924* (Studies in Baptist History and Thought 4; Carlisle: Paternoster Press, 2001), pp. 77–84, 180–2. However, Shepherd takes a more negative view of the continuity of Superintendency with Baptist history and practice than I do here.

111 Shakespeare, *Churches at the Cross-Roads*, p. 83.

CHAPTER 10

The Understanding of Salvation in the Baptist Tradition

Let us begin with a story, from the beginning of the allegory of salvation written by John Bunyan in his *Pilgrim's Progress*. The Pilgrim has just been handed a scroll on which is inscribed, 'Flee from the wrath to come'.

> ....looking upon Evangelist very carefully, [he] said, 'Whither must I fly?' Then said Evangelist, pointing with his finger over a very wide field, 'Do you see yonder wicket gate?' The man said, 'No'. Then said the Evangelist, 'Keep that light in your eye, and go up directly thereto, so shalt thou see the Gate at which, when thou knockest, it shall be told thee what thou shalt do ...
>
> So in process of time Christian got up to the Gate. Now over the Gate it was written, *Knock and it shall be opened unto you*. He knocked therefore, more than once or twice ...
>
> *Christian*. Here is a poor burdened sinner. I come from the City of Destruction, but am going to Mount Zion.[1]

There for the moment we leave the Pilgrim, making his entrance into the Christian life by knocking at the narrow Gate of conversion. Though Bunyan was not a typical Baptist (and has indeed also been claimed for the Congregationalists) he portrays here in colourful terms a central Baptist conviction about salvation through faith that has been held throughout Baptist history. Saving faith means a direct, individual response to the grace offered by God in Christ. Everyone has to knock at the door for himself, or herself. Bunyan has been criticized by some readers for what they see as the 'selfish individualism' of his pilgrim, who sets out on his spiritual journey without his wife or children. But of course this is an allegory, and depicts the way that a person might have to make a solitary decision of faith even *within* the family group. This

---

1   Bunyan, *The Pilgrim's Progress* (ed. Sharrock), pp. 41, 56.

understanding of the event of justification by faith is well set out in the
(General Baptist) Standard Confession of 1660:

.... when men shall assent to the truth of the Gospel, believing with all their
hearts, that there is remission of sins, and eternal life to be had in Christ. And that
Christ therefore is most worthy their constant affections, and subjection to all his
Commandements, and therefore resolve with purpose of heart so to subject unto
him in all things, and no longer unto themselves. And so, shall (with godly sorrow
for the sins past) commit themselves to his grace, confidently depending upon him
for that which they believe is to be had in him: such so believing are justified from
all their sins, their faith shall be accounted unto them for righteousness.[2]

Personal Faith and its Consequences

The necessity for a 'conscious and deliberate acceptance of Christ as
Saviour and Lord'[3] does not mean, however, that there has been any
fixed pattern of conversion experience generally held among Baptists. A
statement approved by the Council of the Baptist Union of Great Britain
in 1948, entitled *The Baptist Doctrine of the Church*, speaks of a
'personal crisis in the soul's life' when someone 'stands alone in God's
presence', but immediately goes on to say that 'such a crisis may be swift
and emotional *or slow-developing and undramatic*'.[4] In this connection,
the Baptist Old Testament scholar Henry Wheeler Robinson noted that a
frequent biblical image for the coming of new life from God is the
dawning of light, and pointed out that while there may be scenes when
'the dawn comes up like thunder', yet 'the normal dawn is gradual and
almost imperceptible in approach'. What is essential is that there comes a
moment when someone can say 'Whereas I was blind, *now* I see'.
However it happens, and in whatever timescale, there has been 'an
awakening of human personality to the presence and power of the
divine.'[5]

Of course, we must add immediately (as do both the witnesses I have
cited), that to be a person is to be more than an individual. Persons are
held in a network of relationships, and so a 'personal' response of faith
always involves the community in or through which faith has been
awakened; as Wheeler Robinson again puts it, 'Christian conversion is
always the discovery of others in God, others whose life is ours for

2 The Standard Confession, art. VI, in Lumpkin, *Baptist Confessions,* pp. 226–7.
3 *The Baptist Doctrine of the Church*, p. 6.
4 *The Baptist Doctrine of the Church*, pp. 7–8.
5 Robinson, *Life and Faith of the Baptists,* p. 76.

Christ's sake.'[6] Baptists through the ages have observed that to be a person *includes* a core of individual identity for responsibility before God and in the face of others; but, theologically, this does not necessarily mean that the individual *precedes* relations with others, that the individual comes first and then enters into relationships. Indeed, an examination of human beings in society might well lead us to conclude that individuality is always created *by* personal relationships.[7]

We must also recognize that this belief in the *personal* nature of justification by faith is not unique to Baptists. They have it as children of the Reformation, in the heritage of Luther, Zwingli and Calvin.[8] What is distinctive about Baptists is perhaps the emphasis they have placed upon this truth, and the rigour with which they have drawn conclusions from it, a rigour that comes from being children more especially of the 'Radical Reformation' (whose inheritance they share to a large extent with present-day Mennonites). To set the scene for a more detailed exploration of what Baptists mean by 'personal saving faith', we ought to notice briefly four of those conclusions they have drawn.

First, personal faith leads to an understanding of Baptism as a sacrament for believers only, that is for those who can already bear witness to their faith in Christ as Lord and to their reception of saving grace. The argument of the Apostle Paul in Romans Chapter 6 has been a constant source of appeal by Baptists from their earliest days, and Paul's view of *identification* with Christ in his death and resurrection through baptism has been expounded as requiring a personal and conscious act of faith. The London Confession of 1644, for example, affirms that immersion in water signifies 'that interest the Saints have in the death, burial and resurrection' of Christ, and glosses this by reference to Romans 6:3-5.[9] In his exegesis of this passage, a modern Baptist New Testament scholar, George Beasley-Murray in his book *Baptism in the New Testament* concludes that according to Paul 'to be baptised ... is to undergo a drastic experience. The overworked term 'existential' is not amiss ... It could hardly be otherwise if baptism be supremely the occasion when God draws near in Christ to a man drawing near to him in faith.'[10] The reference here to the gracious act of God in baptism as well as the human act of faith should not, of course, be overlooked.

---

6   Robinson, *Life and Faith of the Baptists*, p. 76.

7   See Fiddes, *Participating in God*, pp. 22–4, 49–55. McFadyen, *The Call to Personhood*, pp. 7–8, 72–3, uses the geological image of a person as being 'sedimented out' of the flow of relationships.

8   This is emphasized by Payne, *The Fellowship of Believers*, pp. 21–3.

9   The London Confession, art. XL, Lumpkin, *Baptist Confessions*, p. 167; similarly, *A Declaration of Faith* (1611), art. 14, in Lumpkin, *Baptist Confessions*, p. 120.

10   Beasley-Murray, *Baptism in the New Testament*, p. 142.

A second conclusion concerns the nature of the church, as a fellowship of believers. The local congregation consists, in the words of a Baptist Confession of 1611, of 'a compainy off faithful people .....being knit unto the LORD, & one unto another, by Baptisme. Upon their owne confession of the faith. and sinnes.'[11] Personal, owned confession of faith was thus essential for entering into the covenant between God and each other.

A third conclusion flowing from the personal nature of faith and salvation is the defence of freedom of conscience and freedom from persecution. The very first appeal in English for religious liberty for all – not just Christians – was made by the minister of the first Baptist church on English soil. In often quoted words, Thomas Helwys, writing in *The Mistery of Iniquity* (1612) asserted that

> for men's religion to God, is betwixt God and themselves; the King shall not answer for it, neither may the King be judge between God and man. Let them be heretics, Turks, Jews, or whatsoever, it appertains not to the earthly power to punish them in the least measure.[12]

To use temporal powers to destroy false churches, argued Helwys, was contrary to the gospel. Of close relevance to our theme, an argument often advanced by Baptists against persecution was that this obstructed God's personal dealing with those accused, and the possibility of their coming to true faith. Even blasphemy therefore should not fall under the laws of the land.[13]

A fourth conclusion from the need for personal faith and conversion is the prominence that Baptists have given to evangelism and mission.[14] We have already met the figure of Evangelist in Bunyan's Pilgrim's Progress, encountering Pilgrim as he stands bewildered on the borders of the City of Destruction, not knowing where to turn. This passion for communicating the gospel reached a climax with the founding of the Baptist Missionary Society in 1792, and the departure of William Carey for India the following year. The recent confessional statement of the American Baptist Churches USA (1987) begins with an affirmation of the nature of Baptists as a missionary people, saying that

---

11   *A Declaration of Faith* (1611), Lumpkin, *Confessions of Faith*, p. 119; see also the London Confession (1644), art. XXXIII, Lumpkin, *Confessions of Faith*, p. 165.

12   Thomas Helwys, *A Short Declaration of the Mistery of Iniquity* (Amsterdam, 1612), p. 69. See also the Standard Confession, art. XXIV, in Lumpkin, p. 232.

13   So John Murton, a successor of Thomas Helwys as minister to the congregation at Spitalfields, in *An Humble Supplication* (1620), repr. in *Tracts on Liberty of Conscience and Persecution*, ed. by E.B. Underhill for the Hanserd Knollys Society (London: J. Haddon, 1846), pp. 181–213.

14   See also above, ch. 9. pp. 207–10 and below, ch. 11, pp. 252–9.

we are called in loyalty to Jesus Christ to proclaim the Good News of God's sovereign, reconciling grace, and to declare the saving power of the Gospel to every human being and to every human institution.[15]

Already in seventeenth-century England, even within those Baptist churches that stood within the Calvinist tradition and stood by the 'five points of Calvinism', a concern for the awakening of personal faith had led ministers such as Andrew Gifford (Senior), minister of the Particular Baptist Church at Pithay 1661-1721, to make an appeal to his hearers for response. His co-pastor said in his funeral address that Gifford at the close of his sermon would often 'offer Christ to sinners and invite them to embrace him as offered in the most affectionate and pathetic manner.'[16] How this fits in with the grace of God in election as conceived by Calvinism I intend to turn to shortly.

Personal Salvation in Community

Baptists, as I have already observed, have been well aware that persons do not exist in isolation but in relationship, and that salvation involves a corporate dimension as well as an individual experience of salvation. Historically, in fact, a conviction about believers' baptism emerged from the prior question about what was the nature of a true *church*.

The American Baptist theologian James McClendon, as we have noted earlier,[17] proposes that the distinctive mark of Baptists is their self-understanding as a community. There is, he suggests, 'a shared awareness of the present Christian community as the primitive community and the eschatological community.'[18] It is not that the present community claims to be exactly *copying* the structures of the apostolic community, a claim hard to sustain; rather, it feels itself to have an immediate *contact* with the New Testament community of disciples, sharing the same directness of response to the earthly Jesus and the risen Christ. With the same immediacy that the Roman Catholic vision asserts that the eucharistic bread *is* the body of Christ, so (he maintains) the Baptist asserts that 'we *are* Jesus' followers; the commands are addressed directly to *us*. And no rejoinder about the date of Jesus' earthly ministry versus today's date can refute that claim.' This perception, on which McClendon bases his

15   *The People Called American Baptists: A Confessional Statement*, printed in *American Baptist Quarterly* 6/2 (1987), pp. 62–64.
16   Joseph Ivimey, *A History of the English Baptists* (4 volumes; London: Author/ Holdsworth and Ball, 1811–30), II, p. 549.
17   See above, ch. 1, pp. 10–11.
18   McClendon, *Ethics*, pp. 31–33.

whole theological method, is a valuable insight into the way that personal and immediate response to Christ has a community dimension to it.

Consider, for example, the Baptist understanding of baptism. This can only be administered to those who are believers, who can witness to their own *individual* repentance and faith in Christ. But Paul's words in Romans 6 that we have been baptized 'into Christ Jesus' are understood as 'into the body of Christ' in the light of 1 Cor. 12:13, 'By one Spirit were we all baptized into one body'. As the *Orthodox Creed* (1679) expresses it, baptism is a sign of 'ingrafting into Christ, and into the body of Christ, which is his Church'.[19] There has thus been a strong Baptist insistence, especially among General Baptists, that through baptism believers enter upon the active responsibilities of membership of the covenant community.[20] Individual conviction cannot be held in isolation from life in relationship with others, and personal faith involves being commissioned for service to others. Nobody can be baptized without becoming a member of the whole body, or being incorporated more deeply into the body.[21] In many Baptist churches the baptismal service thus includes in succession the acts of baptism, reception into membership and celebration of the Lord's Supper.[22]

Moreover, it would be quite wrong to think that the local church as a covenant community is understood along the lines of a 'social contract' of laissez-faire liberalism. It is not that a collection of individuals have simply decided to band into a group in order to achieve certain aims together. Such a society would be entirely dependent upon the will of the individual members who might withdraw consent if they felt their interests were not being served. When Baptists speak of a 'gathered church', they certainly mean that believers have agreed to gather together, but this is only in response to the Christ who *has gathered* them. *They* do not themselves make the church, but Christ invites them each one individually to become part of it.[23] The statements of the Second London Confession (1677) that churches are 'gathered by special grace' and 'gathered and organized according to the mind of Christ'[24] are echoed

---

19   Art. 28; in Lumpkin, *Baptist Confessions*, p. 317.

20   While this was a General Baptist emphasis, it was not entirely absent among Particular Baptists; see above, ch. 8, pp. 175, 181–2.

21   Above, ch. 7, pp. 137–9, 151–2, I propose a modern Baptist theology of the child and the church, which affirms *both* the connection between baptism and 'church membership' *and* the membership of as-yet-unbaptized children in the body of Christ.

22   See 'The Baptism of Believers and Reception into Membership' in *Patterns and Prayers,* pp. 93–108. This sequence is not however generally followed in Southern Baptist churches of the USA, where candidates can be admitted into membership at the end of any service, by consent of the congregation.

23   See above, ch. 2, pp. 42–4; ch. 4, pp. 77–8.

24   Chs. XXIX, XXXI, in Lumpkin, *Baptist Confessions*, pp. 318–19.

by the recent Confession of Faith of the German Baptist Union, that 'Christ gathers [those who believe on him] into his community in a common life'.[25] The personal response in faith is not thus interpreted as mere individualism; the individual is called into a social reality which already exists before him or her.

This social dimension of salvation is also made very clear in the Baptist concern from earliest days for reform and justice in society. As the modern German Baptist Confession neatly puts it, 'because we have our origin in God's justification of the ungodly, we are called to serve the cause of justice among human beings'.[26] I have already mentioned the early pleas for religious liberty, and to this we could add many examples of social reform from the later history of Baptist churches. In England, for instance, there was the Baptist minister Robert Hall who in 1819 supported the formation of a Union among stocking-makers to enable the payment of benefit to those who were unemployed.[27] Like other Baptists before him in the previous century, Hall also opposed slavery in the British Empire, saying that the slave trade 'introduces the most horrible confusion, since it degrades human beings from the denomination of persons to that of things.'[28]

We notice here the characteristic concern for the person in his or her response before God, and the same theme emerged when William Knibb, a Baptist missionary in Jamaica, opposed slavery in the sugar plantations there. Knibb describes in letters how he went to Jamaica with the intention of bringing an inner spiritual freedom into the personal lives of slaves *despite* their outward chains. He relates, however, that he found the slaves' whole lives to be morally crippled by their situation; they had acquired a 'slave mentality' in every part of their being and could not respond truly to freedom in Christ until they were emancipated from physical bonds. He wrote that, 'the fact that a person could be happy in a state of slavery seemed to me to be one of its most accursed fruits.'[29] To enable personal response to Christ he had to come into conflict with a whole economic system.

Modern Baptist theologians also tend to connect the process of social reform with the personal experience of justification. In the United States of America, for example, the Baptist theologian Harvey Cox was one of the first to come to terms from a Christian perspective with the

---

25   Text in Parker, *Baptists in Europe*, p. 64.

26   Text in Parker, *Baptists in Europe*, p. 70

27   Robert Hall, *An Appeal to the Public on the Subject of the Frame-Work Knitters Fund* (1819), repr. in *Works*, III, pp. 230–97.

28   Robert Hall, *An Address on the State of Slavery in the West India Islands* (1824), repr. in *Works*, III, p. 305.

29   In John Howard Hinton, *Memoir of William Knibb. Missionary in Jamaica* (London: Houlston and Stoneman, 1849), pp. 50–1.

phenomenon of secularization. In his book *The Secular City*,[30] he draws an analogy between the religious experience of personal conversion, and the need for people to experience a moment of 'awakening to reality' which will jerk them out of apathy and motivate them towards social change. We need to stretch our vision, he suggests, about what 'conversion' can mean. In more recent years, in Nicaragua, the Baptist scholar Jorge Pixley has contributed to the literature of liberation theology with his book, *The Bible, the Church and the Poor* – co-authored with a Roman Catholic theologian, Clodovis Boff. The reason, they maintain, for an option towards the poor is having personal faith in Christ who has taken on poverty for us. The poor alone, they point out 'can glory in having the eternal son of God among their relations.'[31]

These are simply examples from history and from theology, to make clear that an emphasis upon personal conversion does not exclude a more social view of salvation, and in fact can actually motivate it. There is a constant Baptist understanding that personal faith in Christ leads to being joined to a community whose members should walk together 'in all the Lord's ways, made known or to be known unto them, whatsoever it should cost them.'[32] It is accurate, I believe, to say that while Baptists have understood justification by faith to be an individual matter in which a person stands alone before Christ, sanctification or growth in grace is a corporate experience in the fellowship of the local church which is serving the wider society. Perhaps what is lacking is the perception that these are two aspects of the same process, and this is an idea to which I wish to return.

Personal Response and the Grace of God

Talk about the personal response of individuals to the gift of life that God offers in Christ may give the impression that salvation is a matter of human decision. This would reduce faith to a work, in which human beings were given credit for making the right choices. In fact, both streams of Baptist life in the past, Particular *and* General, Calvinist *and* Arminian, have emphasized that justification and sanctification depend utterly upon the grace of God. As the General Baptist *Orthodox Creed* of 1679 puts it, 'justifying faith is a grace, or habit, wrought in the soul, by

30   Harvey Cox, *The Secular City. Secularization and Urbanization in Theological Perspective* (London: SCM Press, 1966), pp. 118–122.

31   Jorge Pixley and Clodovis Boff, *The Bible, the Church and the Poor. Biblical, Theological and Pastoral Aspects of the Option for the Poor*, trans. P. Burns (London: Burns and Oates, 1989), pp. 114–16.

32   Covenant of the Gainsborough Church, recalled by William Bradford, *History of Plymouth Plantation*, I, pp. 20–22.

the holy ghost, through preaching the word of God, whereby we are enabled to believe ... and wholly and only to rest upon Christ...'[33] The earlier General Baptist Standard Confession of 1660 affirms that 'there is one holy Spirit, the pretious gift of God, freely given to such as obey him ... that thereby they may be throughly sanctified, and made able (without which they are altogether unable) to abide stedfast in the faith, and to honour the Father, and his Son Christ, the Author and finisher of their faith.'[34]

The real difference between General and Particular Baptists was whether Christ died for all people or only for the elect. The Particular Baptist London Confession of 1644, which pre-dates the strong Calvinism of the Westminster Confession composed by the Presbyterians, states firmly that 'Christ Jesus by his death did bring forth salvation and reconciliation onely for the elect, which were those which God the Father gave him.'[35] This note is sounded even more loudly in the Second London Confession of 1677 which was modelled closely on the Westminster Confession and in which can be clearly found the five points of Calvinism. By contrast, the Standard Confession of the General Baptists (1660) affirms in the words of scripture that Christ 'freely gave himself as a ransom for all' and that 'God is not willing that any should perish', adding that the Gospel should therefore be preached to every creature 'so that no man shall eternally suffer in Hell ... for want of a Christ that dyed for them.'[36]

This same 'Arminian' confession does, nevertheless affirm the election of believers by God 'before the foundation of the world'. Correspondingly we notice that the Particular Baptist Confession of 1677 omits the section of the Westminster Confession on election to damnation, preferring to speak instead of some who are predestined to eternal life, and 'others being left to act in their sin, to their just condemnation.'[37] There are hints here of convergence, and of what I suggest is to be the main Baptist emphasis upon the enabling and initiating grace of God. Put positively, all agree that there can be no turning to God in conversion unless the grace of God empowers it.

This kind of emphasis led at the end of the eighteenth century to what became known as 'evangelical Calvinism', a theology developed by Andrew Fuller under the influence of the New England theologians Jonathan Edwards Senior and Junior. While, as I have mentioned, the

33 *Orthodox Creed*, art. XXIII, in Lumpkin, *Baptist Confessions*, p. 314.
34 Standard Confession, art. VII, in Lumpkin, *Baptist Confessions*, p. 227.
35 London Confession, art. XXI, in Lumpkin, *Baptist Confessions*, p. 162.
36 Standard Confession, arts. III–IV, in Lumpkin, *Baptist Confessions*, pp. 225–6.
37 Second London Confession, ch. III.3, in Lumpkin, *Baptist Confessions*, p. 254.

belief in limited atonement had not prevented a concern for evangelism among many Calvinistic (Particular) Baptists, it did have a dampening effect. Among some, it had extinguished it altogether, and Fuller's theology provided the spark for an explosion in mission at home and abroad, including the formation of the Baptist Missionary Society. Basically, Fuller proposed that while only some people were elected to salvation, *all* people had the positive *duty* to turn to Christ in faith. Technically, he could hold the two propositions together by means of the distinction made by Jonathan Edwards (Jnr) between a general atonement and a limited application of its benefits in redemption, but I leave an exploration of the coherence of this idea to the next chapter.

The ferment of ideas here is captured in the well-known story of a clash between two men. At the Northamptonshire Association ministers' meeting in 1785 William Carey, motivated by Fuller's kind of theology,[38] raised the question as to 'Whether the command given to the apostles to "teach all nations" was not obligatory on all succeeding ministers to the end of the world'. The chairman, John Collett Ryland, who was a Calvinist of a stricter sort, dismissed the question as unworthy of serious consideration and rebuked Carey as 'an enthusiast'. There is a more colourful, perhaps mythical, account of the conflict between the elderly and young minister, which runs that Ryland said, 'Young man, sit down, sit down. When God pleases to convert the heathen He'll do it without consulting you or me.'[39]

Actually these new ideas were, as I have been arguing, not so new after all; they had a strong background in much older Baptist thinking. The *Orthodox Creed* of 1679 had already shown a way forward, affirming *both* that 'we ought not to oppose the grace of God in electing us, nor yet the grace of the Son in dying for all men and so for us'. Both the eternal will of God in election and the revealed will of God in the Gospel must be held together, and we can only say – according to the Confession – that 'here is a great mystery indeed.'[40]

The growing impact of 'Fullerism', against the background of the older convergence, made it possible for the two streams of Baptist life in England to run together into the present Baptist Union towards the end of the nineteenth century. A 'General Union' of Particular Baptist churches was first launched in 1813, and was formally amalgamated with the New

---

38   Carey at this time was probably not influenced directly by Fuller's *Gospel Worthy of all Acceptation*, but by the sermons of Robert Hall senior, whose protegé Fuller was. For a critical account of this incident, see Brian Stanley, *The History of the Baptist Missionary Society* 1792–1992 (Edinburgh: T. & T. Clark, 1992), pp. 6–7.

39   S. Pearce Carey, *William Carey* (London: Carey Press, 8th edn, 1934), p. 54. We should note that Ryland had a basically generous spirit, advocating open communion; see above, p. 180.

40   *Orthodox Creed*, art. IX, in Lumpkin, *Baptist Confessions*, p. 303.

Connexion of General Baptists in 1891, after a century of discussion, controversy and increasing integration.[41] This merger of structures, motivated by the desire for united mission, was so successful that few Baptist church members today are even aware that two groups once existed, or to which their own local church once belonged. Baptists today generally have no clear memory of the debate concerning the saving work of Christ and the sovereign grace of God that once divided their ancestors. They would be hard put to attach the labels of 'Calvinist' or 'Arminian' to anyone. However, the various *ideas* that were once channelled within separate groups are still very much alive, and part of the flavour of Baptist identity is perhaps the way that these ideas are blended in different proportions. The necessity for a personal response of faith certainly remains, and so does a general sense of need for God's grace to initiate salvation and create human response.

It is thus usual to find Baptists today holding divine election and human responsibility as a paradox or (to echo the *Orthodox Creed*) a 'great mystery'. In his style of preaching, C. H. Spurgeon essentially took the same approach, as in a sermon on the double-sided text, 'All that the Father giveth me shall come to me; and him that cometh to me I will in no wise cast out' (Jn. 6:37):

> I am quite certain that God has an elect people, for he tells me so in his Word; and I am equally certain that everyone who comes to Christ shall be saved, for that is also his own declaration in the Scriptures. When people ask me how I reconcile these two truths, I usually say that there is no need to reconcile them, for they have never yet quarrelled with one another.[42]

Spurgeon thought that the two truths met in the fact that no one *wants* to 'come to Christ' unless they are elect and are *made* willing, so that the very desire for salvation is evidence of election; on one occasion he urged his hearers to 'say as an old woman once said, "if there were only three persons elected, I would try to be one of them"'.[43] But Spurgeon was too good a thinker not to realize that some tension between divine action and human freedom remained, and some 'mystery',[44] even

---

41   See Payne, *The Baptist Union*, chs. 2–8. Since 1833 the New Connexion of General Baptists had been accepted as a separate association of the Baptist Union.

42   Charles Haddon Spurgeon, 'The Last Message for the year', *Metropolitan Tabernacle Pulpit*, LVI (1910), 3, 230 (28 December 1873), p. 631. Spurgeon often preached on this text, and the titles are revealing: e.g. 1,762, 'High Doctrine and Broad Doctrine; 2,349, 'All Comers to Christ Welcomed'; 2,954, 'The Big Gates Wide Open'; 3,000, 'Come and Welcome'.

43   Spurgeon, 'Heavenly Worship', *New Park Street Pulpit*, III (London: Passmore and Alabaster, 1858), no. 110 (28 December 1856), p. 29.

44   See e.g. 'Human Inability', *New Park Street Pulpit*, IV (1879), no. 182 (7 March 1858), p. 142.

though he himself took the definite view that limited atonement was part of the doctrine of election. Many, perhaps most, Baptists now hold a more generalized belief in God's election to salvation, without associating this with a limited or particular atonement. This is true not only of Baptists in England, but those elsewhere. The confession of the Federation of French Baptist churches, for example, affirms that 'the Holy Spirit ... produces in those who have been elected through the predestination of God, true Christian life'[45], but offers no hint that Christ has only died for these elect. Nor can I find a single example of limited atonement in any modern confession of faith of a Baptist group connected with the Baptist World Alliance, though among European Baptists the confessions in Germany, France and Hungary affirm the doctrine of the perseverance of the saints, as does the Faith and Message of the Southern Baptist Convention in the USA.[46]

While still holding election and freewill together, Baptists tend now to find some light in the darkness of the mystery by effectively regarding the doctrine of election as a way of speaking of that grace of God which is necessary to initiate human faith. For myself, I believe that we shall only begin to see *how* this kind of grace and human freewill converge if we abandon the view that grace is irresistible. We need, I suggest, a vision of a God who is humble enough to have a gracious offer of life rejected, even of a God who will work by the Holy Spirit in the depths of the human heart wooing human beings to respond, and who is still willing to be spurned. This is an idea I intend to say more about in the next chapter.

For the moment, I want to follow up the strong emphasis in Baptist tradition upon the initiating and enabling grace of God in a different but related direction. It may seem odd, in the light of this conviction, that many Baptists have failed to give due place to the grace of God received in *baptism*. There has been an unfortunate tendency for the stress to fall upon the faith of the person coming for baptism, and for the act to be a 'sign' of dying and rising with Christ only in the sense of a *visual aid* or illustration. It has thus often been reduced to an act of obedience and witness alone. There is, of course, a long Baptist tradition that takes another view, celebrating the presence and manifestation of the grace of God in baptism.[47] In modern times, for example, a prominent advocate of Baptist sacramentalism, the New Testament scholar George Beasley-Murray, has affirmed that the New Testament views the baptism of believers as 'a symbol with power', and that 'there is no gift or power available to man in consequence of the redemption of Christ that is not

---

45   Text in Parker, *Baptists in Europe*, p. 127.
46   Texts in Parker, *Baptists in Europe*, pp. 60, 127, 192, 249.
47   See above, ch. 7, pp. 129–30.

available to him in baptism.'[48] It may seem curious that any other view *could* be taken, given the well-established Baptist understanding (through its Calvinist inheritance) that human faith is always enabled and accompanied by divine grace. If believers come to baptism with faith in their hearts, they must be accompanied in this approach by the power of God's grace.

However, it is easy to see why many have not drawn this conclusion, since Baptists insist that candidates for baptism must *already* have faith in Christ and therefore have already entered upon salvation. God's grace has already been operative in their experience. The resolution of this apparent paradox only comes if we are prepared to see salvation as a process rather than a single point. There is room for the saving grace of God in conversion *and* in believers' baptism if conversion is but one moment in a larger process, in a long story of the saving grace of God that begins with the prevenient work of the Spirit deep in the mysteries of the human heart and ends with the glorifying of the person in the new creation. This is, after all, the New Testament understanding of salvation which is past, present and future. We have arrived once more at the idea of Christian initiation as a journey, [49] but this time from the starting point of the sovereignty of grace, as a power that enables all human response.

From a strictly Calvinist perspective, there is in fact a kind of process between the act of turning in faith to Christ and the moment when the believer receives the *assurance* of salvation (or 'makes his calling and election sure'). These two stages are not present in the Particular Baptist Confession of 1644, but they *are* stated in the Confession of 1677.[50] They are graphically portrayed in Bunyan's story of the *Pilgrim's Progress*, for when we left the Pilgrim entering the Gate of conversion he was still carrying his heavy burden of guilt. It is not until some while later that he arrives at a wayside cross, and

> his burden loosed from off his shoulders and fell from off his back; and began to tumble, and so continued to do till it came to the mouth of the sepulchre, where it fell in, and I saw it no more. Then was Christian glad and lightsome, and said with a merry heart, 'He hath given me rest, by his sorrow, and life, by his death'.[51]

---

48   Beasley-Murray, *Baptism in the New Testament*, pp. 263–4.

49   See above, ch. 7, pp. 137–8, 141–3.

50   Second London Confession, ch.XVIII:2–4, in Lumpkin, *Baptist Confessions*, pp. 274–5.

51   Bunyan, *The Pilgrim's Progress* (ed. Sharrock), p. 70. Bunyan's own long journey from conversion to assurance and inner peace was complicated by the obssessive fear that he had committed an unforgivable sin: see Bunyan, *Grace Abounding to the Chief of Sinners* (London: George Larkin, 1666; facsimile, Menston: Scolar Press, 1970), paras. 182–88, 229–32, pp. 63–5, 79–80.

This particular pattern of salvation experience was not universal among Baptists, even among Particular Baptists, and among Baptists of today a waiting for such a 'moment of inner assurance' is very rare. But the influence of the charismatic movement has resulted in a different kind of 'further blessing' beyond conversion, whether called a 'baptism of the Spirit' or a 'filling with the Spirit'. When Baptist thinkers have simply equated 'baptism in the Spirit' with conversion, they have been perplexed by a phenomenon of grace *later* than conversion whose transforming effects upon a believer's life cannot be ignored. It would be better New Testament theology normally to equate baptism in the Spirit with the baptism-in-water which follows conversion, while allowing freedom to the Spirit of God not to conform to our tidy patterns of belief and to have the capacity to surprise us.[52]

I suggest, then, that among Baptists the older Calvinist and the newer charismatic patterns of experience both point to a story of salvation which is more complicated and extensive than conversion alone.[53] Believers' baptism as an event of saving grace can take its place *within* this story, as a high point in the experience of 'being saved' which does not deny previous entrance into the saving grace of Christ. Understanding salvation as a process like this would also begin to break down the neat distinction made at the time of the Reformation between 'justification' and 'sanctification', an issue that has divided Protestant and Catholic theology since that time.

For Augustine, justification, or the 'reckoning' of righteousness, meant a *bestowing* of God's righteousness upon sinners in such a way it became part of their being, and operated as an inner power which enabled them to act rightly and to do works pleasing to God, so becoming increasingly holy in life (sanctification).[54] For the Reformers, this notion of imparted or infused righteousness seemed to play into the hands of those who saw justification as the result of good deeds. In their view, believers have righteousness reckoned or 'imputed' to them only in the sense that they are *declared* to be in the right with God; while this should result in the grateful response of an increasingly holy life (sanctification), their righteousness remains only in Christ, and so external and 'alien' to them throughout their life.[55] But the more we understand salvation as a journey

---

52   Further on this, see above, ch. 7, pp. 148–50.

53   Above, chapter 2, pp. 39–40, I suggested that the practice of covenant-making also directed us towards the idea of salvation as a story rather than a single point in time.

54   *Augustine on Romans*, ed. P.F. Landes (Chico: Scholars Press, 1982), p. 21, 'the good works we do after we have received grace are not to be attributed to us, but rather to him who has justified us by his grace.' Cf. Augustine, *On Rebuke and Grace*, 35–37; *On Grace and Free Will*, 29–30.

55   Martin Luther, *Lectures on Romans*, trans. and ed. W. Pauck (Library of Christian Classics 15; London: SCM Press, 1961), on Rom. 4:7, p. 134, 'All our good is

and a process, the more possible it becomes to see righteousness as *both* imputed and imparted. The very word of God that declares justification is a ferment working beneath the surface of life. Atonement is not only a giving of a new status, but the giving of a new *relationship* that changes our very being through the transforming power of the Spirit of God. We cannot separate the human response of leading a life in tune with God's purposes from the divine initiative of grace that makes it possible.

While it may seem that the Baptist practice of believers' baptism throws all the stress upon salvation as a crisis of personal faith, in fact it prompts us to see salvation as a developing story.

Personal Salvation and Theologies of Atonement

Salvation is a wider concept than atonement, involving the healing of communities as well as individuals, and spanning the whole story of the transformation of human life, beginning with new birth and ending with the new creation. But atonement is the critical moment of salvation. According to the Christian view of salvation, the universal scope of divine healing stems from one particular event, the death of Jesus for human sins in a Roman execution one Friday afternoon. All roads lead not to Rome, but to a mound of earth outside the walls of a Middle Eastern town in a remote corner of the Roman Empire.

The task of Christian theology has been to explore the link between our experience of salvation in the present, and that particular moment in the past.[56] We have already been considering the relation between the act of God and human response in salvation, but bound up with this is the relation between the decisive event in past history and the continuous effect of it in the present, between the objective and the subjective in salvation. I want now to look into the Baptist tradition to see what it has to say on this question which is both about theology and spirituality.

One of the strongest objections to highly 'objective' or 'transactional' views of the saving work of Christ is that they exclude the believer's subjective response from the actual event of atonement. They portray atonement as a kind of legal settlement between God the Father and God the Son in which we are not involved, despite being the erring sinners who need to be restored to the father's house. To speak of paying a debt to God's justice, either by a gift of honour (Anselm) or as a transferred penalty (Calvin) certainly stresses the once-for-all character of the death

---

outside us; and Christ is this good'; cf. Calvin, *The Epistles of Paul the Apostle to the Romans and to the Thessalonians*, trans. R. Mackenzie (Edinburgh: Oliver and Boyd, 1961), on Rom. 4:3, p. 83.

56   See Paul S. Fiddes, *Past Event and Present Salvation*, pp. 24–34.

of Jesus, but it does not integrate the healing of the human personality here and now into the event of atonement.

Of course, theories like this *add* our response of repentance and trust as a second stage or appendix. But this comes as a later acceptance of what has already been achieved, and so I suggest misses the heart of atonement – the restoring of a relationship between persons. If it is truly to be reconciliation then all the estranged partners must be involved; the prodigal son cannot sit on the sidelines, but salvation is about being embraced by the loving father. It is hard to see the relevance of the human reaction to the atoning act if this is already complete. So Calvin is quite consistent with his transactional theory when he makes the link between past event and present salvation one of election. God includes human beings in the event of salvation *only* in the sense of choosing those who should have justifying faith; they are involved because their names are written into the legal contract.[57] The really consistent conclusion is the one that Calvin's successors drew: that atonement is actually *limited* to the elect.

We may also look at this over-objectivity from another angle. It is usually said that a theory of penal substitution 'takes sin seriously', but I venture to suggest that what it takes seriously is a *debt* which human beings are said to have incurred against God through their sin. The theory does not grapple with sin as a *power* in human existence which warps and distorts personalities and relationships in the present. A substitute penalty (Calvin), like a gift of honour (Anselm) only pays off a debt to the offended dignity of divine justice. The satisfaction provided does not cope with the brokenness of life *here and now* which the holiness of God cannot tolerate. Like a doctor who is implacably hostile to a disease, God wants to root sin out of our lives. This expiation of sin cannot be kept for a second stage of 'sanctification'; it belongs to atonement itself.

Now, we have been exploring the Baptist emphasis upon salvation by faith as personal, individual response to the grace of God in Christ. This precisely does involve the repentant human sinner in the event of atonement. Relationships are re-made here and now. For the reasons I have given this would not seem to fit easily with a highly transactional view of atonement such as Calvin's doctrine of penal substitution, and yet the Puritan-Calvinist heritage in Baptist life is so strong that many Baptists today would assume that this is the only understanding of atonement there can be. There is some tension here with their Calvinistic inheritance, since Baptists have moved away from the view of limited atonement that would have been held by most Particular Baptists in the past, and which I

---

57 Calvin, *Institutes*, II, 3, xxi:5–7, pp. 206–11.

have suggested is a logical consequence of the theory of a transferred penalty.

In fact, we notice that the earlier Baptist confessions were rather undogmatic in their understanding of the *means* of atonement. Relying on the Reformation listing of the three-fold office of Christ as prophet, priest and king, they appealed to the priestliness of Christ in the cross; affirming that he offered himself as an 'acceptable sacrifice', they left open in what sense that sacrifice might be understood.[58] Confessions of Baptist Unions in modern times (in so far as they exist) also often show an openness and flexibility in grappling with this mystery. Typical are phrases from Baptist Confessions which speak of 'perfect obedience and atoning death' (Sweden and Finland), death 'for remission of sins' (France), 'mediating suffering' (Holland) and 'Christ's death for all people' (formerly USSR, now CIS, All-Union Council). The Romanian confession simply states that 'our Lord Jesus was crucified in our place' and the 1963 version of the Baptist Faith and Message of the Southern Baptist Convention (USA) says equally simply that 'in his death on the cross he made provision for the redemption of men from sin.'[59] In the seventeenth century it was not until the two major Baptist Confessions of 1677 and 1679, both under influence from the Westminster Confession, that there was an explicit statement of penal substitution.[60] In modern times this theory has been explicitly adopted in confessions *of some* Baptist Unions in Eastern Europe (e.g. Poland, Hungary, Jugoslavia).[61]

I believe that the typical Baptist combination of emphasis upon the initiative of God in salvation, together with the 'existential' stress on personal response, can in fact lead to an understanding of atonement that does justice to the New Testament witness. It takes a point of departure from the Apostle Paul's account of baptism in Romans chapter 6, where he speaks of the total identification of Christ with the human condition in death. Elsewhere in the New Testament it is said that Christ suffers the consequences of human sin, separation from the Father, and even undergoes the judgement of God against sinful human life. The question

---

58   E.g. *A Short Confession* (1610), art. 13, in Lumpkin, *Baptist Confessions*, p. 106; the London Confession (1644), art. XVII, in Lumpkin, *Baptist Confessions*, p. 160; *The Faith and Practise of Thirty Congregations* (1651), art. 19, in Lumpkin, *Baptist Confessions*, p.178. Of special interest here is the statement in *Propositions and Conclusions* (1612), art. 129, that the sacrifice of Christ 'slayeth the enmity and hatred which is in us against God' (Lumpkin, *Baptist Confessions*, p. 129).

59   For all the preceding texts, see Parker, *Baptists in Europe*, pp. 88, 101, 107, 127, 155, 220, 247. However, the 2000 revision of the Southern Baptist Faith and Message has inserted the word 'substitutionary' before 'death on the cross'.

60   Second London Confession, ch. VIII.4 (Particular Baptist); *Orthodox Creed*, art. XVII (General Baptist): in Lumpkin, *Baptist Confessions*, pp. 261–2, 309.

61   For texts, see Parker, *Baptists in Europe*, pp. 176, 190, 209.

is *why* Christ suffers in this way. Calvin, from the perspective of his own legal culture answers that it was to satisfy the justice of God, a view never explicitly stated in the New Testament itself. Paul in Romans 6 explains that it was to release into human life the power of his resurrection, transforming human personality: 'if we have died with Christ we believe that we shall also live with him.' Christ dies the death we should have died to enable us to share his life. Such a view thoroughly integrates human response in the present with the act of God in the past.

It may be, I suggest, a particular Baptist contribution to atonement theology to affirm the enduring of sin and divine wrath by Christ (Calvinist tradition), while also affirming the central place of human response and human transformation (Arminian tradition). Such a contribution has been made by several Baptist theologians in modern times, notable among them Vincent Tymms in *The Christian Idea of Atonement* (1904) and Henry Wheeler Robinson in *Redemption and Revelation* (1942). Both affirm the suffering of God the Father in the cross of Jesus in sympathy with the Son, both emphasize that Christ endured in himself the terrible consequences of human sin, and both find atonement to lie in the power of the cross to transform human lives in the present. Tymms, like Abelard, finds the power of the cross to be that of revelation; the disclosure of God's love in the cross has the power to create love within our loveless hearts. Unlike Abelard, he affirms the need for Christ to endure the suffering and death which is the consequence of sin, in order to make clear the grief of God over human sin and the costliness to God in offering forgiveness. The atoning act of God is objective in that human guilt is cancelled when the 'human spirit of disobedience is cast out' by the creative impact of the cross.[62]

Wheeler Robinson adds several elements to the approach of Tymms (whom he does not mention). When sin is taken into the very being of God, he affirms, the suffering it causes is changed into the power of forgiveness. Sin is actually *transformed* within God, and he claims that 'the divine reaction to the suffering inflicted upon God by sin is the most "objective" fact in the spiritual history of mankind.'[63] From this achievement flows the power of love that awakens human response and transforms human life. While, like Tymms, Robinson finds that divine love reaches us through revelation, he also draws on his Old Testament studies of 'corporate personality' to hint that human personalities are

---

62   T. Vincent Tymms, *The Christian Idea of Atonement* (Angus Lectures 1903; London: Macmillan, 1904), p. 334.

63   H. Wheeler Robinson, *Redemption and Revelation* (Library of Constructive Theology; London: Nisbet & Co., 1942), p. 276.

changed by their sharing in the divine life itself.[64] In summary, Robinson proposes that:

> By the actuality of a divine transformation of the consequences of sin upon the cross of Christ there are liberated the spiritual energies and influences which eventually transform men from being enemies into being friends and servants of God. Only when that process is completed in all who yield themselves to it will the full victory of God be won on earth.[65]

The past event of the cross is thus an objective act of salvation, in that it creates response to God's love in the present, overcoming human rebellion towards God and so expiating (wiping out) sin. We might, I suggest, spell out this enabling of response in several ways.[66] There is the power of the story of the passion, a narrative into which the community enters in holy imagination, and which shapes its life. There is the effect on the individual of being part of a community, originating in the earliest fellowship with Jesus Christ, which constantly repeats and re-enacts the victory of Christ. But above all, the God who draws near to us here and now to offer forgiveness is one in whose heart is a cross, who in Christ has felt the weight of God's own divine 'no' against sinful human life; our experience of a God of such sacrificial love has the power to break stubborn hearts and win anxious minds. In the sacraments of baptism and the Lord's Supper, enacted in the midst of the community, there is a focus of this story and of this gracious coming of God. Such a theology of atonement cannot be distinctive to Baptists, but there is something about the Baptist emphasis upon both the objective initiative of God's grace and the human existential response that makes it appropriate and convincing.

The Breadth of Salvation

I have been developing throughout this chapter the argument that Baptists combine a view of saving faith as an individual human response to Christ as Saviour, with an equally strong view of the sovereign initiative of God's grace. Whatever the historical reasons for this blend (a kind of spiritual cocktail of dashes of Calvinism and Arminianism), it has led Baptists to have a wide view of the scope of salvation.

---

64   See e.g. Robinson, *The Christian Experience of the Holy Spirit*, pp. 30–33. This is a hint I have developed much more extensively in my own study, *Past Event and Present Salvation*.

65   Robinson, *Redemption and Revelation*, p. 278.

66   Here I follow my account in *Past Event and Present Salvation*, especially pp. 63–5, 99–101, 109–10, 139–42.

It has led Baptists to see themselves as part of a universal church made up of 'all of the redeemed', whatever denomination of the Christian church these belong to. The affirmation of an 'invisible church' has enabled Baptists to be catholic in their view of the boundaries of redemption, though we must immediately add that Baptists have also affirmed the need for the church universal to become as visible *as possible* before the coming of the new creation, and to work for this.[67] The scope of God's salvation for Baptists, we should also note, includes children before the age of moral responsibility. In the words of the Baptist Union of Finland, for example, 'according to Jesus' own words and because of his atonement and death the kingdom of heaven belongs to them.'[68] While declining to baptize infants has sometimes been urged against Baptists as lack of concern for the place of children in the church, and as evidence of a modern individualism, in fact Baptists have seen no need to baptize those who are already included in the kingdom of heaven until they opt out themselves by deliberate transgression.[69]

The sovereignty of God in salvation also led a number of Baptists to affirm confidently that 'God has accepted' all those who show signs of a holy life, regardless of their mode of baptism, and that this should be the basis for open communion and open membership.[70] This language of 'acceptance' by God, derived from a reading of Romans 14 and 15, placed equal emphasis on the objective act of God and the subjectivity of the fruits of the Spirit. Christians were to be welcomed into fellowship, even if they had not been baptized as believers, not just because they could make a profession of faith, but because salvation was in the hands of the Lord 'who is able make them stand' (Rom. 14:4). An example of this approach is to be found in the covenant document of 1780 of New Road Baptist Church, Oxford. Re-establishing an older congregation, with members who were Baptist, Presbyterian and Methodist, and in the face of contrasting beliefs about the subject and mode of baptism, the covenant declares:

.... notwithstanding this difference of sentiment, we promise and agree to receive each other into the same affection and love; and for this, among many other reasons: because we can find no warrant in the Word of God to make such difference of sentiment any bar to Communion at the Lord's Table in particular, or to Church

---

67   See above, ch. 9, pp. 201–2, 206–7.
68   Text in Parker, p. 107. See earlier *Short Confession of Faith in XX Articles by John Smythe* (1609), art. 5, in Lumpkin, *Baptist Confessions*, p. 100; *Propositions and Conclusions* (1612), art. 20, in Lumpkin, *Baptist Confessions*, p. 127; the Standard Confession (1660), art. X, in Lumpkin, *Baptist Confessions*, p. 228.
69   See above, ch. 7, pp. 135–6.
70   See above, ch. 8, pp. 176–7.

fellowship in general; and because *the Lord Jesus receiving and owning them* on both sides of the question, we think we ought to do so too.[71]

In societies which are increasingly multi-cultural and multi-faith, it may be that meaningful dialogue also includes both the elements I have identified – enabling grace and human response. If we are to be responsible to people who have the potential to make a personal response to God manifest in Christ, this requires a telling of the story of Jesus. At the same time, a confidence in the hidden and mysterious initiative of the Spirit requires a humility in the face of what God may be doing among others in sovereign purpose. God, in divine freedom, has ways to bring in the kingdom that we cannot know or guess at, and we ought not to be inflicted with an anxiety that everything depends on us. As God's people discover how these two strands of belief interact, combine and correct each other they may yet be led – in the words of one proto-Baptist church – 'to walk in ways made known *or to be known*, whatsoever it would cost them.'[72]

---

71   Text of covenant in Stevens and Bottoms, *The Baptists of New Road*, p. 25.
72   See n. 32 above.

CHAPTER 11

Mission and Liberty:
A Baptist Connection

The Baptist Old Testament scholar, H. Wheeler Robinson, once wrote that 'The Baptist tabernacle is not always a graceful structure, but at least we may say this of it, that the twin pillars at its door are evangelism and liberty.'[1] He added that 'This has been its attraction to the men and women of low degree from whom its worshippers have been chiefly drawn', reflecting that they have found there both 'the living message of the love of God', and 'a warm sympathy with the toilers of the earth'. The message and the sympathy, the passion for both mission and liberation, are in fact deeply connected. In this final chapter I want to explore their interrelation, and their context in a Baptist theology of covenant. There are those, including some theologians of the Orthodox Church, who will hold literally to the classical four marks of the church as 'one, holy, catholic and apostolic', and who will disagree that mission and liberty are – while admittedly important features of the church – 'of its essence'; but I intend to argue that these aspects belong to the being of the church because they belong to the being of God. In this we shall find some support from thinking in the Orthodox Church itself, with which I want to hold occasional dialogue as we proceed.[2]

Sharing in God's Mission

'As the Father has sent me, so I send you'. These words of Jesus to his disciples after his resurrection, in John 20:21, make clear that mission belongs to the very being of the church. The scene in which these words are spoken is the Fourth Gospel's version of Pentecost, in which the

---

1   Robinson, *Life and Faith of the Baptists*, p. 135.
2   This chapter thus bears the marks of its original context, as a paper given at conversations between the Baptist World Alliance and the Orthodox Ecumenical Patriarchate of Constantinople, in Oxford May 16–19, 1997.

church is born through the receiving of the Holy Spirit (v. 22). At this moment, as Jesus breathes out the Spirit upon his followers and gives them the power of announcing the forgiveness of sins (v. 23), he thus defines the church as those who share in the mission of God. *Mission* simply means a sending (*missio*), and as the Father *sends* the Son into the world, so the Son sends out his disciples.

Agreement that mission belongs to the essence of the church therefore depends upon what is meant by mission. Much also depends upon the manner in which the church engages in mission. In this Johannine text everything is shaped Christologically; the church is to act in the spirit of Christ, being sent into the world in the same spirit of suffering love in which Christ was sent by the Father ('*As* the Father has sent me...), conformed to the ministry of the Christ who proclaimed and manifested the kingdom of God. What this might mean in practice for styles of mission I want to consider later. For the moment it is enough to underline that the church can be characterized as 'apostolic' (one of the four classical marks of the church) in so far as it shares in being sent, just as the witnesses to the resurrection of Jesus were first sent out; we recall that 'apostle' means the 'one who is sent'.[3]

It is true that the community of the church is apostolic in the sense of being the *result* of the sending of the apostles by Jesus. There is a *historical* dimension here according to which the Father sends the Son who sends the apostles who are founders of the churches. The church is the end-product of a historic chain of apostolic action. But there is also a *charismatic* dimension in which the members of the church are empowered by the Spirit to *be* apostolic, to stand in the assembly (*ekklesia*) of the apostles[4] and so not only to witness to the faith of the apostles, but also to be the ones who *are sent* here and now.

The worship of the church bears testimony to this continual involvement of the church in the mission of God: whenever people are dismissed from the Lord's Table with the words 'peace be with you' (as in the Orthodox liturgy of the Eucharist where the cry is 'let us go forth in peace'), they are being sent out to continue the ministry of Jesus as Jesus sent out his disciples from the doors of the locked room with the word of peace (Jn. 20:21): 'Jesus said to them again, "Peace be with you. As the Father has sent me, so I send you".'

As an Orthodox report expresses it, the dismissal from the liturgy is 'a sending off of every believer to mission in the world where he or she lives or works, and of the whole community into the world, to witness by what

---

3   See above, ch. 5, p. 89.

4   This theme is worked out by John Zizioulas (Metropolitan John of Pergamon), *Being as Communion*, pp. 182–7.

they are that the Kingdom is coming.'[5] *Dismissio* is *missio*. It is in fact possible that the way the Fourth Evangelist portrays the meeting of the risen Jesus with his disciples has actually been coloured by the ongoing experience of worship in the earliest Christian communities. The transfiguration of human life that is experienced in worship through the presence of the risen Christ in the power of the Spirit is to be worked out in the transfiguring of society. Thus John Chrysostom urged the church of his time that, just as Jesus went out from the Passover meal to the Mount of Olives, so from the table of the eucharist 'let us go out unto the hands of the poor'.[6]

The reason why mission is of the very being of the church is that mission is not just *imitating* the sending forth of Jesus. It is a *participation* in the Father's own sending forth of the Son. Many organizations in our society today have a 'mission statement', whether they are hotels or car manufacturers. Such statements set out the aims of the company and how they intend to fulfill them. But the church does not have its own mission statement, since mission is not fundamentally a task that is laid upon the church; mission is rooted in the very being of the triune God, and the church is simply summoned to share in *God's* work. 'As the Father has sent me...' says Jesus.

The doctrine of the Trinity tells us that the Father eternally sends forth the Son in the ecstatic love of the Spirit. This 'eternal generation' (as Athanasius describes it) takes historic and temporal form in the sending of the Son into the world, into the dusty streets of Galilee, into the city of Jerusalem. The generous sending of the divine Son into human existence was God's mission from eternity, God's original project to become incarnate in order to raise human life into fellowship with the divine life. God goes out from God's own self in order to bring creatures into God. This is a journey deep into creation that would have taken place, regardless of human fallenness, as God always intended to take on a body of humanity in space and time.[7] But the mission takes the painful form that it does, a mission of suffering love and the establishing of justice in a broken world, as a result of the damage done by sin; because of sin the Son is sent not only into the world, but on the road into Golgotha and to the cross.

---

5   '"Your Kingdom Come", an Orthodox Contribution to the Theme of the World Missionary Conference (Melbourne 1980)', in Georges Tsetsis (ed.), *Orthodox Thought. Reports of Orthodox Consultations organized by the World Council of Churches, 1975–1982* (Geneva: WCC, 1983), p. 37.

6   John Chrysostom, *Homilies on Matthew*, 82 (on Matthew 26:26–28): 5.

7   This has been a widespread conviction in Christian theology. See Duns Scotus, *Opus Oxoniense (Ordinatio)* 3, d.7, q.3; Barth, *Church Dogmatics*, II/2, pp. 101–4, 115–21; Boff, *Trinity and Society*, 186–8; Wolfhart Pannenberg, *Systematic Theology*, II, pp. 63–5.

Mission is thus 'of the being' of the church because in the first place it is 'of the being' of God. There has been a welcome convergence of theology here between the various world communions of the Christian church. There is a shared vision of the founding of mission in the *koinonia* of the triune God, which was expressed for instance in the recent Fifth World Conference on Faith and Order, *On the Way to Fuller Koinonia*.[8]

The church is apostolic because it participates in God's own sending. Recently the Armenian Orthodox Catholicos, Aram I of Cilicia, has linked this with another classical mark of the church, its catholicity (universality). This he identifies as 'a call for a renewed missionary vocation' for 'mission is of the *esse* of the church'. Catholicity is not only given, but is also a task and a call; the church will only be truly catholic, he affirms, through mission, for 'in a sense, mission creates the church'. This is because 'the church has no mission of its own; it participates in God's mission.'[9] The goal of sending is catholicity, the universal praise of God by the creation.

Mission and Covenant

If mission is a sharing in the triune life, then it is also sharing in the divine covenant. From time to time in previous chapters, when considering the gracious partnership of God with the church, we have seen that mission and covenant are intertwined.[10] The theology of the Reformation did not only use covenant language for the activity of God in human life; in the light of this, it perceived covenant in the *eternal* relationships between the Father and the Son, in the fellowship of the Spirit. We have seen that in our time this theme has been developed by the theologian Karl Barth, who finds the covenant which becomes visible at one moment in human history (the life, death and resurrection of Christ) to be the expression of an eternal relationship of love between the Father and the Son in the communion of the Spirit. As the Father makes an eternal decree with regard to the person of the Son, freely determining to be 'God again a second time', so he eternally makes covenant with the human person, Jesus of Nazareth.[11] The two commitments are one and

---

8   Here see especially Metropolitan John of Pergamon (John Zizioulas), 'The Church as Communion: A Presentation on the World Conference Theme', in Best and Gassmann, *On the Way to Fuller Koinonia*, pp. 108–9.

9   Report of the Moderator, Aram I, to the Meeting of the Central Committee of the World Council of Churches, Geneva, 26 August – 3 September 2002, paras. 6.6–7.2; source, www.wcc.coe.org.

10   See above, pp. 32, 36–7, 55–6, 73–4, 189–90, 207.

11   Barth, *Church Dogmatics*, II/2, pp. 161–5.

inseparable. In choosing God's self, God chooses Jesus, and all people along with him. As the Father sends forth the Son – a *missio* – in his desire for communion and in his extravagant love for creation, he makes covenant with created beings. So we can, in contemplation, place ourselves in the heart of this generous movement in God; as a fourteenth century mystic, Jan van Ruusbroec, expresses it, the human spirit 'abandons itself to steep itself in the divine being, and *it flows out again*, along with all creatures, through the eternal birth of the Son, and is established in its created being by the free will of the Holy Spirit.'[12] We can surely sum up this vision of divine mission by saying that God's covenant *with us* is simultaneous with a covenant *within* God's own life.[13]

While early Baptist theologians did not think their covenant theology through in precisely this way, I suggest that it is consistent with their bringing so closely together the 'horizontal' and 'vertical' dimensions of covenant. Somehow, they thought, the covenant that God made through the sacrifice of Christ, arising from an agreement in God, overlapped with the agreement of members between themselves. As Catholicos Aram I puts it in our day, the mission of God creates the church.

There were theological strains here, which Baptist theologians did not entirely resolve. There was, for instance, a good deal of mystery in the way that God's *unconditional* covenant of salvation could become manifest in a covenant in a local congregation which involved free response to God and to each other. They were also inclined to think that God's covenant with any particular local congregation was *conditional* upon its obedience to God in Christ, and there were problems in integrating this with an unconditional covenant of salvation. But despite these mysteries of grace and free will with which thinkers of the church have always wrestled, they found that the eternal covenant of grace was somehow becoming actual in time and place in the covenant promises of the local congregation.

This perspective has implications for the character of the mission in which the church is engaged. It is essentially relational, essentially a matter of making communion and community. On the one hand the announcement of the good news of salvation in Jesus Christ will *result* in new relationships; it will draw people who respond into a new kind of relational existence within the community of the church, and within God's own life. But on the other hand it also means that mission should take the *form* of community; the community of the church 'goes out' by opening up its life to draw in the alien, the outcast and the estranged just

---

12   John Ruusbroec, *The Spiritual Espousals and Other Works*, trans. J.A. Wiseman (Classics of Western Spirituality; New York: Paulist Press, 1985), pp. 116–18.

13   I explain above, ch. 2, p. 36, why Barth himself declines to make this connection.

as God makes room for us in an inner life of communion. The most effective form of mission may be the impact of the community life of the church on its neighbourhood, not enclosed in self-preservation but open in risky welcome. Mission will thus be concerned with making relations at every level of the world, in reflection of the triune God. It will offer prophetic criticism of competitive individualism in society, and seek to encourage political and economic policies that are committed to inter-personal relationships; it will also have a care for the whole natural creation, seeking to foster organic relations between all animal and plant life, in partnership with humanity and beyond it.

These open horizons in mission also derive from another aspect of covenant ecclesiology. As we have seen, it is Christ as covenant-mediator who takes the initiative in drawing the community together. The familiar Baptist phrase 'the gathered community' certainly indicates the personal faith and responsible discipleship which every church member is called to exercise in 'gathering' into the congregation. But the local church is not a 'voluntary society' in the sense that membership depends finally upon the decision of the members to join.[14] Rather, the gathering of the members is completely dependent upon the gracious initiative of Christ in 'gathering' his disciples, to which they respond in obedience. The community is 'gathered', in accordance with the scriptural insight that covenants are not mutual bargains between God and his people, but are always initiated by the grace of God. This aspect of covenant gives mission a totally open quality. The initiative of Christ means that the local church is a community which gathers together a whole range of people, cutting across barriers of age, class, culture and temperament. It cannot be a community of the like-minded, a homogeneous unit, as would be the case with a club based on preference. The local church, in other words, is as 'catholic' as the church universal. Its strength comes from being a gathering of the 'unlike', people quite different from each other. Mission strategies which depend on creating homogeneous units of people who will 'naturally' gather together from one section of society, or from one interest group, or from one kind of job, or from one ethnic group, contradict the principle that Christ is the gatherer.

All this should have meant that Baptists with a covenant theology had mission in the forefront of their minds from the beginning. Unfortunately this was not the case. There was a danger that the concept of covenant would be shrunk to the validation of a narrow, *closed* community. When allied with a hyper-Calvinistic theology of election, and a doctrine of atonement thus limited in its blessings to the elect, members of the local church could rest content with the assurance that *they* had been chosen to be part of the covenant community. They could

---

14   See above, ch. 2, pp. 40–5.

be satisfied with their own privileged position in the mysterious counsels of God, and could see no need to invite others into the life they enjoyed. There was a popular inference from the doctrine of the divine decrees that it was positively wrong to work for the salvation of others, lest they should prove not to be of the elect.[15] This was the story of many Particular Baptist churches in the eighteenth century, which not only failed to regard mission as the *essence* of the church, but were even reluctant to see it as the *responsibility* of the church. Salvation was a matter of God's pre-determination, and so God's responsibility alone.

What changed this situation was a new kind of thinking that emerged towards the end of the eighteenth century, dubbed 'Fullerism' at the time and later named 'evangelical Calvinism'. It combined a Calvinistic stress on God's sovereign covenant of grace with a concern for mission, and so provided the theological basis for both evangelical outreach at home and the birth of the Baptist Missionary Society for mission abroad. Indeed, the first action of the new BMS was to send one of its founders, William Carey, to India in 1793, in partnership with the medical doctor John Thomas. As has been rightly observed, this theological development roused a section of the Christian church that had only little been touched by Methodism and the evangelical revival.[16] Carey was part of a close-knit group of Particular Baptist ministers urging this new theology, including John Ryland (Jnr), John Sutcliff, Samuel Pearce, and Andrew Fuller.[17] It was Fuller who was the main theorist, and particularly in his book *The Gospel Worthy of all Acceptation* (first edition 1785). While a hyper-Calvinistic position maintained that nothing spiritually good could be the duty of the unregenerate, Fuller argued that 'faith in Christ is the duty of all who hear, or have the opportunity to hear, the gospel.'[18]

Fuller, as a Calvinistic Baptist of his time, accepts that the covenant of grace is restricted to those whom God had elected for redemption; but he sets it in a wider context in two ways. First, he appeals to the biblical concept of the image of God in human beings. While the *moral* content

---

15   This popular view actually diverged from the teaching of hyper-Calvinists such as John Brine and John Gill, who distinguished between God's commanding will (revealed in the scriptures) and God's decreeing will (the secret motive for God's own actions): see John Brine, *The Certain Efficacy of the Death of Christ Asserted* (London: Aaron Ward, 1743), p. 151; John Gill, *The Cause of God and Truth* (London: G. Keith, 4th edn, 1775), p. 154. Fuller denied that Calvin's thought, properly understood, undermined the appeal to repentance; on this see Arthur H. Kirby, 'Andrew Fuller – Evangelical Calvinist', *BQ* 15/5 (1954), pp. 195–202.

16   Ernest F. Clipsham, 'Andrew Fuller and Fullerism (1)', *BQ* 20/3 (1963), p. 100.

17   On this group, see L.G. Champion, 'Evangelical Calvinism and the Structures of Baptist Church Life', *BQ* 28/5 (1980), pp. 196–208.

18   Andrew Fuller, *Gospel Worthy of all Acceptation* (2nd edn, 1801), in Works, II, p. 22.

of the image has been effaced as humanity has failed to obey God, he maintains that the *natural* image of God is still there, so that people can be urged to use God-given faculties to respond to the good news in Christ.[19] While they are not *able* to love God without the influence of the Holy Spirit (Fuller was not a Pelagian), the powers of free agency, intellect and conscience remaining within people mean that they do have a moral *duty* to respond to God. The failure of people to believe is thus not a natural incapacity; it is due to a culpable act of the will, though a will that has been fatally injured and imprisoned by sin. In regeneration the divine image is then 're-impressed' on the human person, 'to form in us new principles and dispositions; this he describes as 'a real physical work of the Holy Spirit, whereby he imparts spiritual life'.[20] Mission is thus based both in the gracious gift of God in Christ (the new covenant) and the gifts of God already there in human existence, however defaced (the divine image).

A second way in which covenant thinking was enlarged was in Fuller's view of atonement, which he developed in the second edition of *The Gospel Worthy of all Acceptation* (1801), and to which I have already made some reference in thinking about Baptist understanding of salvation.[21] Fuller accepts that the atonement made in Christ is only *effective* for those who are included in the covenant of grace by election, but maintains that the death of Christ is *sufficient* to cover the sins of all without exception. 'The sufferings of Christ ... are of infinite value, sufficient to have saved all the world, and a thousand worlds, if it had pleased God to have constituted them the price of their redemption.'[22] Fuller thus opposed the hyper-Calvinist view of imputation which maintained a strict, 'quasi-quantitative' equivalence between the sins imputed to Christ and the righteousness imputed to sinful men and women. In this he seems to have been influenced by the New Divinity movement from Yale, led by Jonathan Edwards Jnr, which saw the death of Christ as a demonstration and vindication of the righteous government

---

19   Fuller, *Gospel Worthy of all Acceptation*, in Works, II, pp. 55-..., 82. In this distinction between moral and natural ability, Fuller was indebted to Jonathan Edwards (Snr), especially his *Inquiry into the Modern Prevailing Notions Respecting that Freedom of the Will which is Supposed to be Essential to Moral Agency* (Boston: 1754); on this debt, see Clipsham, 'Andrew Fuller and Fullerism (1)', pp. 110–13; also Clipsham, 'Andrew Fuller and Fullerism (3)', *BQ* 20/5 (1964), pp. 218–20; G.F. Nuttall, 'Northamptonshire and the Modern Question: a Turning-Point in Eighteenth Century Dissent', *Journal of Theological Studies* 16 (1965), pp. 101–23.

20   Fuller, Sermon, 'The Reception of Christ the Turning Point of Salvation', in *Works*, IV, p. 215.

21   See above, ch. 10, pp. 236–7.

22   Andrew Fuller, *Dialogues and Letters between Crispus and Gaius*, in *Works*, II, p. 488.

of God in the universe, rather than as a punishment equivalent to the offences of sinners.[23] In itself, then, the death of Christ was 'equal to the salvation of the whole world, were the whole world to embrace it', but its *particularity* lay in the application of its benefits to the elect 'directed by sovereign wisdom'.[24]

Fuller was obviously limited by the Particular Baptist thought of his time. In this missionary thinking, a theology of the divine image and all-sufficient atonement is being placed *alongside* a theology of covenant to prevent an appeal to covenant in a restrictive way. I suggest that a true understanding of the mission of God needs to *combine* them. A missionary God is always opening up the communion of the divine life for relationships with creation, so that covenant is an open offer and not a privilege confined to a limited number of elect.

For Fuller and his friends, the fact that the elect were known only to God, in the secrecy of the eternal decree, meant that the grace of God could and should be freely offered to all. They were the more confident to do this, believing that all were morally responsible before God, and that the death of Christ was sufficient for the whole world. Moreover, the fact that all people still bear the divine image, the stamp of the king, meant that all must be respected and treated with dignity.[25] The duty of all to repent was matched by the duty of all Christians to obey the command of Christ to 'teach all nations', [26] but what God then *did* with the proclamation of the gospel was in God's sovereign design. The shaping of all styles of mission by the sovereignty of God is indeed a key insight, and it is one that I want to develop further before this chapter ends.

But it is evident that this kind of theology, as expounded by Fuller, has a moral problem at its heart. It may not be illogical to maintain that people have a duty to do a good which in fact they cannot perform (the philosopher Kant indeed maintained something very like this),[27] but there is a more fundamental issue of whether a good God would only deliberately select a few for salvation from a myriad of created beings. I

---

23   On this, see Michael A.G. Haykin, 'Particular Redemption in the Writings of Andrew Fuller (1754–1815)', in Bebbington (ed.), *The Gospel in the World*, pp. 120–8.

24   Fuller, *Gospel Worthy of All Acceptation*, in *Works* II, p. 374. This view was adamantly opposed by Abraham Booth, *Divine Justice Essential to the Divine Character*, in *The Works of Abraham Booth* (3 volumes; London: J. Haddon, 1813), III, p. 61.

25   Fuller, *Expository Discourses on the Book of Genesis*, in *Works*, III, pp. 9, 54; Fuller, *Letters on Systematic Divinity*, in *Works*, IV, p. 664.

26   See William Carey, *An Enquiry into the Obligations of Christians to Use Means for the Conversion of the Heathens* (Leicester: Ann Ireland, 1792), pp. 7–12, 77–80.

27   Kant makes this the basis for a moral argument for the existence of God, in his *Critique of Practical Reason*, trans. L.W. Beck (Indianapolis: Bobbs-Merrill Co., 1975), pp. 128–30.

suggest that the truth within the doctrine of election is the need for God's initiative, for the inner working of the Spirit of God, to enable any human response to the love of God. None come who are not drawn. This is what Augustine saw clearly in his dispute with Pelagius. Grace was not simply outward example and the help of the commandments to live a good life, but an inner secret power which could influence human motivations deep below the surface of the personality.[28] This kind of understanding of grace, however, only results in a limited number of the elect if it is combined with another concept, that grace is *irresistible*. Augustine, and many after him, have assumed that if grace is an internal power, and God is sovereign, then grace cannot be resisted. If people fail to respond to God, the conclusion follows that they were never given initiating grace in the first place.

But, woven through our discussion so far has been an image of a servant God, a God who does not want to force response but who is humble enough to be rejected, even in the intimate depths of the human heart. The human failure to respond to God's offer underlines the extent of God's humility, and the depth of God's suffering which is revealed in the cross of Jesus. We may say that indeed nobody comes to Christ unless they are called; all believers are elected. But others are also called and elect and fail, tragically, to answer. The election of all human beings in the one elect Man, Christ,[29] would not issue, then, in universal salvation as an *inevitable* consequence; but it does open up the *possibility* of salvation for all. Nor is God's sovereignty infringed if God freely chooses to limit God's self in this way, in order to allow created beings to be fully personal

In such a perspective, Fuller's placing of the theology of the image of God alongside covenant becomes more fruitful. The goal of God's mission is the renewing of the divine image in humankind, which means both the transfiguring of the individual within the divine life (*theosis*) and the making of relations in the world which reflect God's own triune communion. As I have suggested in the previous chapter, the power for this transfiguration flows from the all-sufficient death of Christ.[30] Modern studies of the concept of the 'image' of God in humanity have understood it not as some faculty (like reason), but as a point of *encounter* with God. The affirmation of Genesis 1:27 has been understood against the background of religion in the ancient world, where an idol or 'image' of a god was the place where the god met his or her worshippers; it was not confused with the god as being literally the same reality, but was venerated as a representative of the divine and so a

---

28   E.g. Augustine, *On the Grace of Christ and on Original Sin*, 1.25–7.

29   So Barth, *Church Dogmatics*, II/2, pp. 161–76.

30   See above, ch. 10, pp. 245–6.

point of contact.[31] Perhaps, then, the author of Gen. 1:27 is affirming that there is no need for idols because human beings themselves are the image of God, the place where God meets us. This means that the image of God is not only individual but corporate, as God is known and encountered in relationships.[32] Image and covenant thus converge, with image as the capacity for covenantal relationships.

All this makes covenant not an elitist but an all-embracing concept. Although only human beings are declared to be in the image of God, since they are in relationship with all living creatures, covenant promises can be extended to cover the whole community of the natural world. There is already a hint of this in the Genesis story of the God's covenant with Noah, which includes 'the everlasting covenant between God and every living creature of all flesh that is upon the earth' (Gen. 9:16–17).

Covenant and Liberty

From the very beginning of the existence of Baptists as a distinct communion of faith, the Baptist vision has been shaped by convictions about freedom of conscience and religious liberty. It is woven deeply into Baptist consciousness that they have been – and in many places still are – an oppressed people. They are, of course, far from alone among Christians in this, but in a remarkable diversity of places and times Baptists have come into conflict with monarchy, government and established churches. This has been the story – for example – of Anabaptists in sixteenth-century Europe (who have left a spiritual heritage to Baptists), Baptists in seventeenth-century England and nineteenth-century Nordic countries,[33] Black Baptists in the nineteenth- and early twentieth-century USA,[34] and Eastern European Baptists in modern times under both communist and post-communist regimes. Today Baptist communities in several former communist countries suffer intimidation, loss of civil liberties and even violence. The influx of para-church groups and independent evangelicals from outside the countries concerned, without any consultation with Baptist churches which had suffered oppression for long years before the collapse of communism,

---

31   For discussion, see Gordon J. Wenham, *Genesis 1–15* (Word Biblical Commentary 1; Waco: Word Books, 1987), pp. 30–2.

32   Karl Barth regarded the image of God as relations between people, and so as the image of the Trinity: *Church Dogmatics*, III/1, pp. 183–91, 195–6; III/4, pp. 323–4.

33   See Peder A. Eidberg, 'Baptist Developments in the Nordic Countries During the Twentieth Century', in *Global Baptist History. Baptist History and Heritage* 36/1&2 (2001), pp. 138–44.

34   See James Melvin Washington, *Frustrated Fellowship. The Black Baptist Quest for Social Power* (Macon: Mercer University Press, 1986).

has led church and political authorities to react harshly against the Baptist and other non-Orthodox Christian communities; they have been identified as 'foreign sects' and have had their national identity questioned and denied.[35] The situation is exacerbated by the charge of 'proselytism', to which we will return below.

In the light of this experience, it is important to emphasize that Baptists from their beginnings have argued for freedom of conscience and religious liberty for *all* groups, not just Baptists and not even just Christians. In the previous chapter I quoted the declaration of Thomas Helwys (1612) that the earthly king should not usurp the place of the heavenly king in judging human hearts, whether Christian, 'heretics, Turks, Jews, or whatsoever.'[36] Helwys' book – for which he suffered imprisonment and death – had a strong influence on the struggle for religious liberty in the North American colonies through the political activity of such men as Roger Williams. Williams, who founded the State of Rhode Island in 1636, granting full religious liberty to its citizens, had been impressed by a tract by the Baptist John Murton, *An Humble Supplication* (1620),[37] itself drawing on the work of Helwys. Murton's arguments against persecution, written secretly in Newgate Prison in milk on the very paper which had been used as the milk bottle stoppers, were incorporated into Williams' book, *The Bloudy Tenent of Persecution* (1644).[38]

This Baptist influence on the growth of a young nation, together with general support given by Baptists in England to the American Revolution (and the French Revolution for a time), should not be interpreted as meaning that the argument for religious liberty was founded in a merely anthropological view of human freedom. Its theological basis, like much else in the Baptist vision of church and society, is in *the rule of Christ* and so ultimately in the sovereignty of God. This theological root was made clear in another very early Baptist document (1612-14), issued by the congregation of John Smyth:

That the magistrate is not by virtue of his office to meddle with religion, or matters of conscience, to force and compel men to this or that form of religion, or doctrine:

35   For one example, see Theo Angelov, 'Human Rights: Religious Freedom and Tolerance in Bulgaria', in L. A. Cupit (ed.), *Baptist Faith and Witness*, Vol. 2 (McLean: Baptist World Alliance, 1999), pp. 225–9.

36   See above, ch. 10, p. 231.

37   Reprinted in *Tracts on Liberty of Conscience* (London: Hanserd Knollys Society, 1846).

38   Roger Williams, *The Bloudy Tenent of Persecution for Cause of Conscience*, and *Mr. Cotton's Letter Examined and Answered*, ed. for the Hanserd Knollys Society by Edward B. Underhill (London: J. Haddon, 1848), pp. 35–6. Williams became a Baptist in 1639 and founded the first Baptist church in America.

but to leave Christian religion free, to every man's conscience, and to handle only civil transgressions (Rom.13), injuries and wrongs of man against man, in murder, adultery, theft, etc., for Christ only is the king, and lawgiver of the church and conscience (James 4:12).[39]

The context of the rule of Christ – 'lawgiver of the church' – makes clear that this is no mere individualism, or market-place elevation of human choice. We are back in the context of the covenant of grace. The liberty and integrity of the local church is based in the presence of Christ as covenant-mediator in the congregation (Mt. 18:19-20), not in a merely worldly idea of freedom. It is because God in Christ makes covenant with this group of believers that the local church has all the privileges or 'seals of the covenant'. So it cannot be *imposed* upon in matters of 'religion and conscience' by any external human power, whether ecclesiastical or civil, but has the liberty to discern the mind of Christ for itself and so to order its own life. The rule of the risen Christ in the congregation undermines and relativizes all human claims to authority, and, in addition to shaping an understanding of Christian ministry and church government, it is bound to have an effect on the politics of the wider society. Because the liberty of the covenant community is founded not in itself but in the rule of God, this must be extended to all people who stand under the sovereignty of the creator.

The specific struggle for religious liberty has become an important component in a wider and more modern re-statement of human freedom, in terms of 'human rights'. James Wood does not go too far in claiming that 'the *theological basis* of religious liberty is the cornerstone of all human rights'.[40] The whole concept of 'human rights', as a way of asserting that all human beings have inherent worth and dignity,[41] is not however unproblematic. Many different philosophical and religious foundations can be offered for human rights, and these necessarily result in a different listing of what exactly are regarded as rights; some states, for example, insist on a human right to vote, others that it is more important to have a right to work. This situation has been vividly

---

39 *Propositions and Conclusions*, art. 84, in Lumpkin, *Baptist Confessions*, p. 140.

40 James E. Wood, Jnr, *Baptists and Human Rights*. A Publication of the BWA's Human Rights Commission (McLean, VA: Baptist World Alliance, 1977), p. 13.

41 The notion of human dignity is central in the three basic documents of the 'International Bill of Human Rights', consisting of the Universal Declaration of Human Rights (1948), the International Covenant on Civil and Political Rights (1976) and the International Covenant on Economic, Social and Cultural Rights (1976). The Vienna Declaration (25 June, 1993) uses the same language in affirming that 'all human rights derive from the dignity and worth inherent in the human person.' Texts available on the website of the United Nations Office of the High Commissioner for Human Rights: *www.unhcr.ch.*

illustrated recently by the (unsuccessful) application to the European Court of Human Rights of a British woman suffering from motor-neurone disease; she had applied for her husband to be allowed legally to assist her with suicide, on the basis of a supposed 'human right to die'.[42] Moreover, from a Christian viewpoint, 'human rights' seems to place the status of human beings in the centre rather than our relation to a divine creator, with our consequent responsibilities to God and to each other. But it does not really matter that 'human rights' is rather fuzzy talk. We may say that it is a way of speaking, a 'lawspeak'[43] which provides a common forum of discourse. As one legal theorist puts it, 'What matters – what we should take seriously – is not human rights talk but the claims such talk is meant to express: the claims about what ought not to be done to, or what ought to be done for, human beings.'[44]

The Baptist World Alliance and the European Baptist Federation have not been slow to employ the language of human rights, but in doing so they have rooted concepts of human dignity, sacredness and worth in a theological vision of the sovereignty of God and the lordship of Christ.[45] The concept of the image of God as a validation for the dignity and sacredness of human life is an important one; human life has worth because God gives it worth. It must not be oppressed because God gives it the gift of freedom. But it is a typically Baptist approach to place the theology of image in the context of the sovereignty of God (as, we have seen, did Fuller). All human beings have basic rights, because they are participants in the life-giving and liberating rule of God in creation and redemption, a 'kingdom' which is a non-oppressive open space in which human life can flourish. Human beings have dignity because they are not only made in the image of God, but are recipients of the saving love of God in Christ.[46] One influential European Baptist writer on, and participant in, the struggle for human rights, has suggested that the modern movement for human rights, 'to keep human life human', is itself a sign of the providential rule of God in history.[47] In its approach,

---

42   'Final Right to Die Plea Rejected by Court', *The Guardian*, 30 April 2002. The woman, Diane Pretty, died shortly afterwards of ᴜer disease.

43   So Michael J. Perry, *The Idea of Human Rights. Four Enquiries* (New York: Oxford University Press, 1998), pp. 44–6.

44   Perry, *Human Rights*, p. 56.

45   So Wood, *Baptists and Human Rights*, p. 14: 'The right of God's sovereignty is at the heart of all human rights'.

46   See 'Human Rights for All' in *We Baptists*, pp. 76–86; cf. 'Harare Declaration against Racism', repr. in T. Cupit (ed.), *Baptist World Alliance Covenants and Declarations 1990–2000* (McLean, VA: Baptist World Alliance, 2000), pp. 10–13.

47   Thorwald Lorenzen, *The Rights of the Child* (Baptists and Human Rights 2; McLean: Baptist World Alliance, 1978), p. 17; also Lorenzen, 'The Bible and Human Rights'; paper read at the EBF Council, Dorfweil, 1991.

the 'Human Rights Task Force' of the European Baptist Federation (founded in 1994) has been well aware of the scope of God's rule in the world, and has been working with a wide area of rights: personal and social human rights, the economic rights of developing nations and the rights of the natural world. This last aspect appears (in the form of responsibility) in the thirteenth article of an EBF document, 'What are Baptists? On the Way to Expressing Baptist Identity in a Changing Europe'.[48] This statement, we notice, reflects the influence of 'theology of hope', popularized by Jürgen Moltmann, on the issue of human rights:[49]

As Christian Believers, we live in hope of the final appearing of Christ in glory, and the transforming of all creation.

Having hope in God's future, when the lordship of Christ will at last be fully made visible, when all things will be finally reconciled in Christ and when all creation will be renewed, has led Baptists to certain actions in the present. This hope has constantly motivated Baptists to engage in evangelism, to oppose oppressive forces in society, and to be at the forefront of the promotion of social reforms which reflect the values of the coming Kingdom of God. In this generation, in face of pollution and destruction of the natural environment, they also recognise a new responsibility to care for the whole of creation.

Religious liberty, freedom of conscience and human rights are issues that are all associated with a Baptist view of the relation between church and state. The EBF document mentioned above refers in article 12 to a 'separation of church and state', and this language echoes what has become a familiar definition in North America of a Baptist approach to political engagement. Among Baptists in Europe, however (unlike the Anabaptist or Mennonite tradition),[50] it has not been a historic Baptist position to advocate an *absolute division*, along the lines of the 'wall of separation' urged by Thomas Jefferson. That is, engagement of the church in some corporate way in government is not *in principle* ruled out. Nor has the Baptist approach been the Lutheran 'Two Kingdom' doctrine, which can lead to a passivist obedience to the will of the 'Christian Ruler', and suppression of prophetic protest. I suggest that it

---

48   A study paper produced by the Division for Theology and Education of the European Baptist Federation, 1992, revised 1993, received (but not formally adopted) at the Council of the EBF in September 1992.

49   E.g. Jürgen Moltmann, 'The Theological Basis of Human Rights and of the Liberation of Human Beings', in Moltmann, *The Experiment Hope*, trans. M. Douglas Meeks (London: SCM Press, 1975), pp. 147–57.

50   On this difference, see Nigel G. Wright, *Power and Discipleship. Towards a Baptist Theology of the State* (The Whitley Lecture 1996–1997; Oxford: Whitley Publications, 1996), pp. 13–16.

should be the Baptist approach to ask how, *in each situation*, the relation
between church and state accords with the sovereign rule of God and the
place of Christ as the only covenant-mediator in the church.

Article 12 in the EBF document on Baptist identity makes clear that
practices ruled out by the notion of 'separation' are (a) any kind of
establishment in which Christian believers or a certain Christian
communion are privileged above other members of society; (b) a
territorial view of religion in which a country or section of it is designated
by government as the exclusive preserve of one church; (c) any
interference by civil government in church government, or in religious
belief or practices. To these points we should add that Baptists have
always wanted to ask vigorous questions about structures of power and
control, inside and outside the covenant community of the church. Within
this framework, Baptists in Europe have taken a flexible approach to the
relation between church and state. In England, recently, for example, the
Baptist Union of Great Britain has made a response to the proposals of
the Royal Commission on the Reform of the House of Lords, accepting
that in principle a second chamber of Government could contain
representatives of the Free Churches, nominated by an ecumenical
process.[51] That is, without establishment, churches could still participate
in a national forum for debate and decision-making, as long as the
process clearly fostered both justice and liberty.

Liberty and Mission

We have now seen the linking of mission with covenant, and covenant
with liberty. To complete the circle we can now explore the link of liberty
with mission.

Mission and the Liberating Rule of Christ

A passion for mission relates to the passion for liberty first of all through
a common theological foundation in the rule of Christ. Baptist theology
of mission has been strongly shaped by the 'Great Commission' in
Matthew 28:16–20, when the risen Christ – who was crucified –
announces his cosmic lordship ('all authority... has been given to me'),
and in the light of this commissions the apostles to make disciples from
all nations, baptizing them in the triune Name. The rule of Christ, mission

---

51   'Royal Commission on the Reform of the House of Lords. A Response from the
Baptist Union of Great Britain', unpublished paper prepared by the Department for
Research and Training in Mission, Didcot, April 1999.

and baptism are inter-related.[52] Baptists have been quick to deduce from the order of events in this text that the call to faith precedes the act of baptism, and this itself has been a stimulus to the proclamation of the gospel.

Moreover, the call to make disciples, baptize them and teach them the commands of Christ makes clear that the aim of the commission is not to create individual believers but to form churches which, as a fellowship of believers, live under the rule of Christ, make visible the image of Christ crucified and risen, and draw the world more deeply into the sphere of his rule. Church-planting has thus been characteristic of Baptist mission, and received new emphasis during the so-called 'Decade of Evangelism' that ran up to the year 2000. It is notable that the 'Derbyshire Declaration' of the Baptist World Alliance (1992), a 'Call to establish New Churches', placed high on its list of resolves 'to establish churches that enable the character and teaching of Jesus to become incarnate within particular communities'.[53] It is also worth pointing out that this call to plant churches was set within an ecumenical horizon, since its final resolution invited Baptist local churches 'to explore the possibility *of joining with other churches* in establishing' a new congregation. It would be good to see this policy more firmly adopted by local Baptist churches, so that 'going it alone' would only happen where cooperative church-planting is clearly declined by ecumenical partners.

Since mission is grounded in the rule of the Christ who is made visible in community, the act of liberation and the preserving of human rights must itself be part of mission. As an outworking of the rule of Christ, mission includes not only telling the story of Christ but everything that creates wholeness, justice and peace. Mission is a sharing in the mission of God (*missio dei*), and so it will also involve partnership with those who are fostering human health and welfare whether or not they are professing Christians. This is grounded in a view of the sovereignty of God, who is free to work inside or outside the walls of the church. If we are truly to carry through God's 'preferential option for the poor',[54] then we shall have to discern where the grace of God is at work in the world, and seek to cooperate with movements and structures which are in tune with the purpose of God. This, as Leonard Champion suggests in his reflection on the effects of historical 'evangelical Calvinism', is an updating of its principles for our day.[55]

---

52   The Declaration of Principle of the Baptist Union of Great Britain follows these three points from Matthew 28: see Kidd (ed.), *Something to Declare*, pp. 20–22.

53   The 'Derbyshire Declaration' in *Baptist World Alliance Covenants and Declarations*, pp. 7–9.

54   See Pixley and Boff, *The Bible, the Church and the Poor*, pp. 108–138.

55   Champion, 'Evangelical Calvinism and Baptist Life', p. 207.

We often expend a great deal of effort in matters of terminology. Sometimes 'evangelism' – or proclamation – is distinguished from 'mission' as social action, or 'evangelism' is identified as one aspect within an all-embracing activity of 'mission'. But it may well be futile to try and separate 'evangelism' in any sense from 'mission'. Mission and evangelism are simply two ways of describing the same reality. Those who share in God's sending of Christ (mission) demonstrate the good news of the gospel (evangel) through their words *and* their actions of love and justice, just as Christ did. Mission is treading the path of a disciple of Christ: 'That is the basis of the Orthodox theology of mission', concludes a report of the Orthodox Task Force of the WCC, 'to acquire the dynamic, the power of the Spirit of Christ.'[56] It is no less 'evangelistic' to heal the sick, to free the oppressed and to make prophetic protest against the economic and political idols of our society than it is to *tell* the story of salvation. What matters is that 'Jesus' lordship... must become real on earth, as it is in heaven.'[57] For Baptists the missionary activity of William Carey in India from the end of the eighteenth century onwards stands as a paradigm here: proclamation of the gospel was closely bound up with social reform (including the campaign to abolish *sati*, or the burning of widows on their husbands' funeral pyres), social welfare, and an educational enterprise – Serampore College – which deliberately aimed to value and preserve the culture of the region in which it was placed.

We also need some modern paradigms in mission, and perhaps we can find one in a recent event among Baptists in Europe, the 'Albanian Project' of the EBF from 1993 to 1998. In liaison with ministers of the Albanian Government an office was set up in Tirana, which coordinated evangelism, church planting, food aid, the service of medical missionaries, refurbishment of a nursing college, offering of teachers to schools, a farming project, a language school, and help widely with such needs as school equipment and heating. Baptist Unions throughout Europe collaborated within the EBF in this project, and declared their intention from the outset to hand over the whole work and resources to Albanian leaders as soon as possible, and to change their role to that of support and service under a national Union of churches.[58] Care was also taken over the language used, as words such as 'mission' and 'missionary' were aggressive and threatening to the largely Muslim population. It should be added that during the Kosovo conflict, newly established Baptist and other evangelical/Protestant churches in Albania joined together to

---

56   'Your Kingdom Come', in Tsetsis (ed.), *Orthodox Thought*, p. 41.

57   See Thorwald Lorenzen, 'Mission and Discipleship', in Cupit (ed.), *Baptist Faith and Witness*, 2, pp. 43–4.

58   In 1998 the new Baptist Union of Albania adopted the EBF Document 'What are Baptists?' (see above, n. 46) as the basis of its constitution.

provide aid to refugees in a way that 'revealed their... growing spiritual maturity'.[59] Such a story combines issues of mission, human rights and ecclesiology.

This case study shows one other aspect of the liberating rule of Christ in mission, that is the freedom which must be given to churches to be themselves by those who have helped to found them. Just as the 'missionary' churches claim the liberty of Christ to 'interpret his laws', so they must be prepared to grant the same liberty to others. This freedom now often goes under the heading of 'contextual theology'. It was anticipated by H. Wheeler Robinson, in the perhaps excusable language of his time, in his reflection on the two pillars of evangelism and liberty: 'it will mean that the Christian faith will be interpreted by the native mind to the native mind, and that some of the results will not be those which would entirely agree with our Western interpretation.' He adds that 'the liberty that Baptists have claimed and won for themselves they must be prepared to give to others.'[60] There is another dimension of this freedom too, which is the provision of resources to the poor to engage in their own social liberation, rather than thinking that it can be won for them by the affluent and then handed over as an act of charity.[61] That would be simply a new kind of domination.

Mission and the Liberty to Evangelize

Baptists have regarded as a significant part of religious liberty the freedom to proclaim the gospel of Christ, and the freedom of those who hear the Gospel to make a choice about which Christian community they wish to participate in. Churches which have a territorial view of their existence as the body of Christ, such as the Orthodox or Roman Catholic Church are likely, however, to regard evangelism of those who have been baptized or even born within their borders as proselytism, or 'stealing of members', and their oppressive reactions may well infringe the human rights mentioned above. Baptists often feel they are misunderstood about their activities here; they will point out that they are not making any negative judgement on the truth and authenticity of the territorial church in question, but simply telling the story of Jesus and giving persons freedom to respond in their own way, prompted by the Spirit of God. If their spiritual life is newly awakened, or re-awakened after a lapse of

59   See Bernard Green, *Crossing the Boundaries. A History of the European Baptist Federation* (Didcot: the Baptist Historical Society, 1999), p. 211.

60   Robinson, *Life and Faith of the Baptists*, p. 119.

61   For the liberative practices of the poor, see Pixley and Boff, *The Bible, the Church and the Poor*, pp. 202–218.

years, then they should be able freely to choose the church fellowship in which they wish to express their faith and exercise their discipleship.

Of course, Baptists are often blissfully ignorant of the gulf between their ecclesiology and that of other communions. Those who understand a church as having a 'gathered membership' may not understand the view of 'belonging to the church' in churches where society overlaps or is coterminous with church, and so may cause offence when referring to the 'unchurched'. They may also be unaware of how odd 'choosing to belong' to a particular church may sound; indeed, in Baptist thinking itself this needs to be balanced by the conviction that Christ is gathering the community.[62] Liberty here might be better expressed as people's freedom to consent to what they believe to be *a calling from Christ* to commit themselves to a particular community. However, for all this, there are basic human rights which cut across diversity of beliefs. Such liberties to evangelize and choose are enshrined within Article 18 of the Universal Declaration of Human Rights, promulgated by the United Nations in 1948, which states that 'Everyone has the right to freedom of thought, conscience and religion: this right includes *freedom to change his religion or belief*, and freedom either alone or in community with others and *in public or in private*, to manifest his religion or belief in teaching, practice, worship and observance'.[63] Baptists, moreover, urge that these are not merely human values, but rooted in the lordship of Christ.

Proselytism may be defined, in the words of the WCC document 'Towards Koinonia in Faith, Life and Witness' (1993) as 'the conscious attempt to convert Christians to another Christian community by unfair methods which violate the freedom of conscience of the individual.'[64] This is echoed by a German Baptist theologian, Erich Geldbach, who defines proselytism as 'an attempt to win converts from another religious

---

62   See above, ch. 2, p. 42.

63   My italics. The same point is made by Principle VII of the Helsinki Agreement on Security and Co-operation in Europe (1975); text available on the website of the United Nations Office of the High Commissioner for Human Rights, www.unhcr.ch. Cf. the report on 'Structures of Injustice and Struggles for Liberation' adopted by the Assembly of the World Council of Churches in Nairobi (1975), which includes the defence of 'freedom to have or adopt a religion or belief of one's choice...'; see David M. Paton (ed.), *Breaking Barriers. Nairobi 1975. The Official Report of the Fifth Assembly of the World Council of Churches* (London: SPCK, 1976), p. 106. Ernest A. Payne, however, *The Struggle for Human Rights* (London: Baptist Union, 1974), p. 8, points out that the limitations on 'freedom to manifest one's religions or beliefs' in Article 9 of the European Convention for the Protection of Human Rights and Fundamental Freedoms (1953) are potentially of wide application; an example is the limitation necessary 'for the protection of public order'.

64   Best and Gassmann (eds.), *On the Way to Fuller Koinonia*, p. 290.

community by applying ignoble means'.[65] This is a matter requiring great sensitivity and empathy with the offended community, since the 'ignoble means' or 'unfair methods' may be economic, physical, or psychological coercion, and may go unrecognized by those perpetrating them. The signs and trappings of western wealth in a Baptist congregation in Eastern Europe may, for example, constitute an implicit inducement to people. The presence in the church of computers, fax machines, printers and video projectors may be justified as necessary vehicles for teaching and preaching, paid for by Christians in the USA, but they may well present a painful contrast to an Orthodox priest on a survival income. For all this, however, Baptists think that there is a difference between proselytism and the evangelization of those who have no effective or actual relationship to a church community at the time.

Actually, I suspect that if this distinction is to be valid, we must go further than the WCC definition. Proselytism is not just the use of unfair methods, but the 'conscious attempt to convert Christians to another Christian community' *in itself*, by *whatever* methods. It is even dangerous to regard evangelization of non-Christians as attempts to convert them to a particular Christian group. Sharing in the mission of God means, as we have seen, that mission is relational; those who engage in it must therefore be ready for it to have several different kinds of effect. It may well result in the bringing of individuals into new or renewed faith in Christ, and the result will be the growth of the church as they enter the relational life of the body of Christ. The covenant community of the church is 'eschatological', as the Spirit brings the new relations of the new creation into the present, and worshippers have a foretaste ahead of time of the glory of the future kingdom. But *what* Christian community the person joins is a matter of the sovereign call of God and the obedient response of the disciple.

Moreover, going forth on God's mission will also foster healthy relationships and heal broken relationships in society and in the natural world. These results of mission may therefore not be translated here and now into expansion of the church. Mission may issue in some people taking their place within a secular organization, or within the community of another world religion, in a new and more vital way, firmer in their grasp of the values of God's coming kingdom. God will take their lives and work up into the final fulfilment of the divine purposes in God's own way. We must be open to surprises about the effects of our participation in God's mission, and learn not to be anxious as long as we play our part as faithful disciples in telling the story of Jesus. If we claim liberty for ourselves in evangelism, we must allow liberty to the Spirit of

---

65   Erich Geldbach, 'Religious Liberty, Proselytism, Evangelism – Some Baptist Considerations', in L.A. Cupit, *Baptist Faith and Witness*, 2, p. 27.

God. We must learn to trust in God's sovereignty, rather than pinning everything on our own efforts. This lesson too we might learn from Andrew Fuller and 'evangelical Calvinism'.

Conclusion: Mission as *Diakonia*

A good deal has already been said in this volume about a Baptist understanding of *diakonia*, or pastoral service. In conclusion I want draw on insights into *diakonia*, which are relevant to mission, from another tradition and to offer some comparison with the Baptist heritage. In the Orthodox eucharistic liturgy, the *diakonia* of the church is vividly symbolized in the part played by the deacon (*diakonos*). As we have already seen, the church shares in the mission of the triune God because it shares in the *diakonia*, the servanthood, of Christ as his body in the world. Within the Orthodox eucharistic liturgy the deacon typifies this vocation by being *sent* out from the sanctuary into the midst of the people. Within the movement of the liturgy, the deacon moves to and fro between the people and the inner sanctuary, picturing the movement between heaven and earth. It is the deacon who is sent out into the congregation through the 'royal doors' of the icon-screen (*iconostasis*) with the word of scripture, and the deacon who is sent out from the inner altar with the gifts of bread and wine. He is thus a picture of the promise of Jesus, 'As the Father has sent me, so I am sending you'.

In this way he portrays one aspect of the ministry of Christ, humbly serving the people to whom he is sent with the word of life. This Christ-like image of service is echoed in the medieval Pskov Icons of the Descent into Hell. In these icons the 'mandorlas' or halo-like frames which often surround the figure of Christ are portrayed as a kind of door, so that Christ is sent to rescue Adam and Eve through a door to the heavenly world.[66] He steps through a door to grasp the hands of the representatives of the human race, just as the deacon appears through the door of the icon-screen.

The setting of diaconal action in the eucharist, which portrays the passion of Christ, also makes clear that mission is a sharing in the sufferings of Christ. The church continues to bear the salvation of Christ into the world because it bears the cross of Christ; the servant (*diakonos*) is a suffering servant. The witness which the servant makes to the kingdom of God is in word (the deacon brings forth the gospel reading), but it is also in a sacrificial life. The word 'martyr' means, of course, a

---

66   So Irina Shalina, 'On the Interpretation of the Pskov Icons of the Descent into Hell' (1996), now published in Russian in *Atonement. Russian Society of Christian Philosophers. Proceedings of the Second Symposium* (St. Petersburg: International Scholars Publications, 1999), pp. 189–97.

witness and in this sense all witnesses are martyrs. The Orthodox tradition has rightly stressed this element of suffering witness at the heart of mission, and associated it with the concept of *synergeia* or a co-working with God. A key text here is the Apostle Paul's words in Col. 1:24:

> I am now rejoicing in my sufferings for your sake, and in my flesh I am completing what is lacking in Christ's afflictions for the sake of his body, that is the church.

It is apt that Gregory of Nyssa, in his meditation on Stephen, who is commemorated as the first deacon and martyr, reflects that Stephen shared in the sacrifice of Christ, 'pouring out his own blood as a fragrant offering ... covering their sin by his prayer'[67] as he interceded for his murderers.

Sharing in mission with Christ is thus always a process of costly incarnation, which may mean literal suffering and death but which will certainly mean identification with the poor and oppressed. In early liturgical practices, immersion into the culture of the community around was also symbolized in another part of the action of the deacon in worship; it was the deacon who brought up the offerings of bread and wine provided by the people, the fruits of their daily work in the world, to be used in the eucharist.[68] Incarnation is a movement of sending from God to the world, but it also involves taking up the world into God.

The Orthodox eucharistic liturgy graphically portrays the mission at the heart of the church, with the help of the ministry of the deacon. But the traditional Baptist 'liturgy' of the Lord's Supper also has a distinctive and essential role for the deacon, and in this comes closer to Orthodoxy than to other Christian traditions. Both Orthodox and Baptists reflect, in their own way, what seems to have been the very early custom that the deacons served the elements of the Lord's Supper to the gathered people, a function generally lost in the western church.[69] Both, perhaps, are developing the rather vague picture of the deacon as servant of the poor and needy in Acts 6:1-6.[70] Following the Reformation principle that the breaking of bread and pouring of wine should happen in the midst of the people, in Baptist practice there is of course no movement of the deacon from an enclosed inner sanctuary out to the congregation. But the

---

67 Gregory of Nyssa, *Sermons on St. Stephen*, 1, PG 46. 712A. I am endebted to Grigori Benevitch for this reference.

68 See Hippolytus, *Apostolic Tradition*, 4.2.

69 See Dom Gregory Dix, *The Shape of the Liturgy* (London: Dacre Press, 2nd edn, 1946), pp. 135–7.

70 There seems to be no straightforward historical development between this kind of deacon, who 'serves tables', and the later church-office of deacon as a pastoral assistant to the *episkopos*, though Luke may be reading back what he knew of the later deacon into Acts 6; see Schweizer, *Church Order in the New Testament*, pp. 198–200.

deacons sit at table with the presiding minister, and then move from the table to serve the other members who are sitting around in the body of the congregation. In this piece of liturgical drama (though Baptists scarcely notice it as such), the deacon models the *diakonia* of the whole community, which is to leave the table and serve the world outside. Without the 'staging' of an inner area within the building, there is a less obvious depiction of the mission of Christ himself from the heavenly sanctuary, but the deacons still portray the second part of Christ's promise, 'As the Father has sent me, so I am sending you'. In the Baptist version, the deacons, who have been set apart by the local community to lead the ministry of the community,[71] show by example what the whole people are called to do.

In any celebration of the eucharist, at the moment of the transfiguration of worshippers, when the light of the future kingdom breaks into the present as a promise of the new creation, the congregation is invited to share in God's journey of salvation and liberation. Every Christian is to act as a deacon in the world, sent in the spirit of suffering service to bear the word of life, to continue Christ's own work of reconciliation.

As we participate in the movement of 'sending' within God, we are assumed into the relationship between the Father and the Son and discover the movement of the Spirit, opening up new possibilities for life and service. When someone is baptized into the triune Name, and so immersed into the triune life of God, he or she is 'ordained' to *diakonia* (service) and granted a spiritual gift (*charisma*). We have seen that a *charisma* is not a static 'thing' we possess, but an engagement in the dynamic act of the Spirit's *giving*.[72] Christ is embodied in the world through the members of his church, so that he lives a relational life as 'many in one', and all members are endowed with a *charisma* of the Spirit. The experience of the New Testament church provides us with partial lists of *charismata* (for example, prophecy, service, teaching, exhortation, generous giving, leadership, helping: Rom. 12:6–8) but these gifts are bound to differ and diversify in the light of the particular needs of any society. Effective mission will require the coming together of *charismata* distributed to many local communities, and so mission must always be cooperative, drawing upon the resources of many separate churches and many Christian traditions.

If mission is done in the spirit of Jesus, this means the mood of the suffering servant. Witness to the world is a sharing in the sacrifice of Christ, a kind of 'martyrdom', a participation in God's passion for the world. It is thus illegitimate to speak of 'aggressive evangelism' or to use

---

71   See above, ch. 5, pp. 89–91, 93–4.
72   See above, pp. 97–8, 150, 207–8.

the language of military campaigns to describe mission. Mission can never be imperialistic or competitive. It must not impose an alien culture upon people, or make them dependent upon an outside agency. Telling the story of Jesus can only be accompanied by humble pleading; it should never be characterized by coercion, manipulation, the offering of material inducements or any methods that violate the conscience of persons made in the image of God. It must shun all criticism or judgement of other communities in the world-wide Christian church. At the same time we will respect people's own freedom in the way they respond to Christ's calling them into assembly, into a local *ekklesia*, even though we feel the pain and wounds of a divided church.

Mission, then, is of the essence of the church. It is through sharing in God's own mission and God's own freedom that the church becomes one, holy, catholic and apostolic. Mission in freedom is as fundamental to the church as outward-going, self-giving love. Indeed, they are the same reality. It is in mission that the church can follow the traces of a generous God who has gone on ahead, into the future that is promised to the whole of creation.

Bibliography

Abbreviation: *BQ* = The *Baptist Quarterly*

1. Baptist and Baptist-related Publications 1600-1900

Ainsworth, Henry, *The Communion of Saincts* (Amsterdam, 1615).
Angus, Joseph, *The Voluntary System* (London: Jackson and Walford, 1839).
- *Christian Churches. The Noblest Form of Social Life; the Representatives of Christ on Earth; the Dwelling-Place of the Holy Spirit* (London: Ward & Co., 1862).
Association Records of the Particular Baptists of England, Wales and Ireland to 1660 (3 parts; London: Baptist Historical Society, 1974), Part 3. The Abingdon Association, ed. B.R. White.
Beddome, Benjamin, *A Scriptural Exegesis of the Baptist Catechism* (London, 1752).
Booth, Abraham, *An Apology for the Baptists. In which they are Vindicated ... Against the Charge of Bigotry in Refusing Communion at the Lord's Table to Paedobaptists* (London: Dilly, Keith, Johnson, 1778).
- *Divine Justice Essential to the Divine Character*, in *The Works of Abraham Booth* (3 volumes; London: J. Haddon, 1813), vol. III, pp. 3-95.
A Brief Confession or Declaration of Faith, Set forth by many of us, who are (falsely) called Anabaptists (London: printed for F. Smith, 1660) = the Standard Confession, in W.L. Lumpkin, *Baptist Confessions of Faith*, pp. 224-35.
Brine, John, *The Certain Efficacy of the Death of Christ Asserted* (London: Aaron Ward, 1743).
Brown, John, *The House of God Opened and his table free for baptists and pædobaptists, who are saints and faithful in Christ* (London: Joseph Brown, 1777).
Bunyan, John, *Differences in Judgment about Water-Baptism No Bar to Communion* (London: John Wilkins, 1673).
- *The Pilgrim's Progress*, ed. R. Sharrock (Harmondsworth: Penguin, 1965).
- *Grace Abounding to the Chief of Sinners: Or, a Brief and Faithful Relation of the Exceeding Mercy of God in Christ, to his poor Servant*

John Bunyan (London: George Larkin, 1666; facsimile, Menston: Scolar Press, 1970).

Carey, William, *An Enquiry into the Obligations of Christians to Use Means for the Conversion of the Heathens* (Leicester: Ann Ireland, 1792).

Clifford, John, *The True Use of the Lord's Supper* (London: Marlborough & Co., n.d. ?1876).

- 'Conference on the Conditions of Church Membership', *General Baptist Magazine*, 85 (1883), pp. 49-55.

Collins, Hercules, *An Orthodox Catechism: Being the Sum of Christian Religion Contained in the Law and Gospel* (London: 1680).

- *The Temple Repair'd* (London: 1702).

A Confession of the Faith of Several Churches of Christ in the County of Somerset, and of some Churches in the Counties neer adjacent (London: Henry Hills, 1656), in W.L. Lumpkin, *Baptist Confessions of Faith*, pp. 203-16.

The Confession of Faith, of those Churches which are commonly (though falsly) called Anabaptists (London: printed by Matthew Simmons, 1644) = the 'London Confession', in William L. Lumpkin, *Baptist Confessions of Faith*, pp. 153-171.

Confession of Faith Put Forth by the Elders and Brethren Of many Congregations Of Christians (baptized upon Profession of their Faith), In London and the Country (London: 1677) = the Second London Confession, in W.L. Lumpkin, *Baptist Confessions of Faith*, pp. 241-295.

A Declaration of Faith of English People Remaining at Amsterdam in Holland (Amsterdam: 1611), written largely by Thomas Helwys, in W.L. Lumpkin, *Baptist Confessions of Faith*, pp. 116-123.

Dutton, Anne, *Thoughts on the Lord's Supper, Relating to the Nature, Subjects, and Right Partaking of this Solemn Ordinance* (London: 1748).

The Faith and Practise of Thirty Congregations, Gathered According to the Primitive Pattern (London: Will Larnar, 1651), in W.L. Lumpkin, *Baptist Confessions of Faith*, pp. 174-88.

Fawcett, John, *The Constitution and Order of a Gospel Church Considered* (Halifax, 1797).

Fuller, Andrew, *The Gospel Worthy of All Acceptation*, 2nd edition (London, 1801).

- *The Complete Works of the Rev. Andrew Fuller*, ed. A.G. Fuller. A New Edition (5 volumes; London: William Ball, 1837).

Gill, John, *The Cause of God and Truth. In Four Parts* (London: G. Keith, 4th edn, 1775).

- *Complete Body of Doctrinal and Practical Divinity* (1770). *A New Edition in Two Volumes* (Grand Rapids: Baker Book House, 1978 = London: 1795 repr. 1839).

Godwin, Benjamin, *An Examination of the Principles and Tendencies of Dr Pusey's Sermon on the Eucharist. In a series of letters to a friend* (London: Jackson & Walford, 1843).

Grantham, Thomas, *Christianismus Primitivus: or, The Ancient Christian Religion* (London: Francis Smith, 1678).

- *The Loyal Baptist or An Apology for Baptized Believers. In Two Sermons* (London: T. Grantham, 1684).

Hall, Robert, *On Terms of Communion*, in Olinthus Gregory (ed.), *The Entire Works of the Rev. Robert Hall*, (6 volumes; London: Holdsworth and Ball, 1831), II, pp. 9-174.

- A *Reply to the Rev. Joseph Kinghorn, Being a Further Vindication of the Practice of Free Communion*, in Olinthus Gregory (ed.), *Entire Works of Robert Hall*, II, pp. 233-495.

- *An Appeal to the Public on the Subject of the Frame-Work Knitters Fund* (1819), in Olinthus Gregory (ed.), *Entire Works of Robert Hall*, III, pp. 230-97.

- *An Address on the State of Slavery in the West India Islands* (1824), in Olinthus Gregory (ed.), *Entire Works of Robert Hall*, III, pp. 298-326.

Helwys, Thomas, *A short and plaine proofe by the word, and workes off God, that Gods decree is not the cause off anye mans sinne or condemnation. And that all men are redeamed by Christ. As also, that no infants are condemned* (Amsterdam?: 1611).

- A *Short Declaration of the Mistery of Iniquity* (Amsterdam, 1612). Facsimile edition published for the Baptist Historical Society (London: Kingsgate Press, 1935).

Hinton, James, *The Mystery of Pain. A Book for the Sorrowful* (London: H.R. Allenson, 1866).

Hinton, John Howard, *Memoir of William Knibb. Missionary in Jamaica* (London: Houlston and Stoneman, 1849).

- 'What is Anglican Ritualism?'; 'Anglican Ritualism II. The Real Presence'; Anglican Ritualism III. The Miracle of the Altar'; *General Baptist Magazine* 59 (1867), pp. 85-9, 153-4, 215-17.

Ivimey, Joseph, *A History of the English Baptists* (4 volumes; London: Author/ Holdsworth and Ball, 1811-30).

Jessey, Henry, Sermon on Rom. 14.1, 'Such as are weak in the Faith, receive you', printed as an appendix to Bunyan's *Differences in Judgment* (1673).

Keach, Benjamin, *Tropologia. A Key to Open Scripture-Metaphors* (London: Enoch Prosser, 1683).

- *The Glory of a True Church, and Its Discipline Display'd* (London, 1697).

- *The Display of Glorious Grace. Or, The Covenant of Peace Opened. In Fourteen Sermons* (London, 1698).
- *The Child's Delight: Or Instructions for Children and Youth* (London: William and Joseph Marshall, 1702).
Kiffin, William, *A sober discourse of right to church-communion wherein is proved ... that no unbaptized person may be regularly admitted to the Lords Supper* (London: Enoch Prosser, 1681).
Kinghorn, Joseph, *Baptism, a Term of Communion at the Lord's Supper* (Norwich: Bacon, Kinnebrook, 1816).
Knollys, Hanserd, *A Moderate Answer unto Dr. Bastwick's Book; Called, Independency not Gods Ordinance* (London, 1645).
Lumpkin, William L., *Baptist Confessions of Faith* (Chicago: Judson Press, 1959).
Murton, John, *An Humble Supplication to the King's Majesty* (1620), repr. in *Tracts on Liberty of Conscience and Persecution.* Ed. by E.B. Underhill for the Hanserd Knollys Society (London: J. Haddon, 1846), pp. 181-213.
An Orthodox Creed, Or A Protestant Confession of Faith, Being an Essay to Unite and Confirm all True Protestants in the Fundamental Articles of the Christian Religion, Against the Errors and Heresies of Rome (London: 1679), in W.L. Lumpkin, *Baptist Confessions of Faith*, pp. 297-334.
Propositions and Conclusions concerning True Christian Religion, containing a Confession of Faith of certain English people, living at Amsterdam (1612), by John Smyth and others, in W.L. Lumpkin, *Baptist Confessions of Faith*, pp. 124-42.
Robinson, Robert, *The General Doctrine of Toleration Applied to the Particular Case of Free Communion* (Cambridge: Francis Hodson, 1781).
A Short Confession of Faith (Amsterdam, 1610), in W.L. Lumpkin, *Baptist Confessions of Faith*, pp. 102-113.
Sixteen Articles of Faith and Order Unanimously Assented to by the Messengers Met at Warwick, the 3rd Day of the 3rd Month, 1655 (The 'Midland Association Confession'), in W.L. Lumpkin, *Baptist Confessions of Faith*, pp. 198-200.
Smyth, John, *Principles and Inferences Concerning the Visible Church* (1607), in W.T. Whitley (ed.), *The Works of John Smyth* (2 volumes; Cambridge: Cambridge University Press, 1915), I, pp. 249-68.
- *Paralleles, Censures, Observations* (1609), in Whitley (ed.), *Works*, II, pp. 327-46.
- *The Character of the Beast or the False Constitution of the Church* (1609), in Whitley (ed.), *Works*, II, pp. 653-680.
- *Short Confession of Faith in XX Articles* (1609), in W.L. Lumpkin, *Baptist Confessions of Faith*, pp. 100-101.

Spurgeon, Charles Haddon, 'Heavenly Worship', *New Park Street Pulpit*, III (London: Passmore and Alabaster, 1858), no. 110 (28 December 1856), pp. 25-32.
- 'Human Inability', *New Park Street Pulpit*, IV (1879), no. 182 (7 March 1858), pp. 137-44.
- 'The Double Forget-Me-Not', *Metropolitan Tabernacle Pulpit*, LIV (London: Passmore and Alabaster, 1908), no. 3,099 (5 July 1874) pp. 313-24.
- 'The Last Message for the year', *Metropolitan Tabernacle Pulpit*, LVI (1910), no. 3,230 (28 December 1873), pp. 625-633.
- *Till He Come. Communion Meditations and Addresses* (1894; repr. Pasadena: Pilgrim Publications, 1971).
Stennett, Joseph, *Hymns in Commemoration of the Sufferings of our Blessed Saviour Jesus Christ, Compos'd for the Celebration of His Holy Supper* (London: 1713).
Taylor, Dan, *Candidus Examined with Candor. Or, a Modest Inquiry into the Propriety and Force of what is contained in a late Pamphlet; intitled, A Modest Plea for Free Communion at the Lord's Table* (London: G. Keith, 1772).
Tombes, John, *Examen of the Sermon of Mr Stephen Marshall about Infant Baptism* (London: 1645).
Turner, Daniel, *A Modest Plea for Free Communion at the Lord's Table; Particularly between the Baptists and Poedobaptists* (London: J. Johnson, 1772).
- *A Compendium of Social Religion*, Second edition (London: John Ward, 1778).
- *Charity the Bond of Perfection. A Sermon, The Substance of which was Preached at Oxford, November 16, 1780, On Occasion of the Re-establishment of a Christian Church of Protestant Dissenters in that City* (Oxford: 1780).
Whitley, W.T. (ed.), *Minutes of the General Assembly of the General Baptist Churches in England.* Baptist Historical Society (2 volumes; London; Kingsgate Press, 1909).
Williams, Charles, *The Principles and Practices of the Baptists* (London: Baptist Tract Society, 1879).
Williams, Roger, *The Bloudy Tenent of Persecution for Cause of Conscience* (1644) and *Mr. Cotton's Letter Examined and Answered*, ed. for the Hanserd Knollys Society by Edward B. Underhill (London: J. Haddon, 1848).

2. Other Writings 1500-1900

Bradford, William, *History of Plymouth Plantation, 1620-1647*, ed. W.C. Ford (2 volumes; Boston: Massachusetts Historical Society, 1912).

Browne, Robert, *A Booke which sheweth the life and manners of all true Christians* (Middelburgh: 1582), in A. Peel and L. Carlson (eds.), *The Writings of Robert Harrison and Robert Browne* (London: Allen and Unwin, 1953), pp. 221-395.

- *A True and Short Declaration* (1584), in Peel and Carson (eds.), *Writings*, pp. 396-429.

- *An Answere to Master Cartwright His Letter* (London, n.d., ?1585), in Peel and Carson (eds.), *Writings*, pp. 430-506.

Calvin, John, *Institutes of the Christian Religion*, trans. H. Beveridge (2 volumes; London: James Clarke, 1949).

- *The Epistles of Paul the Apostle to the Romans and to the Thessalonians*, trans. R. Mackenzie (Edinburgh: Oliver and Boyd, 1961).

Coccejus, John, *Summa doctrinae de foedere et testamento Dei* (Leiden, 1648).

Edwards, Jonathan, *Inquiry into the Modern Prevailing Notions Respecting that Freedom of the Will which is Supposed to be Essential to Moral Agency* (Boston, 1754).

Fenner, Dudley, *A briefe treatise upon the first table of the lawe* (Middelburg, 1587).

Johnson, Francis, *An inquirie and answer of Thomas White his discoverie of Brownisme* (Amsterdam, 1606).

- *A brief treatise against two errours of the Anabaptists* (Amsterdam, 1609).

Locke, John, *A Letter Concerning Toleration* (London, 1689).

Luther, Martin, *Lectures on Romans*, trans. and ed. W. Pauck (Library of Christian Classics 15; London: SCM Press, 1961).

A True Confession of the Faith, and Humble Acknowledgement of the Alegeance, which we hir Maiesties Subjects, falsely called Brownists, doo hould towards God, and yeild to hir Majestie and all other that are over us in the Lord (1596), in W.L. Lumpkin, *Baptist Confessions of Faith*, pp. 82-97.

Zwingli: *Huldrych Zwingli. Writings*, trans. and ed. H. Wayne Pipkin (2 volumes; Allison Park: Pickwick, 1984).

- *Zwingli and Bullinger*, trans. and ed. G.W. Bromiley (Library of Christian Classics 24; London: SCM Press, 1953).

3. Baptist Writings from 1900

'American Baptists, A Unifying Vision', a resource document for the Commission on Denominational Identity of American Baptists, *American Baptist Quarterly*, 6/2 (1987), pp. 65-113.

Angelov, Theo, 'Human Rights: Religious Freedom and Tolerance in Bulgaria', in L. A. Cupit (ed.), *Baptist Faith and Witness*, 2, pp. 225-9.

Anon., 'Church Covenants', *BQ* 7/5 (1935), pp. 227-34.

Ballard, Paul, 'Baptists and Covenanting', *BQ* 24/8 (1972), pp. 372-84.

The Baptist Doctrine of the Church (1948), reprinted in Hayden (ed.), *Baptist Union Documents 1948-1977*, pp. 4-11.

Baptists and Lutherans in Conversation. A Message to our Churches. Report of the Joint Commission of the Baptist World Alliance and the Lutheran World Federation (Geneva, 1990).

Beasley-Murray, George R., *Baptism in the New Testament* (London: Macmillan, 1963).

- 'Confessing Baptist Identity', in David Slater (ed.), *A Perspective on Baptist Identity* (Kingsbridge: Mainstream, 1987), pp. 75-86.

- 'The Problem of Infant Baptism: An Exercise in Possibilities', in *Festchrift Günter Wagner*, ed. Faculty of Baptist Theological Seminary, Rüschlikon (Bern: Peter Lang, 1994), pp. 1-14.

Beasley-Murray, Paul, 'The Ministry of All and the Leadership of Some: a Baptist Perspective', in P. Beasley-Murray (ed.), *Anyone for Ordination?* (Tunbridge Wells: Marc, 1993), pp. 157-74.

Bebbington, David W. (ed.), *The Gospel in the World. International Baptist Studies* (Studies in Baptist History and Thought 1; Carlisle: Paternoster Press, 2002).

Believing and Being Baptized. Baptism, so-called re-baptism, and children in the church. A discussion document by the Doctrine and Worship Committee of the Baptist Union of Great Britain (London: Baptist Union, 1996).

Birch Hoyle, R., 'Emil Brunner Vindicates the Baptist Position', *Baptist Times*, 30 June 1938.

Bowers, Faith, *Who's This Sitting in My Pew? Mentally handicapped people in the Church* (London: SPCK, 1988).

Brachlow, Stephen, *The Communion of Saints. Radical Puritan and Separatist Ecclesiology 1570-1625* (Oxford: Oxford University Press, 1988).

Brackney, William H., *Voluntarism. The Dynamic Principle of the Free Church* (Wolfville: Acadia University, 1992).

- *Christian Voluntarism in Britain and North America: a Bibliography and Critical Assessment* (Westport: Greenwoods Press, 1995).

- *Christian Voluntarism. Theology and Praxis* (Grand Rapids: Eerdmans, 1997).

Briggs, John H.Y., *The English Baptists of the Nineteenth Century* (London: Baptist Historical Society, 1994).

Bull, Marcus, 'Divine Complexity and Human Community', in Anthony Clarke (ed.), *Bound for Glory?*, pp. 45-58.

Carey, S. Pearce, *William Carey* (London: Carey Press, 8th edn, 1934).

Champion, L.G., 'Evangelical Calvinism and the Structures of Baptist Church Life', *BQ* 28/5 (1980), pp. 196-208.

Child, R.L., *The Blessing of Infants and the Dedication of Parents* (London: Carey Kingsgate, 1946).

The Child and the Church. A Baptist Discussion (London; Carey Kingsgate Press, 1966).

Clark, Neville, *An Approach to the Theology of the Sacraments* (Studies in Biblical Theology 17; London: SCM Press, 1956).

- 'The Theology of Baptism', in Gilmore (ed.), *Christian Baptism*, pp. 306-26.

Clarke, Anthony (ed.), *Bound for Glory? God, Church and World in Covenant* (Oxford: Whitley Publications, 2002).

- 'The Covenantal Basis of God's Trinitarian Life', in Anthony Clarke (ed.), *Bound for Glory?*, pp. 9-19.

Clements, Ronald E., *Abraham and David* (London: SCM Press, 1967).

Clipsham, Ernest F., 'Andrew Fuller and Fullerism (1)', *BQ* 20/3 (1963), pp. 99-114; Andrew Fuller and Fullerism (3), *BQ* 20/5 (1964), pp. 214-25.

Colwell, John, 'The Sacramental Nature of Ordination. An Attempt to Re-engage a Catholic Understanding and Practice', in Cross and Thompson (eds.), *Baptist Sacramentalism*, pp. 228-246.

Covenant 21. Covenant for a Gospel People (London: Baptist Union, 2000).

Cox, Harvey, *The Secular City. Secularization and Urbanization in Theological Perspective* (London: SCM Press, 1966).

Cross, Anthony R., *Baptism and the Baptists. Theology and Practice in Twentieth-Century Britain* (Studies in Baptist History and Thought 3; Carlisle: Paternoster Press, 2000).

- 'Dispelling the Myth of English Baptist Baptismal Sacramentalism', *BQ* 38/8 (2000), pp. 367-91.

Cross, Anthony R. and Thompson, Philip E. (eds.), *Baptist Sacramentalism* (Studies in Baptist History and Thought 5; Carlisle: Paternoster, 2003).

Cupit, L.A. (ed.), *Baptist Faith and Witness*. Book 2. The Papers of the Study and Research Division of the Baptist World Alliance, 1995-2000 (McLean: Baptist World Alliance, 1999).

- *Baptist World Alliance Covenants and Declarations 1990-2000* (McLean: Baptist World Alliance, 2000).

Dunkley, Anne, *Seen and Heard. Reflections on Children and Baptist Tradition* (The Whitley Lecture 1999-2000; Oxford: Whitley Publications, 1999).

Dunn, James M., 'Yes, I am a Baptist' in Staton (ed.), *Why I am a Baptist*, pp. 43-48.

Eidberg, Peder A., 'Baptist Developments in the Nordic Countries During the Twentieth Century', in *Global Baptist History. Baptist History and Heritage* 36/1&2 (2001), pp. 136-52.

Ellis, Christopher J., *Baptist Worship Today. A report of two worship surveys undertaken by the Doctrine and Worship Committee of the Baptist Union of Great Britain* (London: Baptist Union, 1999).

Ellis, Robert, 'Covenant and Creation', in Anthony Clarke (ed.), *Bound for Glory?*, pp. 20-33.

Fiddes, Paul S., *A Leading Question: The Structure and Authority of Leadership in the Local Church* (London: Baptist Union Publications, 1983).

- '"Woman's Head is Man"; A Doctrinal Reflection upon a Pauline Theme', *BQ* 31/8 (1986), pp. 370-383.

- *The Creative Suffering of God* (Oxford: Clarendon Press, 1988).

- *Past Event and Present Salvation. The Christian Idea of Atonement* (London: Darton, Longman and Todd, 1989).

- (ed.) *Reflections on the Water. Understanding God and the World through the Baptism of Believers* (Regent's Study Guides 4; Oxford: Regent's Park College/ Macon: Smyth & Helwys, 1996).

- *The Promised End. Eschatology in Theology and Literature* (Challenges in Contemporary Theology; Oxford: Blackwell, 2000).

- *Participating in God. A Pastoral Doctrine of the Trinity* (London: Darton, Longman and Todd, 2000).

- 'Baptism and the Process of Christian Initiation' in Stanley E. Porter and Anthony R. Cross (eds.), *Dimensions of Baptism. Biblical and Theological Studies* (JSNT Supplement Series 234; Sheffield: Sheffield Academic Press, 2002), pp. 280-303.

- 'Church and Salvation: A Comparison of Baptist and Orthodox Thinking', in Anthony R. Cross (ed.), *Ecumenism and History. Studies in Honour of John H.Y. Briggs* (Carlisle, Paternoster Press, 2002), pp. 120-48.

Paul S. Fiddes, Roger Hayden, Richard L. Kidd, Keith W. Clements and Brian Haymes, *Bound to Love. The Covenant Basis of Baptist Life and Mission* (London: Baptist Union, 1985).

Forms of Ministry among Baptists. Towards an Understanding of Spiritual Leadership. A discussion document by the Doctrine and Worship Committee of the Baptist Union of Great Britain (London: Baptist Union, 1994).

Fowler, Stanley K., *More than a Symbol: The British Baptist Recovery of Baptist Sacramentalism* (Studies in Baptist History and Thought 2; Carlisle: Paternoster, 2002).

Geldbach, Eric, 'Religious Liberty, Proselytism, Evangelism – Some Baptist Considerations', in L.A. Cupit, *Baptist Faith and Witness*, 2, pp. 23-8.

George, Timothy, 'Controversy and Commmunion: the Limits of Baptist Fellowship from Bunyan to Spurgeon' in Bebbington (ed.), *The Gospel in the World*, pp. 38-58.

Gilmore, Alec (ed.), *Christian Baptism. A Fresh Attempt to Understand the Rite in terms of Scripture, History and Theology* (London: Lutterworth Press, 1959).

- 'Baptist Churches Today and Tomorrow', in Gilmore (ed.), *The Pattern of the Church. A Baptist View* (London: Lutterworth, 1963), pp. 114-56.

- *Baptism and Christian Unity* (London: Lutterworth, 1966).

Gouldbourne, Ruth M.B., *Reinventing the Wheel. Women and Ministry in English Baptist Life* (The Whitley Lecture 1997-1998; Oxford: Whitley Publications, 1997).

Green, Bernard, *Crossing the Boundaries. A History of the European Baptist Federation* (Didcot: the Baptist Historical Society, 1999).

Grenz, Stanley L., *Theology for the Community of God* (Nashville: Broadman and Holman, 1994).

- *The Social God and the Relational Self. A Trinitarian Theology of the Imago Dei* (Louisville: Westminster, John Knox, 2001).

Harvey, Barry, 'Re-Membering the Body. Baptism, Eucharist and the Politics of Disestablishment', in Cross and Thompson (eds.), *Baptist Sacramentalism*, pp. 96-116.

Hayden, Roger, *Baptist Union Documents 1948-1977* (London: Baptist Historical Society, 1980).

- 'Baptists, Covenants and Confessions' in Fiddes, Hayden, Kidd, Clements and Haymes, *Bound to Love*, pp. 24-36.

- 'The Particular Baptist Confession 1689 and Baptists Today', *BQ* 32/8 (1988), pp. 403-17.

Haykin, Michael A.G., 'Particular Redemption in the Writings of Andrew Fuller (1754-1815)', in Bebbington (ed.), *The Gospel in the World*, pp. 120-8.

Haymes, Brian, 'Baptism as a Political Act', in Fiddes (ed.), *Reflections on the Water*, pp. 69-84.

- 'Theology and Baptist Identity' in Paul S. Fiddes (ed.), *Doing Theology in a Baptist Way* (Oxford: Whitley Publications, 2000), pp. 1-5.

Heim, S. Mark, 'Baptismal Recognition and the Baptist Churches', in Root and Saarinen (eds.), *Baptism and the Unity of the Church*, pp. 150-63.

Holmes, Stephen R., 'Towards a Baptist Theology of Ordained Ministry', in Cross and Thompson (eds.), *Baptist Sacramentalism*, pp. 247-62.

Johnson, Aubrey R., *Sacral Kingship in Ancient Israel*, Second Edition (Cardiff: University of Wales Press, Cardiff, 1967).

Kendall, R.T., *Calvin and English Calvinism to 1649* (Oxford: Oxford University Press, 1979).

Kidd, Richard, 'Baptism and the Identity of Christian Communities' in Fiddes (ed.), *Reflections on the Water*, pp. 85-99.

- (ed.) *Something to Declare. A study of the Declaration of Principle jointly written by the Principals of the four English Colleges in membership with the Baptist Union of Great Britain*. By Paul Fiddes, Brian Haymes, Richard Kidd and Michael Quicke (Oxford: Whitley Publications, 1996).

- (ed.) *On the Way of Trust. Jointly written by the Principals of the four English Colleges in membership with the Baptist Union of Great Britain*. By Paul Fiddes, Brian Haymes, Richard Kidd and Michael Quicke (Oxford: Whitley Publications, 1997).

Kirby, Arthur H., 'Andrew Fuller – Evangelical Calvinist', *BQ* 15/5 (1954), pp. 195-202.

Laws, Gilbert, 'Vital Forces of the Baptist Movement', in J.H. Rushbrooke (ed.), *The Faith of the Baptists* (London: Kingsgate Press, 1926).

Leonard, Bill, 'Being Baptist. Hospitable Traditionalism', in Staton (ed.), *Why I am a Baptist*, pp. 77-88.

Lorenzen, Thorwald, *The Rights of the Child* (Baptists and Human Rights 2; McLean: Baptist World Alliance, 1978).

- 'Mission and Discipleship', in L.A. Cupit (ed.), *Baptist Faith and Witness*, 2, pp. 41-52.

Martin, Paul W., 'Towards a Baptist Ecclesiology Inclusive of Children', *Theology in Context* 1 (2000), p. 47-59.

McClendon, James Wm. Jr., *Systematic Theology*, Vol. 1, *Ethics* (Nashville: Abingdon Press, 1986).

McWilliams, Warren, *The Passion of God. Divine Suffering in Contemporary Protestant Theology* (Macon: Mercer University Press, 1985).

The Meaning and Practice of Ordination among Baptists. A Report submitted to the Council of the Baptist Union of Great Britain and Ireland (London: Carey Kingsgate Press, 1957).

The Nature of the Assembly and the Council of the Baptist Union of Great Britain. Doctrine and Worship Committee (London: Baptist Union, 1994).

Parker, G. Keith, *Baptists in Europe. History and Confessions of Faith* (Nashville: Broadman Press, 1982).

Patterns and Prayers for Christian Worship. A Guidebook for Worship Leaders. Baptist Union of Great Britain (Oxford: Oxford University Press).

Payne, Ernest A., *The Fellowship of Believers. Baptist Thought and Practice Yesterday and Today*. Enlarged Edition (London: Carey Kingsgate Press, 1952).

- 'The Ministry in Historical Perspective', *BQ* 17/6 (1958), pp. 256-66.

- *The Baptist Union. A Short History* (London: Carey Kingsgate Press, 1959).

- *The Struggle for Human Rights* (London: The Baptist Union of Great Britain and Ireland, 1974).

The People Called American Baptists: A Confessional Statement, printed in *American Baptist Quarterly* 6/2 (1987), pp. 62-64.

Pixley, Jorge and Boff, Clodovis, *The Bible, the Church and the Poor. Biblical, Theological and Pastoral Aspects of the Option for the Poor*, trans. P. Burns (London: Burns and Oates, 1989).

Popkes, Wiard, *Gemeinde: Raum des Vertrauens. Neutestamentliche Beobachtungen und Freikirchliche Perspectiven* (Wuppertal: Oncken Verlag, 1984).

Relating and Resourcing. The Report of the Task Group on Associating, issued January 1998, approved at the Council of the Baptist Union of Great Britain, March 1998.

Robinson, H. Wheeler, *The Christian Experience of the Holy Spirit* (Library of Constructive Theology; London: Nisbet & Co., 1928).

- *Suffering Human and Divine* (London: SCM Press, 1940).

- *Redemption and Revelation* (Library of Constructive Theology; London: Nisbet & Co., 1942).

- *Baptist Principles* (London: Kingsgate Press, 4th edn, 1945).

- *The Life and Faith of the Baptists* (London: Kingsgate Press, 2nd edn, 1946).

- *The Cross of Jeremiah* (1925), repr. in *The Cross in the Old Testament* (London: SCM Press, 1955), p. 184.

Rowley, H.H., *The Missionary Message of the Old Testament* (London: Carey Press, 1944).

Shakespeare, J.H., *The Churches at the Cross-Roads. A Study in Church Unity* (London: Williams and Norgate, 1918).

Shepherd, Peter, *The Making of a Modern Denomination. John Howard Shakespeare and the English Baptists, 1898-1924* (Studies in Baptist History and Thought 4; Carlisle: Paternoster Press, 2001).

Sherman, Hazel, 'Baptized in the Name of the Father, the Son and the Holy Spirit', in Fiddes (ed.) *Reflections on the Water*, pp. 101-116.

Stanley, Brian, *The History of the Baptist Missionary Society* 1792-1992 (Edinburgh: T. & T. Clark, 1992).

Staton, Cecil P., Jr., (ed.), *Why I am a Baptist. Reflections on Being Baptist in the 21st Century* (Macon: Smyth and Helwys Publishing, 1999).

Stevens, W. and Bottoms, W.W., *The Baptists of New Road, Oxford* (Oxford: Alden Press, 1948).

Strong, Augustus Hopkins, *Systematic Theology* (Philadelphia: Griffith & Rowland, 1909).

Summons to Witness to Christ in Today's World. A Report on the Baptist-Roman Catholic International Conversations, 1984-1988. Sponsored by the Vatican Secretariat for Promoting Christian Unity and the Baptist World Alliance (McLean: Baptist World Alliance, 1988).

Taylor, Michael, 'Include Them Out?' in Faith Bowers (ed.), *Let Love Be Genuine. Mental Handicap and the Church* (London: Baptist Union, 1985), pp. 46-50.

Thompson, Philip E., 'A New Question in Baptist History: Seeking a Catholic Spirit Among Early Baptists', *Pro Ecclesia* 8/1 (1999), pp. 51-72.

- 'Sacraments and Religious Liberty: From Critical Practice to Rejected Infringement', in Cross and Thompson (eds.), *Baptist Sacramentalism*, pp. 36-54.

Transforming Superintendency. The Report of the General Superintendency Review Group presented to the Baptist Union of Great Britain Council (London: Baptist Union, 1996).

Tymms, T. Vincent, *The Christian Idea of Atonement* (Angus Lectures 1903; London: Macmillan, 1904).

Walker, Michael, 'The Relation of Infants to Church, Baptism and Gospel in Seventeenth Century Baptist Theology', *BQ* 21/6 (1966), pp. 242-62.

- *Baptists at the Table. The Theology of the Lord's Supper among Engish Baptists in the Nineteenth Century* (London: Baptist Historical Society, 1992).

Ward, W.R., 'The Baptists and the Transformation of the Church , 1780-1830', *BQ* 25/4 (1973).

Washington, James Melvin, *Frustrated Fellowship. The Black Baptist Quest for Social Power* (Macon: Mercer University Press, 1986).

Watts, Graham, 'The Spirit and Community. Trinitarian Pneumatology and the Church', *Theology in Context* 1 (2000), pp. 60-72.

The Way Ahead. A Report on Baptist Life and Work by the Moderator's Commission of the Northern Baptist Association (Darlington: 1960).

We Baptists, Study and Research Division, Baptist World Alliance (Franklin, Providence House, 1999).

West, W.M.S., 'The Child and the Church: A Baptist Perspective' in William H. Brackney, Paul S. Fiddes and John H.Y. Briggs (eds.), *Pilgrim Pathways. Essays in Baptist History in Honour of B.R. White* (Macon: Mercer University Press, 1999), pp. 75-110.

White, B. R., *The English Separatist Tradition. From the Marian Martyrs to the Pilgrim Fathers* (Oxford: Oxford University Press, 1971).

- 'Open and Closed Membership among English and Welsh Baptists', *BQ* 24/7 (1972), pp. 330-34.

- *Authority. A Baptist View* (London: Baptist Publications, 1976).

- *The English Baptists of the Seventeenth Century* (London: Baptist Historical Society, 2nd edn, 1996).

White, R.E.O., *The Biblical Doctrine of Initiation* (London: Hodder and Stoughton, 1960).

Winter, E.P., 'Who May Administer the Lord's Supper?', *BQ* 16/3 (1955), pp. 129-33.

Wood, James E., Jnr., *Baptists and Human Rights*. A Publication of the BWA's Human Rights Commission (McLean, VA: Baptist World Alliance, 1977).

Wright, Nigel G., *Challenge to Change. A Radical Agenda for Baptists* (Eastbourne: Kingsway Publications, 1991).

- *Power and Discipleship. Towards a Baptist Theology of the State* (The Whitley Lecture 1996-1997; Oxford: Whitley Publications, 1996).

- 'Inclusive Representation: Towards a Doctrine of Christian Ministry', *BQ*, 39/4 (2001), pp. 159-74.

4. Other Modern Writings

Agreed Statement on the Eucharist (Windsor 1971), Anglican-Roman Catholic International Commission (London: SPCK/Catholic Truth Society, 1972).

An Anglican-Methodist Covenant. Common Statement of the Formal Conversations between the Methodist Church of Great Britain and the Church of England (London: Methodist Publishing House and Church House Publishing, 2001).

Arendt, Hannah, *The Human Condition. A Study of the Central Conditions Facing Modern Man* (New York: Doubleday Anchor Books, 1959).

Bakhtin, Mikhail, *Rabelais and His World*, trans. Helene Iswolsky (Bloomington: Indiana University Press, 2nd edn, 1984), pp. 19, 26-7.

Balthasar, Hans Urs von, *Theo-logic. Theological Logical Theory. Vol. I. Truth of the World*, transl. A.J. Walker (San Francisco: Ignatius Press, 2000).

Baptism, Eucharist and Ministry (Faith and Order Paper 111; Geneva: World Council of Churches, 1982).

Baptism , Eucharist and Ministry 1982-1990. Report on the Process and Responses (Faith and Order Paper 149; Geneva: WCC Publications, 1990).

Baptism and Church Membership: with Particular Reference to Local Ecumenical Partnerships. A Report of a Working Party to Churches Together in England (London: CTE, 1997).

Baptism and Confirmation. A report submitted by the Church of England Liturgical Commission to the Archbishops of Canterbury and York in November 1958 (London: SPCK, 1959).

Barth, Karl, *Church Dogmatics*, trans. and ed. G.W. Bromiley and T.F. Torrance (14 volumes; Edinburgh: T. & T. Clark, 1936-77).

Berger, Peter, *The Sacred Canopy: Elements of a Sociological Theory of Religion* (New York: Doubleday, 1967).

Best, Ernest, *One Body in Christ. A Study in the Relationship of the Church to Christ in the Epistles of the Apostle Paul* (London: SPCK, 1955).

Best, Thomas F. and Gassmann, Günther (eds.), *On the Way to Fuller Koinonia. Official Report of the Fifth World Conference on Faith and Order* (Faith and Order Paper 166; Geneva: WCC Publications, 1994).

Best, Thomas F., and Heller, Dagmar, (eds.) *Becoming a Christian. The Ecumenical Implications of our Common Baptism* (Faith and Order Paper 184; Geneva: WCC Publications, 1999).

Boff, Leonardo, *The Trinity and Society* (London: Burns and Oates, 1988).

Bonhoeffer, Dietrich, *Sanctorum Communio. A Dogmatic Enquiry into the Sociology of the Church* (London: Collins, 1963).

- *Christology*, trans. J. Bowden (London: Fontana, 1971).

- *Ethics*. Edited by Eberhard Bethge, trans. N. Horton Smith (London: SCM Press, 2nd edn, 1971).

- *Letters and Papers from Prison. The Enlarged Edition.* Edited by Eberhard Bethge, trans. R. Fuller, F. Clarke and J. Bowden (London: SCM Press, 3rd edn, 1971).

Bonino, J. Miguez, *Towards a Christian Political Ethics* (SCM, London, 1983).

Bowie, Fiona, *The Anthropology of Religion* (Oxford: Blackwell, 2000), pp. 55-61, 71-2.

Brand, Eugene L., 'Rites of Initiation as Signs of Unity' in Root and Saarinen (eds.), *Baptism and the Unity of the Church*, pp. 130-37.

Brown, Raymond E., *The Gospel According to John* I-XII (The Anchor Bible; London: Chapman, 1966).

Brunner, Emil, *The Divine-Human Encounter*, trans. A. Loos (London: SCM Press, 1944).

Called to be One. Section IV, Lambeth Conference 1998 (London: Morehouse Publishing).

Christian Initiation and Church Membership. Report of the British Council of Churches Working Party on the theology and practice of Chriostian initiation and church membership (London: BCC, 1988).

Christian Initiation. Birth and Growth in the Christian Society (General Synod 30; Westminster: Church of England Board of Education, 1971).

The Church, Local and Universal. A Study Commissioned and Received by the Joint Working Group between the Roman Catholic Church and the World Council of Churches (Faith and Order Paper 150; Geneva: WCC Publications, 1990).

Cobb, J.B. and Griffin, D.R., *Process Theology: an Introductory Exposition* (Belfast: Christian Journals, 1977).

Cochrane, Arthur C., *The Church's Confession under Hitler* (Pittsburgh: Pickwick Press, 1976).

Coggins, James R., 'The Theological Positions of John Smyth', *BQ* 30/6 (1984), pp. 247-59.

Confessing the One Faith. An Ecumenical Exposition of the Apostolic Faith as it is Confessed in the Nicene-Constantinopolitan Creed (Faith and Order Paper 153; Geneva: WCC Publications, 1991).

Congregation for the Doctrine of the Faith, *Dominus Jesus, Declaration on the Unicity and Salvific Universality of Jesus Christ and the Church*, August 6, 2000: text available at www.vatican.va/roman_curia/congregations.

Cunningham, David, *These Three are One. The Practice of Trinitarian Theology* (Oxford: Blackwell, 1998).

Davies, Oliver, *A Theology of Compassion. Metaphysics of Difference and the Renewal of Tradition* (London: SCM Press, 2001).

Dawson, Andrew, 'The Origins and Character of the Base Ecclesial Community: a Brazilian Perspective', in Christopher Rowland (ed.), *The Cambridge Companion to Liberation Theology* (Cambridge: Cambridge University Press, 1999), pp. 109-28.

Derrida, Jacques, *Speech and Phenomena, and Other Essays on Husserl's Theory of Signs*, trans. D.B. Allison (Evanston: North Western University Press, 1973).

- *Writing and Difference*, trans. A. Bass (London: Routledge, 1993).

Dillistone, F.W., *Christianity and Symbolism* (London: Collins, 1955).

Dix, Dom Gregory, *The Shape of the Liturgy* (London: Dacre Press/ A. & C. Black, 2nd edn, 1964).

Dostoyevsky, F., *The Brothers Karamazov*, transl. D. Magarshack (Harmondsworth: Penguin, 1962).

Douglas, Mary, *Purity and Danger: An Analysis of Concepts of Pollution and Taboo* (London: Routledge & Kegan Paul).

Dunn, James D.G., *Baptism in the Holy Spirit. A Re-examination of the New Testament Teaching on the Gift of the Spirit in relation to Pentecostalism today* (London: SCM Press, 1970).
- *Jesus and the Spirit. A Study of the Religious and Charismatic Experience of Jesus and the First Christians as Reflected in the New Testament* (London: SCM Press, 1975).
- *Unity and Diversity in the New Testament. An Enquiry into the Character of Earliest Christianity* (London; SCM Press, 1977).
- 'Baptism and the Unity of the Church in the New Testament', in Root and Saarinen (eds.), *Baptism and the Unity of the Church*, pp. 78-103.
Dupont-Sommer, A., *The Essene Writings from Qumran*, trans. G. Vermes (Oxford: Blackwell, 1961).
Elliot, John H., *The Elect and the Holy. An Exegetical Examination of 1 Peter 2:4-10* (Leiden: Brill, 1966).
Farley, Edward, *Ecclesial Man. A Social Phenomenology of Faith and Reality* (Philadelphia: Fortress Press, 1975).
Flannery, Austin (ed.), *Vatican Council II. The Conciliar and Post Conciliar Documents* (Dublin: Dominican Publications, 1975).
Forsyth, P.T., *The Church and the Sacraments* (London: Independent Press, 2nd edn, 1947).
Fowler, James, *Stages of Faith. The Psychology of Human Development and the Quest for Meaning* (Harper and Row, San Francisco, 1981).
Gadamer, Hans-Georg, *Truth and Method*, trans. G. Barden and J. Cumming (London: Sheed and Ward, 1975).
Gassmann, Günther, 'The Church as Sacrament, Sign and Instrument' in Gennadias Limouris, *Church, Kingdom, World: The Church as Mystery and Prophetic Sign* (Faith and Order Paper 130; Geneva: WCC, 1986), pp. 1-17.
Habgood, John, *Church and Nation in a Secular Age* (London: Darton, Longman and Todd, London, 1983).
Hartshorne, Charles, *Man's Vision of God: and the Logic of Theism* (Hamden: Archon Books, 2nd edn, 1964).
Holeton, David R. (ed.), *Christian Initiation in the Anglican Communion. The Toronto Statement 'Walk in Newness of Life'*. The Findings of the Fourth International Anglican Liturgical Consultation, Toronto 1991 (Grove Worship Series 118; Bramcote: Grove Books, 1991).
Jung, Carl G., *Symbols of Transformation*. Collected Works of C.G. Jung, transl. R.F. C. Hull, Volume 5 (London: Routledge and Kegan Paul, 1956).
Jüngel, Eberhard, 'The World as Possibility and Actuality. The Ontology of the Doctrine of Justification', in John Webster (trans. and ed.), *Eberhard Jüngel, Theological Essays* (Edinburgh: T. & T. Clark, 1989), pp. 95-123.

Käsemann, Ernst, 'Ministry and Community in the New Testament', in Käsemann, *Essays on New Testament Themes*, trans. J. Montague (Studies in Biblical Theology 41; London: SCM Press, 1964), pp. 63-94.

Kavanagh, Aidan, *Confirmation. Origins and Reform* (New York: Pueblo, 1988).

Khomiakov, Alexis, 'The Church is One', in William J. Birkbeck, *Russia and the English Church* (Eastern Churches Association: London, 1895).

Kinnamon, Michael (ed.), *Signs of the Spirit. Official Report. Seventh Assembly of the World Council of Churches*. Canberra, Australia, 7-20 February 1991 (Grand Rapids: Eermans/Geneva: WCC Publications, 1991).

Kiuchi, N. *The Purification Offering in the Priestly Literature. Its Meaning and Function*. (JSOT Supplement Series 56; Sheffield: Sheffield Academic Press, 1987).

Knox, John, *The Church and the Reality of Christ* (London: Collins, 1963).

Kreider, Alan, 'Lessons from Intentional Communities. Mennonite Perspectives' in *Theology Themes*, 4/1 (1995) (Northern Baptist College, Manchester), pp. 18-24.

LaCugna, Catherine M., *God for Us. The Trinity and Christian Life* (San Francisco: Harper, 1991).

Lampe, G.W.H., *The Seal of the Spirit: A Study of the Doctrine of Baptism and Confirmation in the New Testament and the Fathers* (London: Longmans, Green, 1951).

Lash, Scott and Urry, Jim, *Economies of Signs and Space* (London: Sage Publications, 1994).

Lathrop, Gordon, 'The Water that Speaks: the *Ordo* of Baptism and its Ecumenical Implications', in Best, Thomas F. and Heller, Dagmar (eds.), *Becoming a Christian. The Ecumenical Implications of Our Common Baptism* (Faith and Order Paper 184; Geneva: WCC Publications, 1999), pp. 13-29.

Levinas, Emmanuel, 'Meaning and Sense' in A. Peperzak, S. Critchely, R. Bernasconi (eds.), *Emmanuel Levinas. Basic Philosophical Writings* (Bloomington and Indianapolis: Indiana University Press, 1996).

Locher, Gottfried W., *Zwingli's Thought: New Perspectives* (Leiden: Brill, 1981).

Lohfink, Gerhard, *Does God Need the Church? Toward a Theology of the People of God*, trans. L. Maloney (Collegeville: Liturgical Press, 1999).

Lossky, Vladimir, *The Mystical Theology of the Eastern Church* (London: James Clarke, 1957).

Lubac, Henri de, *Corpus Mysticum* (Paris: Aubier, 1948).

Lyotard, Jean François, *The Postmodern Condition. A Report on Knowledge*, trans. G. Bennington (Theory and History of Literature, 10; Manchester: Manchester University Press, 1984).

Mackie, J.L., *The Miracle of Theism* (Oxford: Clarendon Press, 1982), pp. 162-76.

Macquarrie, John, *Principles of Christian Theology*. Revised Edition (London: SCM Press, 1977).

McCormack, Bruce, 'Grace and Being. The role of God's gracious election in Karl Barth's theological ontology' in John Webster (ed.), *The Cambridge Companion to Karl Barth* (Cambridge: Cambridge University Press, 2000), pp. 92-109.

McFadyen, Alistair I., *The Call to Personhood. A Christian Theory of the Individual in Social Relationships* (Cambridge: Cambridge University Press, 1990).

Miller, Perry, *The New England Mind* (New York: Norton Press, 1939).

Mitchell, Adrian, *Poems* (London: Jonathan Cape, 1969).

Moltmann, Jürgen, *The Crucified God. The Cross of Christ as the Foundation and Criticism of Modern Theology*, trans. M. Kohl (London: SCM Press, 1974).

- *The Experiment Hope*, trans. M. Douglas Meeks (London: SCM Press, 1975).

- *The Church in the Power of the Spirit. A Contribution to Messianic Ecclesiology*, trans. M. Kohl (London: SCM Press, 1977).

Moule, C.F.D., *The Origin of Christology* (Cambridge: Cambridge University Press, 1977).

Not Strangers but Pilgrims. The Next Steps for Churches Together in Pilgrimage (London: British Council of Churches and Catholic Truth Society, 1989), pp. 74-6.

Nuttall, Geoffrey F., *Visible Saints. The Congregational Way 1640-1660* (Oxford: Basil Blackwell, 1957).

- 'Northamptonshire and the Modern Question: a Turning-Point in Eighteenth Century Dissent', *Journal of Theological Studies* 16 (1965), pp. 101-23.

On The Way. Towards an Integrated Approach to Christian Initiation (General Synod Misc. 44; London: Church House Publishing, 1995).

Pannenberg, Wolfhart, *Systematic Theology*, trans. G. Bromiley (3 volumes; Grand Rapids: Eerdmans, 1991-98).

- 'Lutherans and Episcopacy', in Colin Podmore (ed.), *Community – Unity – Communion. Essays in Honour of Mary Tanner* (London: Church House Publishing, 1998), pp. 183-88.

Paton, David M. (ed.), *Breaking Barriers. Nairobi 1975*. The Official Report of the Fifth Assembly of the World Council of Churches (London: SPCK/ Grand Rapids: Eerdmans, 1976).

Perry, Michael J., *The Idea of Human Rights. Four Enquiries* (New York: Oxford University Press, 1998).

Pipkin, H. Wayne, *Zwingli: the Positive Religious Values of his Eucharistic Writings* (Leeds: Yorkshire Baptist Association, 1986).

Plantinga, Alvin, *The Nature of Necessity* (New York: Oxford University Press, 1982).

Pritchard, James B., *Ancient Near Eastern Texts Relating to the Old Testament*, Second Edition (New Jersey: Princeton University Press, 1955).

Reeves, Marjorie, 'Literary Women in Eighteenth-Century Nonconformist Circles', in Jane Shaw and Alan Kreider (eds.), *Culture and the Nonconformist Tradition* (Cardiff: University of Wales Press, 1999),

Ricoeur, Paul, *Freedom and Nature. The Voluntary and the Involuntary*, trans. E.V. Kohak (Evanston: Northwestern University Press).

Robinson, John A.T., *The Body. A Study in Pauline Theology* (Studies in Biblical Theology 5; London: SCM, 1952).

Root, Michael and Saarinen, Risto (eds.), *Baptism and the Unity of the Church* (Grand Rapids: Eerdmans Publishing/ Geneva: WCC Publications, 1998).

Schillebeeckx, Edward, *Ministry: A Case for Change*, trans. J. Bowden (London: SCM Press, 1981).

Schleiermacher, Friedrich, *Brief Outline on the Study of Theology*, trans. Terence N. Tice (Richmond: John Knox Press, 1966).

- *The Christian Faith*, trans. H. R. Mackintosh and J.S. Stewart (Edinburgh: T. & T. Clark, 1968).

Schmeman, Alexander, *For the Life of the World* (Crestwood: St Vladimir's Seminary Press, 1963).

- *Of Water and the Spirit* (London: SPCK, 1976).

- *Church, World, Mission. Reflections on Orthodoxy in the West* (Crestwood: St Vladimir's Seminary Press, 1979).

Schweizer, Eduard, *Church Order in the New Testament*, trans. F. Clarke (London: SCM Press, 1961).

Spears, Larry, and Lawrence, Michele (eds), *Focus on Leadership. Servant-Leadership for the Twenty-First Century* (New York: John Wiley, 2002).

Staniloae, Dumitru, 'The Orthodox Doctrine of Salvation and Its Implications for Christian Diakonia in the World', in Staniloae, *Theology and the Church*, trans. R. Barringer (Crestwood: St. Vladimir's Seminary Press, 1980), pp. 181-212.

Sullivan, Francis A., *Charisms and Charismatic Renewal* (Dublin: Gill & Macmillan, 1982).

Taylor, Mark C., *Erring. A Postmodern A/theology* (Chicago & London: University of Chicago Press, 1987).

Teilhard de Chardin, Pierre, *Hymn of the Universe*, trans. S. Bartholomew (London: Collins, 1965).

Thornton, L.S., *The Common Life in the Body of Christ* (Westminster: Dacre Press, 1944).

Thurian, Max (ed.), *Churches Respond to BEM: Official Responses to the 'Baptism, Eucharist and Ministry' Text* (6 volumes; Geneva: WCC Publications, 1986-88).

Thurian, Max and Wainwright, Geoffrey (eds.), *Baptism and Eucharist. Ecumenical Convergence in Celebration* (Geneva: WCC/ Grand Rapids: Eerdmans, 1983).

Together in Mission and Ministry. The Porvoo Common Statement. The British and Irish Anglican Churches and the Nordic and Baltic Lutheran Churches (London: Church House Publishing, 1993).

Troeltsch, Ernst, trans. O. Wyon, *The Social Teaching of the Christian Churches* (2 volumes; London: Allen & Unwin, 1931).

Trudinger, Ron, *Built to Last: Biblical Principles for Church Restoration* (Eastbourne: Kingsway, 1982).

Ut Unum Sint. Encyclical Letter of the Holy Father John Paul II on Commitment to Ecumenism (London: Catholic Truth Society, 1995).

Vatican II, *Lumen Gentium*. Dogmatic Constitution on the Church (21 Nov. 1964), in Flannery (ed.), *Vatican Council II*, pp. 350-426.

Vatican II, *Unitatis redintegratio*. Decree on Ecumenism (21 Nov. 1964), in Flannery (ed.), *Vatican Council II*, pp. 452-73.

Visible Unity: Ten Propositions (London: Churches' Unity Commission, 1976).

Volf, Miroslav, *After Our Likeness. The Church as the Image of the Trinity* (Grand Rapids: Eerdmans, 1998).

Walker, Andrew, *Restoring the Kingdom. The Radical Christianity of the House Church Movement* (London: Hodder & Stoughton, 1985).

Ware, Timothy (Kallistos), *The Orthodox Church*. New Edition, (Harmondsworth: Penguin, 1997).

Webster, John, *Theological Theology. An Inaugural Lecture delivered before the University of Oxford on 27 October 1997* (Oxford: Clarendon Press, 1998).

Weinandy, Thomas, *The Father's Spirit of Sonship. Reconceiving the Trinity* (Edinburgh: T. & T. Clark, 1996).

Westerhoff, John H. and Kennedy, Gwen N., *Learning Through Liturgy* (New York: Seabury Press, 1978).

Wood, Susan, 'Baptism and the Foundations of Communion', in Root and Saarinen (eds.), *Baptism and the Unity of the Church*, pp. 37-60.

Yoder, John Howard, *The Politics of Jesus* (Grand Rapids: Eerdmans, 1972).

'"Your Kingdom Come", an Orthodox Contribution to the Theme of the World Missionary Conference (Melbourne 1980)' in Georges

Tsetsis (ed.), *Orthodox Thought. Reports of Orthodox Consultations organized by the World Council of Churches, 1975-1982* (Geneva: WCC, 1983), pp. 35-44.

Zaret, David, *Heavenly Contract: Ideology and Organization in Pre-Revolutionary Puritanism* (Chicago: University of Chicago Press, 1985).

Zimmerli, Walther, 'Promise and Fulfilment' in C. Westermann (ed.), *Essays on Old Testament Interpretation*, trans. J.L. Mays (London: SCM Press, 1963), pp. 89-122.

Zizioulas, John (Metropolitan John of Pergamon), *Being as Communion. Studies in Personhood and the Church* (London: Darton, Longman & Todd, 1985).

- 'The Church as Communion: A Presentation on the World Conference Theme', in Best and Gassmann, *On the Way to Fuller Koinonia*, pp. 103-11.

General Index

Cupit, L.A.   10n, 260n, 262n, 266n, 269n
Cyril of Alexandria   186n
Cyril of Jerusalem   110

Dagmar, Heller   147n, 219n
dance, divine   80, 174, 189, 191
Davies, Oliver   100n
Dawson, Andrew   95n
deacons   *see* diakonia
Declaration of Faith of English People (1611)   158n, 230n, 231n
Declaration of Principle (BUGB)   46–7, 49, 50, 52
Derrida, Jacques   1n, 100n
Deuteronomy, Book of   40, 75n, 76, 116n
diakonia   88, 91, 93–4, 99, 223, 270–3
Dillistone, F.W.   108, 110n, 121
Diodore of Tarsus   186n
discernment   102, 153, 154, 212
Dix, Gregory   149n, 271n
Dominus Jesus   204–5
Dostoyevsky, F.   59n
Douglas, Mary   187
Dunkley, Anne   136n
Dunn, James D.G.   88n, 89n, 91n, 97–8, 137, 138n, 148, 149n, 150
Dunn, James M.   13n
Dupont-Sommer, A.   112n, 113n
Dutton, Anne   163n
dwelling, indwelling   42, 67–8, 70, 72–3, 113, 186–90, 216

ecumenism   5, 6, 16, 23, 40, 45, 47, 55–6, 81, 141–2, 161, 170, 176–8, 183, ch. 9 *passim*, 165
Edwards, Jonathan (Jnr)   236, 237, 256
Edwards, Jonathan (Snr)   236, 256n
Eidberg, Peder A.   259n
elders   90, 91n, 92–4, 221, 223n, 224n
election   25–8, 32, 35–9, 72, 78–9, 202–2, 236–40, 243, 254–8
Elliott, John H.   69n
Ellis, Christopher J.   126n
Ellis, Robert   36n

Ephesians, Letter to the   54, 67, 68, 69, 70, 88n, 105n, 112n, 137, 148n, 150n, 197, 199n, 215, 216
Ephraem the Syrian   110
episkope (oversight)   6, 87–99, 101–2, 104, 206, 221–7
eschatology   10, 15, 178, 186, 188, 203, 232, 269
eucharist   *see* Lord's Supper
European Baptists   222, 239, 259, 262, 263, 267
Evangelical Calvinism   39, 236, 255, 265, 270
evangelism   10, 39, 41, 53, 56, 58, 209, 231, 237, 249, 263, 265, 266, 267, 269, 272; *see also* mission
Exodus, Book of   3n, 69, 74, 75
exodus, the   111, 113
Ezekiel, Prophecy of   109n, 112, 116, 188n

Faith and Practise of Thirty Congregations (1651)   31n, 244n
faith   7, 37, 38, 39, 92, 118, 119–120, 126–38, 140, 141, 142, 145–8, 151, 152, 153, 154, 164, 166, 176, 177, 181, 182, 183, 184, 185, 199, 201, 206, 218, 219, 220, 228, 229–32, 233, 234, 235, 236, 237, 238, 240, 242, 243, 246, 247, 254, 255, 265, 268, 269
Farley, Edward   77, 80
Fawcett, John   31
fellowship of believers   35, 72, 125, 157, 159, 172, 231, 265
Fenner, Dudley   64
Fiddes, Paul S.   17n, 18n, 36n, 57n, 62n, 85n, 112n, 114n, 125n, 131n, 143n, 146n, 154n, 170n, 230n, 242n
Flannery, Austin   170n, 204n
Forsyth, P.T.   198n
Fowler, James   136n, 146n
Fowler, Stanley K.   130n
free will   19, 38, 59, 239, 253
freedom of conscience   8, 141, 179–82, 219, 231, 256, 259–61, 263, 268, 275
Fuller, Andrew   19, 39, 48, 64, 92n, 209n, 236–7, 255–8, 262, 270
fundamentalism   50

Studies in Baptist History and Thought

An established series of doctoral theses of high
academic standard
(All titles paperback, 229 x 152mm)

David Bebbington and Anthony R. Cross (eds)
Baptist Identities
International Studies from the Seventeenth to the Twentieth Centuries
This volume of essays comprises the papers from the Third International
Conference on Baptist Studies held in Prague in July 2003.
2004 / ISBN 1-84227-215-2

David Bebbington and Anthony R. Cross (eds)
Global Baptist History
(provisional title)
This volume of essays comprises the papers from the Second International
Conference on Baptist Studies held in Wake Forest North Carolina, July
2000.
2004 / ISBN 1-84227-214-4

David Bebbington (ed.)
The Gospel in the World
International Baptist Studies
This volume of essays deals with a range of subjects spanning Britain, North
America, Europe, Asia and the Antipodes. Topics include studies on
religious tolerance, the communion controversy and the development of the
international Baptist community, and concludes with two important essays
on the future of Baptist life that pay special attention to the United States.
2002 / ISBN 1-84227-118-0 / xiii + 362pp

Anthony R. Cross
Baptism and the Baptists
Theology and Practice in Twentieth-Century Britain
At a time of renewed interest in baptism, Baptism and the Baptists is a
detailed study of twentieth-century baptismal theology and practice and the
factors which have influenced its development.
2000 / ISBN 0-85364-959-6 / xx + 530pp

Anthony R. Cross and Philip E. Thompson (eds)
Baptist Myths
This collection of essays examines some of the 'myths' in Baptist history
and theology: these include the idea of development in Baptist thought,
studies in the church, baptismal sacramentalism, community, spirituality,
soul competency, women, the civil rights movement and Baptist landmarkist
ecclesiology, Baptist bishops, creeds and the Bible, and overseas missions.
2004 / ISBN 1-84227-122-9

Anthony R. Cross and Philip E. Thompson (eds)
Baptist Sacramentalism
This collection of essays includes historical and theological studies in the
sacraments from a Baptist perspective. Subjects explored include the
physical side of being spiritual, baptism, the Lord's supper, the church,
ordination, preaching, worship, religious liberty and the issue of
disestablishment.
2003 / ISBN 1-84227-119-9 / xvi + 280pp

Paul S. Fiddes
Tracks and Traces
Baptist Identity in Church and Theology
This is a comprehensive, yet unusual, book on the faith and life of Baptist
Christians. It explores the understanding of the church, ministry, sacraments
and mission from a thoroughly theological perspective. In a series of
interlinked essays, the author relates Baptist identity consistently to a
theology of covenant and to participation in the triune communion of God.
2003 / ISBN 1-84227-120-2 / xvi + approx. 304pp

Stanley K. Fowler
More Than a Symbol
The British Baptist Recovery of Baptismal Sacramentalism
Fowler surveys the entire scope of British Baptist literature from the
seventeenth-century pioneers onwards. He shows that in the twentieth
century leading British Baptist pastors and theologians recovered an
understanding of baptism that connected experience with soteriology and
that in doing so they were recovering what many of their forebears had
taught.
2002 / ISBN 1-84227-052-4 / xvi + 276pp

Michael A.G. Haykin (ed.)
Fuller as an Apologist
One of the greatest Baptist theologians of the eighteenth and early nineteenth-centuries, Andrew Fuller has not had justice done to him. There is little doubt that Fuller's theology lay behind the revitalization of the Baptists in the late eighteenth century and the first few decades of the nineteenth. This collection of essays fills a much needed gap by examining a major area of Fuller's thought, his work as an apologist.
2003 / ISBN 1-84227-171-7

Michael A.G. Haykin
Studies in Calvinistic Baptist Spirituality
In a day when spirituality is in vogue and Christian communities are looking for guidance in this whole area, there is wisdom in looking to the past to find untapped wells. The Calvinistic Baptists, heirs of the rich ecclesial experience in the Puritan era of the seventeenth century, but, by the end of the eighteenth century, also passionately engaged in the catholicity of the Evangelical Revivals, are such a well. This collection of essays, covering such things the Lord's Supper, friendship and hymnody, seeks to draw out the spiritual riches of this community for reflection and imitation in the present day.
2004 / ISBN 1-84227-229-2

Brian Haymes, Anthony R. Cross and Ruth Gouldbourne
On Being the Church
Revisioning Baptist Identity
The aim of the book is to re-examine Baptist theology and practice in the light of the contemporary biblical, theological, ecumenical and missiological context drawing on historical and contemporary writings and issues. It is not a study in denominationalism but rather seeks to revision historical insights from the believers' church tradition for the sake of Baptists and other Christians in the context of the modern-postmodern context.
2005 / ISBN 1-84227-121-0

Ken R. Manley
From Woolloomooloo to 'Eternity'
A History of Baptists in Australia
From their beginnings in Australia in 1831 with the first baptisms in Woolloomooloo Bay in 1832, this pioneering study describes the quest of Baptists in the different colonies (states) to discover their identity as Australians and Baptists. Although institutional developments are analyzed and the roles of significant individuals traced, the major focus is on the social and theological dimensions of the Baptist movement.
2004 / ISBN 1-84227-194-6

Ken R. Manley
'Redeeming Love Proclaim'
John Rippon and the Baptists
A leading exponent of the new moderate Calvinism which brought new life
to many Baptists, John Rippon (1751-1836) helped unite the Baptists at this
significant time. His many writings expressed the denomination's growing
maturity and mutual awareness of Baptists in Britain and America, and
exerted a long-lasting influence on Baptist worship and devotion. In his
various activities, Rippon helped conserve the heritage of Old Dissent and
promoted the evangelicalism of the New Dissent
2003 / ISBN 1-84227-193-8

Peter J. Morden
Offering Christ to the World
Andrew Fuller and the Revival of English Particular Baptist Life
Andrew Fuller (1754-1815) was one of the foremost English Baptist
ministers of his day. His career as an Evangelical Baptist pastor, theologian,
apologist and missionary statesman coincided with the profound
revitalization of the Particular Baptist denomination to which he belonged.
This study examines the key aspects of the life and thought of this hugely
significant figure, and gives insights into the revival in which he played such
a central part.
2003 / ISBN 1-84227-141-5 / xx + 202pp

Peter Naylor
Calvinism, Communion and the Baptists
A Study of English Calvinistic Baptists
from the Late 1600s to the Early 1800s
Dr Naylor argues that the traditional link between 'high-Calvinism' and
'restricted communion' is in need of revision. He examines Baptist
communion controversies from the late 1600s to the early 1800s and also the
theologies of John Gill and Andrew Fuller.
2003 / ISBN 1-84227-142-3 / xx + 266pp

Frank Rinaldi
'The Tribe of Dan'
A Study of the New Connexion of General Baptists 1770-1891
'The Tribe of Dan' is a thematic study which explores the theology,
organizational structure, evangelistic strategy, ministry and leadership of the
New Connexion of General Baptists as it experienced the process of
institutionalization in the transition from a revival movement to an
established denomination.
2004 / ISBN 1-84227-143-1

Peter Shepherd
The Making of a Modern Denomination
John Howard Shakespeare and the English Baptists 1898-1924
John Howard Shakespeare introduced revolutionary change to the Baptist denomination. The Baptist Union was transformed into a strong central institution and Baptist ministers were brought under its control. Further, Shakespeare's pursuit of church unity reveals him as one of the pioneering ecumenists of the twentieth century.
2001 / ISBN 1-84227-046-X / xviii + 220pp

Brian Talbot
The Search for a Common Identity
The Origins of the Baptist Union of Scotland 1800-1870
In the period 1800 to 1827 there were three streams of Baptists in Scotland: Scotch, Haldaneite and 'English' Baptist. A strong commitment to home evangelization brought these three bodies closer together, leading to a merger of their home missionary societies in 1827. However, the first three attempts to form a union of churches failed, but by the 1860s a common understanding of their corporate identity was attained leading to the establishment of the Baptist Union of Scotland.
2003 / ISBN 1-84227-123-7

Philip E. Thompson
The Freedom of God
Towards Baptist Theology in Pneumatological Perspective
This study contends that the range of theological commitments of the early Baptists are best understood in relation to their distinctive emphasis on the freedom of God. Thompson traces how this was recast anthropocentrically, leading to an emphasis upon human freedom from the nineteenth century onwards. He seeks to recover the dynamism of the early vision via a pneumatologically oriented ecclesiology defining the church in terms of the memory of God.
2004 / ISBN 1-84227-125-3

Linda Wilson
Marianne Farningham
A Study in Victorian Evangelical Piety
Marianne Farningham, of College Street Baptist Chapel, Northampton, was a household name in evangelical circles in the later nineteenth century. For over fifty years she produced comment, poetry, biography and fiction for the popular Christian press. This investigation uses her writings to explore the beliefs and behaviour of evangelical Nonconformists, including Baptists, during these years.
2004 / ISBN 1-84227-124-5

Other Paternoster titles
relating to Baptist history and thought

Paul Beasley-Murray
Fearless for Truth
A Personal Portrait of the Life of George Beasley-Murray
Without a doubt George Beasley-Murray was one of the greatest Baptists of the twentieth century. A long-standing Principal of Spurgeon's College, he wrote more than twenty books and made significant contributions in the study of areas as diverse as baptism and eschatology, as well as writing highly respected commentaries on the Book of Revelation and John's Gospel.

2002 / ISBN 1-84227-134-2 / xii + 244pp

David Bebbington
Holiness in Nineteenth-Century England
David Bebbington stresses the relationship of movements of spirituality to changes in the cultural setting, especially the legacies of the Enlightenment and Romanticism. He shows that these broad shifts in ideological mood had a profound effect on the ways in which piety was conceptualized and practised. Holiness was intimately bound up with the spirit of the age.

2000 / ISBN 0-85364-981-2 / viii + 98pp

Anthony R. Cross (ed.)
Ecumenism and History
Studies in Honour of John H.Y. Briggs
This collection of essays examines the inter-relationships between the two fields in which Professor Briggs has contributed so much: history - particularly Baptist and Nonconformist - and the ecumenical movement. With contributions from colleagues and former research students from Britain, Europe and North America, Ecumenism and History provides wide-ranging studies in important aspects of Christian history, theology and ecumenical studies.

2002 / ISBN 1-84227-135-0 / xx + 362pp

Keith E. Eitel
Paradigm Wars
The Southern Baptist International Mission Board
Faces the Third Millennium
The International Mission Board of the Southern Baptist Convention is the
largest denominational mission agency in North America. This volume
chronicles the historic and contemporary forces that led to the IMB's recent
extensive reorganization, providing the most comprehensive case study to
date of a historic mission agency restructuring to continue its mission
purpose into the twenty-first century more effectively.
2000 / ISBN 1-870345-12-6 / x + 139pp

Mark Hopkins
Baptists, Congregationalists, and Theological Change
Some Late Nineteenth Century Leaders and Controversies
2003 / ISBN 1-84227-150-4

Donald M. Lewis
Lighten Their Darkness
The Evangelical Mission to Working-Class London, 1828-1860
This is a comprehensive and compelling study of the Church and the
complexities of nineteenth-century London. Challenging our understanding
of the culture in working London at this time, Lewis presents a well-
structured and illustrated work that contributes substantially to the study of
evangelicalism and mission in nineteenth-century Britain.
2001 / ISBN 1-84227-074-5 / xviii + 371pp

Meic Pearse
The Great Restoration
The Religious Radicals of the 16th and 17th Centuries
Pearse charts the rise and progress of continental Anabaptism - both
evangelical and heretical - through the sixteenth century. He then follows the
story of those English people who became impatient with Puritanism and
separated - first from the Church of England and then from one another - to
form the antecedents of later Congregationalists, Baptists and Quakers.
1998 / ISBN 0-85364-800-X / xii + 320pp

Charles Price and Ian M. Randall
Transforming Keswick
Transforming Keswick is a thorough, readable and detailed history of the
convention. It will be of interest to those who know and love Keswick, those
who are only just discovering it, and serious scholars eager to learn more
about the history of God's dealings with his people.
2000 / ISBN 1-85078-350-0 / 288pp

Ian M. Randall
Educating Evangelicalism
The Origins, Development and Impact of London Bible College
London Bible College has been at the centre of theological education in
Britain for over fifty years. Through its staff and former students it has had
a significant influence on post-war evangelical life and has in turn been
shaped by evangelical currents. This book is the story of LBC's sometimes
difficult progress through the changing tides of evangelical opinion and
support to its current position as a touchstone for the finest in distinctly
evangelical scholarship.
2000 / ISBN 0-85364-873-5 / xx + 320pp

Ian M. Randall
One Body in Christ
The History and Significance of the Evangelical Alliance
In 1846 the Evangelical Alliance was founded with the aim of bringing
together evangelicals for common action. This book uses material not
previously utilized to examine the history and significance of the
Evangelical Alliance, a movement which has remained a powerful force for
unity. At a time when evangelicals are growing world-wide, this book offers
insights into the past which are relevant to contemporary issues.
2001 / ISBN 1-84227-089-3 / xii + 394pp

Ian M. Randall
Evangelical Experiences
A Study in the Spirituality of English Evangelicalism 1918-1939
This book makes a detailed historical examination of evangelical spirituality
between the First and Second World Wars. It shows how patterns of devotion
led to tensions and divisions. In a wide-ranging study, Anglican, Wesleyan,
Reformed and Pentecostal-charismatic spiritualities are analysed.
1999 / ISBN 0-85364-919-7 / xii + 310pp

Ian M. Randall
Spirituality and Social Change
The Contribution of F.B. Meyer (1847-1929)
2003 / ISBN 1-84227-195-4

Alan P.F. Sell and Anthony R. Cross (eds)
Protestant Nonconformity in the Twentieth Century
In this collection of essys scholars representative of a number of Nonconformist traditions reflect thematically on Free Church life and witness during the twentieth century. Among the subjects reviewed are biblical studies, theology, worship, evangelism and spirituality, and ecumenism. Over and above its immediate interest, this collection provides a marker to future scholars and others wishing to know how some of their forebears assessed Nonconformity's contribution to a variety of fields during the century leading up to Christianity's third millennium.
2003 / ISBN 1-84227-221-7 / x + 388pp

Linda Wilson
Constrained by Zeal
Female Spirituality amongst Nonconformists 1825-1875
Dr Wilson investigates the neglected area of Nonconformist female spirituality. Against the background of separate spheres she analyses the experience of women from four denominations, and argues that the churches provided a 'third sphere' in which they could find opportunities for participation.
2000 / ISBN 0-85364-972-3 / xvi + 293pp

Nigel G. Wright
Disavowing Constantine
Mission, Church and the Social Order in the Theologies of John Howard Yoder and Jürgen Moltmann
This book is a timely restatement of a radical theology of church and state in the Anabaptist and Baptist tradition. Dr Wright constructs his argument in dialogue and debate with Yoder and Moltmann, major contributors to a free church perspective.
2000 / ISBN 0-85364-978-2 /xv + 251pp

Nigel G. Wright
New Baptists, New Agenda
New Baptists, New Agenda is a timely contribution to the growing debate about the health, shape and future of the Baptists. It considers the steady changes that have taken place among Baptists in the last decade – changes of mood, style, practice and structure - and encourages us to align these current movements and questions with God's upward and future call. He contends that the true church has yet to come: the church that currently exists is an anticipation of the joyful gathering of all who have been called by the Spirit through Christ to the Father.
2002 / ISBN 1-84227-157-1 / x + 161pp

The Paternoster Press,
PO Box 300, Carlisle, Cumbria CA3 0QS, United Kingdom
Web: www.paternoster-publishing.com